Creeks and Seminoles

Indians of the Southeast

CREEKS &

SEMINOLES

*The Destruction
and Regeneration of
the Muscogulge People*

J. Leitch Wright, Jr.

University of Nebraska Press

Lincoln and London

First paperback printing: 1990

Library of Congress Cataloging-in-Publication Data

Wright, J. Leitch (James Leitch), 1929–
Creeks and Seminoles.

(Indians of the Southeast)
Bibliography: p.
Includes index.
1. Creek Indians—History.   2. Seminole Indians—
History.   3. Indians of North America—Southern States—
History.   I. Title.   II. Series.
E99.C9W69   1986   975'.00497   86-11281
ISBN 0-8032-4738-9 (alk. paper)
ISBN 0-8032-9728-9 (pbk.)

⊖

In memory of Helen Lee Wright Bynum

Contents

Series Editors' Introduction

For more than two centuries the Indians of the Southeast have fascinated writers and scholars. Since the 1770s, when William Bartram, a traveling naturalist, reported on the Creeks and Seminoles and James Adair, a retired trader, published the first lengthy interpretation of Southeastern Indian history and culture, many books and essays have appeared that have attempted to explain these people and their histories. Some have dealt with the region as a whole, others have focused on a particular group. With few exceptions, however, this substantial literature on Southeastern Indian history has focused on political questions. How did an Indian nation respond to European and American diplomatic pressures? How did it deal with Andrew Jackson's removal policy of the 1830s? Less often, scholars have asked how the various Southeastern nations governed themselves or related to one another. But despite a shift in emphasis from the traditional "Indian-white relations" themes to an analysis of internal issues, the political emphasis has remained.

J. Leitch Wright, Jr., has broken out of this political preoccupation and offers here an interpretation of Creek and Seminole history that stresses ethnic factors. We have long known that the so-called Creek Confederacy was composed of a bewildering variety of autonomous groups that spoke many different languages and had many different cultural and historical experi-

x   ences. Until now, however, no scholar has attempted to explain
the historical implications of this ethnic diversity. Eschewing the
traditional nomenclature of Creek and Seminole as too reflective
of an artificial European political misperception, Wright uses the
term Muscogulge, meaning Muskogee people. The Muscogulges, Wright argues, were divided into two broad groups
based on language. The tensions between those groups best explain both their internal history and their relations with other
Indian nations, Europeans, and Americans.

Wright's interpretation does not ignore political problems;
rather, he argues that ethnic differences of precontact origin
account for the factionalism that so characterized eighteenth-
and nineteenth-century Creek history and suggests that those
conflicts were largely responsible for the establishment of a separate Seminole tribe in Florida. It is an arresting argument that
challenges the traditional interpretations of Creek and Seminole
history and raises significant questions about the nature of eth-
nicity in Native American societies. The series Indians of the
Southeast, was created to "foster study of the internal dynamics"
of Southeastern Native societies; we are pleased to offer *Creeks
and Seminoles: The Destruction and Regeneration of the
Muscogulge People* as the first volume.

Theda Perdue   Michael D. Green

Preface

Accompanied by some six hundred soldiers and a large number of Indian slave porters, Hernando de Soto explored, fought, and plundered his way through the Southeast during the years 1539 and 1540. He did not find an Aztec or Inca empire, but he saw or heard about powerful, presumably wealthy, regional chiefdoms—Calusa, Apalachee, Cofitachiqui, Tama, Coosa, and others. Populous towns in these chiefdoms had platform temple mounds, copper ornaments and weapons, large carved wooden effigies, pearls, peltry, stocks of maize, and much more. Yet in spite of their large population, fighting with the intruders and new diseases introduced by the foreigners led to the destruction of the chiefdoms within a relatively few years, and much of the culture (now known as Mississippian) was shattered. Southeastern Indian peoples were in disarray, and survivors were forced to relocate, merge with, or settle among neighboring tribes, perhaps repeating the process again and again. Sixteenth- and seventeenth-century sources are skimpy or nonexistent and reveal little about the destruction of the chiefdoms and the fate of those who survived.

A variety of English, Spanish, and French accounts disclose a considerable amount about those Southeastern Indians who in the eighteenth century were known as Creeks and Seminoles (or Muscogulges). By that century they had developed a new culture and economy, which reflected both their Mississippian heritage and an adjustment to conditions in the wake of de Soto's entrada. Non-Mississippian aspects of the eighteenth-century way of life included commercial hunting, adopting part of the Europeans' material culture, and adjusting to whites and Africans living in the Indians' midst. This culture, based on commercial hunting, was the only way of life eighteenth- and nineteenth-century Creeks and Seminoles knew. It was the one they fought to preserve, and it was the one Andrew Jackson and his comtemporaries destroyed in the Southeast.

One of the ironies of the American Revolution was that white Americans had reversed their role. After the Revolution, they no longer were colonial subjects of a king four thousand miles away. Instead they were citizens of a new nation that, by winning independence, overnight had become a colonial power: Muscogulges, not whites, now were the North American colonial subjects. Nonwhite and, for the most part, non-Christian Muscogulges were one of the largest and most important Indian peoples on the American frontier. This book is in part a case study of that early United States colonialism; it suited United States objectives to assert that diverse Muscogulge peoples were members of a centralized Creek nation or an unified Seminole nation.

The Indian fighter, border captain, and president of the United States, Andrew Jackson, has come to symbolize American treatment of the Muscogulges. Jackson's policies, however, were not new, and his measures reflected attitudes deeply rooted in the British colonial experience. Born in the years before Lexington and Concord, Jackson started life as a loyal subject of George III, though after 1775 while in his teens he joined the struggle for independence. Many Americans in the Southeast (loyalists or "Tories") fought for, rather than against, George III, and after 1783, despite their defeat, they still were the typical whites who lived among the Muscogulges. Their presence illustrated that though Britain had lost much of her political control over the southeastern Indians she still dominated their economy, and her influence among the Indians was considerable. Muscogulges had not been much concerned with the Boston Tea Party and taxa-

tion without representation, but they understood clearly enough
that after 1783 some English-speaking whites disliked each
other and were now rivals, subjects of either the United States
or of Britain. In an attempt to escape from being treated as
inferiors or dependents and to retain their culture and lands,
Muscogulges played off British subjects against citizens of the
United States and vice versa. One could witness this in 1783
and even as late as 1836 when American soldiers began rounding
up Muscogulges for removal to present-day Oklahoma.

We know far more about what happened to Creeks and Seminoles than to their sixteenth-century predecessors. This book
is primarily about the second destruction of these southeastern
Indians and to a much smaller extent the fate of survivors after
their dispersal to Oklahoma, Texas, Mexico, the West Indies,
and elsewhere. Despite Andrew Jackson, thousands of Muscogulge descendants still live in the southeastern homeland. The
book briefly outlines the different ways in which traditional
culture persevered among twentieth-century Muscogulges in
the Southeast and in their various other residences.

Though eighteenth- and early nineteenth-century sources are
more extensive than sixteenth-century ones, it must be kept in
mind that most Creeks and Seminoles in those years, along with
a majority of Africans and many whites living among the Indians, were illiterate. I have used traditional written historical
sources, but I have also turned to the scholarship of archaeologists, anthropologists, geographers, linguists, and folklorists. To
a limited extent even oral history—interviews with Indians and
Negroes in the late nineteenth and twentieth centuries—has
helped me interpret and reconstruct the earlier period.

Proper clan, town, and linguistic identification is essential to
an understanding of the Muscogulges, but unfortunately these
are often uncertain or unknown. To make a determination in
individual cases I have had to rely on a variety of direct and
indirect, sometimes conflicting, written sources. I have tried to
ascertain if there was a long-term pattern in regard to a particular
Indian's actions and geographic movements; or I have tried to
discover his relations with other Indians whose clan and tribal
affiliation are known. The number of inhabitants of eighteenth-

xiv century Creek towns often fluctuated dramatically. Because of
this population volatility a town's name might not accurately
reflect the ethnic background and language of some of its clans
or even of a large segment of the population living in a particular
town. A similar confusion concerns personal names. The Coweta mico, Eufala tastanagi, or Tuckabatchee yahola mentioned
in an eighteenth-century letter might refer to any one of ten or
twenty Indians having the same title. Two centuries later it is
a challenge to straighten all this out, and sometimes it is impossible. Despite considerable risk of error in individual cases,
the broad pattern of clan, tribal, and ethnic identification and
the evolution of many Creek and Seminole people into two new
divisions or moieties largely along ethnic lines seems reasonably
clear. This is one of the developments that help account for the
Muscogulges' actions during Andrew Jackson's long career
(1767–1845), that clarify why Indians often fought more vi-
ciously among themselves than against whites, and that explain
how traditional culture has survived among present-day Indians.

Several terms are used frequently in the text, and to help
avoid confusion it seems best at the outset to define them.
Muskogee is the language spoken by most Creeks today;
Muskhogean refers to the dominant linguistic family in the
Southeast, which includes Muskogee, Hitchiti, Choctaw, and
other distinct languages and dialects. The term *Muscogulges*
includes those southeastern Indians who were usually known
as Creeks and Seminoles though Muscogulges spoke not only
Muskhogean languages but also those in entirely different linguistic families such as Yuchean, Algonquian, and Iroquoian.
Muskogulge (muskogalgi) is plural, as are *Shawnee, Yuchi*, and
many other tribal names. I—like so many other authors writing
in English—have treated such names as if they were singular,
partly for stylistic reasons, though especially of clarity to English
readers.

Almost none of the various languages spoken by Muscogulge
peoples took on a written form until the nineteenth century. In
the eighteenth and early nineteenth centuries those Muscogulge
words that were written down were, with few exceptions, written by whites. For many reasons (including the fact that Musk-

hogean languages do not have as many vowels as English, Spanish, or French) the same words, names, or titles appeared in various forms. In most instances it has seemed less confusing to retain earlier spellings than to impose an artificial and perhaps incorrect uniformity.

As is indicated in the notes and bibliography, my debt to fellow scholars and institutions is large. Like others writing about the southeastern Indians I repeatedly have turned to the prolific writings of the ethnologist John R. Swanton, whose purview spanned many centuries. However, for the more limited time period covered by this work, my interpretation differs from Swanton's in important respects concerning ethnic composition of towns, moieties, and social structure.

Emmanuel J. Drechsel, James M. Crawford, J. Anthony Paredes, William S. Coker, Thomas Yahola, Charles Daniels (Sakim), Andrew Ramsey (Untolv Haco), and Joe A. Quetone were most helpful in clarifying points or making sources available. The penetrating criticisms of coeditors Michael D. Greene and Theda Perdue have resulted in many improvements, though they disagree with some of my interpretations. Financial assistance from Florida State University and an Albert J. Beveridge grant from the American Historical Association helped make research travel possible. The maps were prepared by James R. Anderson, Jr., Florida Resources and Environmental Analysis Center, Florida State University. Because her own handwriting is illegible, Helen Lee Wright has the ability to read and type that of her father. Polly S. Edmiston, Dianne B. Weinstein, and Wanda D. Mitchell also carefully typed various drafts of this work. Beth Wright's influence appears on every page; as a mentor, colleague, and teacher she has no equal.

The Southeastern Muscogulges

This is the story of an Indian people—the Muscogulges—who were not a people, and of Indian nations—the Creeks and Seminoles—that were not nations. During the late eighteenth and early nineteenth centuries assorted Indians lived in the present-day states of Georgia, Alabama, and Florida. The alternative to referring to them as Muscogulges, Creeks, and Seminoles is to rely on a welter of tribal (or linguistic) names: Yamasee, Tuckabatchee, Hitchiti, Koasati, Alabama, Timucua, Natchez, Shawnee, and Yuchi. The list is a long one, fifty to a hundred or so. By the late eighteenth century these tribes, remnants of those who had greeted de Soto in the sixteenth century, had been incalculably reduced in numbers, and many approached extinction. It would be more accurate to refer to them by their individual tribal names, but it would also be more awkward. Thus, in the name of expediency, we refer to Creeks, Seminoles, and the imprecise but all-encompassing Muscogulge.

Europeans are responsible for most of the onomastic confusion, and we might start with "Creek." One can meticulously examine sixteenth-century accounts of the De Soto and Luna expeditions but find no mention of Creek Indians. Much later, Frenchmen founded Louisiana and established themselves at Mobile in 1702 and at Fort Toulouse near the forks of the Alabama River in 1717. During the eighteenth century for as long as the fleur-de-lis waved over Louisiana, Frenchmen traded, fought, and intrigued with southeastern Indians whom they knew as Alabamas, Tallapoosas, Abihkas, Mobilians, Cowetas, and others—but not as Creeks.

The term Creek is of English origin, and Englishmen in the southern colonies began to use it in the late seventeenth and early eighteenth centuries. When curious Indian traders and historians inquired about the origin of "Creek," the inevitable answer was that southeastern Indians lived in a fertile region watered by many rivers and streams. "Creeks" was applied to these Indians just as Alabamas, Mobilians, and Apalachicolas designated Indians living on those rivers. Near the end of the eighteenth century Alexander McGillivray, claiming to be leader of the Creek nation or confederacy, affirmed that his warriors were known as Creeks because of the proliferation of so many streams throughout his nation.[1]

McGillivray was wrong, but we should not blame him. He had been educated in Charleston and Savannah, and his father was a successful Scottish Indian trader. McGillivray knew that his father and his father's associates employed the term Creek. McGillivray understood what Creek meant to Anglos and used it as his father did in dealings with them. When pressed about its etymology he gave a logical but incorrect answer. The actual etymology is more complex. Oral traditions recount how Hitchiti speakers had lived for many centuries throughout the Southeast, including on the Ocmulgee River in Georgia. Subsequently western intruders (Muskogees) settled on Hitchiti lands. The Hitchiti word for these Muskogees was Ochese. English settlers founded Charleston in 1670, and within a short time Carolinians traded with Indians in the Southeast, among whom were those living on Ochesee Creek (the upper Ocmulgee River). Traders from Charleston and their packhorse trains stopped by Ochesee Creek, bartering manufactures for deerskins. They referred to the Indians there as Ochesee Creeks, Ochesees, and eventually simply as Creeks. In the aftermath of the great Yamasee uprising in 1715, Ochesee Creeks along with other Indians retired westward to the Chattahoochee River and settled various towns near Columbus, Georgia, the principal ones being Coweta and Ka-

sihta. The Indians on the Chattahoochee River were sometimes 3
known as Cowetas and other times as Ochesee Creeks or Creeks.
Similar Muskogees migrating from the west at an earlier period
lived above the forks of the Alabama River. English traders began
to call Muskogees on the Chattahoochee "Lower Creeks" and
those on the Coosa and Tallapoosa above the forks of the Alabama River "Upper Creeks." Eventually all Indians on the Chattahoochee and Flint rivers, whatever their language and ethnic
background, became known as Lower Creeks, and all Indians on
the Alabama and its tributaries the Coosa and Tallapoosa as
Upper Creeks.[2] According to one account the Upper and Lower
Creeks first came together on the Chattahoochee River in the
early eighteenth century, but one would not want to put much
faith in any specific place or date.[3] The important consideration
is that from the British standpoint these Indians did "come
together" and that collectively all of them were Creeks. It was
convenient to assert that virtually every Indian in the Southeast
who was not a Cherokee, Choctaw, or Chickasaw, was a Creek.
At home in white society, Alexander McGillivray understood
clearly what British colonists meant when they referred to
Creeks.

The trouble with all this is that the Indians considered them-
selves what they had always been—Yuchis, Cowetas, Coosas,
Alabamas, Shawnees, Tuskegees, among many others. As far as
we know Muskogee was the language of the true Muskogees, of
Coweta, Kasihta, Coosa, and Abihka, the core or founding towns
of the Creek nation. But most Creeks did not speak Muskogee,
at least not as their first language, and frequently not at all.
Furthermore, by the eighteenth century some of these kinds of
Creeks were living in the founding Muskogee towns. For those
Indians who perhaps did not speak either Muskogee or English,
talk about the Upper and Lower Creeks coming together, and
about a unified Creek nation was bewildering.

In 1763, after Spain had lost Florida and France had relinquished Louisiana, British-controlled territory surrounded the
so-called Creek nation. British subjects were in Georgia and
Carolina in the east, Pensacola and Mobile on the south,
Natchez and Manchac to the west, and on the headwaters of the

4   Tennessee to the north. Muscogulges were addicted to and dependent on the white man's goods, and the only available merchants were British. When British civil and military officials negotiated treaties with these Indians after 1763 and asked their warriors for military service, they called them what they and the traders understood them to be—Creeks. Spain recovered the Floridas during the American Revolution. When Spaniards resumed relations with the Cowetas, Yuchis, and others after 1783 they discovered that in some fashion these tribes had become Creeks. During the 1790s Napoleon hoped to recover Louisiana. Like the Spaniards, Frenchmen learned that their old friends the Alabamas and Tallapoosas had been transformed into Creeks. Eventually Indians themselves, such as McGillivray, in order to let whites of whatever nationality know they were not Choctaws, Cherokees, or Chickasaws, acknowledged that they were Creeks, but often added that in fact they were Alabamas, Yuchis, Natchez, Shawnees, Miccosukees, and so forth.

Some Creeks told the whites they were Seminoles, often to distinguish themselves from Muskogee speakers in Coweta and elsewhere. The term Seminole is of Spanish origin. *Cimarron* (wild and untamed) referred to hostile nonwhites—Indians and Africans—whom the Spaniards had to contend with on their frontiers throughout the New World. Hitchiti-speaking Oconees and their neighbors repeatedly had set out from villages in the Georgia tidewater to descend on Spanish Florida. At some point in the second quarter of the eighteenth century a few of these invading cimarrones settled down permanently on abandoned Timucuan fields in Alachua (near Gainesville, Florida). When Britain acquired Florida in 1763 these Indians identified themselves not as Oconees or Creeks but as cimarrones. However, there is no "r" in Hitchiti or in any of the Muskhogean languages. "R" became "l" and "cimarron" became "cimallon"— in time "Simallone" and "Seminole." When Oconees called themselves Seminoles, they were telling the British that they were Hitchitis and not Creeks, not Indians from Coweta and its vicinity who spoke Muskogee.[4] During the American Revolution, British Indian agent John Stuart, understandably confused, designated all East Florida Indians as Seminole Creeks. Even at that late date, however, Spaniards still knew them as cimarrones.[5]

When dealing with whites, the traditional founders of the Creek nation (the Cowetas, Kasihtas, Coosas, and Abihkas) began to identify themselves as Creeks. The Indian name for these people, at least a majority of whom spoke Muskogee, was Muskogee. However, Muskogee was not a Muskhogean word; it was Algonquian, presumably Shawnee. When Shawnees had moved into the South in the seventeenth century or earlier they had referred to the Cowetas, Kasihtas, Coosas, and Abihkas as Muskogees (people of the swampy ground).[6] In time most Southeastern Indians, including the Muskogees themselves, adopted the term. Before the Shawnees had designated them Muskogees, Hitchitis had styled these Muskogee speakers as Ochesees. Either because they did not know any better or because it suited their purposes, British traders characterized them as Creeks. To compound the confusion, the British began to label almost all Indians in the southeast as Creeks. Indians understood the distinction between Muskogees or Ochesees (who spoke Creek proper), and Alabamas, Hitchitis, Yuchis, and so on who spoke foreign tongues. Whites did not—or at least they pretended not to.

Before leaving this onomastic thicket, it is necessary to return to the Seminoles. The Seminoles of eighteenth- and nineteenth-century Florida had not originated there but came in a series of migrations, which lasted more than a century. They had moved into Florida from Georgia and Alabama and settled on abandoned lands of the earlier inhabitants who now were nearly extinct. In the vanguard were the Hitchiti-speaking Oconees who were followed by the Yuchis, Alabamas, Choctaws, Shawnees, and all the other diverse tribes or bands living in Georgia and Alabama. Some of these spoke Muskogee, though often it had not been the primary tongue of their ancestors. These Indians were survivors of populous tribes and chiefdoms of an earlier day, but warfare and especially disease had taken a grim toll. In the sixteenth century the Florida peninsula had been densely populated with, by some accounts, almost a million inhabitants; by the eighteenth century almost all of these Indians were gone. Seminoles moved down from the north and took over their lands. At first whites associated the term Seminole with the Oconees, though ultimately most if not all Indians residing in Florida were considered Seminoles. A variety of ethnic and linguistic groups constituted both Seminoles and Creeks, and unless these Indians were bilingual they often could not understand one another. Time blurred ethnic distinctions, but even today one merely has to visit the Seminoles in Florida or the Creeks in Oklahoma to realize that such distinctions still persist.[7] It is not surprising that nineteenth-century Americans were confused. Captain Hugh Young, a military engineer in Jackson's army, which invaded Florida in 1818, avowed that the better part of the hostiles in this first Seminole War in reality were Creeks.[8] A decade or so later, Jackson's advisers, anxious to relocate all eastern Indians west of the Mississippi River, recommended that when the Creeks were removed the Seminoles should be included and all established on a single new Creek homeland in Oklahoma.[9]

The Indians that we are dealing with are those in the Southeast who were not Cherokees, Choctaws, and Chickasaws; that is, they were not considered to be part of the other southeastern "civilized" tribes. Refugee bands of Cherokees, Choctaws, and Chickasaws, did live among the Muscogulges and usually were known as Creeks or Seminoles. Muscogulges lived in Alabama, Georgia, and Florida and had geography as much as anything in common. Osceola was a Creek in Alabama and a Seminole in Florida. He did not change—he remained a Tallassee—but white perceptions of him did. A matter of further confusion was the fact that in the late eighteenth century an observer could look closely at these Indians and discover that, though they dressed in the usual native fashion, their skins were black and they had Negroid features. The African influence among these southeastern Indians was considerable.

It is necessary to consider in even more detail Muscogulge ethnic and linguistic components. Because of the great population disruptions and intermingling of tribes, eighteenth-century Indians living in a particular region or village might be newcomers or refugees, and might speak a different tongue from that

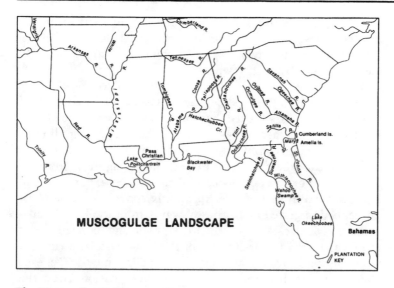

The Muscogulge Landscape

indicated by the village's name. Though there are exceptions, Indians speaking the same primary language in a particular town, in a cluster of towns, or in a group of clans within a town had interests in common and can be regarded as a unit. Despite the complexities and room for error we must attempt to identify more precisely the eighteenth-century Muscogulges. It is best to start with the Hitchitis, who, formerly living in Tama, Apalachee, and other southeastern chiefdoms, supposedly were the oldest, the "original inhabitants" of the soil, and the "elder brother" of the other southeastern Indians. The Hitchitis spoke a dialect in the Muskhogean family unintelligible to those speaking Muskogee proper. From the De Soto narratives it can be deduced that in the sixteenth century, the Hitchitis lived in villages on the Ocmulgee River in Georgia as well as elsewhere in southern Georgia and northern Florida. Much later, after the Yamasee revolt in 1715 and the founding of Georgia in 1733, many of the Hitchitis were to be found in Florida in the Alachua (Gainesville) area and on the lower Chattahoochee River. Other Hitchitis lived among the Lower and Upper Creeks in Alabama

8   and Georgia. It is impossible to establish how many remnants of other tribes joined or merged with the Hitchitis. Chiaha, Oconee, Tamathli, Sawokli, and Alachua were among the eighteenth-century Hitchiti towns.[10]

While some Hitchitis were on the Ocmulgee, newcomers immigrating from the west began to settle on the headwaters of that river. They established themselves on the Ocmulgee's headwaters and elsewhere in Georgia and Alabama. According to tradition, vague references by Spanish explorers, and skimpy archeological evidence, these Indians, including those from the four original or mother towns of Abihka, Coosa, Coweta, and Kasihta, who in early times apparently spoke only true Muskogee, had migrated in a series of waves from the Red River—some say Mexico—crossed the Mississippi, and founded one or more chiefdoms in the interior of the Southeast. The Hitchiti word for these invaders was Ochesee, and in time the Ochesee Creeks gave their name to the entire Creek nation. After the Yamasee rebellion many of the Muskogees retired from middle Georgia and relocated on the Chattahoochee near Columbus. As the eighteenth century progressed there was always misunderstanding about exactly who was a Creek, even among true Muskogee speakers. In 1770 British Indian agents contended that the Abihkas (Muskogees) and Tallapoosas (essentially non-Muskogees) in Alabama constituted the entire Creek nation.[11]

The Alabamas were another influential tribe. Closely associated with the Koasatis, Tawasas, and Tuskegees among others, the Alabamas themselves may have been a separate confederacy before joining the Creeks. Since first contact with Europeans, the Alabamas had moved from the Tombigbee River, to the lower Alabama, and eventually northward to the vicinity of the forks of that river, where most were to be found in the latter part of the eighteenth century. A party of Koasatis, however, attempting to escape Upper Creek hostilities with the Choctaws, had returned southward, seeking a refuge on the Gulf Coast east of Pensacola.[12] Alabamas were known as outsiders, those who spoke a mixed or imperfect language, a blend of Hitchiti and Choctaw, that had much in common with the Mobilian trade jargon. If one could go back in time, one would likely find that there was not one but several Alabama tongues. British trader James Adair noticed that Indians living in different towns within six miles of Fort Toulouse near the forks of the Alabama River spoke at least seven different languages, and the Alabama components had much to do with such diversity.[13] These Indians used Alabamian, a language in the Muskhogean family. Their close neighbors, the Coosas and Abihkas, speaking pure Muskogee, could not understand them. Apparently Hitchitis on the lower Chattahoochee could.[14]

The Yuchis were unique and are even more difficult to fathom than the Alabamas. According to their folklore they had descended from the sun and reputedly were among the oldest inhabitants in the Southeast. There is a tradition that formerly the Yuchis had been a powerful chiefdom—probably known as Chisca to De Soto—located somewhere in the Southeast, perhaps in South Carolina, Georgia, or Tennessee. Their language was distinct, and a Yuchi could not understand a Muskogee, Hitchiti, Alabama, or any other Muskhogean speaker. In the eighteenth century the English trader Timothy Barnard married a Yuchi woman, reared a large mestizo family, and after the Revolution served as a United States Indian agent. He apparently spoke Muskogee and Hitchiti fluently, but Yuchi, his wife's tongue, was beyond his grasp.[15] Diseases, wars, relentless pressure by Europeans, and population losses had forced the Yuchis to move about again and again. Before the American Revolution they were located primarily on the Flint and lower Chattahoochee rivers, but a few Yuchi villages were on the Coosa and Tallapoosa rivers in upper Alabama, and a handful still remained on the Savannah. They retained their language, aspects of their culture and social organization, and a vague awareness of their previous grandeur, and they were conscious of the fact that they were Yuchis, not Muskogees.[16]

In the latter third of the eighteenth century, the peripatetic naturalist William Bartram inaccurately claimed that Yuchis spoke Shawnee.[17] One should not be too harsh on the normally perceptive Bartram. At one time or another Yuchis lived with Shawnees on the Savannah and also the Tallapoosa, which might explain his confusion. Shawnees, however, spoke neither

10   a Yuchean nor a Muskhogean language but one in the entirely different Algonquian family. Few tribes had moved about more than the Shawnees since European contact, and in the seventeenth and eighteenth centuries one could find them in New England, Texas, New Orleans, Detroit, and Saint Augustine. During most of these two centuries a majority of the Shawnees lived in the Southeast, first on the Savannah (Shawnee) River, and later to the west at Tuckabatchee on the Tallapoosa. In the latter part of the eighteenth century many Shawnees moved above the Ohio River. A minority remained in the South, where ultimately they became known as Creeks. Those in the South continued to speak their own language and to live in rectangular lodges having more in common with those of Algonquins in the Virginia tidewater than with the traditional circular wattle and daub ones of the lower South. Near the end of the seventeenth century, Shawnees were in some respects the most powerful tribe in the Southeast; a century later their numbers were greatly reduced, and those who remained had settled primarily in several towns on the Tallapoosa. Despite diminished numbers, their reputation in warfare, religion, magic, and political organization remained high. This helps explain why southern Indians listened so attentively to the Shawnee Tecumseh when he left the Ohio country in 1811 to visit the Creeks.[18]

Like the Shawnees, the Natchez joined the Creeks at a relatively late date. Their homeland was on the Mississippi River in the Natchez region where De Soto in the sixteenth century and Frenchmen over a hundred years later encountered them. After France successfully colonized Louisiana in 1699, the Natchez alternately traded and fought with these Europeans, that is until 1729, the year of the great Natchez uprising, in which at the outset over two hundred Frenchmen were slaughtered. Ultimately the Natchez were defeated, and those who were not killed or sold off as slaves in the West Indies, retired eastward and established new villages among the Cherokees and Creeks. United States Indian agent Benjamin Hawkins in his 1799 enumeration counted Nauchee on Nauchee Creek (a tributary of the Coosa) as part of the Upper Creeks.[19]

Eighteenth-century French accounts reveal much about the

Great Sun, nobles, temple mounds, rituals, and other aspects of   11
Natchez culture. At an earlier period the Natchez chiefdom had
been far more extensive, but pandemics and disruptions had
reduced their numbers and the size of their empire. Other Indians, equally distressed, who perhaps had seen their entire
villages swept away by disease, had sought refuge in the Natchez
chiefdom. These newcomers joined or perhaps formed a lower
class called *stinkards,* which spoke a distinct language. Cata-
strophic disease, the desertion of villages, and the refugees joining and in some fashion being incorporated into other tribes
were common throughout the Southeast after initial European
contact. This helps explain how to an extent the Natchez—like
the Muskogees—were able to sustain their population. We, of
course, are interested in those Natchez survivors who in the
1730s and later settled down at Nauchee Town, elsewhere in
the Coosa Valley, and even in coastal South Carolina, where in
time they became Creeks. The Natchez, however, still passionately hated the French and dreamed of returning to their homeland on the Mississippi. That aspiration remained unfulfilled,
and the refugees remained Creeks.

A puzzle in studying Natchez refugees in the Creek country
is to determine if they were true Natchez or if they were among
those outsiders, perhaps Tioux and Koroa, who, speaking a different language, had joined the Natchez and eventually became
known as stinkards. As will be seen, the term stinkard applied
to many more southeastern Indians than just these refugees
among the Natchez. Natchez exiles among the Upper Creeks
may have dreamed of returning to their Mississippi homeland.
We can only speculate on whether that homeland was where
the Great Sun resided or elsewhere on the Mississippi where
Tunican or another language was spoken. We know that some
Natchez refugees spoke Natchez, but for the remainder we must
wonder if they came from the stinkards and if they needed an
interpreter when conversing with a true Natchez. There are
intimations that true Natchez relocated among the Upper
Creeks, and stinkards among the Lower.

Such questions concerning ethnic backgrounds, many of
which may never be answered, are not confined to the Natchez

12   but must be raised when considering the Shawnees, Yuchis, Alabamas, Hitchitis, and most of the other groups who at some point became Muscogulges.[20] One might refer to the Creek "confederation," but it would be more meaningful to employ "confederation of confederations."

Far more is known about the Natchez than about the Tuckabatchees. Like the Shawnees and others, they had migrated to the South from somewhere in the North, and eventually the largest number of them established themselves at Tuckabatchee on the lower Tallapoosa River. Spread out for several miles along the riverbank, Tuckabatchee developed as one of the largest and most influential Upper Creek towns. They brought, or perhaps acquired after arrival in the Southeast, large rectangular copper plates and circular brass ones, all inscribed with strange characters and motifs. The brass plates had probably been obtained in trade with Europeans; rectangular copper plates were common throughout the South before Europeans arrived. Associated with the sun, sacred fire, and maize, these plates were an important part of the Indian religion. Priests sedulously guarded them, displaying them only at the most important rituals. On the Trail of Tears—the trek to present-day Oklahoma during the 1830s—Tuckabatchee priests carefully placed these plates in backpacks and spoke to no one as they marched hundreds of miles to the West.[21] Numerous other distinct Indian peoples at one time or another appeared in the Southeast and were eventually regarded as Creeks or Seminoles. One was the Koasatis, who "came a great distance from the north" (perhaps the Tennessee River) and in the late eighteenth century resided among the Upper Creeks above the forks of the Alabama River. Theirs was a Muskhogean language distinct from Muskogee proper. As best they could, they retained their language, culture, and the knowledge that they were a distinct people.[22] Another separate people were the Pakanas, in the late eighteenth century concentrated like the Koasatis on the Coosa River and about the forks of the Alabama River in their own villages, with their own square grounds and language.[23]

Still another Muskhogean but non–Muskogee-speaking people were the Okchais, who lived in towns on the Tallapoosa

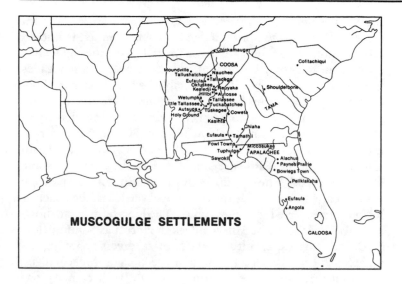

MUSCOGULGE SETTLEMENTS

Muscogulge Settlements

River and even at the end of the eighteenth century retained many aspects of their culture and identity.[24] There were other remnants—the Apalachees, Timucuas, Yamasees, Stonos, Westos (Chiscas or Yuchis), and so forth—among the late eighteenth-century Creeks. Often their languages and much of their cultures had died out, and their progeny began to speak "Creek"; yet by this one can only wonder whether Muskogee, Hitchiti, Shawnee, Yuchi, or Koasati, among other possibilities, was meant.

A measure of geographic stability finally was established among Muscogulge people in the latter part of the eighteenth century. Yet these Indians still were not rigidly fixed in one spot, and it was possible to discern two broad movements, each into a region where there were no whites or at least a minimal white presence. One such area was beyond the Mississippi River and the other was the Florida peninsula. Hunting parties seasonally visited both of these regions, and in time they brought their families and established towns. In the West, Creek settlements appeared on the Red and Trinity rivers and elsewhere beyond

14   the Mississippi.[25] The several Eufaulas illustrate the southern
thrust. The first town of Eufaula about which much is known
is Upper Eufaula, on the Tallapoosa River. During the eighteenth
century an offshoot, Lower Eufaula, "composed of renegades
from all the Creek towns," was established on the Chattahoochee, well below Columbus. Still later, Indians from either Upper or Lower Eufaula who had been hunting in the vicinity of
Tampa eventually founded a new town in Florida. Yuchis from
the Tallapoosa River and the Chattahoochee-Flint river basin
also hunted in the Tampa region, and, like the Eufaulas, some
of them stayed.[26] These Indians in the vicinity of Tampa were
usually called Creeks, but those who had settled in the Alachua
region were referred to as Seminoles. The long-term trend, however, was to label most Muscogulges in Florida as Seminoles.

Despite linguistic, cultural, and political diversity among late
eighteenth-century Creek-Seminole people, or Muscogulges,
two ill-defined divisions, or moieties, can be discerned—one
associated with pure Muskogees and the other with non-Muskogees. The concept of dualism or opposites was common
among peoples throughout the world, including various native
American societies, especially those in the Southeast. European
intrusions had shattered native societies and brought about great
and often confusing changes, certainly in regard to moieties.
With some confidence we can assume that many of the sixteenth-century tribes who later became Muscogulges had
adopted a moiety system as part of their culture before the time
of European contact or soon afterwards. But by the eighteenth
century the traditional dualism that included war (red) and peace
(white) towns had become moribund. After removal to Indian
Territory (present-day Oklahoma) an elderly Muscogulge (Seminole) attested that the concept of red and white towns was not
very important in the West, and there seems little doubt that
this also had been true in the East before removal.[27] Only the
forms, not the substances, of this aspect of the traditional moiety
system remained in the late eighteenth century. A new division
based on ethnic distinctions, unplanned and perhaps unnoticed,
in part brought about by the effects of European intrusions, had
evolved and in large measure had replaced the earlier system.

When we begin to consider the Muscogulge domain in the latter part of the eighteenth century we have to keep in mind that there were two moiety systems, one declining and the other evolving and strengthening.

That in a vague way the two systems overlapped makes it even more difficult to comprehend them. But we must make the attempt, and at first we will turn to the older one. It is important to keep in mind that many Indian peoples had moieties separating towns and also clans within towns, all of which retained much, or at least something, of their vitality long after white contact. Ethnographers in the late nineteenth and early twentieth centuries described in some detail such systems among the Pueblos in New Mexico and certain tribelets in California. Moieties often were exogamous, that is, a member had to marry outside his or her moiety. Sometimes there was a war / peace (red / white) division or a land / water one. Occasionally a child in one moiety was named by members of the opposing moiety, or perhaps those in one moiety buried a deceased member of the other. A recent, and by far the best, treatment of the Choctaws describes how an exogamous moiety system persisted in the East until the Choctaws' removal in the nineteenth century.[28]

But Muscogulges were not Choctaws, Pueblos, or a California tribelet. Despite disruptions in their societies after white contact, the latter tribes maintained a considerable measure of cohesiveness and tribal identity. Muscogulges, in contrast, were an assemblage of numerous peoples. Tribes had merged with or been absorbed by other tribes, and the process could often have been repeated. Shawnees, Natchez, Hitchitis, Yuchis, Tuckabatchees, Alabamas, and others had joined the Muscogulges. Presumably most of the Muscogulge tribes, like others in the Southeast at the time of white contact, or soon after, had adopted some sort of moiety system with red and white, war and peace towns. Our concern is what happened when the Tuckabatchees, Natchez, Shawnees, and other immigrant groups joined and became Muscogulges. We do not know the answer except that change seemed to have been the norm. Possibly immigrants or refugees retained their previous town designations as red or

16   white; probably some of them had never been so labeled to begin
with; or possibly in time they adopted or had imposed on them
the red and white designations of their new neighbors. In Indian
Territory, in the late nineteenth century, Creek or Seminole
towns defeated in the ball game sometimes were force to switch
moieties, to change from red to white if the victor were white
or to become white if red won.[29] There is no record of this
happening at an earlier time in the East, though it may have.
The ball game may have been substituted for war. A defeated
tribe in the East might have been forced to accept the moiety
designation of its conquerors. In these and many other ways
Muscogulges often found that their town's designation changed
from red to white or vice versa and in the process the destination
red or white town, peace or war town, lost its significance.
Because of historical circumstances, by the late eighteenth century many Muscogulge towns were still known as red or white.
This, however, merely reflected a dying system. Members of red
Muscogulge towns did not name children in white ones, and
one could marry into either a red or a white town because it did
not make much difference.

This does not mean that Muscogulge peoples did not have
moieties. Paradoxically, as the traditional war town / peace
town dualism was being enervated, a new moiety dualism based
largely on ethnic distinctions was evolving. On one side were
the pure Muskogee towns and such diverse tribes who had joined
and been absorbed by these towns. (As will be discussed more
fully, a southeastern Indian town was much more than a European one.) On the other side were the Hitchitis and refugees
such as the Koasatis, Alabamas, Tuckabatchees, Yuchis, and
Shawnees who were not absorbed by the Muskogees. Among
the Hitchitis—"the original inhabitants"—and those speaking
closely related dialects were the Chiahas, Apalachicolas, Ta-
mathlis, Sawoklis, Yamacraws, Yamasees, Guales, Oconees,
Osochis, Miccosukees, and possibly Timucuas.

A non-Muskogee moiety did not abruptly appear and at times
never existed. Different ethnic peoples in the non-Muskogee
moiety at times fought among themselves: the Yamasees and
Hitchitis were bitter enemies in the first part of the eighteenth

century, and the Hitchitis and Tuckabatchees persecuted each other in the nineteenth. Despite all this, and although contemporary Indians might not have realized or might even have denied what was happening, the reality was that two ethnic moieties—a non-Muskogee and a Muskogee one—were evolving and strengthening as the older red town / white town division was being destroyed. The best dividing line in the late eighteenth century was not whether one lived in a red or white town but whether it was primarily a Muskogee or non-Muskogee one. This new moiety system tended to be endogamous, which strengthened the cleavage.

Individual towns might have been separated along such ethnic lines, but unfortunately we do not clearly understand much that was happening at the town level. Scholars still debate whether Tuckabatchee, the largest Upper Creek town, was inhabited primarily by the Tuckabatchees, by the Shawnees, or by true Muskogees. Some years ago the distinguished ethnographer, John R. Swanton, was puzzled by the fact that Tuckabatchee was not really Creek (Muskogee).[30] We are also surprised to discover that at one time the *mico* of Coweta, one of the original Muskogee towns, was a Yuchi (or possibly a Hitchiti); and Emisteseguo, before the American Revolution the prominent leader of the Creeks from the Muskogee Upper Creek town of Little Tallassee, in fact was not a Creek, that is, not a Muskogee.[31] It may be best to assume that during the decades before western removal Coweta was Muskogee and Tuckabatchee was not; but Little Tallassee remains an enigma.

In their councils Indians attempted to avoid open disputes and delayed for long periods if necessary in order to reach a consensus. In this fashion Muscogulge towns tended to be democratic. Rarely did a town leader attempt to enforce a policy ruthlessly on all residents. Nevertheless tensions and differences existed, some of which were between Muskogees and non-Muskogees. Time might resolve such disputes, as descendants of refugees adopted the language and culture of their Muskogee hosts. In other instances non-Muskogees moved from the mother town to form a new town—a colony or offshoot—or moved to already existing non-Muskogee towns.

18   Creeks, and the whites associated with them, sometimes designated those in non-Muskogee towns and in certain non-Muskogee clans within a town as stinkards. The etymology of this term is confusing. Today it is best known in connection with the Natchez, or with refugee immigrants who were regarded as inferiors, as stinkards. English traders may have acquired the term from the Natchez or more likely from Frenchmen who traded with these Indians. Another possibility is that the English acquired the word from the Muskogees themselves. Among the Muskogees *estenko (istinko)* meant inferior (literally, worthless hand), and Englishmen may have transformed "estenko" into "stinkard" without reference to the Natchez or to Frenchmen. Throughout the Southeast the terms estenko, stinkard, and their equivalents were commonplace among the Indians and Europeans and, depending on time and place, meant inferior, immigrant, someone speaking a foreign tongue, enemy, or slave. These terms had nothing to do with body odor, though some of the menial tasks performed by stinkard slaves may have been unpleasant, odoriferous ones. True Muskogees applied "estenko" to non-Muskogees. It was a pejorative term, one not appreciated by Hitchitis, Yuchis, Alabamas, and the like, and the use of this term in its various forms contributed to Muskogee/non-Muskogee resentment and division.[32]

Despite the many problems involved, this Muskogee / non-Muskogee split helps explain events in the East before western removal, why more and more Muscogulges became known as Seminoles, and why after 1861 Tuckabatchees sought refuge in Kansas and Cowetas (Muskogees) in Texas when they were not shooting at each other in Indian Territory.

The fact that traditional red / white, war / peace divisions at the town level were becoming insignificant in the eighteenth century should not make us assume that red / white, war / peace divisions at the clan level were also of minimal consequence. The clan system had proved resilient, able to withstand pandemics, warfare, enslavement, and repeated relocations better than most aspects of Indian society, and here the traditional red / white dualism survived.

Each Muscogulge belonged to a totemic clan such as Bear,

Deer, Wind, Beaver, Turkey, Wildcat, Tiger (Panther), or Wolf.   19
The matrilineal clan was an Indian's family, more important to
him than his town or anything else. Wolf, Wildcat, and Alligator
cabins were clustered within a town. Husbands with Wolf wives
were not themselves members of the Wolf clan, but their children were; they belonged to the Wolf mother and to her family,
her clan. Husbands might come and go or be discarded; the
children remained and were educated and disciplined by the
mother's brother or someone of the "same blood." Wind, Bird,
and Bear clans were especially identified with true Muskogees,
whereas the Deer, Tiger, Racoon, Fox, and Potato were more
often best associated with Hitchitis and other non-Muskogees.
There were many exceptions, however. Some refugees were absorbed by and in time became Muskogees, while circumstances
dictated that others remain stinkards. As a result the same clan
might be found in either Muskogee or non-Muskogee villages.
Related clans could be joined into phratries. Among Muskogees,
Bird-Wind-Bear sometimes were so affiliated, as were Tiger-
Wildcat-Potato and Alligator-Tamalgi-Turkey among non-Muskogees. By the late eighteenth century, however, these phratries
seemed to have had only limited significance in Indian society.

A non-Muskogee did not marry into a Muskogee clan and
vice versa, or at least as best we know this was usually true. All
members of a particular clan were in theory descended from a
common animal or similar ancestor and as a result were considered literally kin to each other. In fact, however, the clan totem
served as a badge to identify disparate Muscogulges who for a
variety of reasons considered themselves Bears, Winds, and the
like. When clan members were not related by blood, that fact
perhaps reflected the adoption of many immigrants, individually
and in large groups, by the Muscogulges.

More than anything else, clan membership determined a
Muscogulge's social relationships. If a Wolf visited another town
he customarily resided with and was fed by his Wolf brothers
and sisters. If he were young and courting he might joke with
young Wolf girls who were perfect strangers, but he could court
only a Potato, Alligator, Wind, and so forth. Incest among clan
members, which threatened "to put out the fire," was severely

20 proscribed, and offenders were sometimes punished with the long scratch—as incision made with an awl from the nape of the neck down the spine to the heel. In this and other instances clan vengeance remained the backbone of Muscogulge justice. Murder, adultery, and other crimes were avenged by one's clan. If the culprit escaped, then another member of the clan had to pay by being executed, receiving a beating with sticks, making a monetary payment, or in some other fashion. Such decisions were not reached in the square ground but in that section of town containing the clan's cabins.[33]

We must temporarily put aside the factionalism and disparate elements of the Muscogulges and turn to their culture. Considering their diverse origins, the cultural and social traits discussed assuredly will not apply to all. By the eighteenth century Muscogulge culture was a blend of Indian, European, and African. The prominent Creek leader of the 1780s, Alexander McGillivray, had French, Scottish, and Indian forebears, and his sister Sophia Durand was married to a Negro.[34] The Indian component is what we are now emphasizing. Most Muscogulges had migrated into the Southeast from the west, though Shawnees, Tuckabatchees, Yuchis, and Koasatis arrived from the north. How many Meso-American and Caribbean cultural traits reached the Southeast via the Florida peninsula is unclear; perhaps there are more than the evidence now admits. In any case the most important movement was from west to east, and these Indians brought with them or developed in the Southeast knowledge of the temple mounds and the culture associated with the southeastern ceremonial complex. Clusters of platform mounds have survived, and even today one can see then in Spiro, Oklahoma; Moundville, Alabama; Macon, Georgia; Tallahassee, Florida, and elsewhere in the Southeast. Many were present in the eighteenth century, but they had been built in earlier times. By the eighteenth century, the required population and a powerful state of chiefdom necessary for their construction no longer existed. When the French destroyed the Great Sun's empire after 1729, they extinguished the last vestiges of a Mississippian chiefdom.[35]

Clusters of temple mounds in the Southeast suggest one important fact—Muscogulges were social beings who lived in towns. One did not customarily find among these Indian people or their ancestors a hermit, recluse, or individualist of the Daniel Boone variety. Muscogulges normally lived, died, fought, danced, drank black drink, gossiped, and listened to stories in their square grounds and hot houses in groups.

A convenient starting point in understanding eighteenth-century Muscogulge culture is to look at maize and tobacco. Since grits are such a common food among contemporary southern whites and Negroes and since James Duke created such a southern industry with his cigarettes, one sometimes forgets that maize and tobacco originated with the Indians. They were far more important in Indian culture, however, than they have ever become in those of whites and Negroes. Both plants were cultivated extensively in North and South America and played a vital role in Indian lives.

Of the two, maize was of the most consequence for the southeastern Indians because it was their principal food and it played a significant role in their religion. Introduced into the Muscogulge country centuries beforehand from Meso-America, by the eighteenth century several varieties of maize were being prepared in different ways. The most common was *sofkee*, a gruel or soup, to which pieces of venison were sometimes added. Hardly a household was without a sofkee pot, and family members and visitors ate from it throughout the day whenever they felt the urge. In addition Indians ate corn bread, ghost bread, hard bread, and, for traveling, parched corn.[36] Maize had replaced—though not completely—Indian reliance on *kunti* (zamia) and *smilax* (greenbriar or China briar), both starchy-rooted plants growing in the Southeast, kunti primarily in Florida and smilax in a much larger area. The tubers were grated, dissolved in water, and the residue was pounded into white flour from zamia and red from smilax. Whether growing wild, or in some cases domesticated, kunti and smilax were still harvested on a reduced scale by eighteenth-century Muscogulges. As of old, Indians also cultivated or gathered squash, beans, sunflower seeds, and honey from bee trees (in the eighteenth century often from their own hives).[37]

22   The eighteenth-century Indian diet was more diversified than ever because of the European introduction of fruit trees—apple, pear, peach, orange and other citrus—along with peas, carrots, and similar vegetables. Whether introduced into the Muscogulge territory by Europeans or by other aborigines, sweet potatoes, though native to the Western Hemisphere, were still relatively new in the Southeast in the eighteenth century. Even so, for some Muscogulges, sweet potatoes had become almost as important as maize. This is reflected in the importance of the potato clan, the Ahalaki, the potato people.[38] Poultry, pork, and beef supplemented venison in the diet, and all these new sources of food rendered maize less significant.

But for centuries maize had been the mainstay, literally the staff of life, central to Indian culture and religion. Sweet potatoes, cattle, oranges, peaches, and apples had not changed this. One merely has to consider the *boskita* (busk) or green corn festival celebrated annually when the new maize ripened. The busk marked the beginning of a new year. During this festival a new fire was lighted, the green corn roasted, and the new year commenced. Despite the addition of peaches, oranges, sweet potatoes and cattle, despite a prodigious loss of life to epidemics, despite frequent movements of populations, and despite the adoption of commercial hunting, maize retained both its real and symbolic significance. The sacred fire of four logs represented the sun, the giver of life to maize. The corn goddess, maize, fire, and the sun all remained a vital part of the Muscogulges' religion.[39]

Symbolically, tobacco was second in importance to maize, and like maize was grown extensively throughout the New World. Medicine men carried it in their bundles and used it for medicinal, religious, and ritualistic purposes. Like the black drink, tobacco was associated with sociability, goodwill, and peace. Indians used different styles of tobacco pipes; the most impressive was the *calumet* with a bowl of stone or clay and a long stem adorned with eagle feathers. The calumet was smoked by dignitaries on formal occasions. When a file of singing and dancing Muscogulges approached, the leader holding high a calumet and crying like an eagle, both Indians and whites understood that this was a peace delegation. A calumet raised in this fashion meant far more to Muscogulges than the Europeans' white flag.

Tobacco served many purposes. Early in the morning in a *talwa* one might see an Indian light his pipe—a calumet, pipe tomahawk, or common clay pipe—and, facing the east, blow the first puff to the rising sun, then repeat the process for the other cardinal points. The calumet was passed around at the commencement of treaty and trade negotiations, signifying a commitment to peace and honest dealings. Treaty negotiations and rituals aside, Indians smoked for pleasure. Travellers in the Southeast observed headmen chatting and smoking in the square ground or noted an aged warrior by the fire in his cabin contentedly smoking a pipe tomahawk. Indians still grew and used their own tobacco, but they also acquired it in trade with whites. Often the latter type was milder and more desirable if one were smoking merely for enjoyment.[40]

The precontact Indian culture that is best known is that of the southeastern ceremonial complex identified by large ceremonial platform mounds, sun circles, human hands, and a variety of other motifs. In addition to the surviving artifacts we also have the accounts of early Spanish and French explorers, who described the temple mounds, rituals, and cultural features of these populous Mississippian chiefdoms. By the eighteenth century much of this culture and many of the Indians had disappeared. There were no Muscogulge towns with five, ten, or fifteen thousand inhabitants, and no clusters of large newly constructed temple mounds. The old ones were still there, a source of curiosity to whites and frequently to Indians who had become Creeks and Seminoles. Sometimes Indians had square grounds atop these ancient mounds, even though they did not know who had built them. It was not the temple mounds and large chiefdoms, but other aspects of Mississippian culture—aspects less affected by diseases, drastic population decline, and forced mobility—that survived among eighteenth-century Indians.

Religion is an obvious topic to look at, concerning which the continuing prominence of maize, tobacco, and the busk have

24   already been mentioned. Muscogulge people believed that the earth was flat, probably square, surrounded by water, and that it was overarched by the sky. The sun, moon, and planets were not fixed in the sky but revolved around the earth.[41]

Agricultural societies with urban centers and a priestly class traditionally have been knowledgeable about astronomy. The Mayas kept detailed records charting Venus's path and had an elaborate calendar, all of which were more accurate than those of their European contemporaries. There are many indications that Mississippians had considerable astronomical knowledge; the mounds and stelae at Crystal River, Florida, and Moundville, Alabama, may have been arranged according to the solstices, something like southeastern Stonehenges.[42] After white contact, Crystal River, Moundville, and many other mound complexes were abandoned, and large numbers of Indians and their priests were swept away by disease or carried off into slavery. Eighteenth-century Muscogulges still had their priests, but their proficiency as astronomers seems less than that of their predecessors.

The concept of a three-tiered universe—sky, earth, and underworld—endured. Indians and most animals inhabited the earth. Certain deities were associated with the bottoms of lakes and the bowels of the earth; thus, alligators, frogs, turtles, snakes, and other reptiles and amphibians had a special significance. The Creek shaman (prophet) Captain Isaacs, who went to the bottom of a river and conversed with serpents, was especially revered.[43] Principal deities, however, lived in the sky, including thunder, lightning, and the sun. The relationship between the sun and the ceremonial fire, corn goddess, and maize has already been alluded to. Other celestial deities were Yahola and Hayuya, who might have been lesser gods whom one might call on for breath and strength, or who might have been names for the sun. The supreme god in the heavens was the Master of Breath, again often equated with the sun. In the folklore of the Yuchis, the sun was their mother, and these Indians were known as the Tsoyaha—children of the sun.[44] Birds, especially the eagle, crow, and buzzard, soared on high in close contact with the heavenly gods and were particularly venerated. The eagle-tail dance performed with eagle feathers, the calumet adorned with eagle feathers, the ascending smoke from this sacred pipe, all were identified with the Master of Breath and heavenly deities.[45] It was essential to keep the three parts of the cosmos in harmony. Fowl could not be eaten with venison or bear meat, lest sky and earth be antagonized.[46] For the same reason fire, the breathmaker, should never be extinguished with water.[47] In Muscogulge tradition an eclipse meant that the frog had swallowed the sun or the moon. To prevent calamity, Indians rushed out, shouted, and made loud noises to make the frog release its prey.[48]

Sacred symbols, numbers, and colors retained much of their meaning. Signifying peace, concord, and civil government, white was the most important color. It was not uncommon for "white dirt" to be sent from the square ground of one town to another by a delegation, with their mouths, if not most of their bodies, painted white. Red denoted war. Before battle, warriors painted almost everything red: themselves, the *atasa* (war club), bundles of sticks (the broken days), an elementary calendar, and the tall poles in villages on which scalps were displayed. With increasing emphasis on warfare after European contact, red became of more consequence; by the eighteenth century it equaled or perhaps was superior to white. Black represented death, and when a captive was painted black he knew what was in store. In the eighteenth century blue had a significance that is mostly lost today. At times associated with peace and concord, it may have been a substitute for white, or possibly blue implied female or the underworld. Indian names like Captain Blue, Holata Mico, the Blue Chief, and Blue Mouth Indians, along with blue figures painted on their bodies, had meaning to contemporaries if not to present-day survivors.[49] Muscogulges also associated the four cardinal points with individual colors, though diverse ethnic groups often had different systems. For the Alabama, yellow was north; black, west; red, south; and white, east. For Tuskegees black was north; yellow, west; red, south; and white, east. Despite variations, white was usually east, symbolizing the importance of the sun, maize, and sacred fire among these agricultural people.[50]

Four was a sacred number, associated with the cardinal

26   points, the sacred fire, the sun, and much more. This number repeatedly manifested itself in Muscogulges' culture: in the four sides of the square ground; in crosses engraved on shells or painted on skins and walls; when players danced around the ball pole four times before commencing the game; and when the priest reminded the deceased husband's wife and children that it would take the fallen warrior four days to reach the underworld and that the widow must wait four years before remarrying.

Eighteenth-century Muscogulges buried their dead as they always had, but they no longer built large burial and temple mounds. Instead they laid their dead on the ground and erected a small three-foot-high log structure over the corpse, placed the body on a wooden scaffold, put the corpse in a hollow log, or buried the body in the clay floor and then set fire to the cabin.

Yahola was a resilient title surviving ravages of disease and warfare. As they sat in the square, eighteenth-century traders recounted how the singer passed around what the traders called the black drink. It was in fact dark, but the Indians associated it with purification, peace, and sociability, and they labeled it the white drink. This beverage may have been served in a large conch shell or in a cup purchased from traders. In any case when the black-drink singer emitted long yahola cries—the first deep toned and the latter shrill and held as long as possible—he was following the example of his Mississippian forebears. It is not clear today whether the term yahola signified the Master of Breath, the Sun, or a lesser deity. Obsessed with the Hebraic origins of the Indians, the trader James Adair was convinced that "yahola" was merely the native version of Jehovah.[51] Indians at the time understood yahola's meaning, and yahola was one of the most common Muscogulge titles or names, more common than Jones or Smith among the English.[52] Certain yaholas did far more than officiate at black-drink ceremonies. They might be the talwa's spokesmen, transmitting decisions and policies of village elders and headmen. Yaholas negotiated with whites who often mistook yaholas for more powerful and influential micos. Sometimes knowledgeable whites were aware of the yahola's true function and in 1828 noted that Tuckabatchee Ya-

hola was speaking on his own responsibility—which was exceptional—rather than being the micos' mouthpiece or tongue.[53]
As time passed and the Muscogulge society continued to be
modified, ambitious yaholas expounded the influence of their
position and wielded considerable power, having become much
more than a tongue.

The busk, or boskita, was an important survival from Mississippian times. This annual ritual was enacted in the newly
swept square ground with a ceremonial fire of four logs on new
white sand in its center. Each side had a rectangular lean-to shed
or cabin with benches where, according to protocol and ethnic
background, chiefs, medicine men, warriors, beloved men, and
clan members took their seats. The square ground was in an
elevated spot, perhaps even atop a surviving Mississippian platform mound. The busk, or green corn festival, marked the beginning of a new year, normally at full moon in July or August,
though sometimes later depending on which Indians were involved. At the appointed time Indians congregated and for up to
eight days participated in ancient rites including purging with
black drink, rubbing themselves with new ashes and white clay,
cleansing in the hot house and a plunge in a cold stream, sexual
abstinence, performing the turkey, long, and tadpole dances, and
little or no sleep. Old pottery was broken, old fires extinguished,
unpunished crimes forgiven, and marriages dissolved. Toward
the conclusion, Indians, primarily or exclusively males, took
their assigned seats in the sheds while priests kindled a new fire
by rubbing sticks together. Embers were taken to each freshly
cleaned hearth in town, the green corn was roasted, a feast
ensued, and all joined in the mad dance. A new year had
commenced.[54]

Slavery was more important in Muscogulge life in the eighteenth century than ever before. Indian slavery may have existed
before white contact; certainly it flourished after Spaniards,
Englishmen, and Frenchmen appeared in the Southeast. The
high point was during the 1670–1730 era as tens of thousands
of Indians were captured, put to work on Carolina and Louisiana
plantations, or sold off to the West Indies. Because the pool of
potential captives was depleted, the tempo of Indian slave raid-

Diorama of the Creek busk, or green corn ceremony (Ocmulgee National Monument, Macon, Georgia). Courtesy National Park Service, Southeast Archaeological Center, Tallahassee, Florida. Neg. #03400.

ing sharply decreased after the 1730s. From personal experiences and tales told by their elders, eighteenth-century Muscogulges knew about the fear of going to sleep in their cabins, wondering if hostile Indians, perhaps accompanied by a few whites, might swoop down on their village at night and bind and carry off unfortunates into captivity. Though most Indian slaves were sold to whites, Indian captors retained some who lived in eighteenth-century Muscogulge towns.[55]

In addition to Indian slaves, one also found African slaves among the Muscogulges, and in the decades before the Trail of Tears, African slaves were more numerous and conspicuous than Indian. Some Negro slaves were the offspring of Africans and Indians (zambos), and both zambos and pure Africans lived in Indian villages. In the early nineteenth century separate or autonomous Negro communities emerged in the Indian country, and with some justification whites looked upon them as havens for runaway slaves or maroon settlements.[56]

By the eighteenth century, slavery—Indian, African, zambo —was an established part of Muscogulge life. The actual status of slaves varied in Indian society. Some remained simple chattels having no more rights in the family than herds of cattle or horses owned by wealthy Indians. Some were adopted into a family, a clan, especially females who bore children. In most such cases the children were considered free, like their mothers, members of a clan with a place in native society. In the nineteenth century, autonomous Negro villages appeared. Whether Negroes living in them were slaves or free, in many instances they did not belong to a clan. With their separate villages and existence this was not of much consequence. In a variety of ways Africans and their pure and mixed-blood progeny entered and influenced Muscogulge society, and in some instances the Indians we will be dealing with were these kinds of Muscogulges.

As we know, Indian names were a source of confusion. It confounded whites that males frequently had a succession of three or more names. The first, the baby name, was derived from a physical trait, an event at the time of birth, or a clan reference. At or soon after puberty, the Indian acquired a war or hunting name at the busk. Maturing and assuming more responsibility, he often became a civil official, or a religious or war leader—a *mico, heniha, isti atcagagi, tastanagi, imala, yahola, hoboya, hillis haya,* and so forth. Foremost was the *mico,* the town's principal executive officer or chief, and such a leader was known by his town—Coweta mico or Eufaula mico. Below him was the vice chief, the *mico apokta,* and collectively these lesser chiefs were the *micalgi.* The second man or *heniha* advised chiefs about dances, rituals, public buildings, and communal fields. Even more than micos and micalgi they were responsible for details of civil government. The *isti atcagagi,* or beloved man, was an elder who through exploits in peace, war, commerce and perhaps because of membership in a powerful clan, had risen to prominence. Frequently, though not necessarily, he was too old for fighting and hunting. Muscogulges respected age, and the isti atcagagi was listened to attentively in proceedings at the square ground. A ranking warrior was a *tastanagi* who, after ritualistic purging and fasting, was installed in office. In some

30   towns there was a *tastanagi tako* (big warrior). Advisors and
assitants were *imalas*, while the *tasikayalgi* were common
warriors. Of whatever degree, warriors often had a second
name—*hadjo* (mad or furious in battle), and *fikisiko* (heartless).
Another official title or position was the *yahola*, who among
other duties officiated at rituals by serving the black drink and
giving the long yahola cries, invoking the deity's blessing. *Hillis
hayas* and *kilas* were medicine men. Whites frequently called
them prophets along with an assorted group of *shamans* who
shook, spoke in tongues, had magical powers, and, as in the case
of Captain Isaacs, went to the bottom of a river and conversed
with gods of the underworld. Other titles beyond these mentioned could be found, and particular ethnic groups often used
different words for essentially the same office.

All of this confounded outsiders. The same male Indian might
be known as Coweta mico, Bear, Heniha (Eneah), the Second
Man, or White Lieutenant, and in addition have the surname of
Perryman, McIntosh, or Powell, that of his British father.[57] Females customarily had just one name such as Soyarna, Sofilamaja, and Toakhulga.

Male titles essentially related to towns. There was no supreme mico or political leader of the Creek nation and no grand
tastanagi or overall war chief, despite the fact that from time to
time Indians and whites alike made such claims. The town was
the basic unit. Mention has been made of the Upper Creeks, the
Lower Creeks, and the Seminoles, but it is more appropriate to
consider all these Indians as living in nearly autonomous towns.
One must keep in mind exactly what is meant by a town, a
talwa (tvlwv) in Muskogee. Each talwa had its square ground
and ceremonial fire. The talwa's offshoots or colonies (tvlófv)
might be in villages nearby or miles away. Whatever their population these colonies were not towns; they belonged to the
talwa that contained their fire. Following the whites' example,
some Indians fenced in their fields and lived on isolated farms
and ranches. Nevertheless they still had their tvlwv, their fire,
and their square ground in which to celebrate the busk.[58]

House construction and the talwa's physical layout varied.
Just before the American Revolution, naturalist William Bar-

tram visited the Upper Creek country and described a typical town. In the center was the square ground, council house (rotunda), and plaza. Beyond were houses and streets laid out in a generally regular fashion. Each residential unit was a miniature square ground often containing four structures, one on each side: a cook house and winter residence, a skin house, a provision house, and a two-story building, the lower story for potatoes and the upper a hall for receiving visitors.[59] Less affluent Indians had three, two, or even one structure, but at least the symbolism of the square and the sacred number four remained. Buildings might be rectangular, constructed of logs, or circular wattle and daub structures; roofs were of thatch, bark, or shingles. In major talwas, houses often were dispersed. Around 1800 the northern Florida Seminole town of Miccosukee contained a thousand or more souls, and residences stretched out three to four miles along the banks of Lake Miccosukee. All Miccosukees might not be able to see the council house and square ground, but they usually could spot the tall ceremonial ball pole. The ball pole served many purposes. One was that it, like the sacred fire, symbolized the existence of an autonomous talwa.[60]

Few talwas were without a rotunda or council house, which usually was circular though sometimes square with rounded corners. In Mississippian times rotundas often seated two or three thousand persons, but by the eighteenth century most were smaller, seating hundreds rather than thousands. Regardless of size, their construction was similar: low walls; log rafters from the walls to the high point in the roof's center; an open hole for smoke; roofs covered with bark, thatch, or earth; and a low tunnel entranceway into the council chamber. Dances, rituals, diplomatic negotiations, and assemblies of various kinds were held in the council house, particularly during the winter months, when it sometimes substituted for the hot house.[61]

There was a ceremonial fire in the rotunda's center, but the tvlwv's true fire burned in the square ground, and it was here that the busk and other important rituals were celebrated. Cabins fronted each side, and seating arrangements were clearly prescribed, though arrangements varied from town to town reflecting the Muscogulges' diverse origins. Normally the micos'

32   bed was in the west, and often the warriors' bed in the north, the henihas' in the south, and the youths' and visitors' bed in the east. Micos, tastanagis, henihas and similar officials frequently came from a particular clan, and clan totems—a bird, a bear, an alligator—were conspicuous in front of the respective cabins. These lean-tos might be painted red or white, depending on the primary function of the occupants.[62] Upon occasion women were permitted in these cabins, and exceptional ones addressed the Indians with fervor and authority. Rituals might call for dances by women who were admitted into the square ground from one of the corners. For similar purposes females entered the low tunnel into the council house.

A woman was usually at home where she had her intimate square, and neighboring houses contained her brothers, sisters, fathers, and mothers of her clan. Husbands might come and go or be exchanged, but she kept the house, domestic property, and children. All stayed with her family—her clan. She was the cook, and despite European and African influences on the natives' diet, maize was the staple. She used a large wooden log mortar, about two feet tall with a bowl carved into the top, and a five- to six-foot pestle to grind corn. It was stored outside, becoming as standard a feature as a windmill at a nineteenth-century sod house on the Great Plains, or a television antenna atop houses in 1970 suburbia.[63]

In order to know when to plant and to hold rituals Muscogulge people needed a system of keeping time. By the eighteenth century their knowledge of astronomy had diminished; assuredly the priestly class concerned with it had. Even so, the basic features of earlier centuries survived. Based on lunar months, the calendar began in the summer at the busk or possibly earlier with the first new moon of the vernal equinox. Indian months roughly corresponded to those of the Gregorian calendar: October was the corn-ripening month, February or March the windy month, and June the blackberry-ripening month. Variations existed among the different tribal components. April to October was the ceremonial year with the busk the chief ritual. The day was divided into three parts: morning (the sun coming out of the water), midday, and afternoon.[64] No clocks and bells from gothic church spires summoned Muscogulges to rise, work, eat and return from the fields. The clock, which appeared in Europe in late medieval times, and the Protestant work ethic and mandate not to waste a precious minute, were absent in Indian society.

In recent times census takers have been frustrated because Indians apparently do not know their ages. That figure has had to be estimated or omitted from statistical reports. Despite the census takers' strictures, Indians do know their ages. These ages are calculated, however, on the ancient Muscogulge system. As with the calendar year, one's life was divided into the usual four seasons. In the spring a male child had a baby name, was educated and disciplined by clan elders, and played with clan brothers and sisters. During the summer he received a war name and went on hunting and war parties, and in the autumn perhaps he also became a mico, a heniha, or a hillis haya. The last years—the winter—were spent in his town. Remaining with the women and children while the young men were out hunting, he instructed the youth and passed on tribal lore and medical knowledge. At the square ground, perhaps he was regarded as an isti atcagagi whose advice was sought and respectfully listened to. Throughout the year he might be seen in the square ground, rotunda, or hot house, smoking, drinking black drink, gossiping and passing on traditions. He knew he was in the winter of his life and was confounded that anyone might question or not realize this.[65]

In a general way it is fair to maintain that Muscogulge people were not literate; even so, such a sweeping assertion must be qualified. Since at least Mississippian times Indians used pictographs engraved on stone and shell or painted on hides and clay. Bartram described hieroglyphics or mystical writings on clay walls, and in 1735 Chekilli presented James Oglethorpe a painted buffalo skin that recounted the migration legend of the Creeks, that is of the Muskogees. This buffalo skin and Bartram's clay walls have long since vanished.[66] Bernard Romans, a British cartographer and soldier in West Florida, fortunately copied a few pictographs. They show ten armed men in three canoes setting out against the enemy. On the return, four scalps

34   adorned a long pole. A deer at the top stood forth over all pictographs. This represented a triumph by Muscogulges of the Deer Clan who perhaps successfully had inflicted clan vengeance.[67] A few of the more acculturated Muscogulges wrote in English. Educated by his Scottish father in Charleston, Alexander McGillivray was far more literate than the typical frontiersman who encroached on Creek lands. Another Creek mestizo, John Galphin, son of George Galphin and Metawney, could also write English: "the hole nation is in grate alarm . . . [you must] cum . . . send of an express amadetly . . . I have no paper to rite . . . will wate."[68] A Pulitzer prize, however, was beyond his grasp.

Wampum belts were another means of communication. Wampum beads perhaps were still of shell, though by the eighteenth century, they usually were glass obtained in trade with whites. In treaty negotiations and deliberations at square grounds, belts, after being "read," were delivered, possibly by being thrown on the ground. Emisteseguo in 1770 prepared a belt to bring about peace between the Choctaws and the entire Creek nation, by which he meant Indians living on the Coosa and Tallapoosa rivers. A circle of beads near one end represented the Choctaws; near the other, the entire Creek Nation. Beads in the middle signified Emisteseguo's holding his Choctaw counterpart by the hand. White beads leading to each end represented the path of peace between the Creeks and Choctaws, and black beads at the extremity signified the dark cloud hanging over the two nations. As the belt was read and accepted, the Choctaws were to take tobacco out of an accompanying blue pouch, smoke it, simultaneously pulling off and casting away the black beads. British Indian agent Charles Stuart delivered this belt. If the Choctaws did not accept the peace overtures after reading the belt, they were to return it.[69] Other belts contained tribal history and folklore and were brought out and read by isti atcagagis, hillis hayas, and yaholas or singers. The meaning, if any, of the knots in belts such as Emisteseguo's is unknown.

Whether they were literate or not, Muscogulges needed interpreters because of their ethnic diversity and because they were surrounded by English, Spanish, French, and African neighbors. To an extent wampum belts, pictographs, and a sign language served as lingua franca. Nevertheless interpreters were essential and included every shade and ethnic background. The largest single group, however, as will be discussed more fully later, were pure and mixed-blood Africans—black Indians.

Eighteenth-century Indians moved about as they always had, by walking, running, and paddling dugout canoes; and they also rode horses. More often than not the horse had arrived in the Southeast in connection with trade. In contrast to nomadic Plains Indians, southeastern Indians were essentially sedentary agriculturalists. For the Plains Indians, the introduction of horses had been revolutionary, often a matter of life and death, a fact often recorded in their folklore. Muscogulge stories, however, seldom recount the time when horses first appeared. This is not to say that horses were not important. Southeastern Indians became commercial hunters, and in this regard these animals played a vital role. From time to time Muscogulges also made long journeys to Detroit, Quebec, or beyond the Mississippi. Horseback was the way to go.

Rivers and streams covered the Southeast, and canoes retained much of their utility. They were usually dugout canoes, which is not to say that occasionally northern Indians and French *coureurs de bois* had not brought birchbark canoes and knowledge of their construction into the South. Muscogulges also used portable leather boats. Whenever they had to cross a stream they cut poles, stretched leather skins to form a boat, ferried themselves and supplies across, and then threw away the poles, folded the leather, and proceeded. In earlier times Mississippians had been noted for sailing oceangoing dugouts on the high seas, and in the eighteenth century they still made ocean voyages in their twenty- or thirty-man canoes. Creeks from Coweta and elsewhere on the Apalachicola River paddled or sailed over to Havana, Cuba, and to Nassau in the Bahamas. At one point they invited a white trader to accompany them to Nassau. He agreed—until he saw their dugout. Then he paled. Indians and more adventurous whites, however, went and returned again and again.[70] In the nineteenth century, hard-pressed

36 Seminoles looking for refuge paddled over to the Bahamas to safety. Muscogulge mariners had no compass or sextant, and perhaps not even a map. Like the Vikings, they used the sun and stars and were able to navigate long after land had sunk below the horizon.[71] Most Creeks and Seminoles today live in Oklahoma, and their belts, folk history, and elders reveal almost nothing about their seafaring ancestors. On the Great Plains all of this has a sense of unreality. Diligent scholars seeking information about southeastern Indian maritime exploits may be more fortunate among those survivors in the Florida Everglades and in the Bahamas.

The Indians traveled extensively: to Canada, far beyond the Mississippi, and at times to the islands. When journeying on land it was essential to let foreign Indians know that Muscogulge parties were bent on peace. Assuming there was time, the best way was to paint one's mouth and other parts of the body white and perhaps also to wave white eagle feathers. The intentions of such Indians were clear. Rubbing was a less formal but more common greeting. After approaching one another, Indians shook each other's elbows and stroked parts of the arms and torso.

Eighteenth-century Muscogulge clothing was a blend of European and Indian styles. Shoes were traditional leather moccasins. Leggings might still be of deerskin but more often were woolen as were breechclouts or flaps held fast at the waist by a belt. Brightly colored red and blue woolen flaps were common. If Indians wore shirts, they usually were obtained in trade. Jackets and coats might be of fringed deerskin—Daniel Boone style or made out of imported blankets and strouds. Cloth turbans, belts, beads, and pouches also were often imported. As far as is known, silver did not arrive in the Southeast until the sixteenth century. Like copper, it was highly prized, and in time silver earbobs, beads, gorgets, and armbands appeared. They were obtained in trade and melted and hammered out of coins by native silversmiths. As time passed, Scottish merchants dominated the Indian trade, and with each passing decade the dress of Muscogulge warriors seemed more like that of Highland lairds.[72] Headmen, whose pictures have been preserved, often wore turbans, and ordinary Indians tied silk or cotton handkerchiefs about their heads to hold their feathers or plumes.

In most respects the abilities of native artisans declined after European contact. This can be seen in pottery, shell work, and wood carvings. Frequently a matter of life and death, metallurgy was an exception. The Muscogulges' ancestors, who already knew about copper and lead, fashioned knives, arrowpoints, and other items out of whatever iron and steel they chanced upon after whites arrived. The emergence of native silversmiths has just been mentioned. In the years preceding removal to present-day Oklahoma, Muscogulges who had been apprenticed to farriers and gunsmiths plied their craft in the Indian country. In the main, however, white blacksmiths and gunsmiths serviced weapons that whites had originally supplied.

Southeastern Indians were not as taciturn as they often have been portrayed, as was obvious if one observed their games, especially the ball play. The two principal eighteenth-century ball games employed lacrosse-style racquets: one had a single tall post as a goal, and the other two goals a quarter of a mile or more apart. It has been alleged that in the twentieth century United States football has become a religion of the masses. Without debating this, it should be kept in mind that to a degree ball games were the religion of the Indians. Priests made medicine, and players—fifty to one hundred or more on a side—purged themselves for hours and sometimes days in pre-game rituals. One did not arbitrarily choose sides for a ball game; instead town was pitted against town, clan against clan, and in some instances men against women. Even though games often had great religious and political significance, gambling was rampant. Whatever the ball games' purpose, painted and sweating players, perhaps with panther or buffalo tails tied behind, ran madly to and fro, some falling down groaning with a broken leg or smashed face; hillis hayas chanted and made medicine on the sidelines; blankets, guns, silver ornaments, tobacco, bells, money, and rum exchanged hands with every goal; and young women players, with no more clothes on than the men, shrieked as they scored. A taciturn Indian could not be found.[73] Chunky

38 was another common game in which a spear was thrown after a rolling stone. Few villages were without a chunky yard. Muscogulges spent hours in dicelike games, throwing down cane reeds or grains of corn. Whatever the game, Indians were inveterate gamblers.

Like the ball games, dances served both religious and social functions. Some were sacred, part of the green corn ceremony or to honor the bear and eagle, and were associated with the Master of Breath. Other dances were simply for fun. The repertoire of Muscogulge dances was large, and natives welcomed strangers who could teach new ones. The horse, drunken, and gun dances reflected European influences, and the lively stomp dance was considered by some a "nigger dance," as perhaps was the chicken dance. The eagle-tail dance, often seen at the busk and in treaty negotiations, was identified with peace and customarily performed by white clans; members of red clans frequently enacted the scalp or war dance. A majority of the dances bore animal names—bear, skunk, alligator, bison, rabbit, and so forth. The snake dance was proscribed during the summer so as not to antagonize these reptiles, and the bear dance was not performed in winter while the bear was hibernating. Some dances were for men only, others for women, in others the sexes were mixed. The tendency was for dances *(obangas)* to lose their religious and ritualistic meanings and to be performed purely for enjoyment. Whatever the obanga's function, the Indians danced. Night after night, perhaps into the early morning, accompanied by skin-covered wooden or pottery drums, gourd and turtle shell rattles, and a singer, men and women, separately or together, painted red, yellow, white, and black, in a slow shuffle or wildly animated motions could be seen in the square grounds and rotundas. When scores of shell-shaker girls joined men in a dance with a rapid tempo, the noise was deafening. Able-bodied Muscogulges abstaining from obangas were oddities.[74]

As much as dancing and ball games, war was an integral part of the Muscogulges' life. Without underestimating the many conflicts with white neighbors, as often as not Indians fought other Indians, either to satisfy vengeance or because of tribal

Drawing of Seminole dance at Fort Butler, Florida, 1838, by Hamilton Wilcox Merrill. Courtesy The Huntington Library, San Marino, California.

rivalries. By the eighteenth century they had modified their tactics. They still carried the war club, the atasa painted red, but for the most part, the atasa had become symbolic. The scalping knife, tomahawk, and musket or rifle obtained in trade were the effective weapons. Muscogulges fought in a variety of ways—ambushes, slipping into enemy camps, prolonged sieges, and alongside whites in their campaigns. Whatever the strategy, the tastanagi saw to it if at all possible that he did not lose many men. He could not afford to, because he knew that many Muscogulge components—the Natchez, Yamasees, and Timucuas—had seen their tribes almost completely swept away in a generation or two. In Mississippian times Indians had met each other with massed armies in pitched battles, but that day had passed. The ancient practice of scalping was as common as ever, and upon occasion prisoners were still burned.

When Europeans, primarily the British, made commercial hunters out of the Muscogulge people, they altered all aspects of their life. From time to time we have touched on this. But it is impossible to comprehend Indian society fully without considering commercial hunting and other aspects of their native economy, and it is necessary to consider all this in detail.

Trade

In the late eighteenth century, United States Indian commissioners gave "Chinese hookers" (opium pipes) complete with small silver tubes to the Creeks,[1] but this was not necessary. Indians had long been addicted, not to opium but to European clothing, blankets, hardware, cooking utensils, ornaments, and rum. Powder, ball, firearms, flints, tomahawks, and knives were essential, often a matter of life and death, because without them the Indians risked extermination, starvation, and enslavement. To pay for manufactures the Indians had become commercial hunters, and in the late eighteenth century the concern of many Muscogulges was "whaer . . . shall we get skins to buy what goods our traders shall bring amongst us."[2] Hunting was the answer.

As a result, the life-styles of southeastern Indians differed fundamentally from Mississippian times, and of course, the Indians themselves were not the same. With few exceptions one looks in vain in the eighteenth century for the Calusas, Westos, Timucuas, Yamasees, Guales, and others. The few of them who had survived had blended into the Creek and Seminole nations and had become known as Cowetas, Tuckabatchees, Hitchitis, and Yuchis. Mississippians had been agriculturalists, and maize had been at the center of their subsistence and religion. When whites arrived, Mississippians had two things to exchange for

42 manufactures—slaves and peltry—and for many years when Indians hunted it was uncertain whether their prey had two or four legs. The pool of potential captives after the 1730s was depleted, but the deer, raccoon, bear, beaver, and buffalo remained. Of all these the éco, the white-tailed deer, was the most important by far, and later eighteenth-century Creeks and Seminoles often depended more on selling deerskins than on growing maize. Hitchitis still sang their ancient hunting song: "Hántun talákawati aklig; éyali, sutá! kaya! kayap'hu!" (Somewhere [the deer] lies on the ground, I think; I walk about. Awake, arise, stand up!)[3] But the words had new meaning after the Indians had been transformed into commercial hunters. Prolonged hunting expeditions were required to pay for the white man's goods, and had become an integral part of the Indians' way of life. Male hunters, perhaps but not usually accompanied by their wives, ranged one, two, even six hundred or more miles from their village, their *talwa*, for many months each year.

The trade that had transformed Indian culture was a two-way affair, and it also modified the Europeans' life-style. Englishmen and especially Scotsmen were impelled to abandon their firesides and go live among the Muscogulges for long periods if not permanently. The veteran Scottish merchant, Alexander Arbuthnot, as late as 1817 remarked: "the *honest* trader in supplying their moderate wants . . . of these children of nature . . . may make a handsome profit."[4] The validity of his statement is not impaired by the fact that Andrew Jackson summarily hanged the wizened Arbuthnot. Many of Arbuthnot's European contemporaries had gone to the West Indies, Africa, and the Far East in search of sugar, slaves, and tea; and the populations of these remote regions absorbed increasing amounts of manufactures. In the Muscogulge country, however, it was not sugar, logwood, indigo, or silk, but deerskins that enticed Europeans; and southeastern Indians, whose numbers had finally stabilized and perhaps even were growing, consumed their share of European wares.

Burgeoning European and North American populations increased the demand for leather, and southern deerskins were put to many purposes: saddles, leggings, shoes, gloves, har-

nesses, whips, breeches, and aprons. The price of leather fluctuated, affected by European wars and by cheap woolen and
cotton textiles, which might be substituted for leather in clothing. Nevertheless, as Arbuthnot pointed out, great profits could
be made from the deerskin trade, and he and his fellow merchants continued to descend on the Muscogulge country for as
long as the Indians and the white-tailed deer remained.

Whites, Indians, and Africans were all involved in this commercial enterprise, which was spread out over thousands of
miles. We shall first turn to the Europeans and save the Creek
and Seminole hunters for last. Although the Indians willingly
had become commercial hunters, whites were responsible. One
is struck by the fact that during the eighteenth and nineteenth
centuries essentially the same group of merchants conducted
the Creek and Seminole trade despite the many changes in
sovereignty.

The conflicting territorial claims to the Southeast leading to
the frequent raising and lowering of different national flags,
must have been bewildering. Before 1775 Britain, through her
colonies of South Carolina, Georgia, East and West Florida, and
the interior Indian preserve controlled all of the Creek-Seminole
territory. During the Revolution Georgia and South Carolina
became part of the independent United States, but Spain regained control of East and West Florida. Between 1795 and 1821
the United States, piece by piece, acquired all of both Spanish
Floridas. After the Revolution William Augustus Bowles attempted to establish an independent state of Muskogee in the
Southeast, while partisans of Napoleon endeavored to reestab-
lish French dominion. Overlapping claims and jurisdictions
were enough to send a jurist to Bedlam; but such claims were
resolved not by international law but by force or the threat of
force.

To explain how the same coterie of merchants exploited the
Indian trade it is best to start with Patrick Brown and his firms
of Brown and Company and Brown, Rae, and Company, which
in the mid–eighteenth century dominated the southeastern Indian trade from their headquarters on the Savannah River at or
in the vicinity of Augusta. After Brown died, his successors,

44   John Rae, George Galphin, and Lachlan McGillivray, from their bases in South Carolina, Georgia, and the Indian country, continued the business.[5] When Britain acquired West Florida in 1763, they expanded operations to Pensacola, Mobile, and elsewhere in the new colony.

Breaking out in 1775, the American Revolution strained loyalties and disrupted the Creek-Seminole trade. Not all members of the firm fought on the same side. George Galphin remained in South Carolina at Silver Bluff below Augusta and became the Indian agent for South Carolina and the Continental Congress. His nephews David Holmes and Timothy Barnard and his mestizo children, however, retired to British-held Pensacola or remained among the Indians and helped superintend Muscogulge warriors and the deerskin trade on behalf of the mother country.[6] The elderly Lachlan McGillivray, a loyalist, retired to his Scottish home, turning over his commercial interests to nephew John McGillivray, who remained in Pensacola.[7] Lachlan's mestizo son, Alexander McGillivray, remained at Little Tallassee among the Upper Creeks, became a commissary in the British Indian department, and led the Upper Creeks in support of George III. Young William Panton had come to Charleston before the Revolution, acquired land in South Carolina and Georgia, and trafficked with the Indians. An outspoken Tory whose property was confiscated, he fled to East Florida where he continued trading with the Creeks and Seminoles.[8] Panton in British East Florida was doing the same thing for George III as George Galphin at Silver Bluff was for the Whigs. It is unclear what pre-Revolutionary relationship existed between Panton and his associates and Galphin and his partners. Nevertheless, a decade after the Revolution the arch-Tory Panton could not refrain from noting how much he esteemed the Whig partisan Galphin.[9] It may have been that when the Revolution broke out, merchants who had formerly been members of or loosely associated with Brown, Rae, and Company, found it expedient to have representatives in each camp.

A paradox of the American Revolution was that Panton and his Tory friends, who fled to the Floridas and fought for Britain in a losing cause, in the long run won; while Galphin and his

Silver Bluff colleagues, who fought for the victorious Americans, lost. To comprehend this one merely has to follow William Panton after 1783. He remained in the Spanish Floridas, was given a monopoly of the Indian trade, moved from East Florida to Pensacola in West Florida, and with his associates dominated the Creek-Seminole trade even more than had Brown, Rae, and Company, retaining his ascendancy for almost as long as the deerskin trade remained of consequence.[10] Before, during, or after the Revolution, it was Brown, Rae, and Company, those connected with it, and their descendants, who managed the trade of the Creeks and Seminoles.

From the Indian standpoint there was more continuity and stability than the abrupt changes in sovereignty suggested. Each Indian village normally had one or more resident factors who might be white men (Indian countrymen), mestizos, Indians, or, in certain cases, Negroes. Americans and Europeans eagerly read newspapers for news of military campaigns, peace treaties, and political convulsions. Such newspapers were rare in the square grounds and rotundas. Native hunters still brought peltry to their same village factors, who as usual sent packtrains off to Silver Bluff, Pensacola, and elsewhere. For the hunters the skins' destinations did not make much difference.

Merchants involved in the Creek-Seminole trade, whatever their nationality, concurred that there should be a well-regulated commerce, by which they meant a monopoly or something approaching one. This was not surprising considering that Adam Smith, the advocate of free trade and *laissez faire*, did not publish his *Wealth of Nations* until 1776, and in that year he was a prophet or reformer, hoping to scrap mercantilism and its regulations. Just after the Revolution the greatest opposition to monopoly and special privilege could be found in the United States. Yet in this regard Americans made an exception regarding Indian commerce, and the reasons were military and political rather than economic. The best way to manage the "independent" Indian nations and to render them protectorates was to control their trade. Even the republican arch-foe of privilege, Thomas Jefferson, both as secretary of state and later as president, professed in the case of the Creeks and Seminoles that a

46   monopoly was justified, even essential.[11] The alternative was to
have these Indians provided with goods by unlicensed and perhaps disreputable traders, forcing the Creeks and Seminoles to
turn to foreign merchants and alien powers, and posing a danger
to the republic's exposed southern frontier.

From the 1760s until just before removal to present-day Oklahoma, white neighbors of the Creeks and Seminoles, though
subjects of different colonies or countries, regulated Indian commerce. The provisions were similar, and as an example we might
look at those of British West Florida. Britain acquired this province in 1763, and the center of the southeastern Indian trade
began to shift from Charleston and Georgia to Pensacola. In
1770 West Florida, assuming jurisdiction over territory not only
within its boundaries, but also to the north in the unorganized
hinterland—the Creek country—passed an act regulating commerce. Traders in West Florida had to have a license, post a
bond, list their packhorsemen and other employees, and be responsible for their conduct. Factors were required to traffic with
only one designated village where they had to have their truck
house. They could not deal with any other village or "trade in
the woods" on the sly. Factors were prohibited from entertaining
other factors and white travellers, whatever their origins, for
periods exceeding four days. Traders were required to attend
general Indian councils, to support the military and diplomatic
objectives of the province, and to pay proper respect to the great
medal chiefs. It was made clear, however, that traders were not
the diplomatic and military agents of West Florida. Traders were
prohibited from employing any Negro, mestizo, or Indian who
considered himself an Indian or anyone "who from his manner
of life" was regarded as an Indian. It was no easier in the eighteenth century than in the twentieth to agree on what made one
an Indian. For better or worse, rum was an essential part of the
Indian trade, and traders were allowed eighteen gallons every
three months. Credit was essential, but it too had its limits.
Each hunter might be furnished annually in advance no more
than five pounds of powder, twelve pounds of bullets, and goods
equal in value to thirty pounds of skins. Regulations included a
schedule of prices, which valued blankets, silk ferrets, scissors,

earbobs, hatchets, and a long list of other goods.[12] After 1783
similar regulations were enacted when Spain authorized Panton,
Leslie, and Company to trade exclusively with the Creeks and
Seminoles and when the United States established its warehouse, i.e. factory, system. Regulations were promulgated in
Pensacola, Saint Augustine, Charleston, Washington, and elsewhere, but not in Indian square grounds. Whites appreciated the
advantages of a well-regulated trade (a monopoly) far more than
did the Indians.

Overlapping jurisdictions and petty quarrelling made the Indians wonder who spoke for the white man. Before 1775 each of
the four British colonies bordering the Muscogulges contended
that it should supervise affairs in at least part of the unorganized
hinterland, and in the individual colonies it was unclear whether
the representative assembly or the royal governor should make
the basic decisions. In London George III had different ideas, and
he appointed a superintendent who was to oversee Indian affairs
for all Indians below the Ohio River. These disputes continued
after 1783 as Georgians, the United States national government,
and Spaniards simultaneously insisted that they were responsible for most or all of the Muscogulges. At the same time British
subjects told the Indians that George III had reluctantly given
up the southern colonies and that he was going to return and
take the Indians under his wing; and Napoleon was reminded
that French blood flowed in the veins of Alexander McGillivray
and other Creeks and that the first consul must do something
about it.

We must put aside jurisdictional disputes and rival colonial
ambitions and trace the evolution of the Creek trade from the
mid-eighteenth century until the 1830s. The overall character-
istics are fairly clear. Up until the Revolution South Carolina—
and perhaps for a few years Georgia—dominated the trade
through firms such as Brown, Rae, and Company and through
individual planter-merchants like Henry Laurens who bought
packs of skins in Charleston and disposed of them in Europe.[13]
Up until 1763, the French at Mobile also had a stake in the
Creek trade, and Carolinians, who had to freight their lead,
powder, and other goods hundreds of miles by packhorse, fretted

48   about the French in Mobile, who could conveniently ship goods up the Alabama River to Fort Toulouse in the Upper Creek country. Carolinians also worried about the effects of French Jesuit missionaries, contrasting them with Carolinian packhorsemen who were but loosely regulated.

Before the Revolution South Carolina also had another rival—Georgia, which had been founded in 1733. Liberally interpreting the new colony's limits, James Oglethorpe and his successors asserted control over much of the Creek commerce and required traders to get licenses and post bonds in Savannah rather than in Charleston. An increasing amount of peltry arrived at Augusta, Savannah, and Frederica, but much of it was forwarded to Charleston before shipment to Europe. South Carolina, rather than Georgia, French Louisiana, or Spanish Florida was undeniably the focal point of the Creek trade before the American Revolution.[14] In one sense the Georgia–South Carolina dispute was artificial, because it was often difficult to tell which colony the merchants involved belonged to. Each claimed George Galphin, Lachlan McGillivray, and William Panton, and it was symbolic that Galphin's trading post at Silver Bluff was on the Savannah River boundary.

Having defeated Spain and France in 1763, Britain created the new colonies of East Florida and West Florida out of the spoils. Saint Augustine was the capital of the former and Pensacola the latter. Merchants from Georgia and South Carolina constructed warehouses on the Saint Marys and Saint Johns rivers to serve Creeks in East Florida and established other warehouses in Pensacola. Lachlan McGillivray sent nephew John McGillivray to Pensacola to open a branch.[15] An increasing number of packhorse trains laden with skins began to make their way to Spalding's Upper Store on the Saint Johns River, to John McGillivray's Pensacola warehouse, and elsewhere in the Floridas. Wealthy merchants like George Galphin and Lachlan McGillivray did not care much whether factors in Creek towns sent their skins to Pensacola, the Saint Johns River, Silver Bluff, or Charleston. Whatever their immediate destination, many of them eventually arrived in Charleston, and South Carolina retained its commanding position—that is until 1775.

The American Revolution convulsed the Muscogulge trade, though often appearances were deceiving. This was because a high percentage of factors in Indian villages and wealthy merchants in coastal cities remained faithful to George III, becoming Tories. There are various reasons for this. One is that many of them were Scots, who as a group throughout America remained fiercely loyal to the mother country. Quickly putting his affairs in order and salvaging what he could of his estate, the elderly Lachlan McGillivray retired to the Highlands. Other Scottish merchants—William Panton, Thomas Forbes, John Leslie, James Spalding, and William Alexander—fled from Georgia and South Carolina to East Florida.[16] Lachlan McGillivray's nephew John remained in Pensacola and, in return for an annuity paid to his uncle, took over the business.[17] George Galphin stayed at Silver Bluff and South Carolina appointed him agent to the Creeks,[18] but his nephews David Holmes and Timothy Barnard joined Tory John McGillivray in Pensacola.[19] The effect of all this was that an increasing amount of the Creek-Seminole trade was funnelled through the Floridas, especially West Florida, and it was during the Revolution that Pensacola replaced Charleston as the key port for the southern Indian trade. Before 1775 John Stuart, Britain's superintendent for the southern Indians, lived in a fine house near the Charleston waterfront. In 1776 the Scottish superintendent arrived at Pensacola, where he spent his few remaining years.

Despite bitter guerrilla fighting between Whigs and Tories in the Southeast and major campaigns against Charleston and Savannah, life in Creek-Seminole towns continued in the usual pattern, which is not to say the Indians were unaffected by hostilities. But the traditional rhythm persisted. In the fall, hunters went to the factor who often, but not always, was a Tory, and from him got supplies. After the hunting season Indians brought peltry to the factor who loaded the furs and skins on packhorses and sent them off. The only difference was that their destinations were posts on the Saint Marys and Saint Johns rivers in East Florida and especially Pensacola in West Florida, rather than Silver Bluff or Charleston.

Pensacola's status as the most important port in the southern

50   Indian trade suffered a setback in 1781 when the young Spanish
      captain, Bernardo de Gálvez, captured the West Florida capital.
      British merchants who had not fled to the interior retired with
      the British garrison, and packhorse trains with their peltry
      stopped arriving. Few trading goods were to be found in the
      holds of arriving Spanish ships.

      Gálvez realized that in order to win the Indians' goodwill it
      was essential to supply them. Spain's dilemma was that her
      manufacturing and her ability to extend credit lagged. Therefore
      she turned to her Bourbon ally France, and Gálvez in New Or-
      leans made arrangements to import goods into Louisiana and to
      distribute them among the southern Indians. But British ships
      captured some of the French vessels, there were other setbacks,
      and by the time peace was restored it was obvious that the
      venture had failed.[20]

      The 1783 treaty awarded both Floridas to Spain. She had
      already captured West Florida and proceeded to establish her
      authority in East Florida. The thousands of British loyalists in
      East Florida began to evacuate. Spanish authorities in New Or-
      leans, Pensacola, and after 1784 Saint Augustine realized they
      had to supply the Creeks and Seminoles and their neighbors at
      once and reluctantly turned to William Panton, John Leslie,
      Thomas Forbes, William Alexander, and Charles McLatchy,
      Scottish traders, most of whom had fled to East Florida. During
      the Revolution they had continued to trade with the Creeks and
      Seminoles, and after 1783 they asked Spain to let them remain
      in the province and continue this commerce. With representa-
      tives in Indian villages and dependable sources of supply in
      Britain, they insisted that they could effectively manage the
      trade in Spain's behalf. Spain did not trust these Scottish Tories,
      but the alternatives were worse. The arrangement with France
      had failed, and the impatient Indians had to have supplies.

      Reluctantly Spain allowed Panton, Leslie, and Company to
      remain in East Florida, then to build a warehouse in Apalachee
      on the Wakulla River, and in time others at Pensacola, Mobile,
      and elsewhere. In 1784 Panton himself moved from Saint Au-
      gustine to Pensacola to resume trade with the Indians, which
      had been disrupted since Gálvez had captured the city in 1781.

Panton, Leslie, and Company gradually expanded its operations
from Saint Augustine to the Mississippi River and in time was
conceded a virtual Spanish monopoly of the Indian trade
throughout the entire Southeast. There were competitors—dis-
affected British merchants, especially those who had abandoned
Pensacola in 1781 and were infuriated that Panton had appropriated their trade, American merchants on the Georgia frontier,
and Spanish soldiers who illegally bartered rum for skins. Yet
even after one takes all this into consideration, nothing alters
the fact that Panton and his associates, because of their Spanish
monopoly and business acumen, dominated the Creek-Seminole commerce for decades.[21]

After moving to Pensacola and outwitting and supplanting
his British loyalist rivals based in Mobile and New Orleans,
Panton had to contend with subsidized United States trading
posts or factories in the 1790s. They were first established in
1795 to take advantage of territorial and economic concessions
won from Spain in the Pinckney Treaty. Spain agreed that West
Florida's northern boundary was the thirty-first parallel (only
forty miles above Pensacola) and in so doing relinquished claim
to much of the Creek country. The United States constructed a
government-owned factory at Coleraine on the Saint Marys
River, whose purpose was to take over the Creek trade and to
wean the Indians from Panton, Spain, and British or French
adventurers. From 1795 until the factory system was abandoned
a quarter of a century later, there was always a Creek trading
house, though it moved westward from Coleraine near the coast,
to Fort Wilkinson on the Oconee River, to Fort Hawkins on the
Ocmulgee, and finally to Fort Mitchell on the Chattahoochee.
Employees at the Creek trading house furnished the Indians
with goods almost at cost and were prohibited from swapping
rum for skins. If the Indians and packhorsemen were determined
on a saturnalia, rum could be supplied, but only after trade was
completed. Drunken Indians were not to be cheated out of their
skins. From time to time these Creek factories gave Panton stiff
competition, but in the long run the factory system failed.[22]
Most Creeks and Seminoles looked to Panton, Leslie, and Company (Forbes and Company after 1804) or to Spain rather than

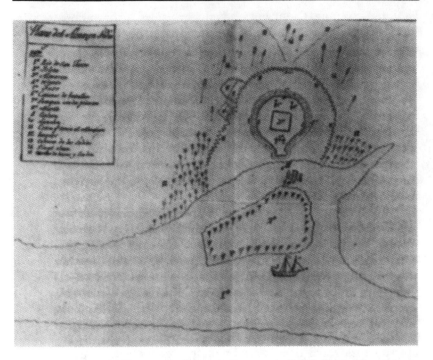

Concepción (Panton, Leslie, and Company's fortified warehouse on the upper St. Johns River), as depicted by Lt. Fernando de la Puente in 1792. From the East Florida papers, courtesy Florida State University Library, Tallahassee.

to the American factories. Winning the Revolution had cost Americans much of the southeastern Indian trade.

Panton, Leslie, and Company's success can be explained on many grounds: intimate knowledge of the Indian trade, business savvy, tradition, and the fact that it extended credit and the United States did not, or at best only a limited amount. The basis of the firm's prosperity depended on the Spanish-Indian trade monopoly, but from this foundation it branched out into manifold legal and illegal activities: supplying the white civilian population of the Floridas with food and manufactures, speculating in land, bribing governors in Saint Augustine and Pensacola, manufacturing salt at Exuma and Turks Island in the Bahamas and importing it to the Southeast, and much more. Contrasting Panton, Leslie, and Company with the United States government–run factories illustrates the advantages of private initiative over state-operated concerns.

For the Muscogulges the important consideration was that from before the American Revolution until removal in the Andrew Jackson era assorted warehouses or factories ringed the Indian country. It was to these stores—to Galphin's at Silver Bluff; to Panton's at Concepción on the Saint Johns, at San Marcos in Apalachee, and at Pensacola; to American factories at Coleraine or Fort Wilkinson; and to hastily built log warehouses thrown up near the coast by foreign interlopers—that the Indians brought their skins. The "Indians" involved customarily were village factors and their employees, who collected the peltry, loaded it on packhorses, and dispatched them to the appropriate (usually the closest) warehouse. But traders were flexible and, depending on conditions, would send their small, sturdy packhorses one hundred or even four hundred miles out of the way. Panton understood this. He had his monopoly, and his high prices reflected it. Even so, he and his successors realized that if they were too greedy there was the danger that village traders might direct their packtrains to American factories in Georgia or to the warehouses of interlopers. This tempered Panton's conduct and kept his prices, though high, at least within reason.

The Indian trade was conducted at three levels: in individual villages where hunters brought in pelts and settled accounts with the factor; at substantial warehouses on Muscogulge frontiers where packhorse trains arrived with bundles of peltry; and in London where ships, their holds filled with chests and barrels of skins and furs, arrived from Pensacola, San Marcos, Coleraine, or wherever. London remained the market for the bulk of the Creek-Seminole peltry, despite the fact that after the Revolution Panton often shipped his through the Bahamas, and the United States through Savannah and Philadelphia. Although Spain sometimes required Panton to consign peltry to Seville, and although Liverpool, Paris, and Amsterdam also received southeastern furs and skins, London remained preeminent.[23]

54   This trade, carried on at various levels over thousands of
miles, illustrates how the Yuchis, Cowetas, Tuckabatchees,
Shawnees, Hitchitis and other Creeks and Seminoles in isolated
villages were affected by and caught up in the dynamic growth
of European commercial and industrial capitalism. In London,
at the center, Panton turned to Strachan and MacKenzie and to
Penman, Shaw, and Company for supplies, but the United States
relied on a variety of separate firms scattered about England
from London to Lancashire.[24]

Experienced in the American Indian trade, these firms readily
procured a wide assortment of goods. One might stroll through
a dimly lit warehouse, the only sounds being river traffic on the
Thames and waves lapping against the quay, and even though
the closest Indians were thousands of miles away, a look at the
goods on the shelves and in half-packed chests revealed how
much the southeastern Indians' life-style had changed since
Columbus's day. Clothing included expensive ruffled shirts,
plain shirts, and common-Creek checked shirts, shoes, shoe
buckles, wool and cotton stockings, leggings, buff jackets, hats,
handkerchiefs (silk and cotton) for turbans, black ostrich feathers for plumes, gloves, and buttons. Shawls, petticoats, and shifts
had long appealed to Muscogulge women. A myriad of textiles
was available: plain and striped blankets from Lancashire, the
more costly ones thicker and warmer and better able to shed
water. From Stroud in the west of England came cheap, coarse,
bright-red strouds, popular and commonly used for breech-
cloths. Muslins, wool, serge, linen cloth and table linen, plain
and colored cotton cloth and a wide variety of other textiles
were to be seen. Silver armbands, wristbands, earrings, gorgets
and razors were made in shops in metropolitan London, as were
silver and steel pipe tomahawks, black-drink cups, brass wire,
sleighbells, and cowbells. Occasionally silversmith's tools were
provided, for since the sixteenth century the southeastern Indians themselves had been fashioning headbands, gorgets and
the like by hammering or remelting silver coins and ingots in
clay crucibles. In London and elsewhere a prodigious number of
beads were produced, which the Indians used for wampum belts,
to adorn the necks of their wives, and for decorative purposes.

Riding saddles and spurs and pack or hunting saddles with sur-
cingles signified that two centuries after the era of the conquistadores, the Creeks regarded the horse as a friend. Indians as
well as whites appreciated that gauze mosquito nets were an
improvement over thick smoke and bear's grease in deterring
insects. Tin, copper, iron, steel, and pewter, cooking and eating
utensils were conspicuous as was iron hardware from nails to
door locks. Children's horns and Jew's harps for all ages often
were of steel. An occasional assortment of carpenter's tools was
to be seen. Dozens of iron hoes suggested how much Creek
agriculture had changed and the degree to which it had remained
the same. No Mississippian precedent existed for reaping hooks.
Fish hooks, nets, beaver, and wolf traps all made the Indians
more efficient fishermen and hunters. It was the smooth bore
musket and long rifle from London or Birmingham and the
Midlands, of course, that had revolutionized Indian hunting.
Factors and wealthy merchants like Panton rather than the ordinary Indian had need of the steelyards. Needles, thread, scissors, and thimbles were for sewing. Blue, black, red, and white
glass beads served for decoration and for belts of wampum.
Paint—blue, vermilion, verdigris—was to adorn the Creeks and,
along with combs and mirrors, help prepare them for rituals and
games. At an early date Creeks had appreciated the value of flint
and steel for fire making. Sometimes one saw barrels of rice,
sugar, and flour, hogsheads of rum, and twists of tobacco, though
often these commodities were acquired in North America and
the West Indies. British flags, large drums, and silver medals
with King George's bust were especially conspicuous when the
king had need of Creek and Seminole warriors.[25]

Eventually orders from America were filled, and goods packed
in chests and barrels were sent off to America, where they eventually were unloaded at Galphin's warehouse at Silver Bluff,
Panton's in Pensacola, or elsewhere. These employees broke
them up into fifty-pound parcels and transferred rum from large
barrels into small kegs. Powder and lead were split up into fifty-
pound packs or kegs, packs and each packhorse normally carried
twice as much lead as powder. Packhorses from the interior
were loaded with goods for the return trip to the villages. Storing

56   these wares in his truck house, the factor outfitted hunters at the beginning of the season, and kept goods on hand to dispense from time to time throughout the year.

To their chagrin, Spaniards realized that Britain after 1783 still controlled the Indian commerce. They were never sure just what to do but were aware that all trade was based "on this system of credit and confidence."[26] The era of bartering trinkets for pelts had long passed. Credit was vital and had to be made available at every level—London, warehouses on the Muscogulges' borders, and village truck houses. A year or even two might elapse before ships laden with peltry returned to the Thames and Panton settled accounts with Strachan and Mac-Kenzie. It might take almost a year before packtrains from Indian towns arrived at Silver Bluff and Pensacola to reimburse Galphin or Panton for goods advanced earlier in the season. In the Creek and Seminole villages, hunters got their powder, ball, and other supplies in the fall but did not pay for them until their return from the hunt in the spring. Almost everyone involved in the skin trade was in debt. Panton and Galphin passed debts on to village traders who in turn extended credit to the hunters. The latter, however, were at the end of the chain and usually could handle debts and continue to get trading goods only by extending the hunting season and ranging even farther from their talwas.

No Indian system of bankruptcy existed, but there were alternatives to dealing with oppressive debts. One was to ignore them and start a fresh account—not with another of Panton's factors, but with a trader from the United States, or perhaps with interlopers who established warehouses on the coasts, or possibly with itinerant traders, whatever their origins, who from time to time roamed the woods. Land cession provided another option, and planting a tomahawk in the village factor's skull offered still another way out. The Indians' concern was not debt, but a dependable source of guns, powder, and manufactures. The United States, perhaps making a virtue out of necessity, advanced little or no credit to the Indians at the Creek factories. London was the world's financial capital, and Panton's ability to exploit this had much to do with his success.

Muscogulge hunters sank deeper into debt, and hunting,

which took them away from home for up to one-half a year and
sometimes even more, represented a form of peonage. The com-
pulsion to devote ever more time to hunting in order to pay off
at least part of their old balance and obtain more goods on credit
represented something new in Muscogulge life. Commercial
hunting had been foreign to pre-Columbian Mississippians and
to Creek ancestors living in Spanish missions. Though far removed from the workshops of London and the mines and factories of the Midlands, Creek and Seminole hunters had more
in common with English workers during the early stages of the
Industrial Revolution than met the eye.

Only a few Creeks and Seminoles ever visited the Old World
and glimpsed England's manufacturing and financial centers.
Indians regularly saw a sample of European manufactures in the
factor's truck house, and a wider display was available at warehouses on the edge of the Muscogulge country. These warehouses were more than just single small log structures. One
could see this by looking at Galphin's establishment at Silver
Bluff on the South Carolina side of the Savannah River, the
principal entrepôt of the Creek trade before the Revolution. On
high ground overlooking the river, his brick residence allowed
Galphin to view his slave quarters, store, skin house, barns,
outbuildings, cow pens, and indigo fields. If dust rising in the
distance was not from cattle being driven to his cow pens it was
from packtrains—four hundred or more animals yearly—plod-
ding toward Silver Bluff. Slaves unloaded the skins, stored them
in the warehouse, and repacked them for shipment by water to
Savannah or Charleston. During their stay the packhorsemen
were entertained and outfitted with rum, munitions, and goods
for their return trip. With buildings of various description, scores
of slaves, thousands of acres, assorted wives, mistresses, and
children, the unlettered Galphin prospered on the expanding
frontier.[27]

After Pensacola became the most important center for the
Creek peltry trade, Panton's establishment in some respects
became more extensive than Galphin's. In 1801 his employees
of diverse ethnic backgrounds, mostly nonwhite, numbered
eighty-five, 12 percent of the city's civilian population. They

58   kept his books, loaded and unloaded oceangoing vessels, weighed skins on beams and scales, turned screws to press the skins together before packing in one-thousand-pound hogsheads, or occasionally in large chests. They beat loose skins weekly to prevent worm damage; they worked in his tannery, cow pens, and stables; they attended to the traders and packhorsemen coming in from the Indian country; and they performed a myriad of other tasks. White employees, often fellow Scots and kinsmen, joined Panton in entertaining ship captains, village traders, Indian delegations, the Spanish governor, or provincial officials. Panton's Negro employees lived throughout the town, in the warehouse and outbuildings at his headquarters, in his own house, in newly built cottages, and in houses abandoned by British settlers in 1781 and not purchased by the incoming Spaniards. Absentee owners of these houses had made Panton their agent. During the warm months when Panton had thousands of skins in his warehouse and his tannery was in operation, the citizenry was thankful to be blessed by a stiff sea breeze.[28]

Panton had branches elsewhere in the Spanish Floridas including ones on the Apalachicola, Saint Marks, Saint Johns, and Saint Marys rivers. The branch at Prospect Bluff on the Apalachicola River, established in 1804, was only fifteen miles from the mouth, easily reached by oceangoing vessels. Here the storekeeper had his residence with a nearby storehouse for trading goods, a skin house, cabins for Negro workers, a granary, barn, miscellaneous outbuildings, thirty acres of fenced cropland, a cow pen, and twelve hundred cattle.[29]

Less pretentious were single, hastily thrown-up log structures, such as those built by the interloper William Augustus Bowles near the mouth of the Ochlockonee River. They could serve for a season or two, and if authorities destroyed them, they could be rebuilt on the same spot or near the mouth of another convenient river.[30]

It is impossible to get precise figures about peltry exported by the Creeks and Seminoles. Over the long run Panton, Leslie, and Company handled the bulk of this trade. Their records that have survived, which are considerable, usually are the ones they showed to Spain, and by no means did they tell everything to the Spaniards. United States accounts at the Creek factories are more complete but relate to only a fraction of the trade. Surprisingly little is known about George Galphin's operations at Silver Bluff, and even less is understood about smuggling by interlopers like Bowles, by soldiers or white employees stationed in the Indian country who traded on the sly, and by unregulated traders who traversed the woods with kegs of rum, trying to inveigle hunters out of their skins.

Nevertheless, assorted data disclosed something of the magnitude of the trade. On the eve of the Revolution 250,000 pounds of deerskins—306,000 pounds in 1768—most of which came from the Creeks, were exported annually from Georgia, and these exports approximately equalled those of Charleston.[31] Soon after Panton arrived in East Florida he exported 32,000 skins (almost 100,000 pounds), and reported that with any encouragement and luck he could ship out 100,000 skins annually, the entire output of the Lower Creeks and Seminoles.[32] After he had relocated in Pensacola during the 1790s he declared that he always exported at least 124,000 skins.[33] In 1803 his Pensacola exports were 79,500 skins (203,200 pounds).[34] Upper Creeks furnished a majority of the skins exported from Pensacola. When the United States Creek factory was established it handled 50,000 pounds of skins annually.[35] An overall estimate is that 8,000 Muscogulge hunters brought in 300,000 or more pounds of deerskin annually, or roughly 40 pounds per man. If one makes allowances for inexperienced young boys and old men, the average take for a veteran hunter must have been considerably higher. All of these figures are for deerskins; none takes into account the bear, raccoon, beaver, fox, muskrat, and other furs whose value was far less.

Hardly ever were Indians compensated for their peltry with money; instead they were paid in "chalks" or "marks." Each chalk was worth twenty-five cents or two Spanish reales or "bits." There were eight reales in the Spanish peso or dollar.[36] Traders credited hunters with so many chalks when they brought in their skins and in payment for other purposes. During the Revolution British agents promised the Indians one hundred chalks or twenty-five Spanish dollars for every live prisoner.[37]

60   The chalks outstanding were entered into the ledger which Indians might examine. Counting was not by arabic numerals but
by marks. A four-chalk balance was indicated by "llll." Eighteenth-century Muscogulge pictographs reflected such a system
of counting, though it is not known whether they inherited it
from Mississippian forebears or learned of it from Europeans.
Trading goods were valued in chalks or pounds of leather, and
one chalk (twenty-five cents) per pound of deerskin long remained the standard. Prices of trading goods could be and were
increased, however. As much as anything these chalks entered
on the factors' ledgers symbolized the extent to which the Muscogulges had become part of the capitalistic market economy of
the western world.

A key, sometimes the most important, personage in an Indian
village was the factor. He might be adopted by a clan or born
into one, and possibly he was a beloved man or a tastanagi. What
gave him much of his influence was that he had the weights and
measures; kept the accounts; and had supplies essential for the
winter hunt, a petticoat for the hunter's wife, and trinkets for
his children. All of this was done on credit, and the books were
not settled until skins were presented in the spring. If the hunter
died, ran off, or took his skins elsewhere, the trader was out of
pocket. The factor outfitted and supervised between 20 and 150
hunters, depending on the town's size, and he stayed at the truck
house until all hunters were in and accounts settled, lest the
Indians decided to go elsewhere.

The factor might be a white man or even a Negro, but usually
he was a mestizo. Often the son of a white trader and a Muscogulge woman, these mestizo Indians are best known to posterity, at least to outsiders, by their father's surnames. Alexander
McGillivray has already been mentioned, though as a member
of Panton, Leslie, and Company he was more than an ordinary
village trader. Indian chiefs in the 1813 Creek War, who fought
both against and with Andrew Jackson, included Peter Mc-
Queen, Josiah Francis, William Weatherford, Wiliam McIntosh
and Timpochee Barnard; all were mestizo factors. Osceola repeatedly proclaimed he was a pure-blood Muskogee, but his
mother's spouse was the trader William Powell, and during

Oceola's lifetime whites most often called him Powell. Early in the nineteenth century Bowlegs became a common Seminole name, and the interloper-adventurer William Augustus Bowles may have been responsible. The prevalence of so many Indians named Grayson (Grierson), Perryman, McIntosh, Moniac (Manac, Monthack), and Barnard can be attributed to white traders.

Mestizo offspring often were genetically more white than Indian, because white traders frequently married mestizas rather than pure-blood Indians. As far as is known, Alexander McGillivray was at most one-quarter Indian. His father was a Scot and his mother's father a Frenchman. For good reason Abigail Adams, the vice-president's wife, remarked when Alexander visited the nation's capital that she hardly suspected him of being Indian: he "dresses in our own fashion, speaks English like a native . . . is not very dark, [and is] much of a gentleman."[38] Bowles's wife was a mestiza as was McIntosh's, and so on.

Mestizo factors had their father's surnames, were members of their mothers' clans and had Indian names and titles. As such they were part of two cultures, belonging to both and to neither. They were uncertain whether their father's surname or mother's clan was paramount. Some mestizos blended into white society. In their youth George Stiggins and Thomas Woodward dressed as Indians and were so regarded, but in their old age they were wealthy planters, championing virtues of the peculiar institution and the white South.[39] Even for mestizos who remained among the Indians the pull of white culture was strong. At the end of the ninteenth century the Creek Graysons in Oklahoma traced their lineage through male Scottish ancestors instead of along matrilineal clan lines.[40] Asserting his Mississippian background, Alexander McGillivray always insisted he was little interested in storing up wealth, that money really was of little use to an Indian. But his multiple plantations, numerous slaves, salaries, pensions, sharp bargaining, and propensity to put his hands on any Creek annuity, were odd ways of displaying his Mississippian heritage.[41] McGillivray and other mestizo factors were conscious of the fact that they had well-known white surnames and also belonged to prominent Indian clans. The

62 white father by design often married into a leading clan. But whenever a mestizo had to decide whether at heart he was a McGillivray, McIntosh, Perryman, or McQueen, or instead a Tiger, Wind, Panther, or Alligator, there was mental anguish and not infrequently bloodshed.

Mestizo factors had one trait in common: they tended to put getting a supply of goods above all other loyalties, possibly even those of clan relationships. McGillivray has been touted as an American Talleyrand because he served and played off against one another various powers ringing the Creek lands. A close inspection, however, discloses a profusion of Muscogulge Talleyrands. At one time or another Robert Grayson (Grierson) of Hilibi among the Upper Creeks was a British Tory, a licensed Spanish trader, and an informant for the United States;[42] and Timothy Barnard's,[43] John Galphin's,[44] and James Durouzeaux's[45] careers among the Lower Creeks were similar. During the era of the War of 1812 William Hambly, who may not have had any Indian blood, simultaneously or in rapid succession, served Britain, Spain, and the United States in dealing with the Lower Creeks and Seminoles. Traders did whatever was necessary to continue getting goods and to protect their property.

Discussion of the village factors, Silver Bluff, Panton's operations, the United States factories, and British commercial firms has merely touched the periphery of our central interest, that of the eight thousand or so Muscogulge hunters. Many never visited Panton's warehouses or an American factory, and only a handful ever came to London, where sailing ships disgorged cargoes of peltry. The hunter's principal—and vital—contact was with the factor and his truck house. Virtually all male adult Muscogulge hunted, from the teenager who had just received a war name at the busk to venerable micos, beloved men, and hillis hayas who were still sound in body and limb. It would be only a slight exaggeration to claim that they and their families would starve and freeze without hunting. The main exception was the factor, an able-bodied male who remained in the village during hunting season. From time to time McGillivray told the Georgians or the Spaniards that he could not meet them in a treaty council or run the boundary line because he had sent all of the men out to hunt.[46] The men were in fact on the hunt, but it was hardly in McGillivray's power to order them out. At the end of the eighteenth century, in contrast to pre-Columbian times, warriors had no choice but to set out on the hunt if they expected to obtain essential European manufactures.

The time spent hunting increased as game became scarcer, prices of manufactures rose, and native dependence on and propensity for European wares intensified. At the end of the eighteenth century it was customary for hunters to go off in October or November and return in March or even April. In addition there might be a brief summer hunting season. The males' absence for such prolonged periods reinforced the already pronounce matrilineal tendencies of the Muscogulges. Before departing in the fall the hunter visited the factor, who was well acquainted with him, possibly belonging to the same clan. Based on past performance, the factor, after marking up his goods 100 percent or more, advanced powder, ball, and other necessities. Before the hunter left he looked at the ledger to see how many chalks he owed, and upon his return he deposited his skins and furs at the truck house. After noting their quality and weighing them, the factor credited the Indian with so many chalks, some of which were used to buy clothing and food for his family. If he were a successful and dependable hunter he could come to the truck house during the spring and summer and get a new petticoat for his wife, a horn or Jew's harp for his children, and rum to celebrate a recent triumph at ball play. In the fall the hunter again came to the factor, reviewed how many chalks were still due, received new supplies, and once again set out from his talwa for possibly half a year. Neither the Indian nor the factor had much choice in all this.

Different towns and the various Muscogulge ethnic components had their own hunting grounds. There they sought the white-tailed deer roaming open forests and grass lands in herds of fifty or more. Our understanding of the boundaries of these hunting grounds is murky today, though the Creeks and their Cherokee and Choctaw neighbors knew where they were at the time. The Chehaws hunted on the Altamaha, the Cowetas between the Oconee and Ogeechee, the Alabamas on the lower

64   Alabama River, and the Tallassees on the Cumberland. The Yuchis were among those who went to mid-Florida and Tampa Bay, and as time passed, the southernmost part of the Florida peninsula became the principal hunting ground of many Seminoles and Creeks. The Koasatis joined other Upper Creeks, who hunted on the Trinity River in Texas and elsewhere beyond the Mississippi.[47] Occasionally men took their wives along, and while the parties were absent from their village they lived in one or more temporary hunting camps. Few descriptions of these camps have survived. Literate mestizos and white Indian countrymen customarily remained behind in the villages, where they reviewed the number of chalks owed, and anxiously awaited to see how many pounds of leather straggling hunting parties would bring in. The United States agent Benjamin Hawkins travelled extensively throughout the Creek country, leaving an invaluable description of Creek customs. But as far as is known he never visited a hunting camp, and he only rarely mentioned that he saw an abandoned one in the distance as he was going from town to town.[48] The naturalist John Bartram, in addition to his observations of the flora and fauna in East Florida, briefly noted that his party passed by "an Indian hunting cabin covered with palmetto-leaves."[49] During the Second Seminole War of the 1830s American soldiers were impressed that their adversaries could put up a simple palmetto-thatched shelter almost as quickly as troops could erect tents.[50]

There are few indications that large numbers of the Mississippians had strayed far from their talwas and none at all that they were absent for half a year. In contrast their Creek descendants, attempting to satisfy the appetite of the London market and calculating the worth of each kill in chalks, hunted for a much longer time and over a far larger area. As of old they might set off by foot or dugout but they usually had riding horses and pack animals. Streams and rivers covered the Muscogulge country, and in the spring vessels drawing up to ten feet of water sometimes brought supplies to Alexander McGillivray at Little Tallassee on the Coosa.[51] Nevertheless more often than not it was impossible to get from one point to another by water. It is not exaggeration to assert that the horse had effected a transportation revolution; without it commercial hunting could never have played such an important role in Indian life. At times Indians mounted on horseback rushed in among herds of deer after their quarry.

Fifty to one hundred and fifty hunters typically lived in each Muscogulge village, and in the fall parties of five to thirty or more with their small sturdy ponies set out on the hunt. Indians in these parties often belonged to the same or closely related clans, and clan totems such as the bear, beaver, raccoon, and deer were their prey. It was permissible for Indians to kill a totemic brother so long as the appropriate propitiatory rituals were observed. Day after day hunters slew bear, beaver, raccoon, and especially deer, butchering and skinning the carcasses, throwing part of the meat into the fire as an atonement to the clan's totem and to the fire, sun, and Master of Breath. There was nothing new in this. Mississippians had apologized and made atonement to their totemic ancestors, insisting that their need for food and clothing made it necessary. At a later period, however, one can only wonder what the ancestral spirit of the deer, bear, or panther thought when he saw his two-legged progeny killing so many of those who were quadrapeds, pressing their hides into hogsheds, and leaving the meat to rot. And we really do not know how much, if at all, Muscogulge hunters of the deer clan worried as they indiscriminately slaughtered their brothers and tormented their symbolic spiritual progenitor.

As in the centuries before whites had arrived in the Southeast, fire continued to be a potent ally of Indian hunters. Sometimes Indians set the woods afire, forcing terrified animals to the banks of deep rivers or to the center of a ring of fire where they could be easily dispatched. Each spring the Muscogulges deliberately fired the woods, and fires accidentally started by lightning also did their work all year long. These fires kept the forests open and clear of underbrush, which facilitated killing deer and other large animals. Whites travelling throughout the Southeast remarked that numerous herds of deer were to be seen not only in the open savannahs and prairies—but also in the woods! Such disclosures amused Indian hunters.

With one chalk purchasing no more than ten loads of pow-

66 der,[52] there was an incentive to revert to the bow and arrow and, for small game, to the blowgun. But the trade musket and rifle were the mainstays and best allowed Indians to kill large numbers of deer in the open forests and grasslands. Beaver were trapped in the eighteenth century usually with a steel trap acquired from the village factor. Indians killed hibernating bears in the usual fashion. According to the Carolina trader Adair, she-bears with their cubs retired to hollow trees to sleep off the winter months but their contented "hum um um" gave them away. Indians set the bottom of the tree afire, forcing out their prey, and then the hunters and dogs did the rest.[53] The bear's oil was prized even more than the fur, and there are intimations that only Indians of certain standing in the village were allowed to kill bears.[54]

Peltry had to be prepared and transported to market. In winter camps part of the hunter's duties—and his wife's if she were along—was to dress the skins. They had to cut and scrape flesh from the deer, dry the skin in the sun, soak it in water and deer's brains, more often than not scrape off the hair, knead the skin and finally smoke it over a smoldering fire.[55] The village factor usually did no more than to rearrange skins into fifty-pound packs and load them and empty taffy (rum) kegs on his horses. Each animal could carry about 150 pounds, usually loaded in three packs, one on each side and the third on top. The packtrain was made up with a packhorseman for every ten animals. With sleighbells tinkling, all set off for the appropriate warehouse, averaging about twenty-five miles a day. Whenever they encountered a stream too deep to ford, packs had to be unloaded, placed on skin boats or log rafts, and ferried across, while the animals swam. Americans used wagons to transport loosely packed skins from Creek trading houses at Fort Wilkinson and Fort Hawkins to Savannah.[56] Whatever the method, there was reason to hurry; the hotter the days, the greater the risk of worm damage. At Pensacola or Savannah peltry was processed further. Panton cured some of the skins with salt, perhaps tanned them, and to the dismay of the Indians, cut off the head and shanks of the deer to reduce chance of worm infestation.[57] Then he pressed and packed the skins and sent them off. In Savannah, govern-

ment employees often kept skins in loose bales and were forced
to beat them frequently to combat worms. Loose bales then
were sent to factory headquarters in Philadelphia (subsequently
Georgetown), combined with peltry from other United States
Indian factories, and shipped to London.

Hunting was the most important but not the only aspect of
the Indian economy. Along with the horse, Europeans had introduced cattle and swine, and large stocks of each subsisted
among the eighteenth-century Muscogulges. Almost all village
factors had cow pens in addition to truck houses. Cattle and
swine ran wild, fed on the abundant grass and mast, and were
rounded up once or more a year. A few were slaughtered for
local consumption, but most were driven to markets in Saint
Augustine, Savannah, Pensacola, and Mobile. With their long
whips, drovers (Indian cattle hunters, vaqueros, or cowboys)
conducted cattle, pigs, and even turkeys on long drives averaging
one to four hundred miles. Part of the prosperity of village factors
was due to the fact that they raised cattle. McGillivray hired
white men to supervise stock at his plantations on the lower
Alabama River,[58] and late in the eighteenth century the Miccosukee chief Kinache could not be found because he was in the
north Florida woods with his Negroes rounding up his cattle.
Kinache was not unique, and Panton, Leslie, and Company's
agent reported in 1789 that he expected to receive cattle from
every Seminole village.[59] Factors exported not only buckskins
but also cowhides. Prosperous Indians owned horses, which they
used in the peltry trade or rented. Buying, selling, and stealing
horses was common in the Muscogulge country.

Wealthy Indians who owned stocks of horses and cattle often
were the ones with the largest fenced-in fields worked by approximately twenty slaves and in some instances by several
times that number. In addition to maize, beans, and other traditional cultigens, cotton was grown. Certain pre-Columbian
Indians in the New World had cultivated, spun, and woven
cotton, but there is no indication that the Mississippians had.
At some point, presumably relatively late, whites or foreign
Indians introduced cotton into the Southeast, and after the invention of Whitney's cotton gin in 1793 cotton culture spread

to the Muscogulges on a small scale. Cotton was suited to hoe cultivation, and from the 1790s sacks of short-staple cotton arrived by packhorse and canoe at American factories and Panton's warehouses.[60] Often white or mestizo traders grew the cotton, and owned the spinning wheels, looms and gins, and their wives, children, and slaves frequently did the spinning and weaving. One elderly Creek chief had a white wife, who in 1798 grew, carded, spun, and wove the cotton and outfitted her husband in homespun.[61] In the following century Timothy Barnard's mestizo son built ten spinning wheels for his father's slaves and his own family.[62]

Some Indians who lived close to white towns and farms hired themselves out as agricultural laborers or were paid so much a load for firewood, which they brought in piled high on their backs.

Creeks and Seminoles continued to fish, but it was more difficult because whites had usurped so much of the coastline and so many of the rivers. Indians still gathered oysters and other shellfish along the coast and, like their Mississippian forebears, poisoned fish in streams with buckeye or caught them in weirs. Fishing nevertheless was of less consequence for Creeks and Seminoles than it had been for Mississippians. An exception was the "Spanish" Indians living at and below Tampa Bay, near Pensacola, and elsewhere on the coast. They apparently were Creeks who had migrated to Florida during the eighteenth century. Regardless of who owned Florida, for decades Cuban fishermen had sailed over to Florida's Gulf and Atlantic coasts, established seasonal camps ashore, and carried their catch back to the Havana market. By the eighteenth century some of these settlements or *ranchos* had become permanent. Spanish Indians fished from Augusta until March, and during the spring and summer they raised corn, beans and other crops. Part of the Upper Creeks and Yuchis who migrated to the Florida peninsula joined the ranchos, acquired the art of casting nets in the surf, intermarried with the Spaniards, and they—or certainly their children—learned to speak Spanish, perhaps as their only language. During the Second Seminole War in the 1830s it was in

question whether to characterize these Indians and their descendants as Yuchis, Tallapoosas, Spanish Indians, Seminoles,
or Cubans.[63]

Despite the introduction of cotton, horses, cattle, and in some
instances new techniques of fishing, maize continued to be the
staff of life and retained its ritualistic prominence. Each family
attempted to grow enough or almost enough food for the year.
If the menfolk did not hunt,the family probably would not literally starve. But it would go naked, be cold, be without firearms
and powder, and have to drink black drink rather than rum.
With men so involved in hunting, women assumed more responsibility for cultivation. After returning in February and
March, men helped clear and break up the ground and assisted
with planting, but much of the rest of the work belonged to the
women and children. As the store of maize all but disappeared
in late winter and early spring, the Indians' diet was precarious.
Whites thought this an opportune time to ply them with food
and drink and win a land cession.

After losing so much of their hunting lands during the War
of 1812, Creeks were forced to rely more on agriculture. Villages
fenced in large communal fields where each family planted a
few acres of corn, a patch of sweet potatoes, and another patch
of peas and rice. Woods frequently separated the different
crops.[64] Sometimes there was no communal field, and villages
stretched out for several miles along a river. In such cases, each
family fenced in one-and-a-half to six acres. Reputedly some of
these farms were as productive as those of any white frontiersmen. Neither the Indian nor the white man was likely to use a
plow.[65]

This discussion of agriculture should not detract from the
fact that until their final removal most Indians remained commercial hunters and in debt. A traditional way of paying off
excessive debts was by ceding land. Giving up part of their lands
restricted their hunting, and for this and other good reasons
Indians were reluctant to relinquish any territory. But fearful of
not having a dependable supply of European manufactures, they
often were forced to make a cession. When this happened the

70 Indians who handed over lands frequently were not the ones who lived on them, all of which reflected the ethnic, clan, and linguistic differences and factionalism among the Muscogulges.

The Muscogulges also regarded presents as a way of maintaining their life-style. Britain, Spain, the United States, France, and private adventurers all rewarded Indians with presents for service or to buy their neutrality. If a winter campaign were involved, the Indians protested without much exaggeration that if they could not hunt their families would freeze: they must have presents. Usually campaigns were in the spring and summer and warriors could get one supply of goods from the factor and another through presents. Gifts often were prodigious. Thomas Brown, Britain's Indian agent in East Florida during the Revolution, gave a delegation of six hundred Creek warriors each a shirt, knife, gallon of rum, lengths of stroud, duffle, leggings, gartering, kettles, hoes, axes, hatchets, paint, salt, sugar, molasses, coffee, standard military rations for five days, etc. All of this cost Brown £3,558, a sum that was not an insignificant portion of the entire provincial budget. In addition, every tenth Indian, and all tastanagis, micos, and others of consequence received a saddle.[66] During the same conflict Georgians furnished each warrior with a blanket, shirt, pair of boots, flap, powder, ball, rice, beef, pork, a gallon of rum, and tobacco.[67] Such presents encouraged Creek warriors and their families to travel hundreds of miles to a council, and because of the expense, whites were reluctant to convene such gatherings or to entertain visiting delegations. For centuries the Muscogulges had taken pleasure in dispensing gifts and bestowing hospitality and not in amassing wealth, but by the eighteenth century they clearly recognized that such beneficence was a New World, not a European, tradition.

Annuities provided another means of handling large debts, and almost all were bestowed by the United States in exchange for lands and other concessions. They were given either to the Creek nation, to selected headmen, or to a combination of the two. In any case, individual Indians usually got less than their share and sometimes nothing. The so-called headman was sometimes merely the mestizo factor with little official standing in the clan and talwa. He was, however, often anxious to usurp the traditional authority of the mico and hillis haya. But annuities, presents, spinning, weaving, and the resurgence of agriculture were all peripheral pursuits compared to hunting. Up until the time of the Trail of Tears, the typical male Muscogulge was a commercial deer hunter compelled to spend almost half his days away from his talwa in quest of the éco.

The Black Muscogulges

Meriwether Lewis and William Clark, leading a forty-five-man expedition, slowly made their way up the Missouri River in 1804, exploring the upper portions of the Louisiana Purchase to find a route across the Continental Divide to the Pacific Ocean. When they arrived at the Arikara villages over a thousand miles from Saint Louis, Clark showed the Indians his compasses, surveying instruments, mirrors, and assorted other trinkets, but the Arikaras were most interested in York, Clark's black slave. They "thought him something strange." He danced and sang for the Indians, who repeatedly rubbed his skin in an attempt to remove paint.[1] The Arikaras' fascination exemplified the gulf between the culture of the Plains Indians and that of the Southeastern Indians. Africans had resided in the Southeast for almost three centuries, and in 1804 no Muscogulge rubbed any Negro's skin to see if the paint might come off.

Three groups, or "races," had long lived in the Southeast, and out of this assemblage emerged a people who, for lack of a better phrase, can be labeled black Muscogulges. They were not a cohesive group. By the late eighteenth century, "blacks" or Negroes" or "Africans," whether slave or free, resided in the Indian country in talwas, on plantations, and sometimes in separate black communities. Whatever their domicile, legal status, and ethnic background, they were numerous, and their presence was

74   pervasive. Unfortunately, they have left few accounts of their life among the Muscogulges. Information about these Negroes most often comes from whites apprehensive about the threat "black Indians" posed to the peculiar institution. Occasionally, literate or semiliterate Indian countrymen and mestizo factors commented on Negroes in their midst.

Eighteenth-century black Muscogulges had diverse origins. Some were true Africans, having been born in Africa, shackled, marched to a coastal trading factory or "castle," packed aboard ship on the Middle Passage, and eventually sold in the New World. After their arrival some ran away from their masters or were brought by owners into the Indian country in connection with the skin trade. In any case West African memories remained fresh in the minds of these black Muscogulges. Their dress, however, was of rough cloth, the standard "nigger" or slave garb of the plantation tidewater.

On the other extreme were blacks who were creoles born in America of African parents, or Negroes of mixed blood. These "virtual Indians," or "black Indians," had resided for years among the Muscogulges, and not infrequently had been born in the Indian country. They dressed like the natives—in stroud flaps, moccasins, leggings, linen or cotton shirts, knee-length coats, and cloth turbans often adorned with ostrich feathers. Whites were confused, never sure whether to style these virtual Indians as Upper Creeks, Lower Creeks, Seminoles, or Negroes.

Representatives of the three "races" were readily discernible among eighteenth-century Muscogulges: a new African who had run away from a plantation in the Carolina low country, a Scottish trader who had gone into the interior to make his fortune, and a warrior who could trace his ancestry back to Mississippian times. Thomas Jefferson referred to three distinct types—red, white, and black—in his *Notes on the State of Virginia* published in 1784.[2] But racial mixing over the years caused distinctions to blur in Jefferson's Virginia, and especially in the lower South, where a rough parity existed among whites, Africans, and Indians, and intermixture was common and diverse. Mestizos (mustees), zambos (Afro-Indians), mulattoes, octoroons (mulaHoes of one-eighth African ancestry), black Indians, virtual Indians and a welter of others were to be found. Robert Leslie managed the Panton, Leslie, and Company warehouse at Saint Marks, where several of the company's slaves were expecting children. Leslie professed that "God's light only will reveal their colours."[3]

Prosperous mestizos played an important role in the peltry trade. White traders married Indian women and reared a mestizo progeny, some of whom eventually became village factors and prominent chiefs. Much has been written about Alexander McGillivray, William McIntosh, William Weatherford, Osceola, Peter McQueen and other mestizos best known to posterity. Many others could trace their ancestry to packhorsemen, European soldiers of diverse nationalities, and coastal farmers, planters, and merchants. During the seventeenth and eighteenth centuries thousands of southeastern Indian females were enslaved and brought to the tidewater, where they became concubines or legal wives of whites. Thomas Woodward is one of the few of the progeny of such unions about which much is known. This mestizo came from Carolina into the Creek country. In his youth he dressed and was known as an Indian or at least to have Indian blood, but over the years he adopted more and more of the Europeans' culture and "whitened," subsequently becoming one of the founders of the state of Alabama and a spokesman of the Old South.[4] But unlike Woodward, few mestizos born into white society and moving into the Indian country wrote their reminiscences, and thus little is known about them.

Other racial combinations among the Muscogulges were legion, including mulattoes of white and African parentage and zambos of Afro-Indian ancestry. Red, white, and black tri-racial mixtures had no distinct label and were to be found under any of the many classifications discussed, though their backgrounds are obscure. It is impossible to assign percentages to the principal Muscogulge racial components—whites, Indians, Africans, mestizos, mulattoes, zambos, and tri-racial mixtures—yet all were represented, not in just a token fashion but as an integral part of the eighteenth-century Creeks and Seminoles.

The Black Factor, generally identified as a Lower Creek chief, illustrates the difficulty in ascertaining a southeastern Indian's ethnic background. Born in the mid–eighteenth century, residing on the lower Chattahoochee River until his death in 1811, and bequeathing his surname to a host of Creek and Seminole Indians and black Muscogulges, he was a village factor, a very prosperous one. In addition to his truck house, he owned cultivated fields, herds of cattle and horses, and scores of slaves. Spaniards, the United States Indian agent Benjamin Hawkins, William Panton, and others from time to time mentioned that the Black Factor had his skins ready for delivery, that their employees bought or rented horses from him, or that he had foodstuffs for sale. The Black Factor's lineal and collateral descendants figure prominently in nineteenth-century legal proceedings as they quibbled over the slave inheritance. Fleeting references imply that the Black Factor was a mixed-blood, but in fact he may have been black—an African. Of course this did not have to be the case any more than his Creek contemporary the Blue Chief had to be blue, or the White Lieutenant, white. It is likely, however, that the Black Factor had African ancestry, though one has to conjecture whether he was a true African, or a mulatto, zambo, or tri-racial mixture.[5] We know that the Little Black Factor was a zambo.[6] But confusion and uncertainty surround the racial mix of most other Creek and Seminole traders.

George McIntosh's ancestors provide another illustration of racial mixing in the southeast. Interviewed in Oklahoma in the 1930s, the elderly McIntosh related how his parents and grandparents had been born in the eastern Creek country. His description of his forebears as Creeks, Catawbas, Negroes, and probably whites is a source of as much confusion as clarification. "Creek" could have meant Muskogee proper, Hitchiti, Shawnee, Yuchi, or Natchez, among other possibilities. "Catawba" is equally perplexing. George's mother, Tama McIntosh, was a Catawba, born in Alabama. He ancestors presumably had moved there from the Catawba homeland in western Carolina. Today there is no Catawba language, and scholars speculate whether the ancestral Catawbas spoke a tongue in the Siouan, Yuchean, or Muskhogean family or even a West African one. Tama remains an enigma, and so do George's Negro ancestors.[7] The term Negro is imprecise and was variously applied to transplanted Africans, mulattoes, zambos, and in some instances to Indians with no African genes. Jefferson divided the American population into the three categories: red, white, and black. Unfortunately he left no instructions as to which group one should assign Black Factor, George McIntosh, and so many other Creeks and Seminoles.

The Southeast was not the only region in the Western Hemisphere where the three races and their various combinations existed. Indians in the West Indies had virtually disappeared, replaced by Europeans and Africans, but in coastal Central America, despite the ravages of disease, Indians survived who in time were joined by whites and Africans. Here the three races and their diverse mixtures also were to be found. Afro-Indians, or zambos, lived among the Mosquito Indians and the Garifunas in Nicaragua and Honduras and with the Bush Negroes of the Guianas.[8] The coastal rim of the Caribbean and Gulf of Mexico, including the black Muscogulge homeland in the Southeast, was that part of the New World where one encountered most Afro-Indians and tri-racial mixtures.

Part of the Muscogulges' acculturation was their adoption of white attitudes towards Negroes, which explains why in 1861 Muscogulges in Oklahoma and Alabama donned Confederate grey and fought to keep their slaves and save the Old South. Englishmen in the New World equated the terms slave, black, and Negro, and used them interchangeably. By the first part of the nineteenth century at least a few wealthy Creeks and Seminoles were doing the same thing. All of this incorrectly assumes, however, that the Muscogulges' attitudes toward slavery evolved as had those of Anglo-Americans.

After Mississippian society began to shatter in the sixteenth century—and perhaps earlier—again, again, and still again tribes whose numbers had been drastically reduced joined or merged with others. Muskogee speakers in Alabama and Georgia characterized these newcomers who joined them as foreigners, enemies, slaves, and sometimes "stinkards." Most enemies or immigrants were not actually slaves but were regarded as inferiors, and a minority of them were literally chattels owned by other Indians. By the time of the American Revolution it was not considered appropriate or just for Washington's contemporaries, citizens of a new republic, to enslave the noble savage. Whites continued to enslave Indians, but to avoid unnecessary criticism after 1783 they usually called the enslaved Muscogulges "Negroes." Muscogulges did not have to concern themselves with such sophistry. Their enemies or rivals had always been inferiors or slaves, and after 1783 when Indians owned other Indians the chattels were known as slaves, foreigners, or Indians—not as Negroes or blacks.

Sidestepping the issue of who was a Negro, it is clear that Negroes bore the brunt of racial discrimination in the Southeast at the hands of both whites and Indians. Because of historical determination, psychological factors, and diverse other reasons, some Europeans, especially those associated with plantation slavery and the slave trade, had long regarded Africans as different, less civilized, savage, pagan, and subhuman, mere chattels, like cows and sheep. Whites living in or on the fringes of the Muscogulge territory shared these views, and some Indians themselves began to hold similar feelings. Creek and Seminole traditions that have been handed down deal with the origin of races. In this folklore either the Indians or the whites were most favored by the Master of Breath. Three boxes came from heaven: that of the whites contained pens, ink, and paper; of the Indians, clubs, knives, and traps for hunting and war; of the Negroes, axes, hoes, and buckets. Negroes were to use these tools for menial labor and to serve the Indians and whites.[9] In other stories whites came out of the water while it was clear and pure, Indians followed, and finally when it was muddy and dirty Negroes emerged.[10]

In the late nineteenth and early twentieth centuries George Washington Grayson was characterized as being "the most prominent and intelligent of all Creek Indians of his time,"[11] and just before Grayson's death President Wilson appointed him head chief of the Creek nation in Oklahoma. Descended from the white loyalist "Indian countryman" Robert Grierson, George Washington Grayson studied his family genealogy and Creek history in general. Grayson was dismayed by the "lasting cloud over his family's name" because loyalist Grierson's mestizo daughter had borne two children in Alabama by a Negro father. After removal to the West Grayson saw the tri-racial offspring, John and Annie, at a distance in Oklahoma, but "we haven't ever met socially." Even worse, according to Grayson, Grierson's mestizo son had married a Negro female slave, had lived with her in both Alabama and Oklahoma, and had reared a large family.[12]

George Washington Grayson lived in the latter nineteenth and early twentieth centuries, and, as a largely acculturated mestizo, he shared many white sentiments. Not surprisingly, he was ashamed of the "lasting cloud" hanging over his family name. But at a much earlier time Grayson's great-great-grandfather's mestizo son and daughter had been born and lived in the eastern Creek country and married Negroes. The attitudes of Tory Grierson's mestizo children rather than Grayson's are the ones that are important, but no documentary evidence reveals what they might have been. Nevertheless there is every indication that while they were in the East they did not believe they were doing anything unusual; they saw no dark cloud, only the clear Alabama sky.

Creek slaveowners, like their white counterparts in the Old South, distrusted Christian ministers preaching to slaves. They feared that notions of spiritual equality would lead to slave insurrections. At Withington on the Tallapoosa in 1828, the Creeks tied the clothes of a twelve-year-old Negro slave over her head, bound her to a post, and lashed her soundly on her bare back. She had gone to hear a missionary preach.[13]

Negroes living among the Muscogulges clearly experienced racial discrimination. It must be kept in mind, however, that much of our information is derived from a later time, filtered through white and acculturated mestizo's accounts. The heyday of Jim Crowism in the South and of lynchings to preserve the integrity of Caucasian womanhood occurred during the nineteenth and early twentieth centuries. This also was the era when, because of the influence of Darwin and Nietzsche, the concept of a master, fittest, or super race prevailed. That race, of course, was white or Anglo-Saxon, though the Muscogulges presumably had hopped out of the water before it got too muddy.

80   Yet if one is truly to understand the culture and perceptions of Creeks and Seminoles before removal, it is necessary to look back to a time before Darwin, lynchings, Jim Crow, and an irrational emphasis on separation of the races. In so doing it becomes apparent that among the Creeks and Seminoles and throughout the South in general, relations between the races were more relaxed and intimate than has often been perceived.

As an example one might mention the soldier, engineer, cartographer, real estate promoter Charles B. Vignoles, who for a time resided in the Southeast. After the United States acquired Florida, he moved from South Carolina to the new American territory. In 1823 he published a book to encourage immigration. Vignoles reflected on Florida's population: "the only difference in man, laying aside his color, is the difference of opinion." All three races—Indian, African, and white—"no matter where born or by whom begot" have provided skilled workmen, artists, and writers. Vignoles readily acknowledged his debt regarding conditions in East Florida to George J. F. Clarke, a white planter-merchant whom some considered to have been the leading citizen in Spanish Florida. Clarke, who remained in Florida after 1821, had a black wife, and he considered his many children to be the equals of any, "no matter where born or by whom begot."[14]

Mixed marriages were common among Creeks and Seminoles. James Factor, "a Seminole or Creek Indian," had a Negro wife.[15] Powell or Osceola, also a Creek or Seminole, may also have had a Negro spouse. Frank Berry, an elderly Negro living in Jacksonville, Florida, during the 1930s, claimed that he was Osceola's grandson, that Indians had carried off his Negro grandmother from Tampa, and that Osceola had married her. Except for infrequent periods when Osceola visited white settlements or was imprisoned by whites, much of his life went unrecorded. In all likelihood, however, he did have a Negro wife, and Berry's account is accurate.[16] The Negroes John and Abraham who were employed by the United States Army in the Second Seminole War, each had Indian wives.[17]

By marrying Negroes, Indians to an extent merely followed the white example. Few Creeks had not heard of George Galphin, and a considerable number had visited Silver Bluff. His will, probated in 1782, is revealing. He had at least four wives or mistresses: Rachel Dupree, whose children were Thomas and Martha Galphin; the Indian Nitshukey, mother of Rose; the Negro Sappho who had two children, Rachel and Betsy; and the Negro Mina, mother of Barbary (Barbara).[18] The entire area around the fall line of the Savannah River, which included Silver Bluff, South Carolina, and Augusta, Georgia, was a region where in the eighteenth century the three races converged. One glimpses this repeatedly. Polly Russell, a free black woman who lived just below Silver Bluff, married a "free man of mixed blood." After the American Revolution white men broke down the door, carried off Polly and her three children, and sold them all in Creek territory.[19] Some of the Galphins were patrons of the Negro Baptist Church at Silver Bluff. Henry Francis, one of the earliest black ministers about whom anything is known, lived at Silver Bluff until forced to leave by the hostilities of the American Revolution. One of Francis's parents was an Indian and the other a white, and this so-called Negro minister had no known African ancestry.[20]

Saint Augustine and its environs in East Florida was another area where the three races interacted. One of the five original partners of Panton, Leslie, and Company, the loyalist John Leslie, resided in Saint Augustine, managing the company's warehouse overlooking Matanzas Bay. The East Florida Indian trade was less extensive than that of Pensacola in West Florida. Nevertheless, Indians visited Leslie, and he made forays into the interior. Leslie did not get along well with his white wife, perhaps because she was an alcoholic. When they separated, Leslie's Negro house servant became his mistress and bore him a son. Leslie provided for his son's education, made arrangements for him to learn a trade, and gave him a house in Saint Augustine.[21] Other prominent Saint Augustine whites also had Negro mistresses or wives. Leslie's younger friend, Zephaniah Kingsley, also a loyalist, lived north of Saint Augustine on Fort George Island, where he was a successful merchant, planter, and slave trader. This did not deter him from marrying at least two Africans, who helped him manage the slave business. He married

82   one of his wives, Anna, in a non-Christian African ceremony.
Kingsley lived well into the American period, until after the
Seminoles had been defeated and the Creeks expelled. He realized in his later years that some of his new neighbors in Florida
had misgivings about Anna, but in his will the fiery Kingsley
denounced "the illiberal and inequitable laws of this territory
[which did not afford Anna justice] due to civilized society."
Just before or after his death, Anna, his daughter Micanopy, and
other family members moved out of the territory to Haiti.[22]
William Wanton, a white man employed by Panton, Leslie, and
Company to superintend the company store and cattle pens on
the Saint Johns River south of Saint Augustine, had a Negro
wife. He was infuriated when in 1815 American slave raiders
carried off and sold his five children.[23] Leslie, Kingsley, and
Wanton all lived in Spanish Florida, and it might be argued that
their behavior was appropriate to the Latin American custom of
demonstrating more racial tolerance than Anglo-Saxons. But in
this instance the argument is inappropriate because Leslie,
Kingsley, and Wanton were Anglo-Saxons, loyalists who had
fled to British Florida, but remained after Spain regained
possession.

Similar examples occurred in the United States. We have
already discussed Galphin, and as a final illustration we might
mention the Kentuckian Richard M. Johnson, frontiersman and
Indian fighter, who reputedly had killed Tecumseh in 1813.
Johnson had a love / hate relationship with the Indians, ruthlessly shattering those standing in the way of American expansion, but at the same time endeavoring to civilize and uplift
defeated and cowed unfortunates so they could be absorbed by
the expanding republic. In this latter connection he maintained
an Indian school, and during the 1820s and 1830s young Creek
and Seminole scholars attended Colonel Johnson's Choctaw
Academy on his plantation in Scott County, Kentucky. That
Colonel Johnson's wife or mistress was a Negro and that his
children were mulattos did not deter him from being elected as
Van Buren's vice-president in 1836.[24] Muscogulges who visited
Johnson in Kentucky, Galphin at Silver Bluff, Leslie at Saint
Augustine, Kingsley at Fort George Island, or Wanton on the

Saint Johns River deemed it neither appropriate nor safe to refer to the dark cloud of miscegenation lying over the land.

At the end of the eighteenth century the African influence was pervasive not only on the Muscogulges' borders but also in the heart of their territory. Black immigrants passed through no single port, no Ellis Island, and no documents have survived revealing exactly how many and at what time they arrived. Nevertheless it is possible to discover in a general way how and when Africans reached the Muscogulges. Blacks had accompanied sixteenth-century Spanish explorers and had helped found Saint Augustine. During Florida's First Spanish Period (1565–1763) roughly 10 percent of the populace were Negroes, though the entire Spanish population numbered only 5,000 or so. Probably the Africans' greatest impact on the Indians came from the diseases they introduced.

Not until the eighteenth century did large numbers of Africans arrive in the Southeast, imported by Britain, the leading slave-trading nation. British subjects had founded Charleston in 1670, and during the following century Carolina's population grew dramatically, accompanying the expansion of rice and indigo culture. Over half of eighteenth-century Carolinians were black. After Georgia was settled in 1733 the trustees proscribed African slavery, though slavery became legal when Georgia was made a colony in the 1750s. On the eve of the American Revolution the colony's black population almost equalled the white. Britain acquired East and West Florida in 1763, and by 1775 the ratio of blacks to whites in East Florida was two to one, and only somewhat less in West Florida. Blacks equalled and usually outnumbered whites in the four British colonies bordering the Muscogulges. The great spurt in numbers of black Creeks and Seminoles occurred in the eighteenth century, and Negroes typically had come from or passed through one of the four neighboring colonies. Both in Britain's southern colonies and among the Muscogulges it was a new phenomenon in the eighteenth century to have so many blacks.

Before the American Revolution Negroes often reached the Indians illegally, having run away from owners in South Carolina or another British colony. Whites contracted with neigh-

84   boring Indians in private arrangements and formal treaties to track down fugitives, offering a bounty for scalps or the entire head if runaways could not be returned alive. Only one of their intentions was to redeem valuable property; whites also set the Indians on Negroes to foment hatred between the two groups. Southern whites, in the minority, shuddered to think that there might be "an intimacy" between their numerous potential enemies.[25]

The terms Negro and black were used loosely; a number of fugitive "Negroes" were zambos or even Indians. During the late seventeenth and early eighteenth centuries, southeastern Indians, especially females, had been captured and put to work on plantations in the Carolina Low Country. They were housed in slave or Negro quarters, and their mates were often newly arriving Africans. A zambo progeny emerged that might be labeled African or Indian, depending on one's inclination. In any case some of the runaways were pure- or mixed-blood Indians, who fled to the interior in search of their talwa and clan.

Fearful of "an intimacy" between the two groups, all of Britain's southern colonies prohibited traders from taking Negroes into the interior. But it was one thing to pass a law in the provincial capital and another to enforce it in the interior. Traders, who lived in Indian villages and were notoriously uncontrollable free spirits, were remote from Charleston or Pensacola. Complaints reached the South Carolina governor in 1757 that, in violation of the law and their bonds, most of the traders had brought Negroes into the Creek nation: John Brown, one Negro boy; Thomas Devaal, two; Daniel Douglass, one; James Germany, one; John Ross, one; Moses Nuñes, one; and John Kitt, one.[26] Galphin at Silver Bluff and factors in native villages all employed Negroes. The alternative was for Galphin and Indian countrymen themselves to load bales of skins on pack animals or to scour the woods for cattle.

The American Revolution created a surge in numbers of blacks among the Muscogulges. Many loyalist traders were forced to flee South Carolina and Georgia. Lachlan McGillivray retired to the Scottish Highlands, and William Panton to Saint Augustine. But Alexander McGillivray, Timothy Barnard, David

Holmes, and other loyalists withdrew to the interior, if possible taking their slaves with them. During the latter years of the Revolution Britain shifted her main campaign to the South, resulting in some of the bitterest fighting of the war, pitting neighbor against neighbor, loyalist against patriot. Britain succeeded better than the rebels in enlisting support from the Creeks and Seminoles, which increased the number of blacks in the Indians' midst. George III's officers distributed presents to the Indians and promised them part of rebel booty, including slaves. Especially during the latter years of the conflict, royal officers offered freedom to blacks who deserted rebel masters and came into British lines. As soldiers or civilians, able-bodied Negroes were given axes, shovels, hoes, and muskets so they could support George III's cause. Most of these Negroes, numbering twenty-five thousand or more, migrated to Charleston and other British-occupied ports. But some Negroes joined British forces in the back country. After the defeat at Yorktown large numbers of these Negroes sailed away with British forces to the West Indies, the Mosquito Shore in Central America, Nova Scotia, or even the mother country. Others headed for the Indian country, creating an influx among the Muscogulges.[27]

After 1783 neither Spain nor the United States made any effort to prohibit traders from employing Negroes. Alexander McGillivray and Charles Weatherford among the Upper Creeks, and Timothy Barnard and the Black Factor among the Lower Creek-Seminoles, along with many others who owned a few or several score slaves resided in or close to almost every village. Negroes, perhaps without masters, sometimes lived in separate villages.

The population ratios among the three races in the Southeast were established in a rough fashion by 1783, though Negroes seeking refuge still joined the Indians. John Forrester, a Panton, Leslie, and Company employee in East Florida, did not pay the "free fellow Bill" his wages, so, despite the price on his head, Bill ran off to the Indians in 1792.[28] When "the raskally Negroe Tom," a company slave in Pensacola, shot Panton's nephew in the foot, the Indian country seemed particularly inviting to Tom.[29] Occasionally the movement was in the opposite direc-

86   tion: it is not known, however, why Sambo, who belonged to the Chehaw Tiger King, fled from the Apalachicola River to Pensacola.[30]

The specter of separate, independent Negro Maroon bastions in the interior frightened whites. Maroons were groups of Africans, Indians, or a combination of the two, scattered throughout the Western Hemisphere. They had fled from white European control to inaccessible regions and when necessary fought to maintain their autonomous existences. Eighteenth-century Jamaica was replete with one Maroon war after another as slaves fled to the mountains and successfully fought for and retained their independence. Other Maroon wars and settlements could be found in South America, and in 1859 John Brown had the notion of a Maroon refuge in the vastness of the western Virginia mountains. Brown failed, and with the advantage of hindsight it is apparent that the best North American examples of Maroon sanctuaries occurred among the Creeks and Seminoles. This was the southern whites' concern when they avowed that there was "not trust in any black Indian."[31] It was appropriate that Maroon and Seminole were essentially the same words, both being derived from the Spanish word *cimarron*.

Florida had a reputation of being identified with and receptive to Maroons, at first symbolized by Spanish Fort Mosa (The Negro Fort) just north of Saint Augustine, and part of that city's outer defenses. Fugitive slaves from South Carolina and subsequently from Georgia ran away to Florida, where Spain confirmed their freedom, gave them land near Fort Mosa, and enrolled them in the militia. When called upon they were to man the Fort Mosa defensive line and, along with Indians in the vicinity, help defend the capital. This community at Fort Mosa was one of the earliest black settlements in territory that later became the United States. Spaniards did not regard Fort Mosa Negroes as Maroons, but South Carolinians and Georgians did. When Britain took over Florida in 1763 Fort Mosa blacks almost to a man wisely sailed away to Cuba with the departing Spaniards.[32]

The next instance when Maroons became conspicuous or notorious in the Southeast was during the era of the American Revolution. Even before 1775 from time to time Georgians had hired local Indians to explore inhospitable swampy regions of the lower Savannah to discover furtive Maroon camps.[33] But in the confusion of 1775 to 1776, as royal authority disintegrated, on their own initiative or perhaps because they had been offered freedom by British commanders, slaves ran away from rebel masters, sometimes fleeing to the interior, though usually to the coast. Hundreds of defiant Negroes congregated on Tybee Island at the mouth of the Savannah River, which alarmed the Carolina merchant Henry Laurens. He was anxious to send in troops and get on with the bloody and "awful business" lest the contagion spread.[34] British forces withdrew from all southern colonies except the Floridas during 1775 to 1776, though several years later the Royal Army returned in force and the South became the principal military theater. During the attendant confusion thousands of Negroes asserted their freedom. At the end of the war most but not all departed with British forces; the remainder returned to their old haunts on the lower Savannah or fled farther inland and joined the Creeks and Seminoles. As a result an unprecedented infusion of blacks among the Muscogulges occurred. Negroes lived in native villages and plantations as well as in their own separate communities. Before 1763 Fort Mosa was the most notorious Maroon abode. After the Revolution Maroon encampments proliferated and were to be found on the Chattahoochee River, at Miccosukee in northern Florida, at Tampa farther south and in other transient locations. These "black Indians" were those Indians whom Americans so feared and distrusted.

There are almost no extant inside views of Maroon settlements. We do, however, know something about the one at Miccosukee, east of Tallahassee near the Georgia-Florida boundary. In 1800 the Indian village here was the largest Lower Creek–Seminole town, and the Negro settlement a mile and one-half off may have constituted the largest concentration of Maroons. After the Revolution, loyalist William Augustus Bowles attempted to establish a British protectorate in the Southeast, the "State of Muskogee," and around 1800 Miccosukee was his capital. Blacks served in Muskogee's army and navy; they ran away from their masters to join Bowles, and those who would

88   not voluntarily flee and come to Miccosukee were captured and
brought there.

A terrified young black female, a slave on a Matanzas River
plantation below Saint Augustine, was in this latter category.
In later life she recounted her experiences, how "Seminoles"
had swooped down and captured her, her brothers, sisters, and
mother, how they had scalped one of her brothers and how she
had survived forced marches for twenty-four days and lived for
months with blacks and Indians at Miccosukee. She made passing references to the hardships of daily life. Her account repre-
sents one of the few, albeit brief, captivity narratives of its
kind.[35] Most blacks at Miccosukee were there voluntarily. Unfortunately they have left no narratives, and even their names
are rarely known. After Bowles's downfall in 1803 and after
Andrew Jackson's sweep through the area in 1818, the Negroes
at Miccosukee moved away, perhaps to found another Maroon
colony, possibly to join the Indians in their towns and plantations, or, as in the case of the frightened young female captive,
happy enough to be saved from the "black Indians" and returned
to a white master on the Matanzas.

In 1823 the American William H. Simmons visited a Negro
village in Florida near Big Swamp below Alachua and described
how he slept on a bed of deerskins in a large new building that
the Negroes had erected in the town's center. It was constructed
in Indian fashion without nails; the boards and shingles were
lashed to the posts and rafters with strips of oak. Large, almost
gigantic Negroes cultivated crops in fields that had been abandoned by the Indians long ago, and the blacks were healthy and
seemingly content, though ever vigilant for the appearance of
soldiers or pro-American Indian raiders.[36]

This Maroon encampment and the one at Miccosukee are
only two examples of those scattered about the Southeast. They
existed—or flourished—in the same era as the Haitian revolt.
In the 1790s blacks on Haiti rebelled, killed or forced into exile
thousands of whites, and founded a Negro republic. Stories about
Haitian atrocities circulated throughout the South and con-
sciously or subconsciously influenced the whites' perception of
"black Muscogulges." A case can be made that these Musco-

gulges posed a greater danger to the peculiar institution than did John Brown later. Regardless of whether this argument is justified, white fears were real and help explain why American forces lost more men in the Second Seminole War than in any other Indian conflict.

It is necessary to keep in mind that many black Muscogulges linked Great Britain with Negro freedom. Although he was called a tyrant by American Whigs in Fourth of July orations, George III was regarded as a friend and protector by black Indians until his death in 1820. This is not to imply that every British subject was an abolitionist. Panton championed the institution, engaged in the slave trade, and depended on slave labor to run the business. Few were more bitter than Panton about those saints, those enthusiasts, who wanted to prohibit the slave trade or, even worse, abolish chattel slavery altogether. But many other British "enthusiasts" passionately disagreed with him and helped associate the Union Jack with black liberty. This is the group that must be considered.

Though more numerous and vocal with each passing decade, abolitionists were in the minority all during the eighteenth century. Our concern, of course, is not with their dissentient emergence in Britain but with what if any effects they had on the Southeast. An appropriate time to start our examination is 1773, when Georgia was founded and slavery and the slave trade flourished as never before. Few questioned the institution on moral, economic, or any other grounds. The Georgia trustees, however, prohibited African slavery in their colony; and James Oglethorpe and John Wesley, who served in the trustees' utopia, were part of the miniscule group who questioned many aspects of slavery. The trustees outlawed African but not Indian slavery. As a result, colonists who thought African slavery desirable and even essential avowed that their slaves were really Indians, not Africans, or that at least they were zambos.[37] During the 1730s and 1740s it was apparent to at least a few Negroes and Indians that some British authorities opposed enslavement of Africans. When Georgia became a royal colony in 1752, however, Negro slavery became legal and soon flourished. The trustees' abolitionist legacy faded.

It was during the American Revolution that large numbers of southern blacks for the first time linked the British government with liberty. British subjects never tired of making the point that George Washington, Thomas Jefferson, Patrick Henry, and other slaveholders were paying mere lip service to liberty and rights of man. Because they continued to own slaves, they were hypocrites and frauds. Taking this line merely to lash out at spoiled, ungrateful colonists, supporters of George III and Parliament often gave little thought to the blacks themselves. But some who criticized slavery had the Negroes in mind, and they joined the small, strident British abolitionist coterie who denounced the institution on moral grounds. Regardless of their personal feelings, hard-pressed British commanders, thinking in military terms, realized that blacks made up one-third of the population in the Chesapeake Bay region and an absolute majority in the lower South. Using the same logic as President Lincoln in his 1862 Emancipation Proclamation, British commanders contended that freeing rebel slaves would weaken the enemy. In addition, able-bodied males could be enlisted in George III's forces, and Governor Dunmore did just that before he was finally run out of Virginia in 1776.

Events in the lower South rather than the Chesapeake Bay directly affected the Muscogulges and the blacks in their midst. When Britain directed her main thrust to the south in 1778 she realized if she were to prevail she must rely more than ever on white, red, and black Americans. Each side suffered from lack of manpower, and each considered, as did Lee and Davis at the end of the Civil War, the slaves' military potential. But only Britain acted. Again and again George III's commanders promised slaves freedom if they came into British lines. Males joined the Royal Army and Navy, serving not only as musicians, body servants, and pioneers, but also as soldiers armed with Brown Bess muskets and foot-long bayonets. The British Army garrisoned Charleston and Savannah on the coast, and Augusta and Ninety Six in the back country. Gathering up his wife and children, a male slave could sneak off to British lines, be fed, clothed, armed—and free! It was this, rather than philosophical musings of the Georgia trustees in London at an earlier period,

that made so many southern blacks associate the Union Jack
with liberty.[38]

The career of Thomas Brown illustrates how the Revolutionary experiences of blacks, whites, and Indians in the South were
intertwined. Before the Revolution Brown was a prominent land
speculator, planter, and Indian trader in the Silver Bluff–Augusta region. His biographers are of little help in disclosing
whether he was connected with Brown, Rae, and Company.
When the Revolution broke out, he became an outspoken loyalist and for almost nine years led provincial troops in the bitter
partisan fighting in South Carolina, Georgia, and East Florida.
He received numerous wounds and was even scalped three
times. American patriots regarded Colonel Brown as the quin-
tessential Tory: he wantonly pillaged civilian property, tormented innocent women and children, and unceremoniously
hanged the menfolk, taking diabolical satisfaction in their final
contortions. Brown was commander of the East Florida Rangers,
reorganized as the King's (Carolina) Rangers, and was also the
southern Indian superintendent for the eastern division, which
included the Creeks, Seminoles, and Cherokees; as a result
whites, blacks, and Indians all served under him. When rebel
slaves ran away to join British forces, Brown was sometimes the
commander. His polyglot forces captured and carried off rebel
slaves, which contributed to the unprecedented infusion of free
and slave Negroes among the Muscogulges.[39]

Like Thomas Brown, Lord Dunmore was a British commander who encouraged southern blacks to regard George III as
a protector and liberator. Run out of Virginia at the beginning
of the Revolution, he retired to the mother country, but in 1781
he returned to America, expecting to resume his Virginia gov-
ernorship. Cornwallis's defeat at Yorktown dashed that hope,
and Dunmore got no farther than British-occupied Charleston.
During 1781 and 1782 he had the greatest opportunity to be a
liberator when the fate of thousands of loyalists, including
blacks whom British commanders had freed, came to the forefront. Through force or diplomacy Britain hoped to regain Pensacola and all of West Florida from Spain, and Dunmore urged
joining West Florida to East Florida and possibly Georgia, which

would create a large British colony in the South like Canada in the North. This colony could be a refuge for George III's suffering white and Negro loyalist refugees. When the definitive peace settlement was made in 1783, Spain kept West Florida and acquired East Florida, so Dunmore's project failed.[40] But the concept that Britain was the protector of Negroes, Indians, and white loyalists, and that the Southeast should be their refuge, persisted, and this notion was not extirpated from the Muscogulge country until the diaspora of the 1830s.

William Augustus Bowles followed in the tradition of Brown and Dunmore. A loyalist officer, he served with forces that defended British West Florida. After Pensacola capitulated in 1781 he sailed away, but in a few years he returned and until his death in 1805 endeavored to establish the Indian state of Muskogee, in reality a British protectorate. He had a mestizo Hitchiti wife, a Cherokee wife, and possibly others, and he had numerous Indian followers. For a period he lived with black Maroons at Miccosukee, and Negroes were one of the mainstays of Muskogee. Bowles, director general of the Creek nation, repeatedly avowed that George III was on the verge of sending redcoats back to Muskogee to oversee the well-being of loyal Negroes and Indians. Although he spoke with some justification, and although as governor of the Bahamas between 1786 and 1796, lent a helping hand, during Bowles's lifetime, promises of massive British support came to naught.

These assurances bore fruit during the war of 1812, however, less than a decade after Bowles's death. During the war of 1812, Britain repeated her abolitionist policy of the American Revolution. Short of manpower and recognizing the southern slaves' military potential, she realized that freeing them could strengthen British forces, and cause grief to the southern Republican slaveowners, who allegedly were responsible for hostilities. The British abolitionist crusade had grown. Antislavery forces had abolished slavery in the mother country, had outlawed the slave trade, and were pressing to do away with slavery throughout the empire. Freeing southern slaves seemed appropriate, and British commanders encouraged Negroes—and Creeks and Seminoles—to rally around King George. During the conflict several hundred Negro soldiers could be seen drilling in the streets of Pensacola or at the British (Negro) fort on the Apalachicola River. They, the Indians, and a few British troops were to invade Georgia's interior and liberate the slaves.[41] This project and the attack on New Orleans failed, and in 1815, at the conclusion of the war, Britain withdrew her forces from the Gulf and Atlantic coasts. Disbanded soldiers remained on the scene, however, still arming and drilling Negroes, Creeks, and Seminoles, still helping them to protect or recover their lands, and perhaps collaborating with other forces in Central and South America who were attempting to overthrow Spanish rule.

Britain's recruitment of and reliance on southern Negroes serves to bring the Maroons among the Muscogulges into sharper focus. One hears about them, particularly from Americans concerned about runaway slaves, living at or near the British (Negro) fort on the Apalachicola River, at Miccosukee, Palatka, Tampa, and elsewhere. These Negroes, along with those in Indian villages and on Indian plantations, from time to time visited the Bahamas to beseech George III not to forsake them. The British flag flying over the fort commanding Nassau's harbor snapped in the breeze, and Negroes witnessed at first hand the implications of Britain's abolition of the slave trade. That black Muscogulges regarded George III as their friend, protector, and liberator worried Andrew Jackson, and this was one reason why he seized Pensacola in 1814 and swept deep into Florida four years later during the First Seminole War.

Archaeologists in the twentieth century excavated a slave cabin on Cumberland Island that presumably had been occupied by Ned Simmons. British forces had taken possession of this island in 1814, and among the artifacts discovered was an 1808 military button. Ned was one of the many southern slaves whom Britain had liberated, armed, and dressed in British uniforms, and it was during the War of 1812 that the slave Ned became the freedman Ned Simmons, a soldier in His Majesty's forces. For whatever reason, Ned Simmons remained behind when British forces sailed away, and he is best remembered as an elderly slave who was liberated again by Union troops during the Civil War. He kept and treasured his British regimental button, as-

94   sociated with the first period when he was free, Mr. Simmons, a real man. So goes the theory, admittedly a heavy one to hang on just one button. But it could be valid. The real significance, however, is that similar experiences could have been reenacted in Negro quarters throughout the Southeast from 1775 until after the War of 1812.[42]

The reason it is difficult to reconstruct the culture of black Muscogulges is that often they were labeled Creeks or Seminoles, or the surviving evidence is no more than a button. In most respects their economic life mirrored that of the Indians. Negroes cultivated maize, rounded up cattle and horses, set out on winter hunts, loaded packs of skins on pack animals, and occasionally spun cotton. Negro slaves labored as domestic servants and waited upon wealthy Indians, and, of course, Indian slaves did the same thing. Coming from coastal plantations and agricultural districts in West Africa, Negroes might have been more efficient farmers than the Indians, and there may have been an indefinite arrangement whereby Indians hunted, fought, and provided security while Negroes remained at home and furnished food. This is no more than a theory, and it may be an erroneous one.[43]

Muscogulge culture combined white, Indian, and African influences, and the African, though significant, was the weakest. This is reflected in the names of black Muscogulges, which customarily were European or Indian. If they had surnames, which was not usually the case, they were those of their white or Indian masters or former owners. As a result black Muscogulges were named McIntosh, McGillivray, Perryman, Barnett, Elasey, Holtuklomico, and Miconopy. Given names, at least the ones that have survived, often are English: Abraham, Jack, Nelly, Joe, and Sally. At times one finds Cudjo, Juba, and Mundy (all West African day names for a child born on Monday), Cumba ("to roar or to be scandalized" in Kongo), Haga[r], ("lazy" in Mende), and Buno ("to be assembled" in Efik). These and similar names may be traced back to West Africa with some confidence.

Lists of inhabitants of Creek and Seminole towns were ocassionally preserved, and along with obviously Muskhogean names one sometimes encounters Indians named Monday, Fri-

day, and March. The practice of naming children after days—
and sometimes after months—was a West African custom. Today one can only speculate about the ethnic background of such
"Indians." Much of the information about names has been filtered through the eyes of literate whites and acculturated Indians. A new African may have protested that he was Kwaku and
should not be called Bill, McIntosh, or even the Anglicized Jack;
the problem was: who else was around from the Gold Coast
who understood Twi and could talk to him in his native tongue?
Even in Maroon villages Negroes often were Creoles or had at
least been in the New World for decades, and they conversed in
English, Spanish, Hitchiti, Yuchi, and similar languages. Protests from a Twi-speaking West African that he should be called
Kwaku, the name given him because he was a male child born
on Wednesday, grew fainter and fainter.[44]

In time blacks adopted much of the European and Muskhogean religions, at least outwardly, though again information
often has come from white sources. Because southeastern Negroes, as compared with those in the West Indies or Brazil, were
relatively less numerous and more mobile, it was difficult to
preserve the African heritage. Either because the Master of
Breath, Corn Mother, and similar Indian deities had much in
common with those of non-Muslim and non-Christian West
Africa or out of sheer boredom, Negroes enthusiastically participated in the busk rituals. Much later, after removal to Oklahoma, Negro Alex Blackston related how as a youth he used to
go to the Creek busk and stomp dance, where Indians tied shells
on their ankles and beat drums while the medicine man distributed black drink. At first he was reticent and stood aside, but
soon, caught up in the excitement and frenzied rhythms, "Negroes like myself mixed, mingled, and danced together with the
Indians."[45] Muscogulges traditionally welcomed new dances,
and some that were performed in the Southeast were of African
origins. A white observer noted that southeastern Indian dances
were "highly martial and graceful" while those of blacks were
lively, awkward, and vulgar.[46]

Southeastern whites owned scores of slaves, and, like slaveowners throughout the South, gave their slaves Christmas week

off. In the long run this constituted part of the Christianization process of Africans. Whether Christmas week had any religious significance to Indian and mestizo masters and their Negro slaves, none of whom were Christians, or whether the week off and "the frolic of rum drinking and dancing" represented no more than a holiday is unclear.[47]

Some Negroes, especially those on plantations and in Maroon settlements, remained aloof from many aspects of Muscogulge society. This could be seen in Negro marriages and family ties, which often were outside the Indian clan system. After the Revolution, Indians carried off a young Negro man and wife from Liberty County in the Georgia tidewater. The captives were taken among the Creeks and Seminoles, where they lived for many years and raised children and grandchildren. In 1820, over three decades after their capture, their Georgia owner was still attempting to recover his chattels and their numerous progeny who somehow had remained together or in close contact with one another.[48] Negro family bonds were much stronger in the Indian country than one might expect. It often was essential to keep Negro slave families together lest spouses and offspring run away. Both Panton and mestizo masters found out about this to their cost.[49]

Regardless of the specific form of the marriage ceremony, Negroes clearly understood when and to whom they were married and who belonged to their families. In Oklahoma during the 1930s the elderly Creek freedman Philip A. Lewis related his family history, which had been passed down from generation to generation. His Negro ancestors in the Old Creek country had been slaves and had belonged to John and Kendall Lewis (Indian countrymen with Creek wives), to the mestizo Roley McIntosh, and to other wealthy whites and mestizos. Philip's great-grandfather was the Negro King Kernel. According to family tradition King Kernel was at an auction in the East at which Philip's great-grandmother, a pretty young light mulatto, was offered for sale. Smitten at first sight, King Kernel asked her if she would marry him, if he could get his master to buy her. She said yes, and King Kernel's master obliged. Through Indian civil wars in the Southeast, Jackson's incursions, and removal to

Oklahoma, they clung fast to one another, and saw a growing number of children, grandchildren, and great-grandchildren. The elderly King Kernel died in 1873 and his beloved wife a decade later, in an era when they and all their progeny were free. But slave or free, in Alabama or Oklahoma, King Kernel never left his wife's side: "King was a big man."[50]

The black experience in the Southeast forced Negroes to adopt much of white and Indian culture, and nowhere was this more apparent than in regard to language. A West African tongue served little purpose: Negroes had to learn one and usually several other languages, including English, Spanish, French, Creek, Hitchiti, Yuchi, Alabama, Shawnee, Gullah, and Geechee. As a result they became versatile linguists in great demand as interpreters.

In 1770 the *Georgia Gazette* published a notice advertising that a twenty-year-old Negro fellow from the Bumbo (Bumpe?) country, who had escaped from a ship at Pensacola and lived among the Indians for twelve months, had finally been recaptured. He spoke "African" and "Indian" and was at Savannah, where he could be redeemed by his master. Whether he was redeemed is unknown, and, except for the advertisement, this Negro is lost to history.[51] Even so, more is known about him than about other Africans among the Muscogulges. The Bumbo fellow spoke "Indian," which is comparable to speaking "European," and might signify one or several distinct languages. Neither his native language from the Bumbo country nor his knowledge of "Indian" would be of much use in the Savannah workhouse. If he remained in coastal Georgia, English and Geechee were essential. Other Negroes had comparable experiences to those of the Bumbo fellow, and they were required to learn a variety of languages, or at least pidgins. This is why they were in such demand as interpreters and spies. Supposedly the Master of Breath fished Africans out of the water last. Both Indians and whites, however, relied heavily on black linguists, and this gave the Negroes status and power—even if the water had been muddy.

These black interpreters are repeatedly mentioned in extant accounts. When a Creek delegation unexpectedly arrived in Nas-

98   sau in 1802 only Panton's Negro, who happened to be there,
could tell authorities what the Indians wanted.[52] Director General
Bowles depended on the Black Prince and Hector to communicate
with both blacks and Indians in the state of Muskogee.[53]
Early in the nineteenth century, white cattle buyers went
among the Upper Creeks, and Indians called on Black John to
supervise the sale.[54] Not infrequently Negro women served as
"linguisters." Lower Creek John Walker was not so acculturated
that he did not have to ask his slave, the Afro-Indian Rose, to
tell him what the whites were up to.[55] Seminole Chief Bowlegs,
whose photograph appeared in *Harper's Weekly* in 1858, and
who was one of the last Indians to relocate in Oklahoma, spoke
English; even after arriving in the West, he still communicated
with whites through his trusted Negro interpreter.[56] Muskogees
occasionally referred to Negroes as "outsiders," those speaking
a foreign tongue; but the foreign languages involved were not
West African, but English, Spanish, Yuchi, Hitchiti, and other
Indian languages, all of which were incomprehensible to Muskogee
speakers.

The legal status of black Muscogulges almost defies comprehension.
Whether a particular Negro was slave or free or who
was his master often depended on whom one asked. This was
the case regarding Negro slaves brought by Creeks into the
Florida peninsula. The Creeks wanted to return to Alabama, but
their slaves would not let them go, because they knew that
Alabama whites would claim them. Between 1775 and 1815
British military commanders had freed tens of thousands of
Negro slaves who ran away from their American masters and
sought sanctuary with British forces. Some of these Negroes
eventually became free black Muscogulges. White American
slaveowners, however, vehemently denied any British liberation.
Occasionally the movement from white to Indian settlements
represented a transition from freedom to slavery. Creeks
might capture a free black woman from the Augusta region and
sell her and her children as slaves in the Indian country.[57]

Part of the confusion about whether a Negro were slave or
free reflected the difference between the European legal system,
which recognized property inheritance through the male line,

and the Indian matrilineal custom. Wealthy, acculturated mestizos—Alexander McGillivray, John and George Galphin, and William McIntosh—successfully contended that they were entitled to an appropriate portion of their father's property, including slaves. In contrast, one can look at Kinache (Kinhega) and the Black Factor, prosperous Seminole (Lower Creek) chiefs owning large stocks of cattle and slaves. Each died in the first part of the nineteenth century, and their sons, the descendants of their mothers' brothers and sisters, and whites who had purchased the slaves from the "legal" owner, all claimed the valuable slave inheritance. One can follow this dispute in Florida during the Seminole Wars, and through the move to Oklahoma Territory, on which agents of the rival claimants dogged the Indians' footsteps. The controversy was resolved in Oklahoma only with passage of the Thirteenth Amendment, which abolished slavery.[58]

Due to their own efforts or sometimes those of their masters, black Muscogulges at times gained their freedom. Through farming, hunting, and so forth, a few earned enough money to purchase their liberty. Early in the nineteenth century, Negro Jim, belonging to Chief Walker, purchased his freedom for $330.[59] Later in the same century, the Negro Abraham and the Seminole Sam Factor appeared before white authorities. Abraham emancipated his son Washington, and Factor emancipated his Negro wife and children.[60] Previously, in 1798, David Randon, probably an illiterate mestizo, visited Benjamin Hawkins at the Creek agency to free his wife Suckey and his five mulatto children.[61] Lower Creek–Seminole Chief Bosten (Boatswain) employed Negro slaves and free Indians who at times intermarried. When one of his black slaves married an Indian, he or she also became an Indian and automatically became free.[62]

Some black Muscogulges were much more incorporated into Indian society and culture than others. Regardless of their status, for the time being we will have to put them aside. It is not possible to leave them permanently, however, because in the Southeast, as in other regions of the Western Hemisphere, the three races persevered, constantly influencing and interacting with one another.

Relations with Britain, Spain, & France

It was essentially outsiders who created the Creek and Seminole "nations," which is why foreign relations were of such consequence. The year 1763 was decisive for the Indians. Britain had soundly defeated France and Spain in the Seven Years' War, and the Paris peace negotiations largely concerned which captured territories Britain would keep and which she would return. The final settlement awarded all of Spanish Florida and the eastern half of French Louisiana, including Mobile and Fort Toulouse, to Britain. Thus for the first time Britain completely encircled the Muscogulges. To the east and south lay the royal colonies of South Carolina, Georgia, East Florida, and West Florida. Far to the west British soldiers and merchants established themselves at Manchac and Natchez on the Mississippi. The Cherokees resided immediately to the north, but if one continued even farther north, British merchants were to be found at Pittsburgh and Detroit.

For years French Canadian *coureurs de bois* had paddled down the Maumee-Wabash route up the Tennessee River to trade. Some married Cherokee women and settled in Cherokee towns, and a few remained after 1763 with their families, still obtaining goods from Canada. But the Union Jack, not the fleur-de-lis, flew over Canada, and the trading companies and merchandise were British. It perhaps was a comfort to the Southern

Indians to know that Frenchmen were still bringing trading goods down from Detroit to the Cherokees, and that Upper Creeks on the Coosa and Tallapoosa might continue to buy manufactures from them. But Indian countrymen and village factors—and one suspects the Indians themselves—understood that George III was now the master of the familiar *coureurs de bois* who brought European merchandise to the southeastern Indians.[1]

The Cherokees, of course, not the British, were the Creeks' immediate northern neighbors, and the numerous Choctaws were their neighbors to the west. Written sources and folklore alike demonstrate that Choctaw–Upper Creek animosity had long been intense. The powerful Choctaws had been the main trading partners of Frenchmen in Louisiana, and French merchants and influence lingered after 1763. But moving into Mobile and elsewhere in recently ceded Louisiana, British merchants aggressively took over the trade. If by chance an Upper Creek decided to go not to Mobile but instead through the Choctaw country—an often risky or foolish enterprise—he encountered the Union Jack flying over the old French Fort Rosalie at Natchez on the Mississippi River.

Creeks and Seminoles had no claustrophobia about being surrounded by the British, because the small white population was widely scattered. After 1763 whites in the two Floridas numbered little more than 5,000, sometimes not that, and only 10,000 to 15,000 lived in Georgia. Indians often composed a majority. Much open space remained, especially in southeastern Georgia, the Florida peninsula, and the mountainous region to the north. The Muscogulges' most numerous immediate neighbors were the Choctaws and the Chickasaws, who outnumbered whites in the two Floridas and Georgia combined.[2]

Even so there was no escaping the fact that after 1763 Britain encircled the Muscogulges. Indian countrymen, mixed-blood factors, micos, and tastanagis first realized this, and so in time did ordinary men and women who gossiped and drank black drink in the square, conducted business in the truck house, and talked among themselves in isolated winter hunting camps. British authorities promised to "pour in goods upon you like the

floods of a great river when it overflows . . . if you behave well."[3]
Regardless of which direction Muscogulges looked, George III's
presence was manifest, and when British subjects traded and
negotiated with the Muscogulges, the Indians involved became
at least to outsiders what Britain asserted they were: "Creeks"
and "Seminoles."

In the final decades of the eighteenth century Alexander
McGillivray was probably the best-known Creek, head chief or
soul of the Creek nation, paid by Spain, member of Panton,
Leslie, and Company, and feted and given a commission by the
United States in 1790 when he went to New York to negotiate
a treaty with President Washington. Confusion exists about
McGillivray's Indian ancestry and about his date of birth, though
presumably it was in 1759. He may or may not have been a true
Muskogee, because according to varying accounts he was a Tuskegee, a Koasati, an Abihka, or a Coosa. Biologically this mestizo
was more white than Indian, and he was part of two cultures. It
is the Indian side of his nature that we are now concerned with.
Possibly he was a true Muskogee—an Abihka or a Coosa. Even
if he was not, he or his mother had adopted or absorbed the
Muskogee language and culture and he was a member of the
Wind clan, which was prominent in the Muskogeee moiety. In
his adult life McGillivray was a spokesman for the "Creeks,"
which more often than not meant the Muskogees.

Lachlan McGillivray was his father, and the French mestizo
Sehoy his mother. For some time British traders did not consider
Alexander's ancestors to be Creeks.[4] In 1720 Carolina authorities enumerated the Indians: 2,406 Ochesee Creeks on the Chattahoochee River; 1,773 Abihkas; 2,343 Tallapoosas; and 770
Alabamas, all on the Alabama River and its tributaries. Alexander's forebears in 1720 were among the 1,773 Abihkas or
others living near the forks of the Alabama, whereas the
"Creeks" were the Ochesees on the Chattahoochee.[5] At some
point after 1720 the Abihkas and others on the Alabama and its
tributaries also came to be known as Creeks—the Upper
Creeks—but whether Lachlan McGillivray regarded his new son
as an Abihka, a Coosa, a Tuskegee, a Koasati, or as a Creek is
unknown. After the American Revolution, Spaniards, Scottish

partners of Panton, Leslie, and Company, and George Washington all professed that McGillivray was the head chief, the dictator, of all Creeks, Upper and Lower. McGillivray was comfortable with these titles and did not worry about his ancestry or how he had become head of the new Creek nation. His confused subjects must, however, have wondered, since there never had been a Creek nation, how McGillivray had become its head, its soul. After 1763 British officials and traders insisted that most of the Muscogulges belonged to the Creek nation, and reluctantly, or in McGillivray's case, enthusiastically, more and more Indians at least outwardly concurred.

In this same fashion British authorities made an increasing number of Muscogulges in Florida admit that they were Seminoles. After 1763 whites sometimes contended that Florida Indians were Seminoles, at other times Creeks, and upon occasion Creek-Seminoles. British colonists did not try to make logic out of all this, which was just as well. The long-term trend, however, was for British colonists to regard most nonwhites in Florida as Seminoles. The first documented use of the term Seminole was in 1771 during the British era. The term, an anglicized corruption of the Spanish *cimarron*, was first applied to Muscogulges who had migrated to Alachua, and later to those who settled in Apalachee. The Indians regarded themselves as Oconees, Hitchitis, Yuchis, Yamasees, Miccosukees, among others.[6] Regardless of their ethnic and linguistic backgrounds, an increasing number of Indians in Georgia and Alabama after 1763 were identified as Creeks, and a growing number in Florida as Seminoles. Often bewildered, the Indians nevertheless had to take note.

British subjects living on the Muscogulges' borders or, as in the case of Lachlan McGillivray, among the Indians, had three primary concerns: land, trade, and their own security. Defense had a high priority, which could be seen when George Galphin converted Silver Bluff into Fort Galphin during the American Revolution, and two decades later when William Panton moved his Apalachee warehouse under the shadow of the cannons at Fort Saint Marks. In 1763 British subjects had been frightened by the prospect of a native uprising involving western Indians from Canada to the Gulf of Mexico, including the Muscogulges.

Pontiac's Rebellion, one of the bloodiest Indian wars in American history, for the most part was limited to the area above the Ohio River. But Pontiac and his confederates from the Great Lakes region had friends and relatives in the South. Authorities in Georgia and the Floridas and traders in the interior were apprehensive, and when Britain occupied her new conquests won from Spain and France, doubts persisted about exactly who surrounded whom.[7]

The royal proclamation of 1763 attempted to shield George III's colonists. It created the two new colonies of East and West Florida, and a line ran from them to Canada, which separated Indians from whites. Immigration was directed to the seaboard colonies and to the Floridas, and the interior above the Floridas and west of the Appalachian Mountains remained Indian country open only to soldiers and traders. The royal proclamation created an undisputed northern boundary for East Florida, and this northern boundary separated the Seminoles from the Creeks in Georgia. Before 1763 Florida, of course, had had a northern boundary, but in the three-way rivalry in the Southeast, Spain, Britain, and France each had a different conception about its location. After 1763 Britain controlled all the Southeast, and no foreign power remained to dispute that East Florida's boundary ran from the Atlantic Ocean up the Saint Marys River to its source and thence to the forks of the Apalachicola River. Before 1763 Spain had designated hostile Oconees both in British Georgia and in Spanish Florida as *cimarrones*; after 1763 Britain contended that these "Semillones" were merely those Indians in the vicinity of Alachua in East Florida. Their Georgia relatives were still designated as Creeks.

Britain had always dominated Muscogulge trade, and after the Seven Years' War she almost monopolized it. French troops and merchants in the Upper Creek country at Fort Toulouse had loaded all their equipment and trading goods on bateaux and let the current of the Tallapoosa and Alabama rivers speed them away to Mobile. Fort Toulouse, a bastion and commerical center on French Louisiana's eastern boundary, lay deserted, and was slowly reclaimed by nature or destroyed by vandals. But when the French flag was also lowered at Fort Conde in Mobile, the introduction of French manufactures into the Muscogulge country via the Alabama River ceased. Ambitious British merchants from South Carolina and Georgia arrived in Mobile to replace the French. Bateaux making their way up the Alabama River now had manufactures from London and the Midlands, not from Paris.[8]

Before Spain evacuated Florida, it had been she who furnished Indians near Saint Augustine and the fort in Apalachee with manufactures. Upon occasion Spanish expeditions had visited Coweta, had distributed presents and attempted to build up a following, and Indian delegations had come to Saint Augustine or even to Mexico City to witness Spain's power and wealth. Coweta chiefs after 1763 might reminisce about prior visits to Saint Augustine or Havana, and Indians in Florida might still wear crucifixes and speak broken Spanish, but the Union Jack now waved over Saint Augustine, Apalachee, and Pensacola.

Britain's commanding position in one sense was misleading. Concentrated in present-day Georgia, Alabama, and Florida, the Muscogulges on the eve of the American Revolution probably outnumbered the combined white population of Georgia and the two Floridas. If one adds the Choctaws, Cherokees, and black Indians, the balance shifts clearly in favor of the Indians. Including African slaves on tidewater plantations makes it even more apparent that southeastern whites were a minority, and all of this tempered British dealings with the Creeks and Seminoles.

Unable to enforce their will on the Muscogulges arbitrarily, British authorities resorted to the old policy of divide and conquer, of keeping alive traditional rivalries, and of encouraging Indians to kill each other rather than to turn on whites. It was not difficult to enflame ancient disputes: that of the Upper Creeks with the Choctaws; of both the Upper and Lower Creeks with the Cherokees; of Muscogees with Yuchis and Seminoles; and of any Indian with another in a different moiety. From the British point of view, the most useful of all these disputes, the one involving the largest number of Indians, was that between the Upper Creeks (Abihkas) and the Choctaws. John Stuart, Britain's superintendent for all southern Indians, with satisfaction and relief reported to his superiors that he had kept Upper Creek–Choctaws hostilities alive, and as a result each side looked to him and British merchants for guidance and security.[9]

Though having overlapping and conflicting jurisdictions, British officials generally agreed that Stuart's divide-and-rule policy was judicious. But they quarreled about disposition of Indian lands and about who was responsible for the disposing. Ambiguities concerning exactly who was in charge—the southern superintendent, provincial governors, councils, assemblies, or the privy council in London—came to the forefront. Authorities not only bickered about who should grant the lands, but also about whether they should be disposed of at all or if instead the Indians should remain commercial hunters. Diverse jurisdictions and contradictory policies reflected flaws in Britain's imperial administration which she never rectified.

Misunderstandings were muted at first, because all parties agreed that to facilitate colonization the Indians should cede lands near Saint Augustine, Pensacola, and Mobile. Accordingly Stuart and the East Florida governor met first with the Creeks and then with the Seminoles, winning from them, without overly worrying about distinctions between the two or which Indians really owned the land, a narrow coastal strip running along all East Florida. Saint Augustine was the principal settlement, and in its vicinity the boundary extended inland over thirty miles to just beyond the Saint Johns River.[10] Stuart and the West Florida governor also met with the Upper Creeks and secured a similar though smaller concession near Pensacola, which included a coastal strip about fifteen miles deep.[11] In no instance was it assumed that the Indians really owned the lands. Sovereignty had already been handed over to Britain by Spain— and in case of Mobile, by France—in 1763. British negotiators at Paris never inquired how Spain and France had obtained these lands from the Indians. In British eyes what the Indians conceded in the Florida treaties was their right of occupancy, and use of the soil or usufruct. George III, of course, already owned all the lands in question.

The Muscogulges were confused by formal treaties between two independent nations of which one was not a sovereign nation but a protectorate or tributary. Part of the misunderstanding reflected differences between the two cultures and legal systems. The Indian economy was based on communal agriculture, droving, and commercial hunting, and no centralized Creek and Seminole government or nation existed. Although there was an ancient Indian tradition of ceding lands of inferiors or enemies in return for presents, rum, and annuities, Indians actually residing on the lands often were bewildered when whites showed them treaties certifying that their lands had been deeded and paid for. This happened in the Florida treaties: Cowkeeper and Seminoles in Alachua were never sure why Creeks in Georgia should be compensated for lands south of Saint Augustine.[12] And it was not clear why Creeks on the Coosa and Tallapoosa should be paid for lands around Pensacola.

John Stuart, governors of the southern colonies, and Indian delegations met at Augusta in 1763, and the natives ceded lands on the north side of the upper Ogeechee. Coupled with agreements made in Florida, this treaty established a white-Muscogulge boundary from Georgia to West Florida, and these agreements, along with the proclamation of 1763, delineated a large interior Indian preserve.[13] Georgia's white population was growing rapidly. In one fashion or another Georgians were determined to have additional Indian lands, and they paid no more attention to Stuart's treaties and George III's proclamation than necessary.

George Galphin had been at the Augusta conference. Like most Indian traders, he was a land speculator. One of his wives, Metawney, was a Creek, presumably a Yuchi. Galphin met with the Yuchis in 1772 on the Flint River, and requested a generous land cession for Metawney and her mestizo children.[14] Galphin knew that in British eyes it was legal for Indians to transfer their right to the use of the soil among themselves. For Galphin that was merely the first step: he wanted that land on the Flint for himself. He realized, as did other land speculators, that in 1757 authorities in London—the Earl of Camden, the attorney general; and Charles Yorke, the solicitor-general—had issued an opinion: "Such places, as have been or shall be acquired by treaty or grant from the Grand Mogul or any of the Indian princes or governments, your majesty's letters patents are not necessary, the property of the soil vesting in the grantees by the Indian grants."[15] Contending that Columbus really had not erred and that an Indian was an Indian, Galphin assumed that what was appropriate for the Grand Mogul in the Far East was suitable for Yuchis on the Flint. Rather than acting as a principal, Galphin operated through Metawney. As an Indian she could obtain the land and not violate Stuart's treaties or George III's proclamation. However, in English law, unless some special provisions were made, a wife legally existed only in the person of her husband, who owned and managed her property. Nevertheless, many a successful Indian trader had founded a landed dynasty, and by manipulating the legal systems of the Yuchis, Bengalese, and English for his own purposes, Galphin intended to be among them.

Another Georgian, Jonathan Bryan, had the same idea, and his eyes were set on Alachua (Payne's Prairie) and Apalachee. Each formerly had contained a dense aboriginal population and had been dotted with Spanish Franciscan missions and cattle ranches. In the nineteenth century they would become part of the Old South's cotton kingdom. Just before the American Revolution Seminole hunters and herdsmen occupied Payne's Prairie, and Hitchiti-speaking Miccosukees, Yuchis and others lived in or were moving into Apalachee. For a consideration, Bryan got Lower Creeks in Georgia to cede Creek lands in Florida that included Payne's Prairie. Chief Cowkeeper, the Hitchiti-speaking Oconee chief at Payne's Prairie, was furious: how dare Oconees in Georgia bargain away lands of their Florida kin? There were several reasons why in the eighteenth century Oconees had drifted into Florida, and one of these was dissension among the Indians themselves. Bryan capitalized on this.[16]

Bryan's purchase threatened to bring on hostilities. Frontiersmen were alarmed and in 1774 authorities pointedly asked Cowkeeper and other so-called Creek chiefs in Florida if they were bent on war or peace.[17] Fortunately the crisis passed. Bryan retreated, denying that he had purchased an enormous tract in northern Florida, and claiming that he had merely leased a small area to graze cattle. The American Revolution, breaking out in

1775, overshadowed Bryan's purchase. But Bryan never took his eyes off northern Florida's fertile lands; he was determined to have them by purchase, lease, or conquest. Chief Cowkeeper never forgot Bryan's ambition nor that his rival, the Oconee King, was Bryan's collaborator.

Land-grabbing schemes of Bryan, Galphin, and others like them periodically threatened the peace after 1763. Whenever a dispute seemed to be getting out of hand Britain resorted to the old policy of a trade embargo, a potent weapon since Britain surrounded the Muscogulges. Even so it was not as effective as one might think. Authorities might successfully embargo goods at Silver Bluff, Savannah, Saint Augustine, and Pensacola, but at the same time the factors' truck houses in the interior, depending on the season, might be bulging with trade goods. Thus, there was a time lag before Indians felt the pinch. Licensed factors had always faced competition from unregulated interlopers roaming the woods, attempting to purchase skins anywhere, and paying little heed to proscriptions of Superintendent Stuart or provincial governors. A trade embargo proffered interlopers a chance for quick profits, an opportunity that many were anxious to exploit. At the time of Bryan's purchase, Creeks killed over a dozen settlers on the upper Savannah. An embargo was imposed, and eventually Oktulkeo, one of the ringleaders, was put to death by the Indians. The other culprits never were punished, and one reason was that the embargo did not hurt as much as it should have considering Britain's position.[18]

Though Britain designated certain Muscogulges as Creeks and others as Seminoles, traditional ethnic, clan, and dual divisions persisted. The Yuchis afford a good example. Scattered among the Muscogulges from the Tallapoosa, to the Flint and Chattahoochee, to Silver Bluff, and to the Florida peninsula, the Yuchis were the largest non-Muskhogean people among the Creeks. A chiefdom (Chisca) in Mississippian times, in all likelihood their homeland had been in eastern Tennessee. After European contact they drifted southward, settling in various places that in time the English insisted belonged to the Creeks. Yuchis joined other non-Muskogee components. "Yuchi" and "slave" upon occasion were synonymous, and the Yuchis were among those enslaved and sold to the whites or kept by Indian masters. Dispersed and sometimes enslaved, the Yuchis in 1763 still remembered the preeminence of their Chisca chiefdom, stubbornly held on to their language, and resented their subordinate or slave status. Regardless of what Superintendent Stuart and provincial governors said, the Yuchis chafed at their assigned role as members of a Creek nation dominated by Muskogee speakers. They often lived apart from pure Muskogees, joining Shawnees on the Tallapoosa and Hitchitis on the lower Chattahoochee, or they lived in their own separate villages on the Flint River, on the Savannah near Augusta, and at or near Tampa Bay.

Around 1763 Chief Tonaby (Tunape) resided at Coweta and was known as the Coweta mico, an influential Lower Creek leader. Before they relinquished Florida, Spaniards had recognized Tonaby as a non-Muskogee Indian, by which they probably meant a Yuchi, though perhaps a Hitchiti. For some years before 1763 Tonaby had lived near the Spaniards at Saint Marks, and while the Spaniards were in Florida they had invited him and his relatives to visit Saint Augustine and Havana. Enticed by an independent source of trading goods that could help maintain their identity, Tonaby and his relatives accepted Spanish overtures. After the Spaniards left Florida Tonaby had no choice but to go to Havana to see his old friends. But in their own vessels or in those of Cuban fishermen this was not difficult, and Tonaby, Escochabey (Escahabe), Alligator, and other Yuchis or Hitchitis arrived in Havana to barter skins for manufactures and receive presents from Spanish authorities. The Indians returned to Tampa, Saint Marks, and the mouth of the Apalachicola River and made their way to their respective villages. Coweta Mico (Tonaby) and some of his people after 1763 removed from Coweta (near Columbus) and established themselves—in reality reestablished themselves—in fertile, thinly populated Apalachee. Tonaby located his village on the site of the future Florida capital (Tallahassee), maintained commercial contact with Cuba through the nearby port at Saint Marks, and flew the Spanish flag at his square ground. Others relocating near Tampa Bay did essentially the same thing, all of which indicated their dissatisfaction with being known as inferiors, slaves, or "stinkards."[19] Upon occasion British expeditions arrived at Tallahassee and suggested that Tonaby fly the British rather than the Spanish ensign.[20]

The Shawnees were another non-Muskogean people scattered about the Creek nation. They too were exasperated at their "stinkard" appellation, and still remembered their former ascendancy. In the 1680s Shawnees (Savannahs) had been concentrated on the Savannah River and for a time served as the principal middlemen for English traders. In the eighteenth century many of them moved westward and became part of the assemblage known as Creeks. They continued their migrations, going above the Ohio, though some returned to the Creek country. The general thrust of the migration, however, was northward. At the close of the eighteenth century Efau Haujo, addressing Indians at the Tuckabatchee square, professed that Tuckabatchee and Shawnee fires were one.[21] In a literal sense this was probably true. A few years earlier Great Lakes Indians and others had met in a general council on the Maumee River south of Detroit. The speaker strode to the center, threw down a belt of wampum, and began his harangue urging native unity: the southern Indians were present for "you see there the Creeks sitting by us." Many and probably most of those Creeks were Shawnees.[22]

The Tuskegees, like the Shawnees, Tuckabatchees, and Yuchis, were non-Muskogees closely associated with northern Indians. Laboring under the same disabilities as the Yuchis and Shawnees, some of them also relocated. Sometime before 1812 Tuskegees from the village of that name, accompanied by Tallassees and others, moved southward into Florida. A young Tallassee boy accompanied them, who, when he became of age, was given the title *asi yahola*, "the black drink singer or crier." This was a common title and the numbers of asi yaholas among the Muscogulges was legion. Little or nothing is known about most of them, but this particular young asi yahola has not been forgotten; he has gone down in history as Osceola, the redoubtable Seminole war leader.[23]

The imprecise terms Creek and Seminole served a purpose; they identified Indians of diverse origins who had congregated in certain geographic areas. British authorities and traders often equated the term Creek with Muskogee, the largest ethnic group, and more often than not concluded economic arrangements for all Creeks through the Muskogees. This accentuated the slave, inferior (stinkard) status of non-Muskogees, and helped explain why the Yuchis, Shawnees, Tuskegees, Tallassees, Hitchitis, Miccosukees, and Alabamas were restive. Making Creek and Muskogee synonymous accentuated the cleavage between the two opposing moieties.

The American Revolution gave new life to non-Muskogees who hoped to preserve their languages and identities. Overnight the British encirclement was broken, and Muscogulges, whatever their background, could turn to Britain, Spain, or Americans in Georgia and South Carolina. Contacts with Spain at first were through Cuban fishermen who continued calling at Florida's Gulf Coast. As the fighting progressed, Spain captured Mobile (1780) and Pensacola (1781), and before or after their surrender, Alabamas arrived at Mobile and Yuchis and others at Pensacola. These tribes sold cattle and foodstuffs to the Spaniards and listened to what the victors had to offer in the way of presents and long-term commercial arrangements.[24]

At the outbreak of hostilities Britain had sent agents and commissaries to live with or periodically visit the Muscogulges: David Taitt and Alexander McGillivray among the Upper Creeks, Timothy Barnard and William McIntosh among the Lower Creeks, and Thomas Brown and Moses Kirkland among the Seminoles. Brown, Kirkland, and Governor Patrick Tonyn of East Florida contended that all Indians in East Florida were Seminoles and thus under their jurisdiction and. not that of Creek agents.[25] Creeks in Florida must have been surprised to discover they had become Seminoles.

In general, pure Muskogees supported Britain, and those in the opposing moiety looked to the United States and Spain. There were exceptions, notably the Hitchiti Cowkeeper. He knew that his Hitchiti kinsmen had sold his Florida lands to the resolute Georgia rebel, Jonathan Bryan, and that Bryan and his associates were determined to have Payne's Prairie and more. Whenever Bryan and his Georgia friends invaded East Florida,

Governor Tonyn and Superintendent Brown called on Cowkeeper for aid. Though Seminoles far to the west were slow to respond or did not show up at all, Tonyn could always depend on Cowkeeper and his followers at Payne's Prairie. Between 1775 and 1778, before Britain had recaptured Georgia, the East Florida–Georgia frontier experienced some of the most savage partisan warfare anywhere in America. Cowkeeper's Seminoles were partly responsible.[26]

Americans and Spaniards most often found their followers among non-Muskogees, including the Hitchitis, Yuchis, Alabamas, Tuckabatchees, and others, many of whom belonged to the Tiger—a predominantly non-Muskogee—clan. Followers of the Tame King (Hoboithle Mico, the Tallassee King) among the Upper Creeks, and the Fat King (Cussita Mico or Eneah Mico, probably a Hitchiti or Yuchi) on the Chattahoochee, though in a minority, looked to the Georgians; and the Alabamas and Yuchis turned to the Spaniards. All three white belligerents asserted that their subjects alone could supply the Indians with manufactures. Despite the fact that so many Georgia traders were Tories who had abandoned the colony during the early years of the Revolution, Georgia maintained a limited commerce with the Indians. Britain's military successes and her seapower, however, made it difficult for Georgians to obtain munitions, textiles, and necessary manufactures. They did have cattle and rum, the latter brought in from the West Indies despite the vigilance of British cruisers. Making a virtue of necessity, Georgians professed that cattle were just the thing for Indians: raising them would imbue the natives with the virtues of private property and serve to uplift and civilize them. Rum was not intended for a debauch but to numb the Indians' minds so they would not realize that Georgia's pack animals brought no guns, powder, blankets, pipe tomahawks, and Jew's harps.[27]

Meeting in Paris in 1783, diplomats concluded a general peace that ended a world war. The terms confirmed the independence of the United States, turned over the Floridas, whatever their boundaries, to Spain, and forced Britain to relinquish title to all Muscogulge lands. The several treaties ended a world war and ushered in a period of peace—but not for the Indians. No Muscogulge had been in Paris, though Indians soon became aware of the terms. With Spaniards on one border and Americans on another after 1783, many Creeks and Seminoles bemoaned the withdrawal of our "beloved white men," those British commissaries and agents who had lavished them with presents.[28]

By no means did all, or even most, of Britain's beloved white men retire. The elderly Lachlan McGillivray had returned to the Scottish Highlands, but his mestizo son, a British commissary, remained at Little Tallassee among the Upper Creeks. William McIntosh left the Lower Creek country, and after passage of time settled down in eastern Georgia. His mestizo son, however, remained on the upper Chattahoochee.[29] William Panton joined the general exodus from Saint Augustine to the Bahamas in 1784, but in 1785 he began establishing himself in Pensacola. William Augustus Bowles, a young officer in a loyalist regiment, left Pensacola after the Spanish capture in 1781, and in the ensuing years schemed in New York and the Bahamas. But by 1785 he had returned to his Indian family and friends on the Chattahoochee. Indian countryman Samuel Mims joined other Tories in moving westward from the Chattahoochee River to Tensaw above Mobile.[30] Countless other Indian countrymen and mestizos, veterans of the Indian trade, remained in their villages, and after the Revolution sent their skins not to Silver Bluff, Savannah, and Charleston, but southward to Spanish Florida, especially to Pensacola.

After 1783 the Muscogulges were surrounded by subjects of at least three powers—Americans in Georgia, Spaniards in the Floridas, and former British loyalists who lived among the Indians and in the Spanish Floridas. Britain had relinquished title to lands in the Southeast, but the British flag still flew over the nearby Bahamas, Detroit, and Canada. Meanwhile Frenchmen, one of whom was Napoleon, thought it was a good idea to raise the French flag once again over Fort Toulouse.[31] The Southeast was a hotbed of international intrigue and land speculation.

Among the Muscogulges, who were at the center of all this, one could detect three trends, sometimes complementary and other times conflicting. One was an attempt to create a centralized Muskogee-dominated Creek nation. The second was the countervailing tendency by the Yuchis, Hitchitis, Alabamas, Shawnees, and other non-Muskogees to prevent this. And the third was an inchoate nativistic, pan-Indian movement, an endeavor by Native-American reformers to join all western Indians from Canada to the Gulf of Mexico in order to protect their lands and culture. Such solidarity required overcoming traditional rivalries between Muscogulge factions, Upper Creeks and Choctaws, Choctaws and Chickasaws, and Mohawks and Shawnees. The task was formidable.

The mestizo Alexander McGillivray was the one most identified with forging a unified Creek nation, and he was not unhappy to be called the soul, dictator, or *isti atcagagi thlucco* (great beloved man) of the Creek nation. No portrait of McGillivray exists, and surprisingly little is known about him. He was born and lived at Little Tallassee until his father sent him to be educated first by his cousin, Farquhar McGillivray, Presbyterian minister in Charleston, and subsequently to a countinghouse in Savannah. From time to time observers reported that McGillivray did not speak good Indian. He may have had difficulty with Shawnee, Natchez, Alabama, and other Upper Creek languages, but Muskogee was a lingua franca, the language of trade and diplomacy, and McGillivray was fluent in Muskogee: it was either his native or adopted tongue. He also spoke English, probably using it more than any other language. His mother belonged to the Wind clan—probably the most influential white clan among the Muskogees. McGillivray used his clan ties, his knowledge of Muskogee, the commercial legacy bequeathed by his father, and his relationship with Panton, Leslie, and Company in his endeavor to unify the Muscogulges.[32]

One of his objectives was to strengthen and control the National Council, which, depending on the time, met at Tuckabatchee, the Hickory Ground, Coweta, or elsewhere. The National Council was as much a creation of the whites as the Indians. Whether such a centralized government ever existed, it suited the purposes of whites to insist that one did. When war had broken out between Britain and Spain in 1739, James Oglethorpe had rushed to the Creek "capital" at Coweta and negotiated a treaty with the Indians whereby the "Creek nation" pledged its full military support. But only 200 warriors showed up for the attack on Saint Augustine; the majority of the Creek gunmen, ignoring transactions in the Coweta square ground, remained in their talwas.[33] During the American Revolution both Britain and the United States simultaneously avowed that the Creek nation sided with them and had even agreed to land cessions. After 1783 McGillivray's ties to Panton, Leslie, and Company, his numerous and influential clan kin, and his assertion that he could protect Indians allowed McGillivray to strengthen the powers of the National Council and his hold over it, and to insure that it met more often among the Upper Creeks. The southernmost Muscogulges, that is the Seminoles, were often represented in such councils at Tuckabatchee, the Hickory Ground, and elsewhere among the Upper Creeks. From time to time the council directed or suggested that Seminoles follow a particular policy, which Seminoles heeded or not as suited their interests. During the 1780s until McGillivray's death in 1793 the trend toward Creek centralization was just that: a trend, more of a hope than a reality.[34] After McGillivray's death others—including Benjamin Hawkins, Big Warrior and William McIntosh—attempted to fulfill McGillivray's dream, but like him, they failed.

The countervailing tendency was to maintain the status quo, the identity of ethnic minorities, the autonomy of the talwas, and the non-Muskogee opposition to a Muskogee-dominated National Council. During and after the Revolution British traders had the strongest ties with true Muskogees. Those opposing centralization, usually not true Muskogees, alternately or at the same time looked to Americans or to British interlopers, who were excluded by Panton's monopoly. These interlopers included British merchants based in the Floridas and in Canada.

Despite the fact that Georgians and Tennesseans were threatening Creek lands and that southeastern Indians were constantly at war with aggressive frontiersmen, a pro-American faction persisted for a time among the Creeks after 1783. The Tallassee King's (Hoboithle Mico's) relatively new village was on the Tallapoosa. He supported Americans during the Revolution, threatened to run British agent David Taitt out of Upper

118   Creek lands, ceded territory to Georgians, and, though he eventually turned against the Americans, until his death in 1813 he
remained a symbol of opposition to the Wind family and to the
true Muskogees.[35] The career of the Fat King (Eneah Mico) of
Kasihta on the Chattahoochee, in all probability a Hitchiti or
Yuchi, was similar, and he collaborated with the Tallassee
King.[36]

In and out of the Southeast for the two decades after 1783,
William Augustus Bowles strove to create a British protectorate,
the state of Muskogee in the Southeast. An examination of his
supporters further illustrates persisting clan and ethnic rivalries.
At one time or another his followers included the Tame King,
the Fat King, and others who, chafing under Muskogee moiety
dictation, alternately turned to Bowles or the United States.
Among the Lower Creeks, including the Seminoles, Bowles
drew his greatest support from the Hitchitis, Miccosukees, Yuchis (one of whom had adopted Bowles), Osochis (Timucuan
remnants), Apalachicolas, and Shawnees; his Upper Creek adherents included Hilibis ("refugees from other towns"),[37] Okfus-
kees (Coosa remnants), Natchez, Tallassees, Shawnees, Tuckabatchees, Kealedjis (perhaps a branch of the Tuckabatchees), and
Fushatchees. It is impossible to identify accurately all the linguistic, ethnic, and clan distinctions of Indians who rallied behind Bowles. Most of them, however, were not pure Muskogees.
His adherents among the Upper Creeks included those who after
Bowles's death in 1805 migrated southward to become known
as Seminoles. The town, Kealedji, in the 1790s was on a tributary
of the Tallapoosa; in the 1830s the Kealedji Mico was head man
of an important Seminole village near the mouth of the Suwannee River in Florida. Relocation of the Tuskegees, Tallassees,
and others to Florida, including the young Upper Creek Osceola,
has already been mentioned.[38]

The incipient pan-Indianism that was sweeping over the
western Indian country affected the Muscogulges. Both whites
and Indians, each in their own ways, encouraged native unity.
Before 1763 Frenchmen from Canada to Louisiana had urged
western Indians to join, align themselves with France, and stand
together to bar expansion of the British colonies. One of the

ironies of history is that Britain assumed this French role. After 1763 Britain controlled Canada, the Floridas, and the intervening territory, and when the thirteen colonies rebelled, British agents—Stuart, Brown, Taitt, and McIntosh in the south, and their counterparts in the north—urged the Indians to unite, throw themselves under British protection, and, fighting side by side, deny territorial encroachments by the American rebels. Britain lost the Revolution, but in one fashion or another she still dominated the commerce of all western Indians after 1783; almost to a man British merchants from Florida to Canada were former loyalists. Many of them longed for, and in fact expected, the British flag to again fly over all the West, and, as during the Revolution, they urged Indians to unite and stand ready.[39]

At the same time French subjects made similar appeals. They had not forgotten that Louis XIV had given his name to Louisiana and that French-speaking colonists remained scattered about the Mississippi Valley. They wanted to see the French flag restored, and, as of old, urged Indians to unite and await orders. One of these Frenchmen was LeClerc de Milfort who lived with Alexander McGillivray for a decade or two at Little Tallassee, married McGillivray's sister, and proclaimed himself "grand war chief or tastanegy," commander in chief of all warriors in the Creek nation. Milfort returned to France in the late 1790s to apprise the directory and Bonaparte that the Muscogulges and all western Indians anxiously awaited the French. To promote this undertaking, Milfort hastily published an historical account of the Creeks, a useful but not infallible source for Muscogulge culture.[40]

White appeals for unity made sense to the natives, though not necessarily for the reasons put forth by Milfort, Bowles, and Indian countrymen. Indians were not impressed by grandiose plans of empire emanating from London and Paris. For them the reality was that their ancestors had been decimated by disease and warfare, that survivors had relocated again and again, and, that to seek refuge in the interior, they had to incorporate with other tribes. The deaths of so many clan relatives and fellow townsmen and, in the case of micos, tastanagis and other village officials, perhaps the loss of status, created a spirit of malaise and despair, and this made the Europeans' rum particularly tempting. Appeals for temperance accompanied pan-Indianism. These reforms were often most strongly supported by the Yuchis, Shawnees, Hitchitis, Tuckabatchees, Tuskegees, Yamasees and other non-Muskogee speakers.

Indians from the Gulf of Mexico to Canada advocated solidarity. A large northern Indian delegation from above the Ohio, which included representatives of the Great Lakes Indians and of the Six Nations, arrived at Tuckabatchee in 1783 and insisted—as did Tecumseh in 1811—that all western Indians must hold one another fast by the hand. From Tuckabatchee the 1783 delegation journeyed to Picolata near Saint Augustine, where British officers praised the concept of Indian unity.[41] The Revolution had badly divided the Six Nations, shattering much of their military and diplomatic influence. Leadership and initiative of the northern Indians shifted from the Iroquois to the western Algonquins, among whom the Shawnees were prominent. At the instigation of British officers, a northern Shawnee delegation in 1777 visited the Creeks, defiantly threw down their war belts in the squares, denounced the rebel Americans, and urged native collaboration. Some of the northern Shawnees were considered Creeks,[42] and as we know when Creek delegations arrived at Detroit in 1783, 1790, or whenever, members often were in reality Shawnees.[43] Creek warriors helped northern Indians defeat the American General Arthur St. Clair's army near the headwaters of the Wabash in 1791, and Shawnees were conspicuous among these Creeks.[44] Northern Shawnees or Creeks, outfitted by British merchants, were back at Tuckabatchee in 1793, pleading for unity and, asking for warriors to help oppose General Anthony Wayne's army in the Old Northwest.[45] But the following year Wayne defeated the Indians at Fallen Timbers (below Toledo), and Britain, at least for the time being, refused to support the Indians actively, all of which checked the pan-Indian momentum. After Fallen Timbers Canadian authorities filed away letters—some with their original seals—received from Creek chiefs at Coweta, Tallahassee, and Tuckabatchee.[46] But the dream of pan-Indianism could not be relegated to a cubbyhole.

The tortured career of Savannah Jack (John Haig or Hague) elucidates the mobility, vexation, and prominent role of the Shawnees, or Savannahs. There are conflicting accounts about whom his white father might have been. Some reports insist that his father was John Haig; others, that his father was Simon Girty; and still others that he was Girty's younger half-brother. Simon Girty was a loyalist Indian trader who had fled from Pennsylvania to Detroit at the outbreak of the Revolution, and, along with his Indian allies, became noted for his hostility and cruelty to frontiersmen. It is unknown whether Savannah Jack was the son of Simon Girty and a Shawnee wife, whether he was Girty's younger half-brother, or whether he was related to Girty at all. Some contend that Savannah Jack was a Yuchi; others that he was not an Indian at all but a white man. There is perhaps some truth in all this; Savannah Jack was not very dark, and Yuchis and Shawnees were closely associated and often confused. Even so, it seems best to consider Savannah Jack to be what contemporaries called him—a Savannah, that is, a Shawnee. There is no question that after 1783 Savannah Jack had the same reputation in the South as did Girty in the North. Thomas Woodward asserted that Savannah Jack "was the most hostile and bitter enemy the whites ever had among the Creeks";[47] J. D. Driesback, related by blood to many well-known Creeks, in recounting the 1813 war, contended that everyone stood in awe of Red Eagle (William Weatherford), Jackson's implacable opponent. Even Savannah Jack did—but "not much."[48]

Relatively little is known about Savannah Jack, but from time to time he emerges from the obscurity of the frontier. Presumably before the American Revolution he had lived at or worked in a store at Augusta. By 1789 he was in Pensacola, where Spanish authorities became furious when he killed a local cowkeeper.[49] A decade later, at the head of a party of twelve Shawnees, he was living at Miccosukee, collaborating with Bowles in schemes concocted in the Director General's fertile mind.[50] Savannah Jack served with the Creeks in 1814, survived the bloody defeat at Horseshoe Bend, and subsequently retired to Florida. At some point his ears were "cut like an Indian's," indicating that Jack had paid a price for his roving eye.[51] Savannah Jack is an enigmatic figure, but the fragmentary evidence suggests that this Shawnee mestizo identified himself with the Indians and, like other Shawnees, enthusiastically supported pan-Indianism.

The attempt at Creek centralization, opposition by non-Muskogees to such unity, and the western pan-Indianism movement, all bedeviled Indian countrymen involved in the skin trade, cattle raising, and intensive agriculture. They were never sure whether to pin their hopes on Panton, Leslie, and Company, British merchants who were Panton's rivals, Spain, the United States, or Frenchmen. Until after the War of 1812 it was uncertain whether the United States', Spanish, British, French, or even the state of Muskogee's flag would wave over the lands of the Creeks and Seminoles. Indian countrymen and mixed-blood factors repeatedly shifted allegiances, often maintaining several simultaneously. Timothy Barnard, George Galphin's nephew, married to a Yuchi, served as British commissary to the Lower Creeks during the American Revolution and led war parties against American rebels. Yet the 1783 peace treaty hardly had time to be formally ratified before Barnard made up with the Americans, resumed sending his skins to Silver Bluff, and in time became an Indian agent for the United States.[52]

Regardless of the ambitions and territorial claims of other powers, Spain assumed after the American Revolution that Muscogulge lands and the entire Old Southwest were either included in the Floridas, or that most Indians below the Tennessee River were in the Spanish sphere of influence. Spanish posts bordered Muscogulge territory from Fernandina and Saint Augustine on the east; to Saint Marks, Pensacola, and Mobile on the south; to Fort Confederation on the Tombigbee in the west. Having recovered the Floridas during the Revolution, Spain expected to make the Gulf of Mexico a Spanish lake and to secure vital sealanes to Mexico. Spanish occupation of the two Floridas and Louisiana deterred foreigners from approaching New Spain's silver mines by land. Still another way to protect Mexican mines was to encourage frontiersmen in Kentucky and Tennessee to separate from the East and align themselves with Spain.

Indians also were to play a key role in defending the Spanish

Floridas, Louisiana, and Mexico. Panton, Leslie, and Company
was the nexus between truck houses in the talwas and Spanish
garrisons on the coast. Spain did not like this arrangement and
did not trust these Scottish Tories, but the alternative of relying
on the Americans seemed worse. Panton's bribes in any case
assuaged some of the distress.[53] In addition to garrisons at scattered posts, Spain stationed a handful of Indian agents in the
interior to watch both the Indians and Panton's employees. After
McGillivray went to New York in 1790 and signed a treaty with
President Washington, Spain dispatched Pedro Olivier to Little
Tallassee to help supervise the Upper Creeks and to keep an eye
on and intimidate McGillivray.[54] Juan Antonio Sandoval, a Mexican, one of the few Spanish subjects who had remained in the
Southeast after the evacuation in 1763, traded with the Indians,
had an Indian wife, and during the 1780s became a Spanish agent
at Kasihta among the Lower Creeks.[55] During the same decade
the Canary Islander, Lucas Perez, who had made his way from
Spanish Louisiana into the Spanish Floridas, became a packhorseman and trader, and served as an agent among the Lower
Creeks.[56] With limited success Spain attempted to place her
own interpreters among the Indians so she would not have to
depend on Panton, Leslie, and Company to find out what the
natives were up to. Fernando Alsar served as interpreter at Saint
Marks, but when he bestowed the presents he was to distribute
to local chiefs instead on his paramour's parents and on Indians
tending his cattle, the Saint Marks commandant asked for his
recall.[57]

Packtrains bringing peltry to Panton's warehouse and Indian
delegations arriving at the West Florida capital reminded governors at Pensacola how numerous the natives were and how
important they were in protecting Spain's colonies. At one point
the governor had inflamed the venerable Upper Creek–Choctaw
feud as a means of protecting Spanish interests, but in the 1790s
it seemed appropriate to align these two with all southern Indians so that they and the Spaniards could present a common
front to the Americans.[58] Usually Spain, through Panton, Leslie,
and Company or on her own, saw to it that Muscogulges had
ample guns and munitions for hunting and defense. Yet when-

124   ever she courted American frontiersmen, hoping that they
would secede from the East and throw themselves on Spanish
protection, Spain curtailed the Creeks' and Seminoles' munitions. The danger, however, was that in currying favor with
Tennesseeans and Kentuckians, she would alienate and lose the
Indians. As time passed Spain realized that she would have to
rely on either the frontiersmen or the Indians, and that she could
not expect both to act in concert. More often than not, circumstances dictated that she depend on the Indians. In the late 1780s
Arturo O'Neill, a professional Irish soldier in Spanish service
and the governor of Pensacola, was ever suspicious of the arrangement with Panton. To help guard the Floridas and intimidate Panton, he urged creating at least six Indian companies of
one hundred men each. Indians, including mestizos, would serve
in these Indian companies. In addition O'Neill wanted to send
a missionary among the Indians and to encourage mixed Christian marriages; he regarded a mestizo population as a source of
military and economic strength. The governor did not get his
six companies, but the mestizos' presence was conspicuous in
the West Florida capital, and O'Neill continued to ponder their
utility.[59]

Despite the misgivings of O'Neill and other authorities, Spain
had to employ Panton, Leslie, and Company. She depended on
the hostility of these old Tories toward the Americans to keep
them in line with Spain's interests. In the long run, however,
O'Neill's suspicions proved well founded: though their property
had been confiscated and some had been tarred and feathered,
members associated with Panton, Leslie, and Company began
to make up with the Americans. During the 1780s Panton's
reputation on the southern frontier had been almost as bad as
Simon Girty's in the north. Yet time proved to be a great healer,
and as the years passed the arch-fiend Panton and his associates
put aside the bitterness of the Revolution, and during the late
1790s they drew ever closer to their old republican enemies.
Diverse reasons explain this rapprochement, one being the 1795
Spanish-American Pinckney Treaty, in which Spain reluctantly
conceded that West Florida's boundary was the thirty-first parallel. This meant she gave up claim to most of the Old Southwest

including the greater portion of the Muscogulges' lands. Panton was incensed; he felt Spain had dealt his firm an underhanded blow, which would make it difficult or impossible to collect his large debts. By any measure, these debts were considerable. Panton realized that the Pinckney Treaty would enhance the United States' influence in the Old Southwest and that the growing republic was in a position, if so inclined, to help him collect these debts.

Another reason for Panton's accommodation with the United States was their common fear of radical French republicanism. Americans, especially Federalists, were aghast at the guillotining of the French king and queen and at excesses of the Terror. When Britain declared war on France in 1793, for conservatives she became the bastion of traditional values in western civilization. During the later half of the 1790s American Federalists drew closer to George III in order to prohibit the spread of French republicanism anywhere in the New World. Appointed United States agent to the southern Indians in 1796, Benjamin Hawkins, who did not want to see France return to the Gulf Coast and to recover Louisiana, began corresponding with his "old friend," the former Tory William Panton, and in 1797 even visited Panton in Pensacola. Hawkins promised that to the best of his ability he would see to it that Indians under United States' jurisdiction paid Panton.[60] When John Forbes went to Washington in 1804 he had powerful supporters and reason for optimism, though in the end he was not successful.[61]

On the eve of the War of 1812 members of the firm, assuming that Spain was losing her grasp on Florida, simultaneously urged the United States to seize Pensacola, and Britain to come to Saint Augustine to take possession of Florida.[62] The long-term trend after 1783 was for Panton and his successors to draw away from Spain and even from Britain and to have their closest ties with the Americans. Shortly after 1815 the firm went over to the United States completely, selling out the Indians in the process. Eventually it dawned on non-Muskogee components and pure Muskogees alike what was happening.

Pressure from the United States coupled with the desire of Muscogulges to be closer to sources of supply—Panton's ware-

126   houses, those of British interlopers, and Cuban fishing vessels—
drew more and more Muscogulges southward. Another attrac-
tion was the fertile lands formerly occupied by the Apalachees,
Timucuans, and other Florida Indians who had become virtually
extinct. Their lands were for the taking. In the mid–eighteenth
century Chief Cowkeeper led Oconees from Georgia to Payne's
Prairie, and by the time of the American Revolution, Payne's
Prairie was the largest Seminole village. Soon after the Revolution Apalachee, scene of deserted and ruined Franciscan missions, contained an increasing number of Seminoles. In 1775
Miccosukee was just another Indian town, yet when Bowles
made it his capital around 1800 and until Jackson invaded Florida in 1818, Miccosukee was the largest of all Seminole towns.
The mestizo Kinache was its chief. Best known as Tom Perryman in his early life, during the Revolution he lived above the
forks of the Apalachicola River, an active partisan in Britain's
behalf. After 1783 Perryman and many of his Hitchiti followers
relocated at Miccosukee, where they become identified as Seminoles and Tom Perryman became known as Kinache (Kapitca
Mico, Lye Drip Mico, Opie Mico, the Far Off Warrior).[63] As we
know, Osceola and his contemporaries in northern Alabama also
migrated to Florida early in the nineteenth century. Permanently or for extended periods, others moved beyond the Mississippi, above the Ohio River, or to the Cherokee country.
Creeks and Seminoles were not provincial, and their delegations
could be seen in councils at Detroit, Montreal, Quebec, New-
foundland, the Bahamas, Havana, Washington, New York, and
London.

When whites such as Benjamin Hawkins, William Bowles,
or LeClerc de Milfort discussed Indian population they customarily asserted that there were between 20,000 and 40,000 Creeks,
a rough approximation.[64] The mobility of the Muscogulges and
exactly how to define them made them difficult to count. Diseases continued to take a toll, though not as heavily as in previous centuries. Out-migration, such as Alabamas who moved
to Texas, and Shawnees who relocated north of the Ohio, resulted in population losses. But there were counterbalancing
accretions: Cherokees who sought refuge among the Creeks

during and after the American Revolution, and Choctaws who at roughly the same time joined the Creeks. Muscogulges who lived in Florida and were usually known as Seminoles doubled; in 1800 they numbered just over 5,000; in the 1830s, almost 10,000.[65] Whether to incorporate thousands of black Muscogulges and lesser numbers of tri-racial elements added further confusion.

If one takes a comprehensive view of who was a Muscogulge and includes Seminoles, black Muscogulges, and Indian countrymen, it is apparent that, despite disease and out-migration, at the end of the eighteenth century Muscogulges were increasing. A minimum of 40,000 seems an appropriate, and indeed a very conservative, estimate. Eight thousand or more Muscogulge gunmen could not resist Americans forever. Nevertheless there were grounds for optimism. Muscogulges were growing and, if a McGillivray, McIntosh, Big Warrior, or Bowles successfully linked them with other Mississippi Valley Indians, the number of gunmen increased considerably. Spain, Britain, and France, as well as various Muscogulges thought such solidarity an excellent idea. The alternative was for the Creeks and Seminoles to join the Alabamas beyond the Mississippi or to suffer a worse fate. The threat from the United States was serious, which made it imperative to count everyone a Muscogulge and to seek as many allies as possible.

Manifest Destiny

Part of the revolutionary effervescence that created the United States was a restless determination to expand. Jonathan Bryan and his Georgia friends had their eyes on East Florida, enthusiastically joining Americans who in 1776, 1777, and 1778 marched southward in unsuccessful attempts to liberate that province. Other Americans fared no better when they tried to capture West Florida, and as a result during the Revolution either Britain or Spain occupied most of the Southeast. Nevertheless aggressive demands of the emerging republic were manifest in the peace negotiations, and her diplomats won from Britain the Mississippi River as the western boundary and the thirty-first parallel as the boundary on the south. This was a diplomatic rather than a military coup: Spanish soldiers still manned forts well above the thirty-first parallel, and the Indians, including the Creeks, denied that they had been conquered..It remained to be seen after 1783 whether the United States could control the immense region in the south that was resolutely claimed and tenaciously occupied by Spain and the Creeks.

This insatiable demand for Indian lands should not be attributed solely to Georgians of the Revolutionary era; it can be traced back to Columbus's time and even to medieval Europe, with the rise of cities, the revival of coined money, and the mounting search for new markets and raw materials. A tradition

130   had evolved in medieval Europe that pagans and heretics, being outside the true church, had no valid title to their property. Therefore when Europeans made their first settlements on the North American Atlantic coast—Spain at Saint Augustine and England at Jamestown—they both denied the Indians, because they were pagans, any title to lands in the New World. After the founding of Charleston in 1670, Carolinians, especially those living nearby at Goose Creek, aggressively extended their sway to the Mississippi River, the Gulf of Mexico, and even the Florida Keys, along the way trading with or enslaving Indians, and occasionally converting them to Christianity. Southeastern Indians who became known as Creeks or Seminoles knew enough about Goose Creek men to be apprehensive about them and their descendants. After 1783 Indians perceived Georgians as heirs of Goose Creek men.

Britain had assumed France's former role in North America. She occupied Canada, and her subjects from Canada to the Gulf of Mexico traded with the Indians and urged them to unite. Together they could restrict the Americans to the Appalachian Mountains. Americans resented this, and, in the tradition of Goose Creek men, resolved to settle on the Mississippi River, to have Pensacola, Mobile, and Saint Augustine, and to take over most if not virtually all of the Muscogulges' lands. Soldier and veteran of the Revolution, Major Caleb Swan, visited Alexander McGillivray in 1791 and examined much of the Creek terrain: "At present it is but a rude wilderness, exhibiting many natural beauties, which are only rendered unpleasant by being in possession of the jealous natives."[1]

In the mid–nineteenth century the resolve by the United States to expand from the Atlantic to the Pacific was termed manifest destiny. But this expansionist force was not a nineteenth-century development; Swan followed in the tradition of Americans who before and after 1775 had invaded the Floridas and insisted that their dominion reached all the way to the Mississippi. The twin props of idealism and greed undergirded American expansion. The idealistic rationale for expansionism was to spread to benighted areas the blessings of republicanism—democracy; dignity of the common man; abhorrence of aristocracy, monarchy, and special privilege; trial by jury; and religious toleration, at least for Protestant Calvinistic sects. Greed used these same arguments as justifications for colonialism and land grabbing.

Muscogulges were apprehensive about descendents of Goose Creek men and their notions of manifest destiny, whatever its theoretical underpinnings. The first American colonial empire containing nonwhite, non-Christian subjects did not abruptly materialize in 1898 and 1899 when the United States acquired the Philippines, Hawaii, and Samoa, but had emerged a century before, when Americans took over the lands of the Muscogulges and their neighbors. The development of this first American colonial system could be seen when the United States concluded treaties with the "sovereign" Creek nation and when Protestant missionaries intensified efforts to uplift Creeks and redeem them from savagery.

Both the Articles of Confederation and the new Constitution that replaced it conferred—or seemed to confer—on the central government responsibility for Indian affairs, and after 1783 a national concern was what the government's Indian policy should be. Conflicting opinions and contradictory advice were proffered, and the government from time to time shifted its position.

Veteran Indian trader James Adair published his account of the southeastern Indians in 1775, and despite his conviction that the natives were descendents of the ten lost tribes of Israel, his account contains an enormous amount of useful information. A contemporary of Lachlan McGillivray, John Rae, Patrick Brown, George Galphin, and other South Carolina and Georgia merchants, Adair had accompanied packtrains into the interior since 1735, had watched village factors store goods in their truck houses, and had observed horses being loaded for the return trip. Adair made most of his money from the skin trade and from serving as Indian agent, yet he realized that many an enterprising American had invested his profits from the Indian trade in land, and had taken his place in the landed gentry. Though Adair spent most of his adult years among the Indians, he looked to the future: "Our rulers ought not to allow so mischievous and dangerous a body as the Muskohge to ingross this vast forest, mostly for wild beasts. . . . [We must defeat] this haughty nation . . . or drive them over the Mississippi."[2] Swan and his contemporaries in the new republic thought Adair's point well taken.

Quaker naturalist William Bartram also traveled among and lived with the southeastern Indians. In the years just before and after 1775 Bartram made scientific explorations in the Southeast and much later from his notes and journals, he wrote a famous account of the native Americans and of the flora and fauna. In scrutinizing this 1791 work, the reader is confused about the exact year when Bartram was in Georgia, the two Floridas, and the Indian country, and is almost unaware that a momentous revolution was in progress. Such vagueness may have been because Bartram was a Quaker. Most American Quakers were lukewarm for independence or were outright loyalists. In 1791 Bartram may not have wanted to explain why during the Revolution he was consorting with Tory Indian countrymen and merchants who encouraged Creeks to take patriot scalps.[3]

For our purposes this is not important. During the Revolution he returned home to Philadelphia, where he became increasingly famous as a naturalist and a friend and correspondent of Franklin, Jefferson, and other Americans interested in science and natural history. There seems little doubt that Bartram was author of the "hints and observations concerning the civilization of the Indians" submitted for consideration in the early 1790s to Washington's cabinet or at least to Secretary of War Henry Knox, the cabinet member most concerned with Indian affairs. These "hints and observations," now to be found among Knox's papers, are signed by the initials W. B., who is identified as one who had spent much time among the Creeks and their neighbors. W. B., or Bartram, who had been in the Creek country in 1776, reports that at heart southeastern Indians are pro-American and rejoiced at news of the Declaration of Independence. He contends that the Creeks, though children of the forest, have the same form and intellect as whites, worship the same great spirit, and are endowed with the same inalienable rights. Even though the Creeks are the "abandoned posterity of the friends of our progenitors," W. B. insists that because we are all brothers, we must treat the Indians as true equals without prejudice. The Creeks must be civilized, but this will be easy because the Creek emperor, or the great mico and his council, have always considered Europeans as worthy of being the Indians' guardians and protectors: we can secure "peaceful dominion without violence." In a powerful, but friendly manner, the United States should introduce its language, legislation, religion, arts, and sciences among the natives. The Creek language is beautiful, so it will be easy to translate the Bible and other books from English. Muscogulges will be happy to have missionaries and schools. "Let us support our dignity in all things [and our] actions . . . be as a mirror to succeeding generations."[4]

Knox shared Bartram's views, regarding the Indians as "more sinned against that sinning."[5] Secretary of war both under the Articles of Confederation and in Washington's administration, Knox as much as anyone realized that well over half the national budget was devoted to negotiating with or fighting the Indians. It was inevitable that the New Englander Knox became deeply interested in the Creeks, the most numerous and powerful of the Indian people on the white frontier. He assumed that for humanitarian, philosophical, and practical financial reasons, the United States must civilize the Creeks. The national treasury was nearly empty, and the alternative was expensive. There was constant pressure for a military campaign against the Indians. But, as Knox pointed out in 1788, it would cost the government $450,000 to protect the Georgia frontier with a 2,800-man army for a term of nine months.[6] According to Knox, the Creeks could field 6,000 gunmen, and whether 2,800 whites could defeat 6,000 Creeks and their allies was an open question. Cost estimates for these campaigns obsessed the secretary of war. If the Creeks could not be civilized as Bartram had recommended, Knox saw no alternative to hostilities that might last twenty-five, thirty, or more years.[7] The secretary of war winced at multiplying $450,000 by twenty-five or thirty. The infant government was weak, beset by a multitude of forces that threatened its success. An expensive protracted Indian war must be avoided. Negotiation and civilization were the appropriate policies, ones befitting the new nation.

Although many Americans shared the views of Knox and Bartram, it was not hard to find those who regarded Creeks as savages unlikely or unable to be civilized. They contended that instead of squandering money to uplift or wage war against the Creeks, the appropriate course was for settlers relentlessly to farm more and more of the Creeks' lands, thereby driving out the game. Without game, the Indians would not be able to continue commercial hunting. Their fate, even if considered, made little difference . . . maybe they would disappear. In any case white farmers would have their lands.

In 1788 a tall, lanky young man with an unruly shock of sandy red hair, a scar from a saber-wielding British officer on his forehead, and much of his worldly possesions in his saddle bags, escaped an Indian ambush and made his way from North Carolina over the mountains to the raw frontier community of Nashville on the Cumberland River. Andrew Jackson sought and found his fortune in the West. His campaigns against the Creeks and Seminoles, the appropriation of their lands, and the eventual relocation of the Muscogulges beyond the Mississippi River in no small measure contributed to his popularity, to his election as president, and to the success of Jacksonian democracy. He did not keep his views on the Indians to himself. In 1794 he viewed the Indians this way: Experience teaches us that treaties with the natives serve no purpose but to open the door for Indians to pass through and butcher our citizens. All Indians are collectively guilty of crimes committed by any; our troops should march to their towns and scourge the entire nation.[8] Jackson was last of the Goose Creek men.

The Quaker Bartram considered Creeks his brothers, and Knox wanted to civilize them as quickly and painlessly as possible. Jackson did not share these sentiments. He was anxious to march and if Knox and others in the national capital would not support him, then "this country will have at length [to break] or seek protection from some other source," by which he meant the British in Canada or the Spaniards in Florida and Louisiana.[9] In the 1790s such statements were branded as rank treason in Philadelphia but not in Tennessee. Threatening secession if necessary to deal with the Indians, young Jackson was not the nationalist of later life who promised to horsewhip or hang Calhoun and anyone else tampering with the Union.

Presidents, cabinet members, and congressmen received abundant advice about the proper Indian policy, and with few exceptions they assumed it was the national government's responsibility to implement such a policy. This ignored that the United States had a federal system of government and that sovereignty was divided. Individual states, notably Georgia, claimed that they had the primary obligation to manage their own Indians. Indians living anywhere within that state were her subjects, her responsibility, and Georgia's boundaries were extensive, reaching all the way to the Mississippi River. Near the close of the Revolution Georgia, like other states, had promised to cede her western lands to the central government, but she procrastinated until 1802. Until then Georgians regarded the Lower Creeks on the Chattahoochee and the Upper Creeks on the Alabama and its tributaries as her wards. Though living in Spanish Florida, the Seminoles were really Creeks, subject to the will of the National Council meeting at Tuckabatchee, Coweta, or nearby talwas, and these square grounds lay in the sovereign state of Georgia. The Creeks considered themselves independent, the owners of their lands. Furthermore, for some time after the Revolution they outnumbered white Georgians. It was not in Georgia's power to occupy Tuckabatchee and Coweta in the heart of the Indian country and to dictate to the Muscogulges. Immediately after the Revolution controversy centered on the easternmost part of the Creeks' hunting lands between the Oconee and Ocmulgee Rivers and used primarily by the Lower Creeks. Squatters put up log cabins, built cow pens, and cleared the forest for crops, and briefly in 1794 revolutionary hero Elijah Clarke maintained a nearly independent trans-Oconee republic.[10]

When Creeks worried about what Georgians were up to they had to look not only to the Oconee in the East but also to the Mississippi in the West. In 1789 and again in 1795 Georgians granted land companies vast western acreage in the vicinity of the Yazoo River and elsewhere on or near the Mississippi. Part of the 1795 grants bordered the western and northernmost

136   reaches of Muscogulge territory. Regardless of the specific location of the lands, it is clear that speculation was rampant.
McGillivray warned Spain and Panton about Georgians' heading
for the Mississippi and vowed that his hunters would watch for
them and interdict their progress.[11]

The Georgians' plans were of enormous interest to the Muscogulges, and one way the Indians found out about them was
through commerce. After the Revolution, Americans kept part
of the Creek trade, and their merchants were usually Georgians
or licensed by that state. They labored under disabilities that
included difficulty of obtaining goods and furnishing credit, the
Indians' knowledge about how badly Georgians wanted native
lands, and stiff foreign competition. At the close of the Revolution Georgians had professed that for the moment they did
not have any goods but as soon as affairs returned to normal
they were sure manufactures would become available.[12] This
was not a reassuring beginning. Even after traffic recommenced
in the 1780s, the Creeks complained that American wares were
inferior and that unscrupulous profiteers laced taffy (rum) with
pepper and tobacco juice.[13]

Despite such impediments, Georgians secured part of the
Creek trade. As we know, Timothy Barnard at the close of the
Revolution left the British service and began sending skins to
Silver Bluff. Elijah Clarke, as he drew up his wagons in a circle
and appropriated Indian lands in his trans-Oconee Republic, also
traded with the Creeks from his store on the Ogeechee. For a
brief period in 1784 his goods had been one or two chalks cheaper
than Panton's.[14] The old Indian countryman James Durouzeaux,
who lived at Coweta with his Indian family and was employed
by Spain and Panton, also sent a few skins to the Americans and
served as their interpreter—if only to keep his options open.[15]
After 1783 American stores appeared to the south on the Atlantic coast, though McGillivray jubilantly reported in 1788 that
the ones on the Altamaha had been broken up.[16] James Seagrove's store at Coleraine on the upper Saint Marys River was
more fortunate, and the proprietor traded with Muscogulges on
both sides of the Florida line.[17]

The Creeks realized that trafficking with Georgians made

Indians dependent on Americans and placed Creek lands in jeopardy. In 1783 at Augusta, 1785 at Galphinton, and 1786 at Shoulderbone, Georgians signed treaties with the "Creek nation," in fact with Indians who for the most part were not Muskogees. The Tame King, the Fat King, and their followers ceded most of the region between the Ogeechee and Oconee rivers and another large tract between the Altamaha and Saint Marys rivers.[18] A price had to be paid, but this was one way for non-Muskogees to escape pure Muskogee domination. Secure in obtaining wares from Panton, McGillivray and the Muskogee moiety damned the Fat King and the Tame King and told Georgians if they wanted the land they must "come and take it."[19] Georgians feted the Tame King and the Fat King, passed around and smoked the sacred calumet, insisted that these chiefs and their retainers were the true voice of the nation, asserted that the cessions were legal, and declared that neither McGillivray at Little Tallassee nor any politician in the United States national capital was going to stand in the way.

The United States denied the validity of these state treaties on a variety of legal and constitutional grounds. One was that both the Articles of Confederation and the 1789 Constitution conferred treaty-making power on the central government. The Creeks were an independent Indian nation, and only the national government was authorized to negotiate with them. This is not to say that the United States regarded the Creek nation in the same light as it did France or Russia. As a result of centuries of experience the concept of usufruct had become entrenched, and the United States considered the Creeks her dependents, her wards, who must be civilized and converted to Christianity. One merely had to consult the 1783 peace treaty with Britain to realize that the United States thought that she already owned the lands in question.

The first treaty the United States signed after adoption of the Constitution was the one at New York in 1790 with the Creek nation. In this and subsequent treaties the United States portrayed itself as the Indians' friend because she demanded less from the Creeks than Georgians had. This was true, but the conduct and objectives of the national government differed from

138   those of the states only in degree, and the year 1790 is as good
as any to mark the beginning of the American colonial system.
Officials in the national capital, like their counterparts in Georgia, were determined to open Indian lands to white settlement.
The difference was that Washington and Knox in New York
pondered the Creeks' fate more than did Georgians. Even so
Washington and his colleagues had not decided whether the
Creeks should remain in the Southeast and become acculturated
and perhaps assimilated, or be removed. That Creeks at least
outwardly were a sovereign nation made the president, his cabinet, the Congress, and the United States Army pay attention
to the treaties and to the rights and privileges guaranteed by
them to the Indians. Not to do so was illegal, because treaties
approved by two-thirds of the Senate were the supreme law of
the land.

Alexander McGillivray, who during the 1780s had railed at
the Fat King's and Tame King's concessions to the Americans,
in 1790 personally led a delegation of thirty-odd Creeks to the
national capital in New York. Revolutionary veteran Marinus
Willett and a detachment of soldiers conducted McGillivray's
entourage in carriages and on horseback from the Creek country,
through Georgia and the Carolinas, to Philadelphia, and ultimately to New York, where President Washington and Secretary
of War Knox awaited. It was the possibility that goods supplied
by Panton, Leslie, and Company and by Spain might be cut off
as a result of an expected Anglo-Spanish war that had inspired
the sickly McGillivray to make the long journey. His delegation
was housed in the Indian Queen Tavern, and after delay and
intrigue a treaty was signed.

This treaty contained fourteen articles, six of them secret.
One of the most controversial, a secret one, was that if war
disrupted McGillivray's Spanish monopoly and the Creeks' traditional commerce through Pensacola, Saint Marks, and elsewhere in the Floridas, then Washington would give McGillivray
and his friends an American monopoly notwithstanding that
monopoly and privilege were incompatible with the new republic. Under this monopoly, Indians could import goods duty free
through an American port on the Saint Marys River, the boundary with Spanish Florida. The treaty stipulated that at least some

of McGillivray's merchant friends had to be American citizens. Panton had numerous partners, correspondents, and relatives associated with his firm, some of whom could easily become, if they were not already, United States citizens, and perhaps Panton himself might make the switch. Or possibly McGillivray might abandon Panton and select other merchants for his American monopoly, but, whoever they were, there was an excellent chance that they, like McGillivray, had recently fought for George III.

Other secret articles concerned McGillivray's $1,200 salary, his commission as a United States brigadier general, and $100 salaries for selected great medal chiefs and beloved men. In the public articles the Creeks ceded the Oconee lands but not those below the Altamaha that were claimed by Georgia. Both Washington and McGillivray and his delegation signed the treaty, which was celebrated with a bonfire and a more sedate ceremony in Federal Hall.[20] In 1789 when considering preliminaries of this treaty, Washington had visited the Senate to get their "advice and consent," but the Senators were embarrassed and intimidated by the Father of His Country in their midst. They stalled, Washington stalked out, and neither he nor his successors returned. After this, the executive merely sent signed treaties for consideration, which the Senate could approve or not. It quickly gave its assent to the 1790 treaty submitted in this fashion.[21]

This compact apparently was between two sovereign powers, the United States and the Creek nation, but the issue of sovereignty, of who owned the Southeast, was far more complicated. This is obvious if one considers the diverse individuals in New York in 1790 who attempted to influence negotiations. Two were José Ignacio de Viar, Spain's representative in the American capital, and Carlos Howard, secretary of the East Florida governor. "For his health" Howard had hastily sailed from Saint Augustine to New York with $50,000 aboard. Spain asserted that all Creeks lived in the Floridas, or in some fashion were under Spanish control, and Spain's legal claims were as good, if not better, than those of the United States. Viar and Howard warned McGillivray not to do anything detrimental to Spanish interests.[22]

Senators William Few and James Gunn from Georgia were

140   also in New York. They were conscious that though they were in the nation's capital, they were citizens of the sovereign state of Georgia. Their constituents at home never let them forget the state's treaties with the Creeks and that the Indians had already ceded the Oconee lands and those south of the Altamaha. These senators had no objection if Washington and Knox wanted to sign a treaty reconfirming all cessions to Georgia. Anything less was unjust, unconstitutional, a violation of states' rights.[23]

Confusion about the Treaty of New York persists when one considers the Indians. McGillivray claimed to speak for all Creeks or Muscogulges, including those known as Seminoles. Yet with few exceptions his twenty-four man delegation representing "the whole Creek nation" was comprised of Muskogee speakers, most of whom were Upper Creeks. Of the ten towns represented, seven came from the Upper Creeks and three from the Lower Creeks. Two-thirds of the delegation were Upper Creeks, and the Chawookly mico was the lone representative from Broken Arrow, a village not far below present-day Columbus. Villages south of Broken Arrow, whether known as Lower Creek, Yuchi, Seminole, or whatever, had no representatives in New York and were conspicuous by their absence. This was the point made by Thomas Dalton, a loyalist, Indian trader, and lieutenant of Bowles, who posed as the "true spokesman" for Creeks in New York. He had just returned from London, and on both sides of the Atlantic he contended that McGillivray was interested merely in lining his pockets. He had no authority to speak for the Hitchitis, Yuchis, Shawnees, and similar Creeks, and he had no right to hand over Oconee lands or any others.[24] McGillivray understood Muscogulge factionalism well enough, and he saw to it that the Tame King from Tallassee, who was in New York, and a Seminole chief of Miccosukee, who was not, received $100 annual salaries to ensure their support.[25] McGillivray returned home in September, and the ensuing months bore witness to internal Muscogulge dissension. Spain and the Indians, especially non-Muskogees, put such pressure on McGillivray that he refused to see the new boundary surveyed, and the portly Knox began to seek out another "soul" of the Creek nation who would.[26] For the moment the Treaty of New York had little effect.

Others did, however, particularly the Pinckney Treaty (1795) and the Treaty of Coleraine (1796). In the Pinckney Treaty between Spain and the United States, Spain agreed that the thirty-first parallel was the Florida boundary, which meant that she relinquished her claim to almost all of the Creek country.[27] Indians had not been represented in the negotiations and felt they were not concerned with or bound by that settlement, but in fact they were. Because of the French Revolution and the wars spawned by it, Europe was in turmoil. Americans emphasized that the Creeks could not rely on Spain or even Britain, and they must come to terms with the United States. This happened in 1796 at Coleraine, a small American trading post on the upper Saint Marys River. Here Creeks, primarily Upper Creeks, reaffirmed concessions made at New York, and this time the boundary was marked.[28] With Spain withdrawing to below the thirty-first parallel, the United States expected to take over most of the Creek trade. She established subsidized trading factories, and appropriately the first one was at Coleraine. The business of the Creek factory at Coleraine—moved to Fort Wilkinson on the Oconee in 1797—steadily increased for several years.[29]

International developments had much to do with the Treaty of Coleraine and with subsequent Creek-American treaties in 1802 and 1805. Between 1799 and 1803 Napoleon threatened to take over Louisiana and the Floridas; Britain planned to seize them to keep them out of French hands; and Bowles strove to vitalize the state of Muskogee. This meant that if Muscogulges could no longer rely on Spain, they might turn to France, Britain, or Bowles. But in 1802 Britain made peace with France and withdrew support from Bowles, whom the Spaniards subsequently captured; in 1803 Napoleon sold Louisiana to the United States. The effects of foreign withdrawal from the Southeast were manifest in the 1802 Creek treaty at Fort Wilkinson and the 1805 Treaty of Washington. In these treaties the Creeks ceded additional lands between the Oconee and Ocmulgee and south of the Altamaha.[30]

In all the treaties, from New York in 1790 to Washington in 1805, payments were made for lands and for salaries to prominent headmen, often designated as great medal chiefs. Annuities were made to the Creek nation as a whole, and individual chiefs

142   drew their salaries. In practice, however, the same Indians often got their hands on most of the money, assuming an enterprising white had not appropriated it beforehand. In the Treaty of New York, McGillivray was paid a large salary and he also was primarily responsible for distributing the $1,500 Creek annuity and additional trade goods. How much he kept for himself and how much the non-Muskogee half of the nation got is unclear.[31] Indians often received their portions of the annuity in goods rather than in money. When the headman had a truck house, or his silent white partner did, the possibility of chicanery and profit existed. As a result of various treaties, by 1806 the Upper and Lower Creeks each received an $8,000 annuity, roughly fifty to seventy-five cents per Indian. This annuity had to be unevenly distributed in order for a few to profit.[32]

The United States repeatedly asserted that it wanted to wean the Indians from holding property in common, inculcate the virtues of industry and frugality, and sever Creeks from dependence on presents. In the years after 1783 the amount of presents distributed was curtailed and did not compare with those formerly dispensed by Britain or even France. Imbued with the Calvinistic work ethic, Americans were galled at the practice of giving presents to Indians merely because they came to a council or even to buy their neutrality. Annuities were used for a wide range of manufactures, but Americans expected, and at times insisted, that Indians buy plows, looms, spinning wheels, metal working tools, and the like, to speed the process of civilization. Even after taking all this into consideration, there was no hiding the fact that annuities, and, to a lesser extent, salaries to great medal chiefs, served the same ends as presents. In each case, the Creeks became pensioners and dependents. Although Henry Knox, Thomas Jefferson, Benjamin Hawkins, and others extolled the virtues of self reliance, they knew what they were about in making prominent chiefs and ordinary Indians dependents. In 1811 the United States withheld part of the Creek annuity to make Creeks locate and punish Indians who had murdered whites on the frontier.[33]

Whatever the exact line of conduct adopted by President Washington and his successors, the American policy became of increasing concern to the Creeks. In 1783 the United States was weak, out of funds, and declining in population because of the exodus of loyalists. But the government soon began to grow stronger, the treasury filled, her population increased, and the United States eventually made good its claim to the thirty-first parallel. Georgia no longer had a meager white population; Tennessee was admitted as a state in 1796; and by 1798 the American flag waved over Natchez. Only Pensacola and the other Gulf ports prevented a complete encirclement.

The conduct of the Creeks, the largest group of Indian people on the American frontier, was of great interest in the nation's capital. On the eve of Jefferson's inauguration as president in 1801 the American government had finally developed a policy for the Creeks. The plan seemed just to all, in harmony with the idealism and fair-mindedness of the republic. In essence the plan was to acculturate the Indians, make small yeoman farmers out of them, and encourage them to abandon commercial hunting and voluntarily sell excess lands. The monies they received for these lands could be used to buy agricultural implements, tools, and spinning wheels. The Creeks would retain part of their lands, and, depending on circumstances, would still live in their own communities or intermarry and intermingle with the whites. Washington's secretary of war, Henry Knox, and his secretary of state, Thomas Jefferson, had had much to do with devising this policy.[34]

In the Southeast no other individual was more associated with this design of civilizing the Indians than Benjamin Hawkins. He had served in the Confederation Congress and the United States Senate, presumably was a Federalist, and in 1796 Washington appointed him agent to the southern Indians. Hawkins was also Jefferson's friend and in time may have become a Republican. In any case in 1803 Jefferson appointed him agent to the Creeks and Seminoles. Whatever his exact title, from 1796, when he took up his duties among the southern Indians, until his death in 1816, Hawkins lived among the Creeks, and they always were his main concern.

Hawkins thought that the only way to civilize the Creeks was to constitute a stable Creek nation with a centralized gov-

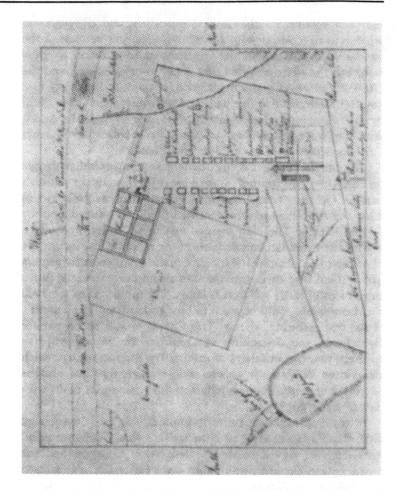

Benjamin Hawkins's Creek agency on the Flint River in the early nineteenth century. Courtesy the Moravian Archives, Bethlehem, Pennsylvania.

ernment based on the white man's ways and values: "Generations yet unborn will have abundant reason for blessing the memory of your character."[35] If the Creeks wanted to keep their hot houses, pray for rain, and continue to drink black drink, that was acceptable. But in Hawkins's mind there was little doubt that as the Indians became civilized they would shed most of their culture.

The mestizo Alexander Cornells (Oche Haujo), Hawkins' interpreter and Alexander McGillivray's friend, in 1804 observed: "We must associate with [the Americans] or the wild beasts of the forest, and in the latter case we must fly our country and go to the wilds in the west."[36]

A feature of Hawkins's program was vitiating the clan system, a Muscogulge institution that had withstood many shocks since De Soto's entrada. A nominal bachelor for most of the two decades he lived on the frontier at the Creek agency, Hawkins did not come into contact with many white females. Young Indian women, however, stopped by the agency, and, as Hawkins informs us in one of his few surviving personal letters, he was attracted to and aroused by these visitors. Nevertheless, he avowed he would never accept an offer of marriage unless he be allowed to discipline and educate the children. To the Creeks, this meant snatching the children from their families, their clans; and this was one reason Hawkins never took an Indian wife.[37]

Another way to weaken the clan and strengthen the National Council was to proscribe clan vengeance. Hawkins insisted that it was the duty of the national government to mete out capital punishment. Creeks must look to the National Council, not to their clan, for satisfaction. If an Indian should die, "it is the nation who killed him . . . not one man or one family."[38] Though during his lifetime Hawkins witnessed and contributed to a weakening of the clan, the institution proved resilient. The clan persevered, continuing to be an integral part of Creek life, and it and ethnic factionalism remained of more consequence than the better-publicized National Council.

The United States exerted pressure to civilize the Muscogulges through its armed forces, financial measures, disposition of public lands, foreign policy, salaries to great medal chiefs, and tribal annuities. After Americans established themselves at Memphis and elsewhere on the Mississippi River, the United States threatened to prevent or actually prohibited Indians from crossing that river to hunt in an attempt to make them adopt

146 the American program.[39] Sale of lands and intensive farming, not hunting, would allow Indians to make purchases at their truck houses or at American factories. Indian opposition to acculturation and centralization was intense, and in a moment of despondency Secretary of War Henry Dearborn thought that Hawkins's policy was not worth the effort, that it was just as well to let the Yuchis, Alabamas, Hitchitis, Shawnees, and the rest go their separate ways.[40] If all else failed there was always the possibility of a "dose of steel."[41]

Despite differences of opinion and contradictory tacks, the primary United States policy from the end of the American Revolution until the War of 1812 was to nurture a pro–United States, which usually meant a Muskogee-dominated, National Council and through it to acculturate the Creeks and acquire their lands. One result was that during this period the pure Muskogee moiety—and also Panton, Leslie, and Company— shifted from being pro-British and pro-Spanish to being pro-American. At the time of the Revolution Britain had drawn her main support from the pure Muskogee element, and it had been fitting that McGillivray was a British commissary. Indians from the opposing moiety, notably the Tame King and the Fat King, in turn consorted with the rebels and Spaniards.

White and mixed-blood Indian traders were loyalists, and at the end of the Revolution they remained among the Muscogulges, perhaps still wearing their British uniforms, flying the Union Jack in front of their cabins, and listening to British snare drums summon the Creeks to the square ground. These Indian countrymen usually got their trading goods from Panton, Leslie, and Company, which meant they came through Pensacola or elsewhere in the Spanish Floridas. Indian hunters, packhorse men, headmen, runners bearing their messages, and sometimes women and children arrived at Pensacola, Saint Marks, and the Saint Johns River where not only Panton's employees but also Spaniards entertained and humored them. An increasing number of Muscogulges, including large numbers of pure Muskogees, began to realize that Spain really was not so bad.

Indian countrymen securing goods from Panton, as well as Panton himself, were among the first to realize how fragile was

Spain's hold on the Southeast. This weakness became apparent in the 1789–90 war scare with Britain, between 1799 and 1803 when Napoleon threatened to take Louisiana and the Floridas, in 1808 when the Spanish mother country was immersed in chaos and guerilla war, and in 1810 when uprisings against Spanish rule erupted throughout North and South America. Spanish debility was also apparent in 1795 when Spain agreed that the thirty-first parallel was West Florida's boundary.

Panton, his partners, and his successors feared for their Spanish monopoly. At one time or another old Tories in Panton's firm realized that they might have to come to terms with the impetuous republic. In the 1790 Treaty of New York Mc-Gillivray got for himself—and apparently for Panton and his partners—an American monopoly of the Creek trade. Panton would have to shift his base from Pensacola to American soil on the Saint Marys River. In the late 1790s Panton discussed with his "old friend" Benjamin Hawkins how best to keep French troops out of the Floridas and to make Creeks pay their debts. In 1810 John Innerarity, Panton's relation in charge of the firm's interest in Pensacola, hearing reports of rebellion sweeping over Old and New Spain, asserted that "on the timely interference of the American Government depends our safety . . . [the Floridas must soon] be honorably annexed to the U.S."[42]

The main reason Hawkins and other Americans embraced their "old friend" Panton was that his firm could assist in civilizing the Creeks and especially in prodding them to sell their lands. Despite initial successes of the American factory at Coleraine, Panton's firm continued to dominate the Indian trade. Hawkins was not distressed so long as Panton helped with the policy of acculturation and strengthening the National Council. This suited Panton and his associates well enough. All southern Indians owed the firm money, but Creek debts, reckoned at $113,000 in 1803, were nearly twice as much as the others combined.[43] The company used these debts and its commanding position in the peltry trade to prevail on the Indians to adopt Hawkins's plan of civilization. In 1803 the company threatened an embargo unless southern Indians agreed to give up land to the United States.[44] The Creeks acquiesced and in the treaty

148   ceded lands on the Ocmulgee. With Hawkins's encouragement
Forbes rushed to Washington to make sure that when the Creeks
were paid for these lands Forbes would get much of the money.
He was crestfallen when the Senate disapproved the treaty because it contained such a large appropriation: after so much
labor and expense to get the Creeks to cede their lands, "our
debts have been left out of the calculations."[45] The Senate in
1805 voted down a Creek treaty that contained an excessively
high appropriation, and both Forbes and Hawkins were dismayed.[46] Forbes and his associates had taken no vow of poverty
when they left Scotland to sleep on flea-ridden bearskins in
smoky cabins, and make long journeys, swimming or fording
rivers and streams, and swatting mosquitoes from April to
October.

Both Forbes and Company and Hawkins persevered, aware of
the advantages of collaboration. Trading on credit, Forbes and
Company reminded Creeks of their financial obligations. Innerarity patiently explained to Big Warrior the total sum that had
been lent to the Creeks, which unfortunately had doubled because of interest charges. Big Warrior of Tuckabatchee avowed
there was no word for interest in the Creek language, and he
was astounded in 1812 when the sum Innerarity demanded as a
partial payment was the exact amount of the United States
annuity.[47]

Collaboration between the Scottish firm and the United
States usually involved land cessions and debt payment, though
cooperation occurred in other areas. The Hitchitis in 1801 had
captured thirty-eight of Francis Fatio's Negroes on the Saint
Johns River in East Florida, and many of them were taken to
Bowles and his friends at Miccosukee. Fatio, closely associated
with Panton, Leslie and Company, if not a member, asked for
Hawkins's help in recovering the slaves. In his letter to Hawkins, Fatio reminisced and pronounced how delighted he had
been in 1784 when Hawkins and General Nathanael Greene had
visited Saint Augustine. Greene had commanded the American
troops that in bitter fighting at the end of the Revolution had defeated British forces in South Carolina and Georgia. Fatio had
served with His Majesty's troops. But that was long ago, and

Fatio hoped Hawkins would use his influence with Muskogees and the National Council to make the Hitchitis (Miccosukees) return the Negroes. Bowles and his Indian supporters were not inclined to give them up, however.[48]

Between 1775 and 1812 loyalists in Forbes and Company made the transition from being desperately pro-British, to becoming Spanish agents, and finally to an association with and dependence on the United States, and they brought the pure Muskogees and the National Council, however grudgingly, with them. In contrast, during the same period the non-Muskogees shifted from collaborating with the rebels to begging George III to send troops back to the Southeast. McGillivray asserted that during the Revolution he had replaced the stinkard Emisteseguo as leader of the Creeks.[49] At the same time non-Muskogees, such as the Tame King and the Fat King, visited Augusta to receive presents and sign treaties with the Georgians. The Tame King accompanied McGillivray to New York in 1790 but was unhappy with McGillivray's pretensions and that McGillivray got a $1,200 salary and the Tame King only $100. After he got home the Tame King opposed surveying the new boundary. When a federal agent to the Creeks, James Seagrove, came to Tuckabatchee in 1793, the Tame King and his non-Muskogee followers from both the Upper and Lower Creeks tried to kill the American. Seagrove was surprised in the middle of the night visiting a lady friend. He dashed out minus his clothes and found refuge in a nearby lake. His paramour eventually found him and brought him his breeches, but Seagrove, immersed up to his neck for hours in frigid waters, nearly died.[50]

According to Henry Knox and Benjamin Hawkins, the opposition, primarily non-Muskogees, composed of banditti, whores, and rogues, were those Creeks who blatantly defied treaties with the United States, especially articles concerning land cessions. The rascally Tame (Tallassee) King in 1803 had the effrontery to contend that he was head of the National Council, questioned the way Panton's firm calculated Creek debts, and insisted that Creeks not go to Washington or anywhere else to bargain away their lands.[51] The wizened Tame King, who in 1783 had been in Augusta consorting with the rebels, in 1811 journeyed to the

150   lower Apalachicola River and dictated a letter to George III, imploring his assistance lest the Muscogulges be lost.[52] Two years later the Tame King died fighting the Georgians.

The confused rivalries between the ethnic moieties, and the shifting alliances of Creek factions with foreign powers cannot be fully discussed without taking into account the Forbes Purchase. This enormous tract of land was the region on the Gulf of Mexico between the Apalachicola and Wakulla rivers and extending inland twenty or thirty miles. The Hitchitis and other members of the opposition first granted this to Bowles, and after his capture and imprisonment in 1803 Forbes insisted that the opposition give it to him if they wanted trading goods. In 1804 it seemed unlikely that Britain, France, or the United States would or could supply these Lower Creek–Seminoles, so they gave Bowles's concession to Forbes, and it became known as the Forbes Purchase. Bowles was in a Havana prison unable to object. Miccosukees from Florida, Little Prince, the Tame King's deputy from the Upper Creeks, and other non-Muskogees required that Forbes establish a store for them at Prospect Bluff.[53] The National Council was furious, contending that the grant had been illegally made by the opposition: land cessions, and the goods and monies flowing into the nation as a result, were supposed to be negotiated through the Muskogee-dominated National Council.

Though it was "as fair a purchase as ever was made from red men since the treaty of William Penn," Forbes knew he had angered the Americans. He promptly notified them that he would turn this land back to the Indians or over to the United States (which expected to acquire the Floridas) as soon as his debts were satisfied.[54] Indians got wind of this, and Forbes assured them that under no circumstances would unruly Americans be allowed to settle on the grant but instead only responsible sympathetic colonists—"good men"—such as British subjects from the Bahamas.

Non-Muskogees feared being completely encircled by the United States and had awarded these lands first to Bowles and then to Forbes to keep them out of American hands. This American threat was brought home in 1799 when a joint team began surveying and marking the thirty-first parallel, the boundary between Spanish West Florida and the United States. Fresh from laying out the capital district on the Potomac River, Quaker Andrew Ellicott headed the American delegation, and Hawkins got the National Council to send a body of men to assist and protect them. Starting from the Mississippi River, the surveying party made their way eastward, blazing trees and at intervals erecting stone markers.

The closer they got to Muscogulge lands the greater the Indian opposition. At the forks of the Chattahoochee Ellicott and his men were forced hurriedly to abandon supplies and equipment and to flee for their lives to Spanish Saint Marks. Hostile Indians were led by the Miccosukee Kinache and the Tallassee Tame King, who viewed Ellicott's deserted camp with satisfaction, and were even more pleased when they learned that Ellicott had given up marking the Florida boundary and had returned to Philadelphia. Their work completed, Kinache retired to Miccosukee, and the Tame King and his followers to the Upper Creeks.[55]

Hawkins was enraged and prodded the National Council into action. His mestizo subagent, Alexander Cornells (Oche Haujo) at the head of seventy-two Upper Creek warriors, marched to Tallassee on the Tallapoosa, surrounded Isstechah's (Caiupicchau Haujo's) house, burned it and the outbuildings, killed or carried off his cattle and fowl, and at last dealt with Isstechah. This Tallassee was beaten mercilessly with sticks, his ears and part of one cheek were cut off, and finally a sharp stick was thrust up "his fundament." Two other Upper Creek chiefs were caught and beaten. Tastanagi Haujo triumphantly brought one of the sticks retrieved from Isstechah's fundament to the Coweta Tallahassee square ground on the Chattahoochee, declaring it would be delivered to the rest of the Lower Creeks and Seminoles and the appropriate punishment meted out to the culprits. The non-Muskogee opposition was more numerous in the South, however, and Kinache's ears and fundament remained intact.[56] The Tallassee Tame King among the Upper Creeks also escaped chastisement, but like others in the opposition moiety he was alarmed by Hawkins's policies.

Hawkins really wanted the Creeks to abandon communal property holding, do away with the clan, accept a Muskogee-dominated government, and relinquish their territory. He expected the Creeks to give up commercial hunting and their "nomadic" ways and instead to settle down, adopt the plow, and concentrate on agriculture. The plow that Hawkins extolled was, however, little more than a symbol of what he was trying to accomplish. Americans and their European ancestors had used the plow for centuries, but white frontiersmen probably did not use the plow much more than the Indians. The Indian way of farming was to girdle and fell trees and to plant crops between the stumps, and this was probably the method used by a majority of small white farmers on the frontier. In all of the agricultural implements consigned to the Creeks in an 1808 shipment Hawkins did not include a single plow.[57] However, the plow was a symbol of far more than how the soil was tilled. The Tame King understood this, and that is why in 1803 he listened sympathetically to those chiefs threatening to kill any Creek using a plow.[58]

Hawkins's plan of civilization as superimposed on ancient ethnic divisions contributed to tensions in Creek society. Part of his plan and of his superiors' in Washington was to build a road from the Tennessee River to Fort Stoddert, the American post above Mobile. This road would allow overland mail service, would provide Tennesseans access to the Gulf without having to make the long journey to New Orleans, and would make it easier to supply the fort. The proposed road ran through Upper Creek territory, and no Muscogulges were more affected and alarmed than the Alabamas.[59] In 1811, Hawkins through the National Council pressed Creeks to sanction this new federal road. General William Henry Harrison in the Old Northwest fought, and if he is to be believed, defeated Indians led by the Shawnee Prophet at the Battle of Tippecanoe.

The Creeks closely followed events above the Ohio River. Tecumseh, the Shawnee Prophet's brother, visited the Creek country in 1811; Seminoles journeyed to the Hickory Ground (Little Tallassee) among the Upper Creeks to listen to Tecumseh and his entourage; other Seminoles "of the Shawanase tribe"

visited their kin on the Wabash;[60] Creeks and Seminoles fought
and died at Tippecanoe; and some two hundred of them joined
the Shawnee Prophet when he relocated his village to Kicka-
poo.[61] Tecumseh and his brother advocated an anti- American
political and religious revival of all western Indians, which Britain would—and did—support from bases in Canada, the West
Indies, and Florida. Many Creeks were Shawnees, which helps
explain why in 1811 Creeks with red wands in their hands began
dancing the dance of the Great Lakes Indians, and local prophets
began urging the same rejuvenation and reforms tinged with
anti-Americanism as Tecumseh's brother had espoused above
the Ohio. In 1812 reports reached Americans that such prophets
had also risen among the Seminoles.[62] The long-awaited explosion was at hand.

The Creek War, 1813–15

Fort Mims was a typical frontier palisaded fort, rectangular in shape, with a kitchen, unfinished blockhouse, private cabins, outhouses, hastily thrown-up board lean-tos, and tents inside. The fort was located forty miles above Mobile on the Tensaw River. Rumors of Indian hostilities abounded, and local inhabitants sought refuge within. On 30 August 1813 hundreds—perhaps as many as a thousand—Muscogulges approached by a ravine, and, as the militia was eating its meal, rushed the stockade at high noon. Before the sun set, blockhouses, private dwellings, and much of the palisade was in ashes; over a hundred Creeks lay dead; and two hundred and fifty defenders of all ages and sexes were also killed, some burned beyond recognition, others mutilated by tomahawks and scalping knives.[1] Though frontiersmen had experienced minor encounters previously, from the white standpoint the assault or "massacre" at Fort Mims marked the true beginning of the Creek War. As Americans saw it, the conflict was not terminated until the following year with Jackson's March 27 victory at Horseshoe Bend and the ensuing Treaty of Fort Jackson in August. From the Indians' perspective hostilities had begun earlier and lasted much longer.

Whatever the exact dates, this conflict disrupted Muscogulge society as had no other in recent times. It could best be compared to sixteenth-century incursions made by De Soto and similar

156 *conquistadores* who had fought and enslaved southeastern Indians and unleashed unseen microparasites. Though traumatic enough, the 1813 Creek War was not as ruinous as the sixteenth-century disasters: De Soto's battle at Mabila was bloodier than Fort Mims; and because Muscogulges in the early nineteenth century were less vulnerable to European and African diseases, Creek and Seminole survivors remain today, whereas one looks in vain for Timucuans, Apalachees, Guales, and others of De Soto's lifetime.

One cause of the 1813 Creek War and of the Seminole hostilities in Florida can be traced back to before De Soto's day, to an era when, according to tradition, Muskogees had migrated into the Southeast from beyond the Mississippi, coming into conflict with and settling on lands of the Hitchitis. Other tribes also came into the Southeast, and out of all this evolved the major Muskogee / non-Muskogee divisions. The cleavage and rivalry among these groups was as intense and bitter as ever in 1813. As much as anything else this explains why seventy-two indignant Muskogees in 1799 had cut off Isstechah's ear at Tallassee and driven a sharp stick up his fundament, and it would not be hard to find other examples.

In 1813 hostilities broke out on an unprecedented scale. These hostilities touched almost all Indians, and fighting erupted from the Coosa and Tallapoosa in the North, to the Chattahoochee in the East, and to the lower Alabama, Gulf Coast, Alachua, and Saint Marys in the South. In addition to centuries-old feuding between the Muskogees and their rivals, other circumstances converged in 1813 that help explain the extent and severity of the fighting.

One was the nativistic revival sweeping over widely scattered North American Indian villages. The prophets advocated revival and Indian unity, and early nineteenth-century prophets were active from Canada to the Gulf Coast and the Florida peninsula and on both sides of Mississippi. Technically these prophets were shamans, though Americans around 1813 used the term prophets loosely to characterize any Indian prescribing a course other than Hawkins's plan of civilization. In the same way during the McCarthy red scare of the 1950s, anyone who differed with the senator might have been branded a Communist, although these so-called Communists included those who in fact were Marxists, and those who advocated civil rights, integration, unionization, peace, or in some fashion upsetting the status quo. Indian prophets, or "fanatics," sometimes were *hillis hayas*, medicine men, who officiated at religious ceremonies and rituals. They often took the lead in emphasizing native customs, and more than most opposed erosion of native values and the replacement of these values with an American concept of civilization. Little place for hillis hayas would remain if the Creeks abandoned their clans, adopted private property, and turned to white protestant ministers for guidance. Hillis hayas denounced whites' attempts at "civilization," and were unconcerned when Americans dubbed them heathen agitators, wild-eyed grinning prophets.

Other prophets were *tastanagis*, war leaders, who in times of crisis assumed more leadership. It was not difficult for an enraged tastanagi, in the tradition of his Mississippian ancestors, to make an emotional speech in the square, brandish the ceremonial red-painted atasa, and set a date for an avenging expedition against whites. Whites had built roads and introduced rowdy frontiersmen into the vitals of Muscogulge lands. They had enervated warriors with rum sometimes laced with vinegar and pepper. Native Americans had no words for interest and usury, but tastanagis pointed out how difficult if not impossible it was to pay off all the chalks owed to the village factor and that nothing seemed to suffice except extending the hunting season, ranging even farther from home, and, as a last resort, selling lands. It was possible for a war leader also to be a *hillis haya*. Priestly functions and military leadership aside, warriors far from home appreciated the advantages of having a doctor—a hillis haya—skilled in treating gunshot wounds in their midst.

True prophets, sometimes loosely called knowers, were shamans, who as a group were not numerous but nevertheless played a prominent role in Indian society. A shaman might be a healer, a medicine man, but his specialty was not prescribing medicinal roots and herbs. Instead, he conversed with or spied on gods and evil spirits, and disclosed their wishes and schemes

158 to Muscogulges at large. A shaman might fast, sweat profusely, go into trances, retire alone to a cabin, or draw a circle on the ground and sit in its center. Some made no formal preparations at all, but abruptly had convulsions while chatting with friends in the talwa or far from home on a hunting expedition. While a shaman was in a trance his spirit left his body, soared to the heavens, descended to the underworld, or entered the domain of witches. For hours or even days he might not take nourishment, as his eyes rolled back in his head and he grinned and convulsed. Indians had assorted gods, but the sun was the most important, and after recovering from their trances Muscogulge shamans reported how the sun had hovered just above their heads and spoken to them. Because they conversed with the gods, shamans were able to prophesy, even summon to their aid earthquakes, hailstorms, thunder, and lighting.[2] Whites associated magic owls with shamans or prophets. The owl was a symbol or badge for a doctor, for one who had fasted and received instruction in curing diseases and wounds. A hillis haya who had been so schooled was entitled to include an owl's feather in his headdress, to wear a stuffed owl on top of his head, or to carry one in his hand. More often than not the prophets who bore these magic owls were not true shamans.[3] Upon occasion shamans waved five-foot staffs with cow's tails tied to the ends. Muscogulges had long used such staffs or wands, though the cow's tail presumably had replaced that of the buffalo, which had become extinct in the East.[4] In any case the meaning of these staffs has been lost.

Shamans sometimes blackened their faces and wore feather mantles that covered most of their bodies.[5] Indians had worn such mantles in Mississippian times, before Europeans and Africans had arrived, and these birdmen had a special relationship with the eagle, buzzard, owl, or some other bird that soared on high and spoke to Yahola. Prophets could no longer direct the building of large temple mounds, but they could keep alive or rejuvenate powers of the feathered medicine man-priest who had been so important in the religion and culture of the Mississippian peoples. Part of the shaman's powers had been to make a warrior's body a sieve so that arrows, and subsequently bullets, might pass through harmlessly.

Shamans' spirits at times entered the witches' domain. After awakening from a trance shamans pointed out Indians in their midst who had consorted with evil spirits, and as a result some of these sorcerers and witches were put to death. Throughout history societies have tended to kill more witches during times of change and stress, and Muscogulges executed a number early in the nineteenth century. One gets the impression that the frequency of such executions was greater than it had been, but there are no reliable statistics.[6]

A shaman could be of any age, from a teenager who had not long had his war name to an elderly Muscogulge in the winter of life. He might wear distinctive garb such as a feather mantle, or he might dress as did most Indians. Shamans held in common a clearer perception than the average Muscogulge had of what the Master of Breath expected and of who were devils, witches, and God's enemies. God, of course, did not reveal himself in exactly the same way to all shamans, yet early in the nineteenth century one could get a general impression of what he was telling the Indians. The Indians' present distress could be blamed on the fact that they had strayed from the teachings of the Master of Breath, and that too many hillis hayas, micos, fire makers, and yaholas had not paid due respect to the sun, corn mother, and sacred fire. Revival of such respect was essential if Creeks were to be saved. They should return to and emphasize the old ways. Whites were responsible for many of the Indians' distresses, and contacts with them must be curtailed, though not abolished. Europeans had come to the Southeast to stay: that could not be changed any more than the necessity of substituting cow tails for buffalo tails.

The Master of Breath no more expected Indians to return to hunting and gathering than to cut off trade with the whites. Europeans had made commercial hunters and drovers out of the Indians, and this, like the previous adoption of agriculture, had become entrenched in Muscogulge society. Shamans realized that in certain respects European contacts had improved Indian life. Steel knives and hatchets were superior to stone ones; iron and copper pots had obvious advantages over clay vessels; blankets, shirts, strouds, ribbons, and other textiles in most respects were an improvement over skins and furs; and there was obvious

160 merit in raising horses, cattle, and swine. But a Creek could ride his horse, hunt with a musket rather than a bow and arrow, and clothe himself in textiles from Lancashire, and at the same time continue the old ways. He could drink black drink as the singer intoned his long cry; observe the duties and proscriptions of clan membership; and listen to the hillis haya and hiniha's admonitions in the talwa's square ground. This square perhaps still was raised, possibly atop a temple mound built in an earlier day.

It was one thing to draw on aspects of both European and Indian experience, modify Muscogulge culture, and have the synthesis represent new and in some respects improved features. But Hawkins's plan of civilization, his largely Muskogee National Council, and his intended suppression of the clan represented destruction, and rather quickly, of the Indian heritage. A Muscogulge perished spiritually and culturally when yaupon tea (the black drink), but not the yahola cry remained, when his property duly recorded in the county courthouse was merely five to fifteen acres, when in times of sickness he turned to a white physician rather than a hillis haya, or when a Baptist minister explained exactly who was the Master of Breath. This was the prospect revealed by the Master of Breath to shamans in their trances, convulsions, fasts, and dreams. In turn they divulged the danger and yahola's plan of salvation to hillis hayas, micos, tastanagis, and ordinary Indians. The shamans' admonitions swept from talwa to talwa and from clan to clan throughout the Indian country, especially among non-Muskogee clans.

Pan-Indianism was associated with the shamans' appeal. In contrast to religious and cultural revival that emphasized traditional practices (modified by long contact with Europeans and Africans), pan-Indianism was new. However Indians had designated themselves before Columbus's time, they had not called themselves Indians. Native Americans consisted of a welter of diverse linguistic, ethnic, and cultural groups that were often separated by deep-seated rivalries. Powerful, centralized sixteenth-century chiefdoms, such as those of the Coosas, Yuchis, and Cofitachiquis, disappeared after the whites arrived. The Pan-Indianism that swept over the Muscogulge country early in the nineteenth century represented much more than attempts to resurrect a Coosa or Cofitachiqui kingdom. Instead Native-American reformers insisted they were what Columbus had called them—Indians—and that throughout the Mississippi Valley from Canada to the Gulf all Indians were brothers.

All Indians might be brothers, but their society was fragmented. The sun, yahola, and black drink might be of paramount interest in the South, and northern Iroquois and Algonquins might look to the Good Twin and the Upholder of the Skies. No national language existed. When Tecumseh and other Indians advocating unity traveled about the Mississippi Valley interpreters were essential. Tecumseh was a Shawnee living above the Ohio River, yet his mother was Creek, and so were his ancestors. According to one tradition Tecumseh and his brother, the Shawnee Prophet, were born in Tuckabatchee and could trace their ancestry to Governor James Moore of South Carolina, a prominent Goose Creek man around 1700.[7] Other ancestors were reported to be Yamasees and Apalachicolas.[8] Tecumseh's mother, a Creek, was of the Tiger clan, and members of the Tiger (Panther) family entertained and fed him when he visited the Southeast.[9] Tigers were one of the foremost non-Muskogee clans. Tecumseh's Shawnee or Mobilian trade jargon served as lingua francas, but this was not something leaders of pan-Indianism dwelled on. Speaking Shawnee, Muskogee, Choctaw, English, French, or Spanish, as events dictated, Tecumseh's Creek brother (i.e. first cousin) Seekaboo accompanied Tecumseh as an interpreter on his journey into the Southeast in 1811. Seekaboo was first known as a Shawnee, then as a Creek, and finally, when in his mid-forties he moved to Florida after 1814, as a Seminole. But wherever he was and whatever he was called, he urged solidarity.[10]

Shawnees and those identified with them, including Tigers and members of affiliated clans, took the lead in advocating pan-Indianism. Little Warrior, a native Creek, had lived among the northern Shawnees for fifteen years. In 1813 he was at the head of Creeks who murdered seven whites at the mouth of the Duck River in Tennessee, one of the incidents touching off the devastating Creek War.[11] Hillis Haya, the Autauga (Alabama) prophet Francis, was closely associated with the Shawnees, and

162   may in fact have been a Shawnee. He accompanied Tecumseh's party when it visited the Osages and other tribes beyond the Mississippi, pointing out the advantages and necessity of unity.[12] This was the way to accomplish what shamans insisted Yahola demanded.

The Master of Breath enjoined shamans to abstain from strong drink. Lands, chattels, wives, and lives had been forfeited on account of the abuse of alcohol, and again and again shamans, some of whom were reformed alcoholics, preached the virtues of temperance. When several hundred Muscogulges under the prophets' influence visited Pensacola at the outbreak of the Creek War in 1813, John Innerarity was astounded that not one of them touched a drop of taffy, a thing heretofore unknown.[13] Some shamans urged eating venison rather than beef, and turkey rather than chicken, practices that were less traumatic than teetotaling.[14]

More controversial was putting aside the white man's gun and powder and relying on the bow and arrow. This was the best way to escape from commercial hunting, the local factor, and his account books. Such reasoning had some effect on the Muscogulges, though less than contemporary whites thought. More often than not when Indians in the Creek War used bows and arrows they made a virtue out of necessity. Many Indian léaders, including those labeled prophets, were factors. They did not want or expect trade with Europeans to be cut off, and they clearly understood that revitalization and pan-Indianism had to be won and safeguarded by guns, powder, ball, and steel tomahawks rather than bows, arrows, and wooden atasas.

Pan-Indianism and nativistic revival found adherents among all Muscogulges, especially those non-Muskogees who for centuries had collaborated in attempts to retain their languages and customs. Like their southeastern Indian neighbors, Muscogulges of whatever background were commercial hunters, owned cattle, horses, and swine, and were village factors. Few believed that the Master of Breath commanded them to give all this up, but the prophets' appeals that they have nothing to do with Hawkins's plow and the puppet, largely Muskogee, National Council made a great deal of sense.

American determination to build roads from Georgia and the Tennessee River to Fort Stoddert above Mobile was one of several unrelated causes of the Creek War. An 1805 treaty provided for a road from Georgia to Fort Stoddert, and in the ensuing years the United States insisted that another be opened from Tennessee as well. For some time the exact routes were undetermined, though it became obvious that the two roads must converge in the Upper Creek country and follow the Alabama River southward from the forks to Fort Stoddert. This funneled all travellers and all troops using these military and post roads through the Alabamas' domain. Hawkins at the Creek agency issued passports for immigrants heading west, and tradition was on the side of such east-west traffic. Goose Creek men, Brown, Rae, McGillivray, and Galphin had sent packhorse trains from Georgia and Carolina toward the Mississippi for years. But little precedent existed for European soldiers, merchants, and immigrants to descend en masse from the Tennessee River to the Gulf. The proposed road to Fort Stoddert, which in 1811 Hawkins and President Madison demanded be opened quickly, ran through villages on the Coosa, through villages of the Alabamas about the forks of the Alabama River, and then on to the south.[15] The sun had hovered over the head of the young prophet Letecau, who had been reared among the Alabamas. He denounced the Americans and their proposed road. Recognizing Alabama opposition to the new roads, Muskogees in the National Council and Hawkins and the Americans contended that these Indians really were not Creeks. The point was well taken but in 1813 it was also irrelevant.[16]

At the same time that Tennesseans were insisting that a new federal road be run through Alabama villages, Americans were threatening another part of the Muscogulge domain, that of the Seminoles in East Florida. Since the Revolution Americans had demanded this colony; it made no difference that the Spanish flag waved over Saint Augustine and that Indians claimed the province. Jonathan Bryan and other Georgians repeatedly had attempted to liberate the colony, and in 1812 they tried again, optimistic about success. The Spanish empire was shaken and in turmoil, and its debility helps explain how Americans had

164   recently annexed Baton Rouge in Spanish West Florida. A "patriot army" from Georgia seized Fernandina, the Spanish outpost on Amelia Island in East Florida. Saint Augustine was the real objective, and if it fell Spain's hold on the province would cease to exist. The patriot army was an extralegal filibustering force. Nevertheless just as the patriots assaulted Fernandina, United States warships in battle formation took position in the river just off the Spanish fort. The fort's commander made little distinction between the United States Navy and the private patriot army and thought it wise to surrender. Because of diplomatic and military exigencies Madison at first disavowed the patriots and at almost the same time ordered the United States Army and Georgia and East Tennessee militia into East Florida.[17]

No force had ever captured the Castillo de San Marcos in Saint Augustine, and the patriots proved no exception. As a result they looked westward and set their eyes on Alachua. Hitchiti King Payne of Payne's Prairie was alarmed, and like the Spanish governor he made little distinction between Americans who came into East Florida with or without permission. In 1812 Seminoles killed an American officer and a Negro courier between the Saint Marys and Saint Johns rivers and sent their scalps to the Upper Creeks: Muscogulges must stand fast and protect their domain wherever threatened and have nothing to do with the Americans and Hawkins's reforms. Hawkins was dismayed by the peregrinations of the American officer's hair and by Muscogulge unity. He pressured the National Council to dispatch his old ally Tuskegee Tustunnuggee (Big Feared) from Kasihta to the Seminoles to request that they remain quiet and not heed their prophets. The passage of time has hidden transactions in the Seminole square grounds and the number of prophets or shamans. But the message of the shamans, whether the Shawnee Prophet or the Alabama Letecau, was widely disseminated among the Seminoles: of that there was no doubt.[18] The Seminoles, along with the Shawnee Prophet and the Alabama Letecau, of course were all non-Muskogees.

Black Muscogulges in no small measure contributed to the outbreak of fighting and to the bitterness of the hostilities. They were scattered throughout the Indian country, but their semiautonomous Maroon communities were most numerous in East Florida. Patriots storming into that province were promised land and booty, the latter including black Muscogulges who might have been slaves, freedmen, Africans, zambos, or Indians classified as Negroes. Whatever their background, slaves commanded a high price on auction blocks in the lower South's booming Cotton Belt. Black Seminoles understood this. One of them from Alachua went to the outskirts of Saint Augustine to spy on the patriots, and the black Seminoles were happy enough when the scalp of the Negro courier in American employ was circulated throughout Upper Creek towns.[19] Seminoles, many of whom were black, defeated Major Daniel Newnan in a pitched battle lasting days west of Saint Augustine. Despite this defeat and the failure to take Saint Augustine, patriots eventually fought their way to Alachua, where lands were distributed, and the district of Elochaway in the republic of East Florida, though enfeebled, at least existed. In May 1814 Americans overran and destroyed Negro villages, and blacks relocated them toward the Gulf Coast near Tampa Bay.[20]

The great fear of the whites was that black Muscogulges might incite a servile insurrection throughout the South like the one in Haiti, which helps explain why Americans ruthlessly torched black Seminole villages whenever the opportunity arose and were pleased whenever "Indian" prisoners proved to be black.

Britain's long-standing identification with and sympathy for black Muscogulges contributed to fears of a general slave rebellion. In 1812 impressment and related maritime grievances had caused the United States to declare war on Britain. These, however, were merely proximate causes. Previously, British subjects in Canada, the Bahamas, and throughout the Mississippi Valley had urged native unity, and, with or without official authorization, promised British support. Such tampering with the Indians helped cause the American War of 1812 and the Creek War the following year.

Both the Spaniards and the Seminoles in Florida—black and red alike—were relieved when in 1812 British warships arrived at Saint Augustine and at the Saint Marys River to help protect

166   the province from the patriots. Britain was angry with President Madison and his Republican Party, which she felt had stabbed her in the back by declaring war while Britain, standing almost alone, struggled against Napoleon. Britain had no troops to spare, and she resolved to employ Indians, blacks, or anyone else to get even with Madison and his Republican followers. Tecumseh's party in 1811 and other Shawnees in 1812 promised the British aid in return for an Indian confederation, and after the outbreak of the Anglo-American war the Canadian governor asked southern Indians to take up the hatchet.[21] Admiral John Borlase Warren, commanding Britain's fleet on the North American station, had black Muscogulges in mind when he supported efforts of British abolitionists: "the terror of revolution in the southern states can be increased to good effect."[22] From various quarters evidence mounted that Britain was increasing her interest in black Muscogulges and in pan-Indianism.

As has been mentioned, another cause of Creek and Seminole hostilities was the rift between pure Muskogees and those in the opposing moiety. In private letters and in the press, Americans portrayed this civil war as one between the Creeks, who had adopted much of white culture and were anxious to complete Hawkins's design, and those who were primitive and whose prophets advocated reverting to savage ways. Americans characterized the latter as "red sticks" or "red-club men." It was convenient and reassuring for Americans to declare that their Indian friends were civilized and their enemies savages, but this view distorts the reality of Muscogulge society. This becomes apparent when one looks more closely at a sample of the native leaders who fought on one side or the other.

When Americans contended that friendly Indians—more often than not Lower Creeks—were civilized, they often had William McIntosh in mind. Son of a Coweta Creek of the Wind clan and Captain William McIntosh, British agent to the Lower Creeks during the Revolution, young McIntosh remained among the Lower Creeks when his father returned to eastern Georgia and settled down with the whites. Through trade, land speculation, slave raiding, and Creek annuities, the mestizo McIntosh amassed a fortune in land, slaves, and livestock. He had three

wives and two plantations—one at Lockchau Talofau (Acorn
Town) on the Chattahoochee and another fifty miles westward
on the Tallapoosa—that were worked by scores of slaves, and
he built and operated a commodious tavern at Indian Springs on
the upper reaches of the Ocmulgee River. His first cousin,
George M. Troup, became a prominent politician and was
elected governor of Georgia in 1823. During the same period
McIntosh at Coweta assumed leadership among the Lower
Creeks, representing them in Washington at the 1805 treaty,
and, at the head of friendly Creek warriors, he collaborated with
Jackson in his campaigns against the Creeks and Seminoles.
Urged by Hawkins and the National Council, in 1812 McIntosh
led 300 Upper and Lower Creeks (mostly pure Muskogees)
against other Creeks (Shawnees?) who had killed frontiersmen
on the Duck River in Tennessee. Allegedly McIntosh was author
of the "Laws of the Creek Nation" promulgated in 1818 which
reflected many Anglo-American judicial concepts. The Coweta
mestizo McIntosh was well along the road to acculturation.[23]

In contrast, and fitting American perceptions of a fanatical
hostile red-stick warrior, stood the Koasati High Headed Jim.
He was a true prophet, a shaman, who upon occasion went into
trances, lost his breath, convulsed, and grinned, and in battle
exhorted warriors, assuring them that the gods would deflect
the white man's bullets or make American soldiers bog down
in a quagmire as they charged. High Headed Jim lived farther
west near the forks of the Alabama River, where it was easier
for superstition, magic, and primitive religion to survive, or so
it seemed.[24]

Also born and raised not far from the forks of the Alabama
River, the Tuskegee William Weatherford was another hostile
Upper Creek leader. Except that he was illiterate and in the
opposing moiety, he outwardly had far more in common with
McIntosh than with High Headed Jim. Both Weatherford and
McIntosh were mestizo sons of Tory traders and agents; both
owned extensive lands, slaves, and cattle; and both had several
wives. Weatherford, with short hair, a fine black broadcloth
jacket and vest, and elegant boots and hat, dressed and looked
like a white. He was well mannered and courteous, and in the

168   years before his death he was received by the highest Alabama
society, "even when women were present." Like his father before him, Weatherford had a truck house, traded with, and was
indebted to Panton, Leslie, and Company. He and his packhorsemen had made frequent trips to Pensacola to pick up guns,
powder, bullets, and textiles. Weatherford went into no trance,
knew no power that would alter the trajectory of a well-aimed
lead bullet, and had no desire to revert to a more primitive life-
style. Other Upper Creek red-stick "fanatics," such as Peter
McQueen from Tallassee on the lower Tallapoosa River had
backgrounds similar to Weatherford's and shared his views. In
contrast to Weatherford, however, the factor McQueen did not
speak English.[25]

In many respects the Upper Creek red stick Josiah Francis
was in the same category as Weatherford and McQueen. A mestizo factor who was in debt to Forbes and Company ($905 in
1812), he also was an experienced silversmith. In addition he
was a hillis haya, a medicine man. He perceived more acutely
than most, the threat white civilization posed to the Indian
rituals, religions, and way of life. Few were more convinced than
Francis that Yahola required Muscogulges and all western Indians to band together lest their heritage soon be lost. His talwa
was Autauga, just below the forks of the Alabama. His Indian
ancestors probably were Tawasas, though possibly they were
Shawnees or Koasatis who had come from the north. By most
whites he was considered an Alabama. Francis was a friend and
confederate of Tecumseh, and before 1812 they travelled
throughout the Mississippi Valley, among the Muscogulges,
above the Ohio River, and west of the Mississippi preaching the
virtues of pan-Indianism and related reforms; and emphasizing
the power and disposition of the Master of Breath, who spoke
in thunder and could swallow up entire villages. As they
preached, they waved a red wand and danced the animated dance
of the Lakes Indians. Whites described Francis when he visited
Pensacola, Saint Marks, the Osage country, and London, but
they gave no indication that he was a true shaman. He was a
medicine man and like Tecumseh he had a dream. Both wore
British uniforms, appreciated the realities of commercial hunt-

ing and the necessity of trading and allying with Europeans. Both insisted that King George was anxious to ship over rifles.[26]

Big Warrior (Tustunnugee Thlucco), like Francis, Peter McQueen, and William Weatherford, was a wealthy Upper Creek. He seems to have been less involved in trade, perhaps was a full-blood, and had a Shawnee (or Miami) heritage. According to tradition, Big Warrior's son invited Tecumseh to visit the Muscogulges, and Big Warrior watched closely as the Shawnee delegation danced and pled for rejuvenation. Non-Muskogees contained diverse ethnic groups, and for whatever reason in 1813 Big Warrior, though he wavered, allied not with the Alabamas, Shawnees, Tallassees, and other non-Muskogee hostiles but with the Muskogee moiety. As a result, red sticks destroyed his property and forced him to flee to Coweta for his life.[27]

Mestizos, such as the Yuchi (Lower Creek) Timpoochee Barnard, were unsure whether to side with a majority of the Yuchis or with friendly Creeks. Timpoochee's mother was a Yuchi, and most of that tribe were hostile red sticks; yet his father, Timothy Barnard, was Hawkins's friend and trusted employee. Timpoochee was torn between two worlds, two cultures, and unlike most Yuchis, he did not join the red sticks. His Barnard name, rather than clan and moiety affiliation, had the greater pull.[28]

Red-stick leaders arose among the Seminoles, including elderly Kinache, the veteran mestizo factor from Miccosukee. He was not an early militant; he bided his time, noting the actions and successes of the various parties. Much of the white man's culture suited him well enough. But he distrusted Americans who coveted Apalachee; he became incensed whenever the Muskogee-dominated National Council tried to dictate to him; and he was impressed by and succumbed to presents and blandishments of British officers in 1813 and 1814. Kinache and some of his warriors were at the Battle of New Orleans in January 1815. The British commander was anxious to storm Jackson's lines, and that suited the Hitchiti Kinache well enough.[29]

The final red stick to be discussed is the Prophet Abraham (Souanakke Tustenukke), though he was neither a true prophet nor even an Indian. He was a West African, a slave employed in

Timpoochee Barnard. From Thomas L. McKenney and James T. Hall, *History of the Indian Tribes of North America* (1836–44). Courtesy National Anthropological Archives, Smithsonian Institution. Photo no. 45,113.

Pensacola by Forbes and Company (or possibly by a Spaniard), who in 1814 escaped and joined the hostile Indians. At Pensacola and on trips to the interior he had come into contact with southern Indians and had learned their languages. After he arrived at the Negro Fort on the Apalachicola River and even after he moved to East Florida, he served as both war leader and interpreter. The sun had spoken to the young shaman Letecau to reveal what was necessary for Indian rejuvenation, but Abraham was not touched like other Muscogulges because the Master of Breath had not mentioned West Africa. But whatever exactly they were, Abraham's dreams were real: freedom, leadership in a maroon community, possibly even return to West Africa. Abraham was a prophet, a red stick, who collaborated with both hostile Indians and the British. Yet it was easier for him than others to change his friends, clan, and moiety, and pursue his own destiny.[30]

The Creek War and Jackson's victory at Horseshoe Bend have often been recounted, and we will consider only certain aspects. Americans, of course, designated the hostiles as red sticks, perhaps referring to the red wands that Tecumseh's party waved when dancing, possibly signifying the "broken days"—bundles of red sticks sent out to indicate the number of days before a military campaign was to begin—or more likely referring to the ceremonial wooden atasas painted red. Red signified war; it was appropriate that atasas, arrows, and bundles of sticks were painted red and that Americans characterized hostiles as red sticks. Red sticks were principals in every Muskogulge conflict, that of 1813 and those of preceding centuries.

As we have seen, the causes of the hostilities were complex. They included the status of Spanish Florida and the involvement of the United States, Britain, and Spain in the War of 1812; the revival of pan-Indianism; a resolve by many Muscogulges to retain and defend their lands and their commercial hunting-droving economy and not to become civilized; the strident reforms of the prophets; the aspirations of black Muscogulges; and age-old ethnic divisions. In general the Alabamas, Hilibis, Eufaulas, Atasis, Shawnees, Hitchitis, Yuchis, Miccosukees, and assorted other non-Muskogees were hostile or sullenly neutral. There were, of course, many exceptions, and the Tuckabatchee (Shawnee) Big Warrior has already been mentioned. Individual Indians in the same town were pulled in different directions—toward the United States because of the appeal of civilization, fear of American power, or concern over the prophets' radicalism; or toward Britain because of the belief that King George could be the Muscogulges' salvation.

172   From the Indian point of view, hostilities had commenced in 1812 when the patriot army marched into East Florida. The skirmish in southern Alabama at Burnt Corn Creek on 27 July 1813, however, for many whites marked the true beginning of the Creek War. The Tallassee Peter McQueen, the Tuskegee Josiah Francis, and the Koasati High Headed Jim, along with a sprinkling of northern Shawnees, had conducted more than three hundred Indians on the well-worn path from the Upper Creeks to Pensacola. They requested—or demanded—munitions and guns from Forbes and Company and the Spanish governor, pointing out that for years both had enriched themselves at the Muscogulges' expense. Now was the time to restore part of that wealth. Forbes and Company's strongest ties—and also those of the United States—were with the pure Muskogee moiety. The company's representative, John Innerarity, did not want to antagonize the United States, and contended he was intimidated neither at the approach of armed red-stick warriors nor when High Headed Jim began to shake. Instead Innerarity inquired why Francis, McQueen, and other red-stick factors had not paid their debts. Nevertheless in time the Indians secured munitions and clothing from the Spanish governor and from private merchants including Forbes and Company. Reports that Britain and her hard-pressed ally Spain were prepared to support the Indians were not without foundation. Loading muskets and kegs of powder on pack animals, McQueen and his Indians prepared to depart.[31]

Rumors that red sticks were being armed in Pensacola alarmed the scattered populace in southern Alabama and Mississippi. Militia were called out, and women and children sought refuge in wooden forts and stockades. Alabama militia commanded by Colonel James Caller located and surprised McQueen at Burnt Corn Creek ninety miles above Pensacola, capturing the packhorses and scattering the warriors. The colonel and his men began distributing and gloating over the booty too soon: the Indians rallied, turned the tables, and forced the Americans to flee in disorder. Fifteen days elapsed before anyone located the colonel. The encounter at Burnt Corn Creek was a minor one: two Americans died and fifteen were wounded and Creek casualties are unknown.[32]

The red-stick attack on Fort Mims a month later was no insignificant skirmish. At midday Red Eagle's (Weatherford's) warriors secretly approached and when within a few hundred yards let out the war whoop and rushed the stockade. Before night fell, 250 defenders lay dead in the smoking ruins and a lesser number of attackers had perished. By word of mouth and through the press grisly accounts circulated of how defenders were burned and hacked to death, babies cut out of live mothers' wombs, and infants' heads bashed against trees. In Louisiana, Tennessee, and Georgia, armies were set in motion to avenge this savage attack against white frontiersmen.

Many and probably most of the "whites" who perished (or were made prisoners) inside the stockade were Creeks of the pure Muskogee moiety who had adopted much, if not all, of Hawkins's program of civilization. In some respects the "massacre" represented a continuation of the ancient Muskogee / non-Muskogee conflict, though whether to classify certain participants as Indians or whites makes such a distinction difficult. Captain Samuel Mims, for whom the fort was named and who died in the smoking ruins, presumably was a mestizo, and in his youth had been a packhorseman for George Galphin.[33] Zachariah McGirth had grown up on the Tensaw River, married the mestizo Vicey, and fathered eight children. At the time of the attack Zachariah was absent, but not the terrified Vicey. Miraculously she was spared, and after living among the red sticks for nearly a year she finally joined her husband in Mobile. He was struck dumb, having assumed that she was dead and had long ago been buried in the mass grave at the fort.[34] The valiant Captain Dixon Bailey was not so fortunate, though he fought until the end, attempting to protect the women and children. Like Vicey, Captain Bailey was a mestizo, probably McGillivray's kinsman by marriage, educated in Philadelphia as part of the provisions of the 1790 Treaty of New York.[35] Durants, Hathaways, McGirths, and other of McGillivray's relatives in the Wind or closely allied clans also died or were taken prisoner in the fort.[36] Virtually all of the militia, women, and children at the fort were Creeks (or spouses of Creeks), though largely acculturated to be sure. Black Muscogulges fought on both sides, madly rushing toward the fort at high noon or strug-

174   gling for hours in the futile defense. Some blacks in the fort, slaves with little say-so in their conduct, were spared and carried off as part of the booty.

Previous hostilities at Tuckabatchee reflected the complexity and conflicting tensions in Muskogulge society far more than those at Fort Mims. In 1813 Tuckabatchee was probably the largest Upper Creek town. This was not the Tuckabatchee of earlier centuries when Tuckabatchees with their brass and copper plates had settled down on the Tallapoosa River. By 1813 their culture and ethnic composition had been modified, though exactly how is not clear. Nevertheless in 1813 we can identify several amorphous groups. One was composed of Indians who were conscious that they were descendants of the ancient Tuckabatchees with their plates and northern background. Another was the Shawnees, who in the eighteenth century or earlier came to Tuckabatchee in some numbers. Still another included Indians, whatever their background, who were becoming Muskogees by having adopted their language and much of their culture. In Tuckabatchee, of course, as in other Indian towns, there were a few, usually mestizos, who really were more white than Indian.

Nevertheless Tuckabatchees had a tradition of being not Muskogees but outsiders. The principal chief Big Warrior, probably a Shawnee (or Miami), repeatedly bragged about his northern ancestry. But though he wavered in 1813, he did not join Hillis Haya, McQueen, Weatherford, and the prophets: instead he sided with the Americans. The passions aroused in 1813 did not allow much room for a neutral. In the protracted, destructive siege at Tuckabatchee, only McIntosh's reinforcements from Coweta broke the prolonged siege, which allowed the defenders to retire to Coweta. Big Warrior and the other chiefs sought refuge in McIntosh's house. Prophets had destroyed their livestock, fences, and plows, and had carried off their slaves, and McIntosh and Big Warrior retaliated in kind against the property of McQueen, Francis, and other prosperous red sticks. They begged Hawkins for guns, powder, and white militia, and promised Americans red-stick lands on the Alabama if only they would help the Muscogulges destroy their enemies.[37]

This is precisely what the Americans had in mind, and on a far larger scale than McIntosh or especially Big Warrior envisioned. The Americans resolved to send three separate armies against the red sticks on United States soil. One was to come from Georgia, cross the Chattahoochee, and press deeper into Indian Territory. The second, from Mississippi, was to make its way northward up the Alabama River; and the third from Tennessee was to strike southward. Patriots in Spanish East Florida threatened the Muscogulges in still another quarter.

The Georgia force, roughly 1,500 strong, commanded by General John Floyd, and supported by McIntosh, Big Warrior, and up to 500 friendly Creeks bent on vengeance, fought two bitter, hand-to-hand encounters at Autosse and Calabee Creek. Numbers on each side were roughly equal, and both suffered heavily. Indians, whether red sticks or McIntosh's friendly Creeks, lost the most men. Eleven Americans were killed and fifty-four wounded. After the conflict each party withdrew: Floyd to the Chattahoochee, and Indians up the Tallapoosa, where they began to fortify themselves at Horseshoe Bend. Surveying the field after the Battle of Autosse, Americans came across the body of the aged Tallassee (Tame) King, "the greatest conjuror of all the fanatics." The British aid he had requested in 1811 had not yet arrived. The militia sent his calumet, the one he had smoked in 1786 at Shoulderbone, back to Georgia. It was a curiosity of antiquarian interest, for McIntosh and the Muskogees, not those in an opposing moiety now usually made common cause with the Georgians.[38]

At the head of Mississippi militia and Choctaw and Chickasaw Indians, General Claiborne advanced up the Alabama River, fought several skirmishes, laid waste Alabama towns, and before long, primarily because of lack of supplies, withdrew. In the end he had little to show for his efforts. In East Florida the patriots, at times reinforced by American militia, abandoned hope of taking Saint Augustine and turned westward toward Alachua, where they laid out a town and established the district of Elochaway in the republic of East Florida. Their "various efforts made to cultivate the minds and reform the manners of the savage race having failed," they resolved to forget the Indians and keep their lands, and they petitioned for annexation to the United States.[39]

The most destructive campaign against the Muscogulges was

176   that of Tennesseans commanded by Andrew Jackson. He moved his army to the upper Coosa River, fighting sharp engagements at Tallushatchee and Talladega, and inflicting casualties, though not coming off unscathed himself. All armies that invaded Muscogulge territory suffered from lack of supplies, an undisciplined and untrained militia, and fierce Indian resistance. But, in contrast to the other commanders, Jackson overcame these with his iron will, and the result was the crushing Indian defeat at Horseshoe Bend. Refugees from Hilibi, Neuyaka, Fish Pond, Okfuskee, Upper Eufaula, among others, had taken refuge and fortified themselves. The non-Muskogee presence was overwhelming. McIntosh and Big Warrior were with Jackson. The thousand or so warriors defending the town were outnumbered three or four times. Prophets, waving cow tails tied to sticks, drinking black drink, offering tobacco smoke to the gods, and chanting, assured defenders of Yahola's blessing and that he would subvert the aim of Tennesseans and perhaps terrify them with an earthquake. It was comforting to have Yahola's blessing, but Savannah Jack, Menewa, and other red-stick leaders whose names have been lost, understood that this was not sufficient. They had constructed a sturdy, zigzag wooden breastwork with portholes for guns across the neck of the bend in the river, amazing Jackson and his fellow officers by its ingenuity and strength. This breastwork (a *tohopke,* by which name whites knew the Indian town) failed to save the red sticks; considering that they were outnumbered and short of supplies, the outcome was not surprising. Creeks and other friendly Indians swam across the river and threatened the village in the rear with its women and children, and Jackson followed with a frontal assault and overran the tohopke. A general slaughter ensued: friendly Creeks settled old scores and militiamen proudly took home reins for their horses that had been skinned from red-stick bodies on the field. By nightfall forty-nine militia, and less than a dozen friendly Creeks, lay dead; beside them or floating down the Tallapoosa were some eight hundred red sticks. Though perhaps grievously wounded, a number of the Indians escaped and some women and children were spared.[40]

Regardless of whether they had been at Horseshoe Bend, red

sticks could not remain on the Coosa and Tallapoosa, because friendly Creeks, backed up by American forces, scoured their towns, burned their cabins and crops, and carried off their livestock. Some retired to remote areas in the woods, but most fled to Pensacola and the Apalachicola River in Florida. The Muscogulge migration into Florida that had been going on for a century intensified. At first most refugees went to Pensacola because it was convenient and because the long-promised massive British aid was finally arriving. By the summer of 1814 British officers had armed more than a thousand warriors and had clothed and fed their families.[41]

After Horseshoe Bend Jackson descended the Tallapoosa River and built Fort Jackson, an earthen fort on top of the old French Fort Toulouse. He was anxious for a peace treaty and an end to hostilities. Big Warrior and McIntosh had already offered lands of the Alabamas if only American forces would help crush the fanatics.

Federal commander in the South, General Thomas Pinckney, had had instructions to negotiate a peace treaty including such a cession. But Jackson superceded Pinckney, took charge of negotiations, and resolved to have much more than the Alabamas' lands. This is what he got in the Treaty of Fort Jackson concluded in August 1814. The Creeks ceded an enormous L-shaped tract accounting for roughly half of their domain. This included the talwas and hunting lands of many friendly Creeks. Even though they were allowed to retain one square mile per family in the ceded area so long as they and their descendants actually occupied the land, friendly Creeks were furious, and to add insult to injury, they were the Indians forced to sign the treaty. With few exceptions the red sticks were dead, hiding out in the woods, or in Florida. Only one red stick signed the treaty.[42] Jackson commanded friendly Creeks to sign or to join Indian refugees in Pensacola. If they set out for Florida, however, he promised to dog their march every inch of the way. They signed—McIntosh four times—and as Jackson saw it, the Creek War was over. In the ensuing years the settlers who filled up these and adjoining Muscogulge lands forced friendly Creeks off their holdings and became a mainstay of Jacksonian democracy.[43]

Signing of the Treaty of Fort Jackson, 1814, as reenacted by the Poarch Band of Creek Indians and others in *The First Frontier*, a 1986 television documentary. Courtesy Auburn Television. Photograph by Thomas P. Causland.

The Battle of Horseshoe Bend and the Treaty of Fort Jackson gave rise to surprising political changes. Red Eagle (William Weatherford), who had led the assault on Fort Mims but had not been present at Horseshoe Bend, came in alone, almost unnoticed, and presented himself before Jackson's tent at Fort Jackson. After discovering the identity of their prisoner, Jackson's officers wanted to hang him on the spot, but Old Hickory refused and spent much of the evening drinking and conversing with Red Eagle. The Indian leader recounted how he had fought against the Americans to the utmost, but his warriors were dead, their bones whitening the fields at Talladega, Calabee, and Horseshoe Bend. Only sick and starving women and children remained: take Red Eagle's life if that would serve any purpose, but spare them.

This began the depiction of Red Eagle as a noble leader of a doomed race. Today, the view of Red Eagle has much in common with that of Nez Perce Chief Joseph. In the late nineteenth century Chief Joseph had led his followers hundreds of miles in the Pacific Northwest in a vain attempt to hold on to his lands, avoid being forced onto a small reservation, or at least escape to Canada. All failed, and Chief Joseph vowed that he wanted to keep up the struggle but he had no more warriors: "I will fight no more forever." He attracted sympathy when he visited Washington and other eastern cities. Red Eagle never visited Washington, but according to tradition (probably incorrect) he lived with Jackson for almost two years at the Hermitage in Tennessee. Red Eagle did eventually acquire land and establish a plantation in southern Alabama not many miles from Fort Mims. Until his death in 1826 prominent whites from time to time called on him, commenting on his commanding physical appearance, piercing gaze, and courtesy. Accounts of the Creek War described how Red Eagle, when surrounded by the enemy at Holy Ground, had leaped with his white horse from a high bluff into the Alabama River "which opened its bosom to receive the dauntless hero,"[44] and with bullets splattering the water, made his escape. These same accounts made the point that other Indians, not Red Eagle, had slaughtered women and children at Fort Mims. Weatherford left the scene in disgust when his orders to spare non-combatants were not obeyed, and presumably it was a threat of the loss of his property that forced him to take command of the Creek attackers.

When Chief Joseph surrendered to the United States Army he was cut off from escape to Canada and had no other recourse. At the time Red Eagle entered Jackson's tent he did not exaggerate about the distress of Creek women and children. But, unlike Chief Joseph, Red Eagle could have continued to fight. Dressed in British uniforms, the Tallasee Peter McQueen, the Tuskegee Josiah Francis, and the Atasi Homathle Mico still commanded angry red sticks at Pensacola and on the lower Apalachicola River, and these red sticks were anxious to use their new muskets, tomahawks, and cutlasses. The Creek (Shawnee) prophet Seekaboo and Savannah Jack also were in Florida and had not forgiven the Americans. Eventually Jackson captured and executed Hillis Haya and Homathle Mico. Red Eagle, Chief Joseph, and later Osceola became well-known tragic

180   heroes in the American press. Though it was not emphasized, all had had the good sense to surrender. The Tuskegee Red Eagle undeniably had put up a good fight, but when he entered Jackson's tent he truly became the son of his white father Charles Weatherford. Not much is heard about Hillis Haya, Homathle Mico, Seekaboo, and McQueen, but of course most Muscogulges were illiterate, and besides, before long most were killed or expelled from the Southeast, and almost none visited Washington or settled down and lived among the whites.[45]

Like Red Eagle, Big Warrior also switched allegiances. He had suffered at the hands of the prophets and red-club warriors and had fought beside the Americans. Yet the Treaty of Fort Jackson had taken lands perilously close to his talwa, and Jackson threatened him with handcuffs or another Horseshoe Bend unless he signed. Big Warrior from Tuckabatchee was indignant, and it dawned on him that Americans were worse than red-stick fanatics. He petitioned the British King for support, preparing to align himself with Francis, McQueen, and other non-Muskogees, his recent enemies.[46]

Francis, McQueen, and even friendly Creeks like Big Warrior did not presume that the Treaty of Fort Jackson had really ended the Creek War. British marine and naval officers did all they could to promote anti-Americanism and to keep Indians in the field, whether against Jackson in Alabama or the patriots in Alachua. Napoleon had gone into exile at Elba, and in 1814 Europe was at peace. Britain, however, still had one enemy—the United States—and she was determined to settle old accounts. She dispatched veteran soldiers to America, including almost ten thousand to the Gulf of Mexico. New Orleans was the primary objective, though British forces prepared to invade Georgia simultaneously. In these campaigns she expected help from red sticks and black Muscogulges.

British forces arrived at Pensacola and the Apalachicola River, occupied Saint Vincent Island near that river's mouth, and established an outpost over a hundred miles upstream. The largest concentration of troops on the river was at the new British Fort at Prospect Bluff near Forbes's store. On the Atlantic coast British forces occupied Cumberland Island. Britain ordered her marines, accompanied by red and black Muscogulges, to invade Georgia's heartland, and get even with Madison's Republican supporters by liberating their slaves. William McIntosh and his friends at Coweta also would be made to rue the day they had aided Jackson. Colonel Edward Nicholls, commander at the British fort at Prospect Bluff, asked a red stick if he was acquainted with the way to the interior. The old Indian replied he knew it well: it was marked by the graves of his five children.[47]

Whether fugitive plantation slaves or black Muscogulges, Negroes were to play an important role in Britain's southern campaign. The London government authorized enlisting five thousand Negroes from the deep South to serve in provincial regiments, and Colonel Nicholls, Lieutenant George Woodbine, and other marine officers trained up to a thousand blacks at Pensacola, the British fort, and Cumberland Island.[48] Black recruits evoked visions of a general slave insurrection, and their psychological threat was as great as their military potential. Although invitations to desert their masters and come into British lines circulated throughout the South from Georgia and Tennessee to Louisiana, many of the Negroes enrolled in the British service came from Anglo planters and merchants in East and West Florida, especially from Forbes and Company. When Jackson proposed to attack British and Spanish forces in Pensacola late in 1814, John Innerarity rushed 130 company slaves across the bay to keep them out of harm's way. Jackson captured the city, and to Innerarity's consternation, Colonel Nicholls sailed away to the Apalachicola River with the 130 Negroes aboard. Nicholls insisted he was acting on behalf of a philanthropic society, and in any case Innerarity was a traitor.[49] Forbes and Company's slaves also were among those joining British forces on Cumberland Island.[50] After the war most of these slaves remained among the Indians; only a fraction ever returned to the company.

The Innerarity brothers were furious. For years they and other members of Forbes and Company had been drifting toward the Americans, and loss of their slaves—at British hands no less— was an additional reason to seek American protection. The value of cotton they exported from Pensacola early in 1814 slightly

182   exceeded that of deerskins, and James Innerarity was anxious
       for industrious whites to occupy Creek lands.[51] That was where
       lay the greatest chance for profit. But for the time being Britain
       was on the Gulf Coast in force, and company employees fur-
       nished the Indians with munitions and food and served as in-
       terpreters, all the while reminding George III's ministers of their
       suffering during the American Revolution and of their loyalty
       to the Crown. The company, however, did not trust the red
       sticks.

       Observers on both sides of the Atlantic assumed that Britain's
       veterans, aided by Indians and Negroes, would succeed in their
       southern campaigns. Repeated delays prevented the multiethnic
       force from leaving the Apalachicola River for Georgia's interior;
       Jackson shattered British units at New Orleans; and in February
       came news of the Treaty of Ghent. Because of the probability of
       hostilities resuming in Europe, Britain decided to make a quick
       peace with the United States, which she did at Ghent. She
       abandoned her harsh demands and agreed to stop fighting and
       to return to the status quo ante bellum. As a result, between
       March and the summer of 1815 she withdrew her forces from
       the Apalachicola River, Cumberland Island, and elsewhere in
       the South.

       Whatever their ethnic background, many Indians, especially
       non-Muskogees, were disillusioned. They had seen the seas dot-
       ted with British warships and transports carrying thousands of
       regulars; up to a thousand Negroes and as many as three thou-
       sand Indians had been armed, uniformed, and trained; women
       and children had been fed and cared for; and the patriot army
       had retired from East Florida for good. British commanders at
       Detroit, Niagara, and Burlington had promised Creeks serving
       in the North that King George would not let them down.[52]
       Colonel Nicholls, who had made similar promises to the Indians
       and Negroes, delayed leaving the British fort on the Apalachicola
       River until June, hoping that the British flag would not have to
       be lowered, or that, in the tradition of Bowles's state of Mus-
       kogee, British subjects, Indians, and Negroes could sustain a
       British protectorate. The secretary for war and colonies, the earl
       of Bathurst, had this in mind when in December 1814 he in-

structed British officials to use the term "[independent] nations" rather than "tribes" when referring to the Indians.[53] Nicholls's wanting to keep the Union Jack flying or to establish a protectorate involved more than broken promises and his honor: if he stayed he expected to take over and develop the Forbes Purchase.[54]

Nicholls eventually left but turned the fort, with its cannons, muskets, sabers, and kegs of powder, over to the Muscogulges, most of whom were black. Americans now began calling this British fort the Negro Fort. Black families had cabins and plots of land immediately adjoining the fort and extending up and down the river for miles. The Negro fugitive Garçon (Garcia) commanded the fort, and Garçon and Nicholls had been responsible for its becoming the center of the largest and most heavily armed Maroon community ever to appear in the Southeast.

Forbes and Company's recently established warehouse at Prospect Bluff wound up operations after the war. The company had gone over to the Americans completely; it collaborated with Jackson, and waited for industrious Americans to settle Indian lands. The company had always professed—and continued to do so—that it was the Muscogulges' benefactor and protector, but after 1815 most of the Muscogulges realized that they had been sold out. Scores of black Muscogulges, including part of the Negro Fort's garrison, had run away from Forbes and Company and were hostile to that firm. For the first time since the Revolution the company was little involved in the southeastern Indian trade. Commerce remaining after 1815 was in other hands.

Peace at last! Bonfires and patriotic orations had marked news of Jackson's victory at New Orleans and the Treaty of Ghent, and the 1814 Treaty of Fort Jackson presumably had terminated the Creek War. Muscogulgees, however, lit no bonfires. No red stick had signed the Treaty of Ghent and only one the Treaty of Fort Jackson. Muskogee / non-Muskogee passions continued inflamed. Jackson wanted scattered red sticks to settle between the forks of the Alabama, close to Fort Jackson, and he also hoped to put friendly Creeks there, few of whom had forgotten

184   what the red sticks had done.[55] The American garrison at the fort could not prevent clan and moiety vengeance. The Tucka-batchee Big Warrior, the Hitchiti Little Prince, and other friendly Upper Creeks were madder at the Americans than at the red sticks, but Lower Creek Muskogees were less likely to forgive their Indian rivals. William McIntosh became enraged whenever he thought about his plantations, pillaged livestock, and escaped slaves, some of whom now garrisoned the Negro Fort or lived elsewhere in Florida. He was anxious to revenge himself on the militant red sticks. Each for his own reasons, McIntosh and Jackson were determined to plant the Stars and Stripes in Flor-ida. Francis, Peter McQueen, and the Negro Garçon dared them to come. Only in graves at Calabee, Talladega, Fort Mims, and Horseshoe Bend was there peace in the Muscogulges' domain.

Old Hickory and the Seminoles

The Indian defeat at Horseshoe Bend, Jackson's remarkable victory at New Orleans, and the withdrawal of British forces from the Gulf Coast inaugurated one of the greatest land rushes in the history of the American frontier. Eager settlers swarmed into rich bottomlands and large stretches of the Old South's fertile Black Belt that had been ceded at Fort Jackson. Part of this territory lay in Georgia, though most was in the present-day Alabama, and at the outset most immigrants were drawn to Alabama. In 1810 the population of that future state numbered roughly 9,000, but a decade later it contained 144,000, a sixteenfold increase, most of which occurred after 1815. Wagon roads from Athens, Milledgeville, and Hartford in Georgia brought settlers, their slaves, and cattle westward to the new Canaan.[1]

Foreign powers protested that these new settlements were unwarranted, but with little effect. British subjects lingering on the Gulf Coast among the Indians and royal officials in London contended that according to provisions of the Anglo-American Treaty of Ghent the Fort Jackson cession was illegal. Article Nine stated that Britain's Indian allies who had fought against the United States should have all their prewar territories and possessions restored. But President Madison, Secretary of State John Quincy Adams, and Andrew Jackson all maintained that when the Treaty of Ghent was signed in December 1814 the Creeks were not hostiles because they already had made peace the preceding August at Fort Jackson. None of this made sense to Peter McQueen, Hillis Haya, Homathle Mico, Savannah Jack, the Shawnee prophet Seekaboo, and other red sticks who had not gone to Fort Jackson but moved to Florida.[2] The Hitchiti Bowlegs (Istaapaopoya), whom the patriots had forced to abandon Alachua and relocate on the Suwannee, also was furious: "So far from complying with the IXth Article of that treaty they [the Americans] are making daily encroachments and forging treaties (which they pretend are concluded with our people) for cessions and grants of land which were never in existence, and the signatures to which are unknown to the chiefs of the Creek Nation, who alone have a right to assign or transfer the common property."[3] There is question about Bowlegs's literacy, and the Scottish merchant Alexander Arbuthnot doubtless helped the chief with his letter. The sentiments, however, belonged to the Hitchiti chief.

American settlers rushed into the ceded lands as soon as British forces withdrew in 1815. The United States government did not survey and offer for sale any of this territory until 1817, and until then squatters were there with no valid titles.[4] But on they came, usually by land, though sometimes via the Mobile, Tensaw, and Apalachicola rivers.

The Fort Jackson cession punished red sticks far more than the friendly Creeks. The Alabamas' towns near the future Montgomery and Selma, including the prophet's Holy Ground, were all given up, while Coweta and neighboring talwas on the Chattahoochee of McIntosh and his friends remained untouched. Nevertheless the friendly Creeks suffered, especially those on the lower Alabama and Tensaw rivers. Upper Creeks had migrated southward to this region and had established plantations, perhaps intermarrying with Tory refugees or Negroes. These highly acculturated friendly Creeks, usually in the Muskogee moiety, saw the wisdom of Hawkins's plow as they fenced in and tilled their fields. As has been seen, many of them had sought refuge in Fort Mims and been killed. Ranches and farms of surviving relatives and neighbors were on river bottomlands ceded at Fort Jackson. Surging into the Creek domain in 1815, Georgians fixed their eyes on these lands. From the vantage point of the Tensaw and lower Alabama rivers one could best see Alabama's sixteenfold population increase. Though friendly Creeks were allowed to keep their houses and a 640-acre section per family, and to draw on $85,000 set aside for their wartime losses, they had to give up their hunting and grazing lands and the communal lands of their talwas. Those who tried to remain on these reduced holdings often were overwhelmed by Georgia immigrants, and if Indians ceased to occupy their lands they lost title to their 640 acres. Creek protests that they had fought with Jackson, that their relatives had died in Fort Mims, and that at a minimum they should not be dragooned off their 640 acres served little purpose. In 1815 the Mississippi Territory incorporated a large part of the ceded Indian territory into Monroe County, at one stroke wiping out—at least in theory—communal property, matriarchal descent, clan vengeance, and other manifestations of Native American culture. To add insult to injury, Georgians who had travelled hundreds of miles and set themselves down on the best lands in sight taunted acculturated Muscogulges about their mixed ancestry.[5]

In contrast Weatherford lived relatively unmolested in southern Alabama. He had been outside Fort Mims, not within, crawling stealthily up the ravine before rushing the palisade. Apparently when the Indian leader walked into Jackson's tent Red Eagle and Old Hickory had a previous understanding: if Red Eagle would surrender and encourage other hostiles to do the same, in return he could live on a plantation farther south near the coast. He relocated on a relatively unattractive, isolated tract east of the Alabama River in the hinterland between Mobile and Pensacola. Other red sticks followed, settling on Red Eagle's holdings or on nearby pinelands, and all were out of the way of the new white immigrants. From time to time the white newcomers accidentally met or visited Weatherford, and his highly acculturated, pro-American mestizo brother-in-law George Stiggins wrote a flattering biography of the war leader. Stiggins contended, and subsequent historians generally have accepted his view, that Weatherford, though the most outstanding red stick leader, in no way was responsible for the massacre of women and children at Fort Mims.[6] At any rate, assorted circumstances, not just disasters of the recent war, had forced this mestizo to become less of a Tuskegee and more of a white American.

Red Eagle's apotheosis had begun. He and other Indians living near him, for the most part red sticks, were isolated and to a large degree left alone in contrast to Indians on the Tensaw and lower Alabama who were being forced off their lands. It is ironic that in this part of the Muscogulge domain the Americans' friends lost their holdings, and their red stick enemies in a sense were rewarded. Logic and justice, however, did not often characterize the Anglo-Indian frontier.

White immigrants swarmed into the hinterland above Mobile. In 1817 Alabama became a territory separate from the Mississippi Territory, and two years later Alabama had sufficient population to be admitted as a state. Appropriately the first territorial capital was at Saint Stephens on the Tombigbee less than fifty miles from Fort Mims. Indians in this Gulf Coast hinterland were mightily affected. Some of them tenaciously clung to the land, continuing to farm and raise cattle, and in time they or their descendants were absorbed by the white culture. Among these were both friendly Creeks in the Tensaw region and hostile Creeks living to the east near Weatherford. Other desperate displaced refugees, red sticks and friendly Creeks alike, found it difficult or impossible to find a spot to plant their maize and beans in security. They had no talwa and no factor to extend their credit for the hunt, and the white-tailed deer and Indian hunting lands were vanishing. The natives were forced to do what their ancestors had done millennia before— to hunt merely to subsist. Indians wandered about, killing such large and small animals as they could find, and also the white man's cattle and swine, partly out of vengeance and to vent their frustrations, but primarily to keep from starving. These Creeks, now often characterized as Seminoles, lived in swamps and remote hammocks between Pensacola and Mobile and farther east along the Gulf Coast.[7]

When Georgians emigrated to Alabama they frequently crossed the Chattahoochee at Coweta. Selling food and fodder to the immigrants, being paid to ferry them across the river, and putting them up in their homes and taverns, McIntosh and his friends profited from this migration. Some immigrants were destined for bluffs below the forks of the Alabama where Montgomery and Selma began to rise. This was the old Alabama heartland, the center of red-stick fanaticism, the region where prophets had their Holy Ground. With pain McIntosh remembered what the red-club men had done to him, and it bothered him not a whit when whites appropriated their domain.

Due south of Coweta, in an enormous region that was also part of the Fort Jackson cession, Indian opposition was much greater. Americans built Fort Scott above the forks of the Apalachicola, Fort Gaines on the Chattahoochee, and Camp Crawford on the Flint, all in the domain of the Hitchitis, Yuchis and other non- Muskogees. McIntosh signed the Treaty of Fort Jackson four times, but none of these Indians' signatures appeared on that document. Months after the treaty was concluded, the Hitchitis and their friends accompanied British troops to New Orleans hoping to make Jackson pay for what he had done at Horseshoe Bend and Fort Jackson.

The status of the Muocogulges on the Apalachicola River and its hinterland differed sharply from that of Indians above Mobile. Those on the Tensaw were friendly Creeks who had fought and died alongside whites in the recent war. If they did not welcome American settlers at least they did not take up arms against them, and in any case whites soon outnumbered the Indians many times. The United States had seized nearby Mobile from Spain in 1813, and the new colonists had ready access to that port. But at least in theory, Spain still controlled the mouth of the Apalachicola farther east, though she had no port or settlement of any kind there. Only the Negro Fort fifteen miles upstream commanded the entrance to that river. Indians in this region, for the most part non-Muskogees, had remained sullenly neutral or had joined the red sticks in the recent war. They denounced southern Georgia's cession and shot at whites arriv-

190   ing at the Chattahoochee and Flint in southwestern Georgia and
also at the immigrants moving to the Satilla 200 miles to the
east.[8]

With American colonies in revolt, Spain was not likely to
support Lower Creek–Seminoles who opposed American encroachments. With some justification, however, Muscogulges
assumed that Britain might. Hillis Haya led a red-stick delegation to London in 1815; British merchants and recently discharged soldiers remained among the Indians, set themselves
up as semiofficial British agents, and promised that King George
had not forgotten his old allies. At the same time the British
secretary for war and colonies, the earl of Bathurst, asserted that
Americans' settling on the Creek cession probably was a flagrant
violation of the Treaty of Ghent and that the government should
intervene.[9] Cannons and muskets marked with the royal insig-
nia remained at the Negro Fort in the hands of defiant Indians
and blacks.

Whether characterized as Africans, Afro-Indians, Creeks, or
Seminoles, Negroes simultaneously restrained and encouraged
American expansion. Southern white slaveholders were reluctant to bring their chattels into a region where Maroons were
present, but they urged Jackson to take his forces and stamp out
these sources of potential insurrection.

During the past war Britain had armed hundreds of Negroes,
including Garçon at the fort on the Apalachicola and Ned Simmons on Cumberland Island. Black soldiers had served in both
British and Spanish armies, joining British forces attacking New
Orleans and the Spanish garrison defending Saint Augustine.
Black Indians had been conspicuous among Seminoles contest-
ing the patriots' advance toward Alachua. Blacks in the Tensaw
region belonged to or were part of the friendly Creeks and were
soon outnumbered and intimidated by the arrival of thousands
of Georgians. This was not the case farther east. Well-armed
Maroon communities existed at the Negro Fort, Miccosukee,
the Suwannee River, and Tampa Bay, and black Muscogulges
lived among and were an integral part of the Creeks and Seminoles. The "main drift" of the Americans was to destroy these
blacks.[10] A number of them were fugitive slaves, having escaped

from white Georgians, Innerarity and his associates in Florida, and McIntosh and other friendly Creeks. These blacks had good reason not to want Americans to swarm into Indian lands, whether above or below the Florida line.

In surveying conditions after the war in the Southeast—in ceded lands in Georgia and Alabama, near the Negro Fort on the Apalachicola, in new red-stick villages on the Wakulla, and at Bowlegs Town on the Suwannee—it is not hard to explain American reports that the old hostile red-stick party had begun dancing again. Yet it must be kept in mind that the Tuskegee Hillis Haya and the Tallassee McQueen in northern Spanish Florida, Savannah Jack in southern Alabama, the Hitchiti Bowlegs on the Suwannee, and Abraham, Garçon, and the Seminole (Choctaw) chief at the Negro Fort had never ceased hostilities or their war dances. Britain, France, and other great powers might be at peace after 1815, but not these Muscogulges.

Compounding Muscogulge bitterness after 1815 was Forbes and Company's open collaboration with the Americans. This firm and its predecessors had nurtured the Indians and kept their truck houses full for almost a century, but now was preparing to reap benefits from the Fort Jackson treaty cession and assist Americans in fulfilling their manifest destiny. In the new scheme of things little room remained for the Muscogulges, whatever their clan or moiety. William Hambly and Edmund Doyle stayed at or near the Forbes and Company store at Prospect Bluff. The skin trade was unprofitable and shrinking rapidly, and the two looked upstream to American soldiers who were the vanguard of white immigration into the lower Apalachicola hinterland. As Americans constructed Fort Scott just above the forks, Hambly urged Innerarity at Pensacola to rush him foodstuffs and trading goods. The American garrison at Fort Scott was desperate for corn—two reales (twenty-five cents) for twelve ears, and the price rising![11] Realizing that Spain was weak and reputedly longing for a speedy American takeover, Hambly and Doyle furnished intelligence to American commanders about both Spanish and Indian affairs in Florida. Doyle confided to his superior Innerarity in Pensacola: "I hope the damned old blind [Spanish] governor is by this time gone to the devil . . . this country is greatly admired . . . [if the mediated change occurs] we weary travellers shall rest in peace."[12] The Muscogulges did not read this letter but saw the rations that were piled up at Prospect Bluff before being shipped upstream to United States troops, and these Indians were convinced that Hambly had betrayed the Negro Fort to the Americans. Indians seized both company employees, sent them off to Miccosukee and then to Bowlegs Town, and threatened to put a premature end to their weary travels.[13]

The black Muscogulges who had helped capture Hambly and Doyle understood that Forbes and Company was no longer their friend. Company slaves had run away or been liberated during the war, and after 1815 much of the firm's energy was expended in largely unsuccessful efforts to recover these fugitives. Few wanted to return, and they joined and lived among black Muscogulges in East and West Florida, still holding on to their muskets, bayonets, and uniforms.

James Grant Forbes's career further illustrates how the firm was anxious for Americans to acquire Florida after the War of 1812. James Grant had been born in British Saint Augustine in 1769, son of the Anglican minister John Forbes. Another Forbes, Thomas, a kinsman and a founder of Panton, Leslie, and Company, became James Grant's guardian when James Grant's father died at the end of the Revolution.[14] Young James Grant accompanied his mother to New England and in time became an American citizen. But he never forgot Florida and his Forbes relations who were associated with Panton, Leslie, and Company (Forbes and Company). James Grant arrived at Fernandina in 1818, and served as a delegate in the "mock legislature" of Spanish-American revolutionaries Gregor McGregor and Luis Aury.[15] When the United States took over Saint Augustine three years later, James Grant was among the first to arrive. He was appointed marshal of the territory and subsequently mayor of Saint Augustine. As a native son of Florida, he considered himself the most qualified to publish a description of the province. His eye was on the Forbes Purchase and other Florida lands that were claimed by the company. Those promoting this real estate laid out the town of Colinton at Prospect Bluff in a rectangular grid, appropriately with Jackson Square at one end and Forbes Square at the other. James Grant's 1821 *Sketches, Historical and Topographical of the Floridas* was aimed at Georgians: he advised them not to trek all the way to Tensaw when Eden was right at hand on the Apalachicola.[16]

Forbes and Company's abandoning the Indians and joining the Americans in 1815 had created a commercial vacuum, which the elderly Bahamian merchant Alexander Arbuthnot rushed in to fill. At the end of the War of 1812 he established a store at Saint Marks (on the site of Forbes and Company's old store), at Tampa Bay, and at Cedar Keys below the mouth of the Suwannee. Factors could send packhorses to these stores for supplies, or displaced refugee Indians individually might trade skins there. The Muscogulges had lost much of their hunting lands, and the best part of what remained, which still was considerable, lay in Florida and southern Georgia. These Muscogulges were Creeks of non-Muskogee backgrounds who had relocated in Florida, Hitchitis and others who had long been on the scene, and the blacks in their midst. They still hoped to live in their talwas, plant crops, raise cattle, and hunt commercially.

Arbuthnot nurtured this hope. He was not a philanthropist as has been claimed; he was a Scottish merchant who aspired to make his fortune in the Indian trade. He could succeed only if Indians remained commercial hunters and Spain held on to Florida or Britain acquired it. Granted power of attorney by "chiefs of the Creek nation," Arbuthnot became the Indians' advisor. He wrote letters to the British minister in Washington and to authorities in London, insisting that the United States had blatantly violated the Treaty of Ghent by appropriating Indian lands. Britain should protest, reassert her presence among the southern Indians, appoint him or someone Indian superintendent, and consider acquiring the Floridas.[17] Except for recommending a British takeover of the Floridas, Arbuthnot wrote in the same vein to the Spanish governor in Havana.[18]

British soldiers remained in the Floridas after 1815, told the Indians the same things as Arbuthnot, and held forth the prospect of British support. But these soldiers of fortune feuded with Arbuthnot and his fellow traders. Part of the bickering reflected

194   the age-old dislike and mistrust of soldiers for merchants, the latter being regarded as men of few scruples, of inferior birth, and with few interests outside their ledgers.

Among the discharged soldiers who remained in Florida were Robert Ambrister and George Woodbine, who were outspoken abolitionists and drew many of their followers from black Muskogulges, including the "bluff people"—blacks at the Negro Fort at Prospect Bluff. The two were bent on glory, planning to liberate not only Florida but also Venezuela, Central America, and other parts of Spanish America, perhaps joining them in a loose confederation. The merchant Arbuthnot relied primarily on native Americans and did not object to Spain's holding on to Florida so long as she continued his commercial concession and kept the Americans at bay.

But Spain could not restrain the Americans, so she turned to other countries, primarily Britain, for support. The Muscogulges did the same thing, and were even more dependent on King George. Years before Hillis Haya had realized that the prophets' reforms stood little chance of success without British aid. In order to preserve what remained of the Muscogulge lands and culture and to minimize McIntosh's influence, Hillis Haya led a small red-stick delegation from the Apalachicola River to London in 1815. Repeated misfortunes had carried him a long way from his Upper Creek talwa and from the Osage country that he and Tecumseh had visited in 1811. Colonel Nicholls lodged Hillis Haya in his own home and served as his mentor. The Indian leader brought a calumet for the prince regent, George III's son, he presented memorials to the government that described the plight of Creek women and children, and he insisted that Britain should keep her promises and not desert the Indians. While in England the silversmith Hillis Haya used his artistic talents and painted a self-portrait. Though it was not of high quality, Hillis Haya did not appear the wild savage portrayed in the American press.[19]

Despite Hillis Haya's pleas and the American violation of the Treaty of Ghent, Britain refused to sign an alliance with the Muscogulges. She had finally decided that she was not going to recover the Floridas, and she did not want another war with the

Hillis Haya, self-portrait, England, 1817(?). From Ralph T. Coe, *Sacred Circles: Two Thousand Years of North American Indian Art* (1976). Courtesy the Arts Council of Great Britain and the Trustees of the British Museum. Eth. doc. no. 1311.

Hillis Haya (Francis) as portrayed by whites. From John Frost, *Pictorial Life of Andrew Jackson* (1847). Courtesy Florida State Archives, Tallahassee.

United States. Hillis Haya was sent off with a new silver pipe tomahawk, £100, travel expenses for him and his delegation back to America, and vague promises that the Muscogulges would be provided for when it was truly necessary.[20] Nicholls made arrangements for Hillis Haya's son, perhaps the one born in London, to remain and be educated in England, though it is uncertain whether this occurred. The Tuskegee red-stick leader and most or all of his family returned to the Bahamas, sailed over to Ochlockonee Bay, and made their way inland to Tallahassee. He informed the Indians that though the prince regent had given him only minimal support, Arbuthnot and his Bahamian friends would see to it that Muscogulges had powder, ball, and clothing.[21]

While Hillis Haya was in London other Muscogulges petitioned the British minister in Washington. Advised by Arbuthnot, McQueen wrote Minister Charles Bagot how American settlements at Tensaw and on the lower Chattahoochee had notoriously violated the Treaty of Ghent. Though sympathetic, Bagot was noncommittal, and when the cabinet's position finally became clear, he refused to take any action. Nevertheless the possibility existed that Britain might have a change of heart, that the Union Jack might yet wave over Florida, and that King George might come to the rescue of his old Indian allies. This kept alive the hopes of McQueen, Hillis Haya, Kinache, Abraham, Garçon, and Savannah Jack, none of whom were Muskogees.[22]

Before Hillis Haya returned to Florida, Americans destroyed the Negro Fort. Spaniards and Indians had debated about which of the two owned Prospect Bluff. Americans understood that the fort stood on foreign soil—not that this made any difference. They regarded the fort, its munitions, and the Negro cabins stretching out for miles up and down the river as a dangerous Maroon settlement. Beyond this, they claimed that nature had decreed that American ships be allowed to sail from the Gulf upstream with supplies for garrisons at Fort Scott at the forks and for other forts and settlements on the Chattahoochee and Flint rivers. Black Muscogulges Garçon and Abraham, the Tallassee McQueen, the redoubtable Hitchiti Bowlegs, and the Mic-

Destruction of the Negro Fort, 1816. By Arthur M. Mulders, 1982. Courtesy The Museum, Florida Tribe of Creek Indians, Blountstown, Florida.

cosukee Kinache (Tom Perryman) all thought differently, and they resolved to use the Negro Fort's cannons and muskets against any Americans foolish enough to try and pass by Prospect Bluff. Despite a French name bestowed by a former master Garçon, the resolute fort's commander, was determined to oppose the Americans and to show them he was no "boy."

This is why American forces converged by land and sea on the Negro Fort in August 1816. General Clinch with troops from Fort Scott and McIntosh with a large friendly Creek delegation came downstream, and American gunboats sailed upriver from the Gulf. American troops and friendly Indians prepared for the assault. Including women and children, Garçon commanded just over three hundred defenders, most of whom were black Muscogulges. A close analysis of forces arrayed on both sides in and around the fort reveals that the old ethnic divisions among the Muscogulges were far from dead, and McIntosh's warriors skirmished with a vengeance. American gunboats had laboriously made their way upstream. They took their positions and commenced firing with little effect, that is until they began using hot shot. The first hot shot rolled into the open powder magazine and touched off a stupendous explosion—smoke, flame, debris, and mangled bodies all were lifted into the air above the log fort, and soon American soldiers and McIntosh's warriors were inside putting a quick end to any who dared to resist. Garçon and the Choctaw "Seminole" chief were both captured unhurt. McIntosh's Indians tortured, executed, and scalped the two unfortunate leaders. Except for 10 cannons, McIntosh and his followers received the booty: 2,500 stands of arms, 500 carbines, 200 pistols, 500 swords, 1,062 kegs of powder, bars of lead, uniforms, and foodstuffs. Survivors who escaped McIntosh's incursion fled to Miccosukee and other Indian villages. Many of the black refugees returned to or relocated at Bowlegs Town on the lower Suwannee River.[23]

The American flag now flew over the bluff in Spanish Florida and, except for an interval of a year and a half, remained there until 1821 when the United States finally acquired Florida. Early in 1818 the United States Army constructed Fort Gadsden, which adjoined the charred and decaying Negro Fort. The largest Maroon settlement ever to threaten the peculiar institution in the Old South was no more, and the burned Negro Fort and the new Fort Gadsden ensured that this Maroon haven would not be resurrected.

McIntosh's warriors had been among the first into the blown-up Negro Fort. Afterward they enthusiastically guided American forces and scoured the river banks and woods to round up men, women, and children not agile enough to escape. Some of these Negroes had been the property of McIntosh and his friends or of Forbes and Company, and these so-called Negroes were Africans, zambos, and even those who biologically were not one bit African. Yet all were trussed up in rawhide strings and marched off to Alabama and Georgia.[24] An 1807 act of Congress had prohibited the foreign slave trade, the importation of slaves from outside the borders of the United States. But as Arbuthnot, Ambrister, Hillis Haya, and the rawhide-bound slaves could

200   testify, acts of Congress and the Bill of Rights were of little consequence in Spanish Florida.

As McIntosh and his warriors charged into the Negro Fort, scalped Garçon and the Choctaw chief, rounded up unfortunates of diverse ethnic backgrounds classified as Negroes, and carried off arms and munitions left by the British, they were sending a message to non-Muskogees. All Muscogulges must adopt the American scheme of civilization, cut ties with Britain, accept the president of the United States as father, and acknowledge the leadership of McIntosh, his kin, and the National Council. McIntosh's message was the same in 1816 as it had been at the outset of the Creek War. Red sticks and their Upper Creek sympathizers on the Tallapoosa in 1816 still damned Hawkins's plow, but they remained quiet: memories of losses at Autosse and Horseshoe Bend were fresh. Though chastened, McQueen, Hillis Haya, Kinache, Bowlegs, and others in Florida still hoped that Britain or Spain would come to the rescue, and they dared McIntosh to do his worst.

The hostility and militancy of Florida Muscogulges became manifest in November 1817 when they ambushed Lieutenant R. W. Scott's party. Commanding a detachment of forty soldiers and accompanied by seven women and a handful of children, Scott made his way in an open boat from the mouth of the Apalachicola River toward the American fort at the forks. A mile below the fort the lieutenant veered close to the shoreline in order to avoid the strong current. Remembering those who had perished at Prospect Bluff, black and Native American Muscogulges suddenly opened fire, killing or wounding most of the Americans. A few escaped to Fort Scott to give an account of the ambush, but the attackers captured the remaining women, children, and soldiers. The others had been killed and scalped. Surviving prisoners and scalps alike were taken to Kinache's Miccosukee, to Hillis Haya's new red-stick village on the Wakulla, and elsewhere.[25]

Another prisoner, Sergeant Duncan McKrimmon, was captured at the beginning of 1818 (or possibly earlier), and marched to Hillis Haya's village, where Indians blackened his face and prepared him for execution. Just before he was to be put to death,

Milly Francis pleading for Duncan McKrimmon. From Henry Trumbull, *History of the Discovery of America* (1828). Courtesy Florida State Archives, Tallahassee.

Milly Francis, Hillis Haya's daughter, rushed forward and successfully pleaded for the young sergeant's life. Perhaps village elders had been affected by Milly's entreaties or more likely the sergeant's delivery had been planned beforehand, an example of the Indian custom of adoption. Symbolic executions or running the gauntlet "killed" or "beat" the whiteness out of a captive, who then might be adopted, join a clan, marry, and help stem the population loss. McKrimmon did not have a deep knowledge of Muscogulge culture, and he—any more than those in the twentieth century—could not comprehend Milly's motives. But the grateful sergeant washed the soot from his body and was led away by Milly, having suffered no more than one who is smitten by one of Cupid's arrows.[26]

McKrimmon's capture and the death of most of the rest of Scott's party should not obscure the fact that McIntosh and his followers in the Muskogee moiety, backed up by regular United States soldiers and frontier militia, had the upper hand. McIntosh's dream was that all Muscogulges, including those who were black, should recognize his leadership and that of the National Council. This meant that Indians must give up commercial hunting and become acculturated: that was the way to survive, remain in the Southeast, and prosper. Considering the American plan of civilization inevitable, McIntosh and the National Council in 1818 enacted the "Laws of the Creek Nation" to further the cause. Hawkins had died two years previously, but he was likely the author. These laws retained aspects of traditional culture: medicine men could attempt to make rain; fire hunting was allowed; the punishment for adultery was ear cropping; and the ball game was still permitted, though in a somewhat more humane version. However, the new Creek laws also included provisions with no basis in traditional Muscogulge culture: private ownership of property, penalties for nonpayment of debt, patriarchal descent, a Negro slave code like that of the whites, and near destruction of the clan. An exception was that McIntosh and his friends in the same clan or moiety retained power.[27]

The mestizo Hitchiti Bowlegs was a large slaveowner and a factor with a truck house, constantly pestered by his hunters for powder. Partially acculturated, he could accept some of the National Council's laws. But Bowlegs disagreed with McIntosh on one point: the Creek capital was in Florida on the Suwannee, not at Coweta near the falls of the Chattahoochee.[28]

At the end of 1817 and on into 1818 Andrew Jackson and William McIntosh, in a conflict labeled the First Seminole War, swept through villages on the Apalachicola and Suwannee rivers and Lake Miccosukee. The causes of this First Seminole War are not hard to find, and in many respects that conflict represented a continuation of the Creek War. McIntosh had fought McQueen and Hillis Haya's allies at Calabee and Horseshoe Bend, and he was anxious to set out after unrepentant survivors in Florida. Non-Muskogees (the Seminoles) regarded Jackson, McIntosh, and settlers who were encroaching on Indian lands as the enemy. Americans in 1813 had been most alarmed by the prophets' entreaties, whereas in 1817 the danger of black Muscogulges was highlighted. Images of the red or "bloody" flag waving over the Negro Fort were still fresh in the minds of white southerners, and, despite the destruction of the Negro Fort, Maroon settlements remained scattered in Florida, the major one in 1817 being Bowlegs Town on the Suwannee. Americans and those in Spanish Florida who were associated with Forbes and Company assumed that many of these Negroes were fugitive slaves, whereas the blacks considered themselves free, having been given their liberty by Indian masters, British officers, or someone. According to the Americans, British adventurers, usually the same ones active in Spanish Florida in 1814, were still tampering with black dissidents in that colony, threatening the security of the frontier and the South's peculiar institution. Jackson, Secretary of War John C. Calhoun, and McIntosh perceived Bowlegs Town as the main danger and hoped that the Miccosukee Kinache and other non-Muskogee slaveholders would recognize the threat and cooperate in a joint attack. Kinache, however, had other concerns.[29]

Since the American Revolution, the United States had insisted that it must have the Floridas and that if necessary force should be used to make the Seminoles respect the dictates of Washington authorities: "The poisonous cup of barbarism cannot be taken from the lips of the savage by the mild voice of reason alone; the strong mandate of justice must be resorted to and enforced."[30] Spain's New World colonies were beset by revolution. Now was the time to move against defiant nonwhites in Florida—and against Spaniards themselves.

All of this prompted expansionist Secretary of War Calhoun, with the president's approval, to order Andrew Jackson to raise an army, chastize the hostile Indians and Negroes, and, according to the doctrine of "hot pursuit," follow them into their Florida sanctuaries if necessary. This was all the encouragement Old Hickory needed; he was convinced he had authority not only to discipline the Seminoles but also to take Spanish towns. Jackson assembled Tennessee and Georgia militia, United States regulars, and McIntosh's friendly Creeks on American soil near the forks of the Apalachicola River at Fort Scott. Before Jackson arrived an altercation had occurred with the Hitchitis at Fowltown across the river, and in the aftermath the Hitchiti villages had been burned.[31]

204   Jackson descended the Apalachicola River to Prospect Bluff and erected Fort Gadsden, which adjoined the Negro Fort's ruins. At the same time McIntosh's Indians prowled about the right bank of the Apalachicola River, capturing 183 Seminole women and children and 53 warriors. McIntosh decreed that many of these captives were not Indians but Negroes who should be kept or sold as slaves.[32] McIntosh and Jackson's militia marched farther into the Florida peninsula close on the heels of McQueen and his followers. McQueen escaped, but not 97 of his women and children. Their fate and that of captives like them is unclear, but one can guess. Since the heyday of the Goose Creek men, Indians and their white allies had roamed the Southeast in search of slaves, primarily women and children, a practice that only the Civil War ended.[33]

Miccosukee and Bowlegs Town, the two largest Seminole villages in Florida, were Jackson's prime objectives. With at least 300 houses, Miccosukee stretched out for several miles on and near the banks of Lake Miccosukee; and Bowlegs Town on the Suwannee, with Negro refugees from the Negro Fort, Alachua, and elsewhere, in 1818 contained the largest Maroon community anywhere in the South. The Indian village was approximately one mile from the several Negro villages, and Negro houses outnumbered those of the Indians several times.

Closest to Fort Gadsden, Miccosukee was the first to be destroyed. Indians, including black Muscogulges, put up a perfunctory resistance but were outnumbered. Only about a half-dozen were killed, but their houses were burned, and at least 1,000 of their cattle were rounded up. McIntosh and his Indians remained in the vicinity for some days, relentlessly "scour[ing] the country around that place" and asserting the authority of Coweta and the Muskogees.[34] According to American reports 350 scalps, 50 of them fresh and presumably from Lieutenant Scott's party, hung from a tall red pole in Miccosukee's square. Confusion exists concerning these numbers, not the least being that less than 50 individuals of all ages and sexes were killed in Scott's party. American frontiersmen often inflated the number of scalps taken by the "savages," and Indians often inflated the number of scalps by making two or more out of one to collect an extra scalp bounty or to magnify their military prowess. Thus, the exact number and origins of the Miccosukee scalps remain uncertain.[35]

Between Miccosukee and Fort Gadsden lay the Spanish fort at Saint Marks. It was the next to fall, its small garrison offering even less resistance than had Miccosukees' defenders. With five hundred of his men enthusiastically watching, Jackson lowered the Spanish flag and presented it to the Spanish commander. Enhancing Jackson's elation was that the elderly Alexander Arbuthnot had been nabbed. Soon joining this Scottish merchant were Hillis Haya and the Autosse chief, Homathle Mico, both lured aboard American gunboats flying the British flag in the Saint Marks River presumably bringing munitions from the Bahamas. These two Upper Creek red sticks had eluded Old Hickory in 1814, but they were not so fortunate four years later.[36]

Miccosukee had been put to the torch; the Spanish Saint Marks garrison had departed for Pensacola; Arbuthnot, Hillis Haya, and Homathle Mico were in custody. Now Jackson and McIntosh set off for Bowlegs Town. After a grueling seven-day march and a sharp encounter with McQueen and his followers, Old Hickory reached the outskirts of Bowlegs Town. But the defenders had had warning and had escaped with women, children, horses, and cattle. McIntosh and his Indians were first on the scene and did virtually all of the skirmishing with the enemy rearguard at the Suwannee. As he burned the empty town and began his return march northward, Jackson realized that because these Maroons remained at large, he had failed in achieving one of his major objectives. McIntosh was dismayed that he had not punished his enemies and that so many potential slaves had escaped.[37]

The campaign against Bowlegs Town was far from a complete failure, because the town had been destroyed and the inhabitants dispersed. Bowlegs, who was among the fugitives, bemoaned the fact that he and British troops had not killed Jackson at New Orleans in 1815. Another triumph occurred when Robert Ambrister stumbled into Jackson's lines. During the War of 1812 Ambrister had enrolled and trained black Muscogulges for

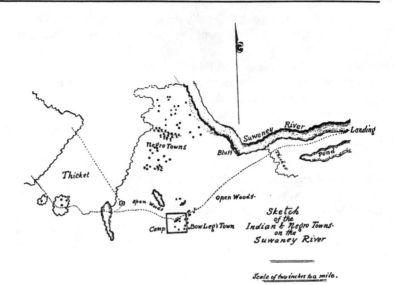

Scale of two inches to a mile.

Bowlegs Town on the Suwannee River (Captain Young's "Sketch Map, 1818). Courtesy *Florida Historical Quarterly*.

Britain. Still relying on these blacks after 1815, Ambrister, in conjunction with George Woodbine, Luis Aury, and other Spanish-American revolutionists, expected to lead them and help liberate Spanish America. In the aftermath Florida might be associated with Bolivar's Gran Colombia or parts of Central America. Blacks and Afro-Indians were insurgents in all these areas. Heading a contingent of black Muscogulges, Ambrister planned to sail from the Suwannee and seize the Spanish fort at Saint Marks. In Jackson's eyes one of Ambrister's greatest crimes was that he did not understand that capturing that fort was part of America's destiny. But when the British soldier was captured and he silently made his way northward toward Saint Marks with Jackson's troops, whatever Ambrister's dreams might have been, they had been crushed.[38]

Arbuthnot and Ambrister, who detested each other and testified against each other, were both tried, Arbuthnot for inciting the Creeks to war and spying, and Ambrister for aiding enemies of the United States and leading them against Americans. Both were convicted and condemned to death. Jurists subsequently questioned the validity of proceedings in the old Spanish fort, but they were not present at Saint Marks River. Arbuthnot was hanged from the yardarm of his own ship and Ambrister was shot. Jackson's subordinate officers petitioned on behalf of Ambrister for a lesser penalty, but Old Hickory was obdurate: he knew both his destiny and Ambrister's.[39]

With no trial and little ceremony Hillis Haya and Homathle Mico were executed, dragged out of the fort by their heels and buried in an unmarked grave. At the same time in the old Alabama heartland, Montgomery, future capital of the Confederacy, was rising on the banks of the Alabama. The great aspirations held by Hillis Haya in 1811 when he had ranged throughout the Mississippi Valley with Tecumseh and in 1814 when British officers had feted him at Pensacola were dashed.

American forces had also killed friendly Indians, or at least those who were noncombatants. While Jackson was in Florida, Georgia militia under Captain Obed Wright attacked "hostiles" in Chehaw Town on the Flint River in Georgia, killing McIntosh's uncle and other friendly Creeks. Some Chehaws had accompanied McIntosh to Florida and others had provided foodstuffs to American forces. Assuming that his promises to McIntosh's friendly Creeks had been broken and his honor besmirched, Jackson was furious at this "perfidious murder," and he demanded that Wright be placed in irons and court-martialed. After a litigious interval, however, little happened to the captain.[40]

McIntosh, of course, had been with Jackson in Florida. At one point he, his Indian followers, and mounted white militiamen came upon a small party of Indians—three men, a woman, and two children—all busily cutting down a honeybee tree. For centuries Indians had relied on honey as a quick source of energy when traveling, waging war, or fleeing from an enemy. Not waiting to inquire whether these particular Indians were hostile or not, mounted Tennesseans and Indians galloped at full speed toward the honey-gathering party, which made no resistance. Nevertheless one man was killed, another wounded, the woman

208   "shot . . . through the body," and the "under jaw of one of the children . . . shot off." The afflictions of the woman and child, who, if not friendly, in any case were noncombatants, did not blemish Jackson's honor. Sometimes, but not always, he was a paladin of children and the weaker sex.[41]

While Jackson was at Saint Marks, reports reached him that, as during the Creek War, red sticks were congregating at Pensacola and being furnished munitions. Although these reports may have been inflated by Hambly, Doyle, and other Forbes and Company employees, Jackson resolved that the only recourse was for the American army to seize the Spanish capital. Making an arduous march of over 200 miles from Saint Marks, Jackson, not without some difficulty, took Pensacola for the second time within five years.[42]

With the American flag flying over Saint Marks, Fort Gadsden, and Pensacola, and Hillis Haya, Homathle Mico, Arbuthnot, and Ambrister dead, the First Seminole War was over. Jackson's invasion touched off international disputes and vitriolic domestic controversies, and in time American forces withdrew from Pensacola and Saint Marks—but not from Fort Gadsden. Continued occupation of the latter was a reminder to Spain that her days in Florida were numbered.

No peace treaty ended the First Seminole War, and for McQueen, Bowlegs, and the prophet Abraham, the Creek War of 1813 had yet to run its course. Nevertheless with the withdrawal of most American troops from the Spanish Floridas relative calm returned to the Indian country. Surveying the Muscogulge domain of late 1818 one characteristic that stands out is that the Muscogulge southern migration was continuing. Red sticks had been forced off lands ceded at Fort Jackson, and a considerable though undetermined number of Indians made their way to the Floridas. Hillis Haya and Homathle Mico, of course, had been executed at Saint Marks in 1818, but Peter McQueen and his followers had found a precarious refuge farther south in the Florida peninsula. Weatherford and his friends had made their peace with Jackson and moved from the vicinity of the forks of the Alabama southward to a comparatively isolated and secure region northeast of Mobile. Black Muscogulges who

had lived near the Negro Fort or at Miccosukee in northern
Florida retreated to Tampa Bay and to coastal islands farther
south.

Both hostile Muscogulges and friendly Creeks participated in
this southern movement. Chief John Blount (Laufauka), a mestizo from Tuckabatchee, had fought alongside Big Warrior in
1813 when the prophets' warriors besieged Tuckabatchee.
Blount had sided with the Americans in 1813, but, unlike Big
Warrior, Blount continued to throw in his lot with the Americans after 1815. During both the 1813–14 Creek War and the
First Seminole War Blount and his followers had served with
Jackson's forces. After destruction of the Negro fort in 1816,
when hostile Muscogulges had moved away from the Apalachicola River, Blount and his Upper Creek kin appropriated fertile
Florida bottomlands above Prospect Bluff, and in Florida they
became known as Lower Creeks, Seminoles, or Apalachicolas.
Blount probably did not realize it and would have been uncom-
fortable with the role, but in fact his new town was an advance
agent of American manifest destiny. Blount recognized, however, that his security and prosperity were tied to the United
States. Even with American troops close by he was in danger.
Most of the Muscogulges in Florida, whatever their color and
ethnic background, did not speak Muskogee as their first language and many did not speak it at all. These non-Muskogees
remembered what Blount and other friendly Creeks had done at
Horseshoe Bend, the Negro Fort, and Miccosukee, and they had
signed no peace treaty in 1814, 1818, or at any other time. Blount
expected American troops at Fort Scott to the north and at Fort
Gadsden below to afford his town protection and usually, though
not always, they did. Nevertheless, not long after he had settled
down, Seminoles, some of whom were Upper Creek red sticks,
attacked Blount and "rifled . . . his family (slaves) from him."[43]
For these and previous losses the United States awarded Blount
$5,000, one-seventeenth of the total set aside at the Treaty of
Fort Jackson to reimburse friendly Creeks. Blount, McIntosh,
and even Weatherford recognized how much it paid to have Old
Hickory as a friend.[44]

McIntosh was victorious: he, Blount, and other friendly

210   Creeks had triumphed over their enemies. Hillis Haya, Homathle Mico, the Tame King, and many of the prophets were dead;
Weatherford had moved out of the Upper Creek heartland and
was quiet; and Peter McQueen, Seekaboo, and Savannah Jack
were skulking who knew where in Florida. Two of McQueen's
sons had been captured, and McQueen himself soon died on "a
barren island" on the east coast of the Florida peninsula. At
some point after 1818 Savannah Jack finally stopped killing
whites in Florida and Alabama, emigrated to the West, and
settled on the Red River.[45] Old Hickory regarded General Mc-
Intosh as "the bravest man I know,"[46] and the Creek general
was busily and successfully storing up treasures on this earth.
His periodic incursions into Florida netted captives that he and
his partner, Creek agent David B. Mitchell, disposed of profit-
ably. In a sense Prospect Bluff, the site of the Negro Fort and the
great hope of the Maroons, had been transformed into a slave
mart, a barracoon. McIntosh and his Indian and white associates
also visited Amelia Island and Charleston to recover "Negroes"
characterized as runaways, and in 1819 McIntosh urged the
government to send him and his friends into Florida. They would
range over the peninsula and bring home many more fugitives
trussed up in strings.[47]

Cattle made up part of McIntosh's Florida booty, and United
States Army officers assumed that livestock would be divided
among warriors who had accompanied the army. McIntosh,
however, sold the cattle on his own account, though he insisted
that Indians had gotten their due portion of the cash.[48] If true,
it is safe to assume that most of this money was spent at Mc-
Intosh's store, and that with no competition from Forbes and
Company or Arbuthnot, McIntosh adjusted his prices accordingly. McIntosh's partner was agent David B. Mitchell, the former governor of Georgia. As part of William H. Crawford's political machine, Mitchell had been appointed Creek agent to
replace the deceased Hawkins. Many Americans went to the
frontier to seek their fortunes, and Mitchell was no exception.[49]

McIntosh's aversion toward those Indians in the opposite moiety,
whether they were called Creeks or Seminoles, was genuine, and he
had no qualms about profiting at their expense. Another

way to do this and further punish his enemies was to get the United States to recognize that Florida Indians were Creeks and not Seminoles. More often than not the United States characterized all nonwhites in Florida as Seminoles. McIntosh, however, contended that those "other Creeks known as Seminoles" were really Creeks, and thus subject to the will of the National Council.[50] McIntosh assumed, as did Jackson and many other Americans, that Florida would not long remain in Spanish hands. After the United States took over and settled Florida, Seminoles would have to be compensated for the loss of their right to use of the soil. When that happened McIntosh wanted the money to go to himself and the National Council, not to those Creeks known as Seminoles. This prospect afforded an excellent opportunity for McIntosh and his friends to enrich themselves while punishing and exerting authority over their enemies.

And McIntosh had still another scheme in mind. According to an 1807 act of Congress, importing slaves from abroad was illegal. But if the United States concurred that Florida lands were Creek lands, this would facilitate bringing slaves across the international boundary, and once in the Creek country slaves might remain with the Indians or be sold to whites in Georgia and Alabama. Whatever the method, money was to be made from smuggling slaves.

Secretary of War Calhoun denied McIntosh's pretensions and decreed that Indians in Florida were Seminoles, and Indians above the line Creeks. McIntosh and his coterie were friends of the United States, but the bonds of friendship did not extend that far.[51] Based on Spanish and British titles, American citizens claimed the best lands in Florida, and neither they nor Calhoun planned to reimburse the Indians. McIntosh protested, insisting that friendly Creeks were being penalized twice: first by the large cession at Fort Jackson and now by not admitting that Florida belonged to them.[52] McIntosh did not always get his way, but around 1820 his wealth, prestige, and influence had never been greater. He had avenged himself on the prophets and their largely non-Muskogee adherents.

It was an expectation of British assistance that had betrayed

William McIntosh. From Thomas L. McKenney and James T. Hall, *History of the Indian Tribes of North America* (1836–44). Courtesy National Anthropological Archives, Smithsonian Institution. Photo no. 45,111-B.

non-Muskogees into presuming that they might successfully ward off McIntosh and Jackson. During the War of 1812 that aid had been substantial, and after 1815 Arbuthnot, Ambrister, and Woodbine continued to promise British support. This was the reason why Hillis Haya in 1818 had confidently boarded a ship in the Saint Marks River that was flying the British ensign and was presumably laden with munitions from the Bahamas. This mistake, as we know, cost him his life. Despite Jackson's sweep through Florida and his summary execution of Arbuthnot and Ambrister, hard-pressed Muscogulges still hoped against hope that King George might be their salvation, either by propping up the Spaniards or by acquiring Florida outright.

The expectation of British aid had dimmed but had not vanished, perhaps because there was no other. Iacohaslonaki (George Perryman) was a Miccosukee chief from the lower Apalachicola region who fled to Pensacola after Jackson invaded Florida. Just before Old Hickory captured Pensacola in 1818 Iacohaslonaki escaped aboard a British ship and in time arrived in Portsmouth, England. Possibly the son or nephew of Kinache or in any case his kinsman, the desperate Iacohaslonaki petitioned the government to relocate him and his 250-man tribe in the Bahamas or another British colony. He reminded the British of their promises to the Indians, which went back to the era of the American Revolution, pointed out how Americans had openly disregarded the Treaty of Ghent by occupying Indian lands, and condemned Jackson's summary executions of Arbuthnot and Ambrister.[53]

These executions had inflamed the British populace, and Viscount Castlereagh, the foreign secretary, averred he had but to snap his fingers and the nation would back him in a popular war.[54] But after evaluating ramifications of another conflict with the United States, the ministry decided not to press its case, which signified that there would be no resumption of hostilities, little likelihood that Britain would recover Florida, and no support for the Muscogulges. The latter was made clear to Iacohaslonaki at Portsmouth. Giving him almost no presents and only few pounds for expenses, the government promptly dispatched him and his delegation back to Florida, instructing naval commanders to bring no more Creek delegations to the mother country.[55]

Individual British subjects believed that these instructions did not truly reflect the government's fundamental policy, or that in any case such a policy would soon be reversed. The reason for their optimism was that the rebellion of Spain's American

214   colonies had brought increased opportunities for British trade. Ignoring the government's official position thousands of British merchants and disbanded soldiers and sailors collaborated with Spanish-American insurgents, making promises that the mother country, at least for the moment, was not prepared to honor. Included among them were promises that, despite many setbacks, Britain still was going to make Florida a colony or protectorate, and that she would not abandon her Muscogulge allies.

This is what inspired eighty-year-old Kinache and twenty-three other Muscogulges to board a Bahamian wrecking vessel at Plantation Key and sail over to Nassau in 1819. Kinache (Tom Perryman) had led warriors in Britain's behalf during the American Revolution, been one of Bowles's most powerful supporters up until the director general's death in 1805, and in 1814 taken his warriors to New Orleans to fight Old Hickory. Four years later Jackson swept through Miccosukee, destroying the town, and in the aftermath Hambly surveyed the battlefield and identified Kinache's body.[56] This identification was an error, perhaps reflecting mutilation or wishful thinking on Hambly's part. Most of the Miccosukees had escaped to the east and south. Kinache now presented himself before Governor William V. Munnings at Government House in Nassau. Kinache described the Muscogulges' plight and used all the old arguments why Britain should aid the Indians. Understanding much about Indian matters in the Southeast and not anxious to have the United States as a neighbor across the Bahama Channel, Munnings listened sympathetically to Kinache, lodged him and his delegation next to the barracks, gave them presents, and arranged for their passage back to Plantation Key. But more he would not do—at least for the moment.[57]

The wizened chief died not long after he returned to Florida. For almost a half-century Kinache had aided and fought alongside British subjects not because he loved the Union Jack but because a British connection seemed to be the best way to supply his truck house with goods, to continue commercial hunting and raising stock, and to maintain the independence of the Hitchiti Miccosukees. In contrast to Weatherford, the mestizo

Kinache never made an accommodation with Andrew Jackson.
Weatherford and his descendants held onto their southern Alabama lands, in time prospering, and in the latter part of the
nineteenth century local authorities erected a stone monument
on this Alabama patriot's grave.[58] Kinache's final resting place
is unknown and unmarked, perhaps unwittingly desecrated by
thousands of visitors swarming to Disney World.

Prelude to Removal

At the conclusion of the First Seminole War 50,000 to 60,000 nonwhite Muscogulges of diverse linguistic and ethnic origins lived somewhere in the Southeast. Upper and Lower Creeks, which composed the largest group, were concentrated in Alabama and Georgia on unceded lands, but many other Creeks, such as those northeast of Mobile, resided in counties where white law theoretically prevailed. Other Muscogulges lived among whites in towns and on farms and may or may not have been considered Indians. It was becoming increasingly common to label all nonwhites in Florida as Seminoles, though John Blount and his followers on the Apalachicola River avowed that they were Upper Creeks or Apalachicolas, but in any case not Seminoles. Several hundred red sticks, primarily Upper Creeks, eked out a living in the vicinity of Pensacola. How visible they were to outsiders depended on whether or not Jackson's army was about. Spaniards called these Indians Tallapoosas (Upper Creeks), and Americans insisted they were Seminoles. Southeastern Muscogulges at Pensacola and elsewhere thought of themselves as Tawasas, Cowetas, Eufaulas, Hilibis or members of another talwa, or as belonging to the Wind, Tiger, Potato, or some other clan. United States Army Lieutenant John T. Sprague was uncertain whether Indians in Florida were Seminoles, Creeks, Yuchis, Apalachicolas, or whatever, and could only refer to them as the "Florida tribes of Indians."[1]

218   Blacks constituted an important component of the Muscogulges, especially of those living in Florida. For years McIntosh
and Jackson had persecuted them, destroying the Negro Fort,
Miccosukee, and Bowlegs Town and sending off prisoners in
strings to Georgia and Alabama. Even so, many had escaped and
during the 1820s lived in swamps, hammocks, and islands in
the vicinity of Tampa Bay. Seminole agent Gad Humphreys
recaptured the fugitive Negro John, who belonged to a Saint
Augustine widow, chained him first about the neck, and subsequently ordered the blacksmith to put on handcuffs and leg
irons. But John escaped again . . . and again . . . and again, in
each instance apparently aided by a black Seminole.[2] Slave and
free Negroes resided in Indian villages scattered throughout Florida, on Indian plantations on the Apalachicola River, and with
whites in Saint Augustine and Pensacola, and they were variously known as Negroes, Negro-Indians, and Indians. A contin-
uous and easy intercourse existed between black Muscogulges
in Indian settlements and Negroes serving in Florida, Alabama, and Georgia on white plantations as field hands or in
Saint Augustine and other cities as domestics, artisans, and
fishermen.

       Spanish Indians also were included among Sprague's Florida
tribes of Indians. Though they numbered but a few hundred,
these Indians in the 1820s and 1830s were considered to pose a
threat to the Old South's peculiar institution. Americans
charged that Spanish Indians, abetted by Cuban fishermen, introduced munitions and seditious doctrines among southern
Negroes and facilitated the escape of fugitive slaves. For many
years these Spanish Indians were regarded as descendants of the
Calusas, who had been numerous in this same general region
in the sixteenth century. But primarily as a result of diseases
introduced in the sixteenth century, the Calusas had become
virtually extinct, so it is unlikely that many Calusa remnants
were to be found among the nineteenth-century Spanish Indians.
From the scattered evidence available, it appears that the Spanish Indians were of diverse ethnic origins, but a majority may
have been Upper Creeks who had migrated to the Tampa Bay
region sometime after the mid–eighteenth century. Spanish Indians spoke Muskogee proper, Hitchiti, and Yuchi, as well as

West African languages, Spanish and English. As Indians and black Muscogulges who became known as Spanish Indians settled down and intermarried, their economy changed and they became commercial fishermen. Their houses were clustered in villages and ranchos on coastal islands, and Spanish Indians for three-quarters of a century had time to develop their own life-style and identity, a subculture of the Southeastern Muscogulges. Yet Americans insisted Spanish Indians were Seminoles.[3]

In a sense the Spanish Indians' diversity mirrored the ethnic distinctions of the Muscogulge people. Such unity or cohesiveness as remained was still along linguistic, clan, and moiety lines. This had not changed despite the large territorial cession at the Treaty of Fort Jackson, Spain's withdrawal from Florida, and American insistence that Indians in Florida were Seminoles and those to the north were Upper and Lower Creeks. Tiger, Potato, Bear, Wind, and other clans were scattered throughout the Southeast. Though often separated by great distances and intimidated and harassed by American frontiersmen, Muscogulges maintained clan ties to a remarkable degree. More internal migration and intercourse occurred than generally has been recognized. Muscogulges in Florida visited relatives in Alabama on the Tallapoosa and then returned to Florida, in so doing, from the American perspective, transforming themselves from Seminoles into Creeks and back again to Seminoles. But whether they were in a talwa, in an isolated cabin, or in the woods with a fugitive band, these Indians remained Tigers, Potatoes, and Alligators—they knew that!

White sources and surviving letters of literate mestizos afford glimpses of this internal migration. Around 1820 Peter McQueen died on an obscure island, apparently one of the keys in southern Florida, and his widow returned to her talwa in Alabama over six hundred miles away and married Peter's nephew.[4] The father of the friendly Creek David Moniac, perhaps just to escape creditors, moved from the Little River in southern Alabama more than a hundred miles back into the Indian country with his kinfolk to the north.[5] And there were many other examples of such Indian relocations.

After Americans acquired Florida in 1821 they recommended

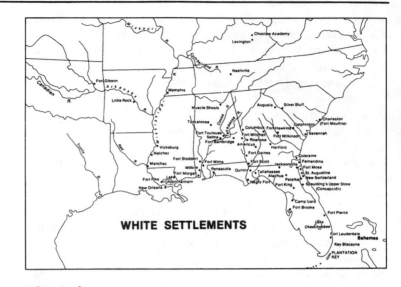

White Settlements

that all red sticks in Florida, by which they meant a majority of the Seminoles, should rejoin their relatives on the Tallapoosa and Coosa.[6] This, of course, was to get the Indians out of Florida and open up lands for settlement. The problem was that Americans were ignoring clan allegiances and that these red sticks, these Seminoles, were bitter enemies of the Upper Creeks, many of whom were friendly Creeks in clans associated with pure Muskogees. Alabama Creeks and Florida Seminoles made it clear that relocating Seminoles in Alabama talwas would ignite an Indian war. Neither whites nor Indians wanted this, and red-stick Creeks remained in Florida and continued to be known as Seminoles.

During the War of 1812, the First Seminole War, and the early years of territorial Florida, the Hitchiti Chief Neamathla rose to prominence. Neamathla had long, wavy black hair, a broad nose, thin mustache, and a resolute but aggrieved countenance. At the outset of the First Seminole War he and his followers lived at the largely Hitchiti Fowl Towns near Fort Scott and defied Americans' attempts to cross the Flint River. After Jack-

son's victory in the First Seminole War Neamathla moved eastward to Tallahassee, the old center of Spain's destroyed Apalachee missions. Tallahassee in 1819 was at least twenty-five
miles from an American or Spanish post. After acquiring Florida
in 1821 Americans had to deal with the Indians and for their
own purposes decreed that Neamathla was the chief of the Seminole nation. They feted him, and in the 1823 Treaty of Moultrie
Creek, Neamathla was awarded a two-square-mile section west
of Tallahassee on Rocky Comfort Creek at Tuphulga (near
Quincy).[7]

A partially acculturated village factor with a truck house, the
Hitchiti Neamathla was determined to defend and retain his
culture, clan, and economic way of life. As an *eneah* (heniha)
theoretically he was a second man, an advisor to the village
chief. With the disruptions and alterations of Muscogulge society it appears that the second man sometimes also served as the
mico, that the offices of principal chief and second man might
have been combined. For whatever reasons it is clear that Eneah
Mathla, perhaps also an *isti atcagagi* or beloved man, long remained a powerful Muscogulge leader. When whites began aggressively to settle the lower Apalachicola River and selected
Tallahassee as their capital, Neamathla and his followers moved
north and returned to Alabama. They were there in the mid-
1830s, when Neamathla emerged as one of the most influential
and bitter Creek leaders who opposed emigration to Oklahoma.[8]

Americans coming into Florida wanted to eject not only Neamathla but all Indians from the territory: where they went was
of secondary consideration. But to the consternation of Floridians the southern migration of Muscogulge people from Alabama
and Georgia into the territory continued, and the Seminole population increased. New red-stick leaders emerged to take the
place of Neamathla, Peter McQueen, and Savannah Jack, all of
whom had died or moved away. Seminoles in Florida lived on
or near the coast and had opportunities to continue trading with
foreigners. Americans tried to keep them away from the Gulf
and Atlantic Ocean, and to relocate them in Alabama or Oklahoma. But during the 1820s and early 1830s they had little
success, and the Muscogulge migration south continued.

222   The great fear of Muscogulge people, whether they lived in
Alabama, Georgia, or Florida, and regardless of which moiety
they belonged to, was that the United States was going to move
them beyond the Mississippi. Government officials reminded
Muskogee speakers that centuries ago they had come from the
West into the Southeast and had taken over the lands; now
whites were justified in doing the same thing. It was appropriate
for Muskogees to return to their ancestral home.[9] The Creek
and Seminole wars had demonstrated the folly of Jefferson's
program. After the Indians had become civilized, Jefferson and
Hawkins had expected many of them to become assimilated by
the whites. It was obvious even in 1800, when Jefferson was
elected president, that this assumption was a delusion, but in
the 1820s more and more people questioned Jefferson's assumption, and pressures and justifications for removal mounted.
Many concurred with Andrew Jackson that white and Indian
cultures were too different; that whites were civilized and Indians savages; that each should remain separate and evolve in
its own way—the Indians, of course, in the West. At the same
time reformers contended that rum and unscrupulous whites
preying on and corrupting Muscogulges were destroying them
and that only by relocating them beyond the Mississippi and
buying time was there any chance for civilization and Christian
conversion. The one thing that the policies of Jefferson, Hawkins, Jackson, and Baptist missionaries had in common was that
Muscogulges must relinquish all or most of their eastern lands.
What Muscogulge people thought of this was inconsequential.
As Calhoun told the Indians: the Great Spirit has made our form
of society stronger than yours . . . you must submit, give up your
lands, and live like whites if you wish to be happy.[10]

        In the 1820s Georgians posed the greatest threat to the Mus-
cogulges. For the moment Alabama seemed to have territory
enough to accommodate most of her settlers. But Georgia,
whose population was dramatically increasing, reminded authorities that in 1802 when Georgia had ceded its western lands
the federal government promised to extinguish the Indian title
expeditiously. Creeks in western Georgia felt threatened.

        One of the paradoxes of all this is that although Americans

were more determined than ever to remove the Indians and take their lands, they were at this time increasing their efforts to save the Muscogulges and convert them to Christianity. Just where the converts would live and their role in the dominant white society was never worked out. But the Protestant missionary impulse, which was deeply rooted in the American experience, dictated that the Muscogulges, like the Cayuses in the Pacific Northwest and Polynesians in Hawaii, must be converted, taught to read the Bible, and be made to appreciate the value of thrift and hard work. Conversion of the Muscogulges had the highest priority: "perhaps the LORD is about to open a great and effectual door among these sons of the forest."[11]

The Muscogulges felt the influence of the religious revivals—the Second Great Awakening—sweeping over the United States, especially frontier regions, during the early decades of the nineteenth century. Evangelical denominations established missions among these Indians. The first was that of the Moravians at Hawkins's agency on the Flint River. The two German missionaries there were artisans rather than ministers, and they enjoyed some success in disseminating skills necessary to be coopers, wheelwrights, cabinet makers, and tin men, but they made few converts during the 1807–1812 era.[12] Of more significance was the Methodist mission founded in 1821 at Asbury below Fort Mitchell on the Chattahoochee among the Lower Creeks, and the Baptist mission established at Withington in 1822 at Tuckabatchee among the Upper Creeks. Supported by public and private funding, these missions existed or flourished for most of the 1820s, stars in the night gleaming over a dismal landscape steeped in decadence and paganism. In the long run, however, all failed.

Southern Baptists and Secretary of War Calhoun had had high hopes for Reverend Lee Compere's Baptist mission at Withington. In 1822 Compere was anxious to begin the "improvement of the unfortunate inhabitants of the forest . . . these poor degraded creatures." Indians, Negroes, Compere's family, and white missionaries all helped construct the log buildings: a twenty-by-eighteen-foot schoolhouse and miscellaneous outbuildings including an eating house with a clay floor, a loom

224   house, smokehouse, stable and a large eight-room dormitory. During its existence from 1822 to 1829, between thirty to seventy children were enrolled annually, though perhaps no more than 25 percent finished the complete course of instruction. Interpreters were required because a high percentage of the students did not understand English. Most of the children belonged to clans that were especially identified with pure Muskogees, such as Wind, Bear, and Beaver; though we know that, despite the opposition of his parents, one young boy from the Alligator clan, often a non-Muskogee clan, was enrolled. Boys wore "Indian frocks" and girls dresses, and all were taught the three Rs. Advanced students read the New Testament and studied geography. Eventually girls were sent to the loom house and instructed in domestic arts, and boys were taught the virtues of plow agriculture, fences, and private property.[13]

Partly as a result of the missionaries' teaching and example, and partly as a result of prodding by the Creek agent and other American authorities, more and more Indians began leaving the talwa's large communal fields and fencing in and cultivating private holdings of five, ten, or more acres. This trend reversed at the end of the 1820s, however, and Indians, despite what was being taught in the missions, shifted from private farms back to communal fields. The reason was not hard to discern. Americans had made it clear that they were resolved to have all Creek lands in the East, not in the remote future but soon, and that destroying the talwa was part of the process. Muscogulges felt they could best resist by remaining in their talwas, as of old joining with neighbors in working and protecting their communal lands.[14]

The Baptist mission of Lee Compere at Withington and the Methodist establishment of William Capers and Brother Isaac Smith at Asbury each lasted less than a decade, and various circumstances explain their failures. One was that some Indians regarded the missionaries as American agents working to take over native lands. Another was the subject matter taught. Instruction in use of the loom, blacksmithing, and agriculture was not the problem. Parents recognized the advantages of learning such practical skills. The problem was the preaching. It was one thing to encourage Muscogulges to modify their technology and economy and another to ask them, especially the more conservative ones, to give up their religion, their souls. Up to a point evangelical missionaries might insist that Christianity and the Indian religion had much in common—the symbolism of the cross, a tradition of the flood, an afterlife, and a similarity between the Master of Breath and Jesus. The Indian cosmos of the sky, underworld, and earth resembled the Christian heaven, hell, and earth, though for the Indians it was easier for men and animals to move back and forth between one another. Despite these similarities, hillis hayas and shamans realized that the trinitarian Christian god was not the Master of Breath, and that missionaries did not understand or care about the sacred fire, sun, and corn mother.

Converting the heathen was the paramount reason missionaries had left their homes and undergone the hardships of living among the Indians. But it seemed worth it. Reverend Capers, in reporting to his Methodist sponsor, the South Carolina missionary committee, described how he was succeeding and how Indian pupils "have continued two or three hours together, weeping and praying to God . . . [losing] no opportunity to be instructed in the religion of the Gospel."[15] Reverend Capers had not previously even "been able to discover [among the Indians] anything identified under the name of religion."[16] Capers was aghast at Creek naughtiness and savagery: the whooping, gambling, and violence of the ball games and the indecent nakedness of the women. When the missionary approached the Chattahoochee he saw the head of a female bobbing on the river, and he suspected she was bathing nude for all to see in broad daylight. Capers waited . . . and waited . . . and waited, until at last a young girl, covered by no more than long black tresses, strolled up on the bank. "Oh Lord! . . . I scarcely had any spirit left." Of course bathing, sweating, the priests' role at the ball games, the purging ("puking") after taking black drink were closely associated with or an integral part of the Muscogulges' religion. The missionary, however, could only contrast human degradation found among the Lower Creeks with the sweet and noble fervor of camp meetings.[17] Considering that many camp meetings consisted of a half-dozen frenzied ministers simultaneously preaching fire and brimstone while members of the congregation swooned, shook, spoke in tongues, barked, and treed the devil, an impartial observer might not have considered the gulf between Indian and white society so great. Neither Jehovah nor Yahola manifested himself dispassionately on the southeastern frontier.

Sometimes the most wealthy and acculturated Indians vehemently denounced missionaries for the same reason whites did: they preached to the Negroes. Baptist and Methodist missionaries, their salaries paid in part by contributions from devout church members in Georgia and South Carolina, some of whom were black, taught for six days and preached on the seventh. No one in the Indian country was compelled to attend services, and African and zambo slaves, partly because they spoke English, often outnumbered Indians in the congregation. In fact missionaries expected their first converts to be these Negroes. Like their white counterparts, Indian slaveholders instinctively distrusted anyone's expounding to their chattels that all were equal in God's eyes, and they were not calmed by assertions that Christianity "commands the obedience of servants."[18] Fearful of insubordination and flight of their slaves, Indian masters vented their hostility on missionaries and Negroes alike. This opposition, coupled with the animosity of hillis hayas who were trying to retain what remained of Indian culture, and with the fear that missionaries were advocating western removal, contributed to the failure of the Withington and Asbury missions.

The American concept of separation of church and state did not apply to the Indian country, and Indians regarded governmental attempts at education and civilization inseparable from efforts to convert them. Opposition to the American program, though widespread, was most acute among non-Muskogee clans, which readily could be seen among the Seminoles. In 1826 Neamathla, Micanopy and other Seminoles informed Americans who hoped to establish a school: we refute that the Great Spirit wants us to read and write. According to Seminole folklore, only two races long ago resided in the South, the white man and the Indians. The Master of Breath presented a book to a blind old man living among them. This blind old man notified whites and Indians that whoever first killed and gave him a deer would be taught how to read. Whites killed a nearby sheep, assuring the blind man it was a deer. "If this cheat had not been practiced" many years ago Indians would now be as literate as whites.[19] Whether such a "cheat" ever occurred is immaterial. The important consideration in the 1820s was that Hitchiti speakers and similar non-Muskogees were set against missionaries and government agents locating a school at the agency in their midst. To avoid confusion and make clear the Master of Breath's intentions, Neamathla explained to the Florida governor that God had put three races in the Southeast, that Negroes were to be laborers; Indians, hunters; and whites, scholars. "It is not my wish [or the Master of Breath's] to have my red children made white children of."[20]

Neamathla was overstating his case because in reality he and most other Muscogulges of diverse backgrounds were attracted to and dependent on European technology and manufactures, and the Hitchiti chief appreciated the advantages of Indian children's learning how to be blacksmiths, gunsmiths, wheelwrights, weavers, and so forth. The danger was that instructors of such practical skills were often inspired evangelicals, and they were determined to spread the light of Christianity. This threatened to destroy the Indians' souls, the clans, the significance of the black drink and sacred fire, and the Muscogulges' cosmos. Furthermore missionaries were rivals to traditional leaders in the talwa.

These dilemmas could be avoided—in a sense having the best of two worlds or cultures—by sending orphans and children with their families' approval away from the Indian country to be educated. For this and other reasons the so-called Choctaw Academy became the most important school for Creek and Seminole children in the years before removal. This name is misleading because the school was not in the Choctaw country and Choctaws almost never composed a majority of the pupils. Located outside of Lexington, Kentucky, the academy was on the plantation of the ebullient Jacksonian Democrat Colonel Richard M. Johnson. He was its mentor and in overall charge, though

228   Baptist minister Thomas Henderson was superintendent and
from the beginning actually ran the school. Funding was provided by part of the Choctaw annuity and private donations, and
in time a portion of the annuities of the Creeks, Seminoles, and
other Indians from above and below the Ohio also were used to
support the school. From its inception in 1826, when twenty
Creeks were enrolled, until the 1840s a succession of young
Creeks and Seminoles attended Colonel Johnson's academy.

Log buildings were erected on the colonel's plantation: a
dormitory; a dining hall; instructions rooms; shops for blacksmiths, tailors, shoemakers, boatwrights, and cartwrights; stables; and miscellaneous outbuildings. Enrollment averaged between 100 and 150, and Indian children came from the tribes
bordering the Great Lakes in the North to the Gulf of Mexico
in the South. As much as possible English was the language
employed, by design and necessity becoming the lingua franca.
Henderson and his white assistants carried on most of the instruction. At times the Lancastrian system was employed,
whereby older pupils who had mastered a subject taught younger
Indians, if possible still in English.

During the academy's early years reading, writing, and ciph-
ering were emphasized along with an elementary liberal education. Students attended classes in geography, English, surveying, astronomy, natural philosophy, moral philosophy, history,
and music, and were encouraged to join the singing society, the
debating society, and the Napoleonic society (etiquette). The
Lycurgus court, in which Indians served as judges, lawyers, and
jurymen "brought to view . . . many species of vice . . . that
otherwise never would have been known or punished."[21] On
special occasions hundreds of whites in the vicinity were invited
to watch the Indians perform. As much as possible Indians were
supposed to dress alike—gray or blue and white coats and trou-
sers, cotton shirts, shoes or moccasins, woolen stockings, cap,
and a dress hat. Just before returning home the graduate might
be given a new coat, boots, and cravat, and if he went by horseback, saddlebags were also provided.[22] Breakfast and supper consisted of tea, coffee, milk, and bread, and dinner included meat,
vegetables, and hominy. Fretting that the boys were inclined to

"gormandize," Johnson urged omitting one of the three meals.[23]

Indians not already having an English name acquired one upon arrival. As a result Richard M. Johnson, Andrew Jackson, Henry Clay, Thomas Hart Benton, John Eaton, Richard Rush, James Barbour, Thomas McKenney, William Duval, and Wiley Thompson could be seen sitting alongside one another on wooden benches in the instruction rooms. The Creek, Elijah Beaver, who in a fashion retained his clan affiliation, was an exception.[24] If an outsider merely read the roll, he might have had the impression that the national government, the Indian agency, and the Florida territorial government were all run from Scott County, Kentucky.

It was not the intention of Colonel Johnson, the Indian agency, the Baptist Church—nor at a much later date of the Indian schools at Hampton Institute and at Carlisle—but giving Indians proper Christian names, instructing them in English, and mingling Creeks, Seminoles, Choctaws, Potawatomis, Pawnees, and others encouraged pan-Indianism. When Indians graduated they were expected to return home, not to join white society, and Indian pupils, from Potawatomis to Seminoles, though they had English names, were conscious that collectively they were Indians and not whites.

Those interested in the Choctaw Academy at times disagreed over what should be emphasized and the school's primary function. At first liberal arts were stressed; then, vocational education. Almost all pupils were male, and the school's patrons wondered if they might not speed up the civilization by concentrating on young girls. This remained little more than speculation, however, and the student body continued to be predominantly if not exclusively male. As far as Baptist teachers were concerned, Sunday school, preaching, and conversion were the academy's *raison d'être*.

Officials in Washington, including Secretary of War John C. Calhoun and Thomas McKenney, head of the Indian office, endorsed these religious and educational objectives, but they also had another: to use the Choctaw Academy to implement the national will. Critics of colonialism have made the point that the flag followed the Bible, and to this the Choctaw Academy

230   was no exception. McKenney encouraged Creek and Seminole students to write home to their parents demonstrating their progress. But at the same time McKenney admonished Henderson to examine and correct their letters, "and make them tend to the great objects of government, in giving them a [western] home . . . on which alone their *very existence* depends. Do not lose sight of this most important part of letter writing."[25] Calhoun phrased it bluntly: if missionaries in government-supported schools did not promote United States policies, the subsidies would be withdrawn.[26] This helps explain why Brother Smith at Asbury and Lee Compere at Withington told the Creeks that it was best for the Indians to go to the West.[27] Calhoun and his successors considered the Indians at the academy to be hostages, that the presence of young Creeks, Potawatomis and others would help prevent massacres like those at Fort Mims, Chicago, and Mackinac.[28]

Students enrolled at an early age, sometimes under six, and they often lost knowledge of their native language, culture, and Indian heritage, occasionally with unforeseen results. The friendly Creek Laufauka (John Blount) indicated that he was willing, even anxious, to leave the lower Apalachicola River and relocate in the West—but only if his son, a student in the Choctaw Academy, were first returned. Authorities in Washington and Florida, anxious to remove any of the Indians, accepted Blount's proposal, and instructed Superintendent Henderson to return the chief's son. Like all the other students, this young Muscogulge had been given a Christian name. To his dismay, Henderson discovered he could not identify Blount's offspring. Part of the difficulty was confusion over exactly what was meant by "father," "family," and "Seminole," and over the fact that Blount, like many adult Indian males, had assorted names and titles. Although Superintendent Henderson quizzed young Henry Clay, Andrew Jackson, and Thomas Hart Benton to see if they were Laufauka's offspring, all efforts failed, and Henderson could only report that the young Indian must have died in a cholera outbreak.[29] Whether he was alive or dead long remained in doubt, but as far as Blount was concerned his son (nephew?) had vanished into a black hole. Though the chief vowed he would not leave until his son was returned, in fact this friendly Creek redoubled efforts to put as much distance between him and the Americans as possible.

Mestizo Muscogulge youths sometimes were accepted by whites and sometimes not. One of McIntosh's sons was educated not at a mission school among the Lower Creeks but with white children at Milledgeville.[30] David Moniac, through the influence of his uncle, the friendly Creek David Tate, enrolled at West Point in 1817 and was commissioned a second lieutenant five years later.[31] In 1818 Andrew Jackson denounced Woodward as "a damned long Indian looking son-of-a-bitch," but Woodward, who had been educated by whites, in the 1820s and 1830s became one of the "founders" of Alabama.[32] More typical, however, was the experience of friendly Creeks on the Tensaw River, young and old alike, who were chided about their mixed ancestry, and forced off their lands. Thomas McKenney, an advocate of Indian education and civilization, took two young Creeks, William Barnard and Lee Compere (Arbor), the latter named for the Baptist missionary at Withington, with him to Washington to continue their educations. When the Creeks dismounted from their stagecoach to eat at a public stand near Augusta, the proprietress was adamant that no Indians were going to dine at her table; they must eat with the Negroes or somewhere else. McKenney insisted that the Indians loved him and appreciated what he and the government were doing in their behalf. Yet after a spell in a Georgetown school the two young Creeks returned home and then one or both headed south to join the Seminoles.[33] These and other Indians understood clearly enough what it meant when they were not allowed to eat with whites, or when Americans in the 1830s notified acculturated Creeks that they might continue to live on small individual farms in Alabama but could never become citizens.[34]

During the 1820s pressure for removing all the eastern Indians was becoming irresistible. Hawkins's and Jefferson's policy of acculturation had failed, party because many Muscogulges, especially those in the non-Muskogee moiety, had refused to accept it, and partly because it had succeeded too well. Not only Barnard and Compere but other Indians, young and old, de-

232   manded to eat at the white man's table. For whatever reasons, the Hawkins plan had turned out badly, and an argument increasingly heard in the 1820s was that the only way Muscogulges could be saved and civilized was through removal, that the only way to make them like whites was to separate them from whites. If the Muscogulge people remained in the Southeast they were doomed. They were being exposed to whiskey sellers, gamblers, land speculators, lawless frontiersmen, and venereal disease "in its worst form." Relocation would buy time for the process of civilization to proceed. Another reason for relocation was that the Muscogulges, especially the Seminoles, associated with "another class" of the population, that is the Negroes.[35] The growing number of critics of slavery, and Nat Turner's 1831 insurrection in Virginia, made white slaveowners throughout the South tremble for the stability of the peculiar institution. Yet the main reason so many whites wanted to relocate the Indians was the fact that Muscogulges claimed or occupied vast stretches of the best lands in the Old South; only by removal could Jackson, "having lighted the torch of freedom," fulfill his destiny and that of the common man.

Whatever the causes and justifications, the threat of eviction was real, and the Seminoles became aware of its growing intensity. More and more it suited United States' purposes to allege that all nonwhites in Florida, except fugitive slaves, were Seminoles. The numbers of the Seminoles included Hitchiti speakers who had long resided in Florida, recent red-stick accretions, Spanish Indians on Gulf Coast ranchos, Yuchis, Shawnees, Choctaws, and remnants from tribes who at an earlier time had lived on the peninsula. Having acquired Florida in 1821 and occupied Saint Augustine and Pensacola, one of the United States' first tasks was to sign a treaty with the Seminoles or at least reach an understanding with them. Somewhat to his surprise, the Lower Creek Neamathla suddenly found himself supreme chief of all the Seminoles, appointed by the United States with authority to head a delegation that would conclude a treaty binding the entire nation.

After delays and confusion Neamathla and other Seminole chiefs met at Moultrie Creek outside Saint Augustine with

American Commissioners William P. Duval, James Gadsden,
and Bernard Segui, who were supported by a military detachment and furnished with food, presents, and rum. In effect this
was a peace conference to recognize the Indian defeat and clearly
end the First Seminole War. War had not been formally declared
in 1817, and technically no peace treaty was necessary. But there
was no confusion about one thing: Jackson had humbled both
Indians and Spain. Though the Spaniards had departed, the Seminoles remained, and they must pay by ceding part or all of their
lands and promising to obey the whites. One reason for the delay
in assembling at Moultrie Creek was that Jackson questioned
whether a treaty was even necessary. Old Hickory had van-
quished the Seminoles, and, according to Jackson, the United
States was infinitely stronger than in past decades and should
merely inform survivors what must be done and not negotiate
at all.[36]

Nevertheless having Seminoles agree that they had been defeated and accept their fate seemed the best way to promote
tranquility and facilitate white settlement. Because the Seminoles had lost, they must relocate; Americans argued only about
where the Indians' new home should be. One solution was to
concentrate them in southern Florida, so much of which seemed
unattractive to white settlers because it was covered with lakes,
marshes, and rivers. Concentrating the Seminoles close to agitators in the Bahamas and Cuba had its disadvantages, however,
and Muscogulges on the lower Apalachicola vehemently denied
that they were Seminoles and vowed never to go to southern
Florida. Another solution, one in time favored by Jackson, was
to move the Seminoles to the Apalachicola River in northern
Florida and southern Alabama. Jackson's assumption was that
white settlers would intimidate and outnumber these Seminoles
and force them off their lands.[37] But for the moment this placed
Hitchiti speakers and other red sticks alongside the friendly
Creek, Chief Blount. This was not the way to provide for tranquility. Floridians, of course, considered it an excellent idea for
Indians to leave the territory and rejoin their Creek kinsmen in
Alabama and Georgia. But despite the different solutions whites
agreed that Florida Indians must move somewhere so that part,

Neamathla. From Thomas L. McKenney and James T. Hall, *History of the Indian Tribes of North America* (1836–44). Courtesy National Anthropological Archives, Smithsonian Institution. Photo no. 45,112-D.

if not all, of their lands could be sold. How else was the United States to acquire the five million dollars required by the Adams–Onís Treaty? Indians had not been consulted in Adams's negotiations with the Spaniards, but they were involved. By giving up their lands they were to provide the necessary money for the United States to fulfill its treaty obligations and obtain Florida.[38]

In 1823 Neamathla led the Indian delegation to Moultrie Creek to negotiate or be informed of the Indians' fate. This

Hitchiti chief, a village factor and slaveowner, had lived in southern Alabama and northern Florida for years, usually at or not more than sixty miles from the forks of the Apalachicola River. Having supported Bowles, Nicholls, and Arbuthnot, Neamathla had long been hostile to the Americans. After the Americans had built Fort Scott and invaded Florida in the First Seminole War, Neamathla retired eastward to Tallahassee. From time to time he shifted his political and economic allegiances. But he had a constant dream: to maintain the independence of his Hitchiti kinfolk and to continue the eighteenth-century Indian life-style based on agriculture, commercial hunting, and droving. This is what he had in mind when he reiterated to Americans that the Seminoles must farm *and* hunt, that they could not be restricted to small individual farms like whites.[39]

Painting themselves white, performing the eagle-tail dance, and smoking the calumet, Neamathla and the Indians negotiated with their white counterparts at Moultrie Creek. John T. Sprague, a young lieutenant in the Second Seminole War and in 1867 commander of federal troops occupying Florida, commented before the outbreak of the Second Seminole War that "it was clearly manifest . . . in justice to all parties . . . that the Florida Indians . . . should be removed . . . the white man or the savage must succumb."[40] Professional soldier Sprague knew who was the stronger. In view of this Neamathla perhaps could have considered himself fortunate with the Moultrie Creek accord. Florida Indians were to be concentrated in a large four-million–acre reservation in central Florida while those Seminoles known as Apalachicolas were allowed to remain in the panhandle on or to the east of the Apalachicola River in rectangular sections averaging four to eight square miles in size.[41] Neamathla, Blount, Mulatto King, and three other chiefs in this group had had some hope that the treaty would permit them to continue their agricultural–commercial hunting life-style. American intentions were made explicit, however, when they ordered hunters from Blount's town at Tampa Bay to return forthwith to the Apalachicola River reservation.[42]

The Seminoles' loss of the First Seminole War resulted at Moultrie Creek in their relinquishing claim to most of northern

Seminole village on the Apalachicola River, nineteenth century. From Francis Castelnau, *Vues et Souvenirs de l'Amérique* (1842). Courtesy Florida State Archives, Tallahassee.

Florida. As compensation they were awarded a $5,000 annuity for twenty years plus an additional $1,000 to establish and maintain a school on the reservation.[43] The Hitchiti Neamathla, off by himself in his reservation in the Florida panhandle, and the Hitchiti Micanopy in central Florida wanted no such schools: the white man had already done enough in the Indian's behalf. If the friendly Creek (Seminole) Blount wanted to send his son to the Choctaw Academy in Kentucky that was his business.

The Treaty of Moultrie Creek did not resolve the issue of the Seminoles' ultimate disposition, but both Indians and whites had an idea of what was in store. The annuity lasted for only twenty years, and when it was renewed the Americans expected the Seminole reservation to be on the far side of the Mississippi River. Neamathla, Blount, and the other Apalachicolas had north Florida sections guaranteed to them and their followers for as long as they occupied them. Should they vacate these lands the titles would revert to the government. Whites continued to raid and carry off slaves from the scattered Apalachicola reservations; steamboats stopped at these preserves, their crews corrupted Muscogulge men and women with whiskey and cash; and in a variety of ways the growing white population intimidated the Indians. Neamathla and his disciples withdrew into southern Alabama, still determined to defend a shrinking Hitchiti domain.[44]

Blount and his friendly-Creek following thought moving beyond the Mississippi an excellent idea, the only solution. Neamathla, on the other hand, expected Muscogulges in the Southeast, despite ancient rivalries, to stand up to the Americans, and Neamathla removed the ears of those who thought emigration a wise policy.[45] At the same time farther north in Alabama the angry Upper Creek Tuskeneha snapped his loaded rifle at pro-removal Alexander Moniac.[46] As Neamathla became obstinate and eventually moved into Alabama, in white eyes he was transforming himself from a Seminole into a Creek, and Americans decided that the acculturated and more accommodating mestizo, the Miccosukee John Hicks (Tuckose Emathla), should be head of the Seminole nation.[47] In a melodramatic and not necessarily accurate account, Washington Irving described how the intrepid Governor Duval single-handedly rode into Neamathla's camp and, though "thirty or forty rifles were cocked and leveled," denounced the chief and subsequently "appoint[ed] another in his place."[48]

The Tuckabatchee Blount had long been the rival and enemy of the Hitchiti Neamathla and other non-Muskogee Indians, having fought red sticks in upper Alabama and ridden with Jackson against Bowlegs Town. Kinsmen of Peter McQueen, Hillis Haya, and Bowlegs lived in central Florida, and Blount knew what he was about at Moultrie Creek when he told the Americans that he could never join these Indians: he must be allowed to remain on the Apalachicola.

238   Blount was distressed that his powerful friendly-Creek ally
McIntosh had been killed in 1825 and especially that the United
States Army and Indian agents after the First Seminole War saw
little need to woo Blount. Seminole agent John Phagan threatened to break Blount as a chief and cut off financial aid unless
he became more conciliatory. In desperation some of Blount's
followers rejoined their Upper Creek kinsmen in Alabama, and
a few moved to the Florida peninsula to the south; but for Blount
and most of his band, moving beyond the Mississippi seemed
the best and almost only solution. Years before, presumably
while Blount lived among the Upper Creeks, his Koasati uncle
Red Moccasin had moved to the upper Trinity River in Texas,
and Mexican Texas, not American Oklahoma, was where the
aged Blount resolved to go. As a youth Blount had hunted with
his uncle on the Trinity and he knew the region well.[49]

William McIntosh's execution had shocked Blount and other
friendly Creeks; McIntosh's death seemed to have the hubris of
a classical Greek tragedy in which the hero, at the zenith of his
power and prestige, was suddenly cut down. Around 1821 Mc-
Intosh's wealth and influence had never been greater. He had
assisted Jackson at Horseshoe Bend and subsequently accompanied him into Florida, and McIntosh's partnership with former
Georgia governor David Mitchell had enriched them both. Visitors at McIntosh's commodious tavern at Indian Springs in
north-central Georgia, east of the Indian country proper, dined
at a well-provided table and enjoyed the finest wines. Whites
considered McIntosh author of the "Laws of the Creek Nation,"
which symbolized Indian progress toward civilization, and they
regarded McIntosh as the speaker, principal chief, or headman
of the Creeks. In addition to his wives (Creek Susanna Coe, and
Cherokee Peggie), plantation, and two-story house at Acorn
Town (Lockchau Talofau) on the west bank of the Chattahoochee, McIntosh had another wife (the mestizo Eliza) and plantation fifty miles away on the Tallapoosa in the Upper Creek
country, and he had supporters among Cherokees and allies like
the friendly Creek Blount to the south.

Yet in 1825 angry Creeks had surrounded McIntosh's house
at Acorn Town, set it afire, forced McIntosh outside, and riddled

his body with bullets. McIntosh had known he had enemies and was in danger. He branded his critics as red sticks, disciples of the fanatic prophets who, despite Horseshoe Bend and Jackson's invasion of Florida, had not been crushed. There was some truth in his assertions: Upper Creek Menawa, his body horribly scarred, had survived Horseshoe Bend. That McIntosh had been there with Jackson still haunted him. Menawa commanded the Upper Creeks who surrounded McIntosh's house and shot him repeatedly when he fled from the burning structure.

Another good, and perhaps the most important, reason for McIntosh's execution was that he had been bribed to cede most of the Creek lands still claimed by Muscogulges in the East. In the 1825 Treaty of Indian Springs he relinquished all territory in Georgia and two-thirds of the native domain in Alabama, and he was paid handsomely for this cession.[50] He had resolved to move to Oklahoma, having fixed his star to that of the whites. His position depended on their benevolence and military support, which he expected to continue after he and his followers relocated in Oklahoma. The mestizo McIntosh wondered how often he and his three wives would be invited to dine at the white man's table if he remained in the East. McIntosh's rivals did not see it that way, which explains why the scarred Menawa and his followers continued to riddle McIntosh's corpse with lead balls long after he had died.[51]

Menawa enjoyed widespread support among the Muscogulge people—Upper and Lower Creeks and Seminoles, Muskogees and non-Muskogees alike. The venerable and powerful Lower Creek Chief Little Prince, a non–English-speaking Hitchiti, collaborated with Menawa and denounced McIntosh's pretensions and his conduct at Indian Springs. Lower Creek Yuchis, according to McIntosh a conquered (stinkard) tribe, joined in the criticism. The Tuckabatchees also turned against McIntosh. Fundamentally the Tuckabatchees were non-Muskogees and rivals of the Cowetas. In 1825 they were incensed by McIntosh's actions, which threatened destruction of the Creek's domain, and they instructed Opothle Yahola, their singer or speaker, to have nothing to do with McIntosh and his Indian Springs concessions. Opothe Yahola was a Potato, and Potatoes, Tigers, and Alliga-

240   tors, most numerous among non-Muskogee people, were conspicuous among McIntosh's critics.

Much has been made of the role of the National Council and
of the "Laws of the Creek Nation." In the events leading up to
McIntosh's death, McIntosh had violated these laws by selling
lands, and the council had therefore broken McIntosh and ordered his death, or at least this is the way it appeared to whites.
McIntosh's execution, decreed by the Creek central government, was thus not an example of primitive clan vengeance but
an illustration of the workings of a modern judicial system.[52] But
both the National Council and the "Laws of the Creek Nation"
were white inspired. A centralized government had never lain
easy on the Muscogulge clans and moieties, and the council had
never had the power and significance whites and interested
Indians claimed.

Furthermore, eastern Indians, including Muscogulges, had a
long tradition of selling lands that did not belong to them; in
this regard McIntosh's actions were not unique. The prevalence
of the practice did not, however, prevent Indians whose lands
were disposed of without their consent from being furious, and
Upper Creeks in 1825 were no exception. The Okfuske Menawa,
presumably a Coosa descendant, had fought against McIntosh
at Horseshoe Bend. He and 125 others, including old red sticks
and friendly Creeks, Muskogees, and those in the opposite
moiety, set off after McIntosh. Menawa and the angry warriors
accompanying him were mad because McIntosh had sold their
lands and they feared that diverse Muscogulges might soon lose
virtually all of their eastern domain. McIntosh and the Coweta
Etomme Tustunnuggee were killed, and the mestizo interpreter,
Samuel Hawkins, was forced to "eat fire" before being hanged.[53]

In the period just before his death McIntosh realized to his
dismay that he could no longer rely on the United States Army.
In the past American soldiers often had accompanied him as he
persecuted red sticks and magnified the importance of the National Council. American troops had been at McIntosh's side at
Horseshoe Bend, at the treaty negotiations at Fort Jackson, and
in the Florida expeditions. Yet after the First Seminole War and

the acquisition of Florida in 1821, American troops were conspicuous by their absence from the Upper and Lower Creek
country. Fort Jackson was abandoned, Fort Mitchell near Coweta had few if any troops, and farther down the Chattahoochee
both Fort Scott and Fort Gadsden lay deserted in the early 1820s.
In 1821 the Americans took over Spanish forts at Pensacola and
Saint Marks, and in 1824 they erected Fort Brooke at Tampa.
Garrisons at these posts, however, were small, and many miles
from McIntosh at Coweta.

McIntosh understood, as did the Indians, that American soldiers could descend on the Indians on short notice, but unfortunately for McIntosh these troops in the early 1820s were likely
to be Georgia militia rather than United States regulars. Mc-
Intosh's first cousin Governor Troup was anxious to send in
state militia to support surveyors, intimidate the Indians, and
clear them out of Georgia. After the invention of the cotton gin
in 1793, Georgia's back-country white population exploded, and
in the 1820s, in contrast to the era of the American Revolution,
whites vastly outnumbered the Creeks. Native Americans living in villages and owning land communally or residing on
isolated plantations barred these Georgians' westward expansion. Citing a variety of treaties, Governor Troup and small
farmers hoping to obtain frontier lands through the state lottery
demanded that Indians surrender all territory in the state. The
fact that some of the Creeks, especially mixed-bloods—and
McIntosh was a good example—had adopted much of the white
culture made little difference. Creeks must go; "should a militia
army [from Georgia] be marched into the Indian territory, there
is reason to apprehend that 'humanity' would not be inscribed
on its banners."[54] McIntosh understood that with the backing
of white soldiers he could stay in the East, but he also knew that
when he no longer had their support he would have to leave.

Acculturated friendly Creeks in Georgia had much in common with friendly Creeks on the Tensaw and Chief Blount and
his followers on the Apalachicola, all of whom were taunted
about their mixed ancestry and pressured to move. In contrast
the red stick Weatherford and his friends in southwest Alabama,

242   off the beaten path, remained on their farms relatively unmolested. McIntosh knew the minds of Troup and the Georgians, and he realized this was not likely to be his fate.

As McIntosh saw it, Creeks had to move, and he was determined to make the best of a bad situation. Through legal payments and bribes he would be compensated for surrendering Creek lands. He would take this money, his slaves, his moveable property, and his friends, and move beyond the Mississippi. As a youth he had accompanied hunting parties up the Arkansas River, and he knew that good farming and hunting lands were available just east of the Great Plains, the "Great American Desert." In a perverse sense McIntosh was like white farmers selling out eastern homesteads and going west to better their fortunes. This helps explain why McIntosh took the lead in concluding the 1825 Treaty of Indian Springs. He and the Upper and Lower Creeks in his party ceded all their eastern domain except a small area in eastern Alabama.[55] According to provisions of the treaty, Creeks determined to remain in the East had little choice but to move to this constricted domain in Alabama, join Cherokees in the North, or Seminoles in the South. None of these eastern areas, except possibly Florida, seemed to offer much of a long-term solution.

McIntosh's son Chilly rode furiously eastward to Georgia's capital at Milledgeville to bring news of his father's death. He and others in the McIntosh faction asked for protection, all the while affirming they supported the Treaty of Indian Springs. He asked them to give the McIntosh faction as much of the treaty money as possible; to protect them, their slaves, cattle, and property; and to help them to move to the western Indian territory as soon as possible. This was one point on which Georgians and federal officials were inclined to agree with the Indians. Beginning in 1827 Roley McIntosh, William's half-brother; Chilly McIntosh, his son; and their followers, travelling directly west overland or by steamboat via the Tennessee, Mississippi, and Arkansas Rivers, made their way to the Indian territory. By the end of 1828 hundreds of the McIntosh faction had arrived at newly built Fort Gibson near the intersection of the Arkansas and Grand Rivers. From there they were soon sent on to their new homeland on the Verdigris River not far away. Well-to-do and first on the scene, the Creeks in the McIntosh faction acquired the best lands, and United States soldiers at Fort Gibson were solicitous of their well-being. Were William McIntosh alive he could not have been displeased.[56]

Receiving timely reports of the departure of the McIntosh faction, friendly Creek (Seminole) Chief Blount feared for his safety, and, for the same reasons as Roley and Chilly McIntosh, resolved to leave. Florida territorial officials were happy to assist, and we know that Blount and his followers departed in 1833. But the Tuckabatchee Blount settled on the Trinity River in east Texas, not with the Cowetas in Oklahoma.

With President Jackson's enthusiastic blessing, the United States Congress in 1830 had passed the famous Indian removal bill, which provided for relocating eastern Indians beyond the Mississippi. It is not fair to credit or blame Jackson exclusively for this controversial measure; it enjoyed widespread support, especially in the southern States where most Indians lived. Critics of this policy merely quibbled over details of removal or used the issue for partisan purposes to get at King Andrew.[57] Even so the Muscogulge peoples would have preferred that in 1788 young Jackson had not made his way over the mountains to seek his fortune in Tennessee. They knew that the Americans expected all Muscogulges, not just the McIntosh and Blount factions, to emigrate. Whether or not they had been signed by corrupt and bribed chiefs, the treaties of Indian Springs, Washington, and Fort Mitchell were valid according to the United States: Creeks had ceded Georgia lands, and state authorities in Alabama extended state law over all the Creek domain in Alabama, which legally annihilated most of the Indians' culture and communal property rights.

In 1832 American agents met with Seminole chiefs at Payne's Landing, and the following year with a delegation at Fort Gibson. There is much confusion over the terms of the two resulting treaties, but Americans insisted that the Seminoles had first agreed in principle to western removal, and then, after examining their new homeland, committed themselves to depart immediately.[58]

244   By 1833 Americans could cite various treaties whereby essentially all Muscogulge people had agreed to relocate in the West. Indians did not think these treaties valid, and perhaps were not even aware of them. They did know that some Indians had gone West, and that Georgians, Alabamians, and Floridians coveted their lands. The Muscogulges were despondent. Some sought solace in drink. Appeals that "our eyes are overwhelmed at the thought" of removal, that we throw ourselves on the protection of the federal government, and that "our only crime was being placed by the Master of Breath in the neighborhood of Georgia," were of no avail.[59] Creek students at Withington grumbled that there seemed little use in getting an education if they had no home to return to: why study and worship God when they might die in the bushes?[60] Dejected Upper and Lower Creeks moved to the South, joining Florida kinsmen and becoming Seminoles. The American threat to Florida seemed less acute partly because, as Creek hunters knew, much of the peninsula was unsuited to cotton cultivation. Nevertheless more and more Muscogulges reluctantly accepted the fact that they must move to the West.

The Defiant Muscogulges, 1835–42

To help prod Seminoles to emigrate, Major Francis Langhorne Dade's command of blue-coated soldiers set out from Fort Brooke at Tampa in late December 1835. Despite his vigilance the major was ambushed enroute to Fort King one hundred miles to the north. Dade and virtually all his men were killed. This "massacre" ignited hostilities that lasted at least seven years, and the conflict engulfed the Southeast from the Everglades in the South to large parts of Alabama and Georgia in the North. Whether inhabited by Indians or recently settled by whites, much of the Muscogulge domain was in turmoil, and, as in 1813, from the Indians' perspective these hostilities represented both a civil and a foreign war. Muscogulge warriors battled regular United States troops and state militias, but at the same time they savagely fought each other. Paradoxically if the Seminole and Creek nations ever existed, it was in the years after Dade's misfortune, when savage warfare and the relocation effort were contributing to their eventual demise.

The length and bitterness of the conflict and the mounting number of casualties surprised whites, not that it was any secret that the Muscogulge people opposed relocation. The Muscogulges, however, were the only southeastern Indians who in any significant way violently resisted removal. Indications of unrest before Dade's ambush were common. Indians killed whites,

246   each other, and in despair committed suicide. Settlers occupied more and more of the Southeast, driving Muscogulges off their lands and forcing them into the woods and swamps to live off swamp cabbage, kunti, smilax, bark, fish, and such game as was available. Those who came back and prowled about their old cabins and square grounds, stole corn from settlers' cribs or green ears from the field, or killed cattle and hogs, were whipped or worse.

According to treaties concluded during the 1820s Musco-gulges had ceded all of their domain in Georgia, and surveyors with their instruments crisscrossed the western part of the state preparing to offer it for distribution by lottery. Yuchis and Hitch-itis on the Chattahoochee and Flint rivers protested in vain that they did not want to move to Oklahoma with McIntosh, to cross the Chattahoochee and live with Creeks in Alabama, or, if they were mestizos, to remain but deny that they were Indians. But Georgians were not to be stopped. They founded Columbus in 1828, took over more and more of the Lower Creek lands, and forced the Creeks to join their brethren in Alabama, to go north and live with the Cherokees near Chickamauga or south with the Seminoles, or else flee to the woods. The Georgia governor threatened to unleash regular troops and swarms of state militia on the Indians—"that lawless band of robbers" more savage than wild beasts—who stood in the way.[1]

Conditions in Alabama were about the same, except that for the moment Creeks tenuously clung to a large eastern domain containing the highest percentage of the Muscogulge people, twenty-five thousand or so. The 1832 treaty assumed, though it did not actually require, that Indians must move to Oklahoma if they did not remain on their individual allotments. Without concern for details of this and previous agreements between the federal government and the Creeks, state authorities extended state law over the Creek Territory, and speculators proceeded to inveigle allotments from any Indian rash enough to consider staying in the East. The cupidity of land-speculating companies in Columbus and Montgomery and abuses associated with "per-sonification" were notorious: "if fraud and corruption ever ap-proximated to perfection, it has done so in this case."[2] If one yahola, tastanagi, emathla (imala), or mico refused to sell his allotment, another Indian having the same title easily could be found and witnesses bribed to attest that this yahola or mico was the true owner. Sometimes legitimate owners were paid a fair price, but through force or trickery the land speculator soon got back most or all of his money. White newcomers grazed livestock on uncultivated lands lying inside fences encircling Indian towns, and settlers denied that village headmen had any authority to expel horses from the talwa's communal fields. Muscogulges having complaints were directed to seek relief in county courts, but, as lawyers for the land companies pointed out, Indian testimony was untrustworthy, and, like that of Negroes, inadmissible. "Hurrah boys! Here goes it! Let's steal all we can."[3]

Experiences of the Lower Creeks at Eufaula illustrate the plight of the Alabama Muscogulges. This old Indian town on the Chattahoochee was in newly created Barbour County. In defiance of treaties and federal regulations, immigrants rushed in, established the town of Irwinton, and began planting cotton and developing a riverboat town on the old Eufaula talwa. They erected log houses on communal fields and the square ground, and they burned or destroyed Indian cabins, unconcerned that the 1832 treaty allowed Creeks to select allotments where their houses stood and that the federal government had promised to protect the Indians. Whites sometimes leased or otherwise got Indian approval to settle on these allotments, but frequently they did not bother. Both Alabamians and federal authorities planned to remove the Indians, only the United States insisted it be done in a legal, methodical, and humane fashion, which took time. As a result in 1832 federal marshals, backed up by regular troops from Fort Mitchell, ran off settlers and burned their cabins. Angry whites returned, accompanied by the local sheriff, and in the ensuing commotion a soldier bayoneted the sheriff. The press in Alabama and elsewhere played this incident up. Coming on the heels of the South Carolina nullification controversy, it was portrayed as a states' rights contest. Though wounded and staining Alabama's soil with his blood, the Barbour County sheriff had manfully stood up to the tyranny of

248   federal troops. Indians were not overly concerned with Calhoun's logic and the fine points of states' rights. The reality for Foshatchemarthla, Yeleka Harjo, and other Eufaulas was that intruders had occupied their houses, fenced and divided the talwa's fields, harvested their ripening corn, and forced women and children along with the warriors to live in nearby woods like animals or to join the Seminoles in Florida.[4]

With less fanfare Irwinton's experience was duplicated elsewhere in Alabama. Wavering Creeks felt compelled to bow to the will of state authorities lest they be forced to join Foshatchemarthla's townsmen in the wilds. Opothleyahola reluctantly accepted the fact that removal was inevitable; from the Tuckabatchee square he counseled anyone who would listen to dispose of his allotment and property and prepare to go west.[5] Many followed his advice. But Hitchitis, Chehaws, Eufaulas, Miccosukees, Yuchis, and others in the Chattahoochee Valley, remembering Irwinton and reluctant to follow the lead of the Tuckabatchee Opothleyahola, sullenly withdrew to the interior, and established new, often inaccessible villages in swamps and pine barrens in the Hatchechubbee Creek Valley between Fort Mitchell and Irwinton. Hunters continued to cross the Chattahoochee River into Georgia, spending several months deep in the woods, having few if any contacts with whites.

The experiences of Muscogulges in Florida before Dade's ambush had been similar to those in Alabama, and one could see the new towns of Tallahassee, Quincy, and Monticello arising on the sites of Muscogulge villages. The difference was that not many Indians were in the vicinity—Jackson had cleared them out in 1818—and those who remained usually were friendly Creeks or transient hunting parties whose remote campfires could be seen dimly at night. A majority of Florida Muscogulges lived on the Seminole Reservation on the peninsula. But Muscogulges in northern Florida, like those in eastern Alabama, saw their square grounds and ball poles desecrated, and they sometimes lashed out at newcomers. The Indians killed cattle and pigs roaming the woods and harvested green ears of maize.[6] When they were caught, culprits were flogged and ordered to prepare to emigrate immediately. With fresh scars on their backs, embittered refugees joined Neamathla on Hatchechubbee Creek in Alabama, or Osceola near the Withlacoochee in Florida. Emigration was not foremost in their minds.

The greatest center of Muscogulge discontent and militancy was on the Florida Seminole Reservation. South of the reservation the entire peninsula was open to the Indians; only Fort Brooke stood in the way and there was some question about who surrounded whom. The white population of Florida, roughly 45,000 in the mid-1830s, was concentrated in northern Florida, and the governors of Alabama and Georgia were reluctant to let their militias out of their states. All of this contributed to Seminole defiance and to the hope that even at this late date they could remain in the Southeast and continue their old lifestyle. With little fanfare, mounted hunters leading packhorses absented themselves from central Florida villages for months, journeying to northern Florida and especially to the peninsula's southernmost tip for game. They exchanged peltry for munitions and trading goods with American, Cuban, and Bahamian merchants. Indians—and sometimes whites—suggested that since southern Florida seemed so uninviting the Indians should keep it.

This was not to be, and as good an explanation as any was the Negro controversy. The southeastern underground railroad ran not north to Canada but south through Florida to Cuba and the Bahamas, and white concerns about fugitive slaves and the collusion of Indian-Negroes with plantation slaves were justified. Such concerns were what Floridians had in mind when they insisted that the Seminoles who were truly Indians must be separated and removed from Negroes and whites in their midst if the Indians were to recover their ancient spirit and vigor.[7]

During all this controversy Powell (Osceola) emerged from obscurity. Like Tecumseh, his roots were in the Upper Creek country. Tallassee refugees, Osceola and his mother had associated themselves with Peter McQueen's band in Florida after the War of 1812. Both Asi Yahola (Osceola) and Opothleyahola were Upper Creek speakers or singers, presumably having a special relationship with the Supreme Being; both yaholas had

250   assumed positions of leadership. But while the Master of Breath
instructed Opotheyahola to be a moderate and reluctantly accept removal, this deity commanded Powell to resist like Peter
McQueen, Hillis Haya, and Savannah Jack. Oceola, a yahola, a
tastanagi, and an emerging war leader, resolved to obey the
Master of Breath, and he vented his hostility on whites and
accommodating Indians alike.

Charlie Emathla (or Emarthla) was the first to die. It is probably impossible to explain accurately his background and moti-
vations. In the 1830s he told the Americans he did not have
authority to speak for or commit the Seminole nation. This was
true for a variety of reasons, one being that Charlie Emathla was
a Creek—from Oswiches (Osochi) Town on the Chattahoochee.
A Lower Creek, whose ancestors in the distant past may have
lived in Timucua, Charlie Emathla was not part of the McIntosh
faction, and he remained behind in the late 1820s when
McIntosh's followers moved to the West. Creeks, however, and
Charlie Emathla was one of them, ceded all of their Georgia
lands in treaties concluded after McIntosh's death. If they did
not retreat into nearby piney barrens and swamps, Georgia
Creeks had the options of moving across the Chattahoochee
to Alabama, of joining the Cherokees, or of going to Florida.
Charlie Emathla opted for the last course, and in the 1830s
he had a small farm and herd of cattle near Fort King on the
Seminole Reservation.

In Florida Charlie Emathla reluctantly decided that he and
his band must do the Americans' bidding and move to the West.
A strident critic of McIntosh and removal, the Upper Creek
Opothleyahola by the 1830s had changed his mind and was counseling Muscogulges to sell their allotments and property and
follow him to Oklahoma. Charlie Emathla followed the same
course. He signed the Seminole removal treaties of Payne's Landing and Fort Gibson and, though denouncing fraud and intimidation associated with them, collaborated with American soldiers and prepared to move. In November 1835 he drove his cattle
to Fort King for sale.

Osceola and his warriors met Charlie Emathla when he was
returning home, shot him, and scattered the money on the

ground by his body. Opothleyahola and Muscogulges accepting removal in Alabama were in the majority, but the opposite was the case among the Muscogulge people in Florida. Charlie Emathla understood this, gambled, and lost. A tastanagi, a warrior of the first rank, Osceola may have felt there was reason why Charlie was merely an emarthla, a warrior of second rank.[8]

According to the best information available, Osceola had two wives, one of whom was a Negro, and it is probable that Osceola himself had African ancestry. For whatever reason Seminole-Negroes deeply concerned Osceola. As whites saw it, Osceola and the Seminoles were refractory in part because of the Negro influence, and whites blamed William Lloyd Garrison and his northern abolitionist friends. One suspects that Osceola and the Seminoles never read Garrison's *Liberator* or knew anything about the tirades against the buying and selling of slaves in the national capital. The abolitionist tradition, deeply rooted among the black Muscogulges, derived not from Garrison but from British subjects including Thomas Brown of the American revolutionary era, and William Augustus Bowles, Edward Nicholls, George Woodbine, and Robert Ambrister of a later period. Blacks at the Negro Fort on the Apalachicola River, even some of those whom McIntosh had taken back to Georgia and sold, in one fashion or another made their way to the Seminole country, never forgetting what the Negro Fort had symbolized.[9]

In 1835 whites became alarmed by Charlie Emarthla's death, the prospect of an Indian war, and the recalcitrance of the blacks. As Major Dade was marching to reinforce Fort King, the militia increased the vigilance of its patrols throughout northern Florida to prevent intercourse between plantation slaves or urban domestics and the Indian country. East Floridians in Saint Augustine repaired old Spanish defenses, unsure whether the greatest danger was from Indians without or the Negroes within.[10] The Negro threat seemed the more acute. In 1835 Hannah, Joe, María García, and other Negroes from Saint Augustine and its environs ran away and joined the Seminoles. Painted Seminoles also attended a Negro dance on an outlying plantation. East Florida sugar plantations had a high percentage of Negroes, and apprehensive whites armed themselves and took precautions.[11]

252   Throughout the southeastern Muscogulge country, one encountered fear, suspicion, despondency, resentment, and violence. Nowhere was this more the case than in the fastness of Big Swamp and below the Withlacoochee where the obdurate tastanagi Powell, surrounded by Upper Creek red-stick refugees, Seminoles proper, and Negroes, had built villages and planted maize and rice in secluded locations still unknown today.

Fort Brooke at Tampa and Fort King to the north lay on the edge of these villages. Indian belligerency made it essential to reinforce the undermanned, exposed garrison at Fort King. Major Dade set out from Fort Brooke on 23 December 1835 with just over one hundred men, aware of the danger and that he was vastly outnumbered by followers of Powell, Micanopy, and other hostile chiefs. After six days out, despite precautions, he was surprised on terrain that had become less swampy and more open. Lining one side of the military road, Seminoles ambushed the command, and killed the major and half his men in the first volley. Dazed survivors huddled together, threw up a triangular log breastwork, and, with their cannon bravely firing, held the enemy for several hours. But surrounded in an exposed pen, they dropped one by one. Muscogulge warriors strode over the battlefield, stripped corpses of arms and clothing, jubilantly dismantled the cannon, and threw it in a nearby pond.[12] Word of Dade's misfortune spread as fast throughout the Indian country as it did among white settlements. Two and one-half weeks elapsed before citizens of Tallahassee and Mobile heard about Dade's undoing.[13] According to contemporary accounts the Indians took no scalps, but Negroes, after all danger was over, rushed in and, despite the "loud cries and groans [of the wounded] with hellish cruelty, pierced the throats of all" before scalping them.[14] Muscogulges exulted in their triumph, as well they might, because it was the last one of this magnitude they would ever know in the Southeast.

Indians behind oaks, pines, and palmettos were concealed from Dade in the nineteenth century and in many instances remain obscure in the twentieth. Nevertheless it is essential to examine as closely as possible those who lay in wait for Major Dade or who soon joined the hostiles. Even though this massacre was overshadowed by a worse one at the Alamo, much has been written about Dade's downfall. These accounts reveal at least something about the Indian enemy.

Over a long period of time Muscogulges, including those who were black, had been drawn or pushed into central Florida. Muscogulges continued to be attracted to Florida, and the Seminole population increased. Taking the broad view, the most obdurate Florida Seminoles were nineteenth-century Creek immigrants, the Tallassee Osceola (Powell) being the most famous. While Indians were preparing to ambush Dade, Osceola and some sixty followers were not there but almost fifty miles to the north outside Fort King, where Wiley Thompson, the Seminole agent, made his headquarters. Thompson symbolized to Osceola all the evil the white man had inflicted on the Indians. When the agent strolled outside the fort to smoke, Osceola and his companions riddled his body with fourteen balls, stabbed and scalped him, and killed a half-dozen other unfortunates. Osceola, of course, was not a native of Florida and had spent his youth as an Upper Creek on the Tallapoosa in Alabama. He became the best known Seminole war leader because of his military leadership, because he killed Thompson, and because just before his death his portrait was painted and widely disseminated.[15] Another Upper Creek refugee, Jumper (Ote Emathla), was older than Osceola. This red-stick warrior—"the last survivor of 'some ancient' tribe"—after arriving in Florida had married Micanopy's sister. In 1813 Jumper had rushed through the gate at Fort Mims, and twenty-two years later he was at Micanopy's side firing at Dade's men. Few Muscogulges ever saw more dead white soldiers.[16]

Osceola associated with the Miccosukees. Some of them had accompanied him to Fort King, and many more had hidden along the military road awaiting Dade. Miccosukees had migrated from the Flint and Chattahoochee rivers in Georgia and Alabama, to Apalachee in Florida, and then to the Seminole Reservation. In Georgia and Alabama these Hitchiti speakers were known as Lower Creeks. The fanatical Halleck Tustenuggee, who with his teeth ripped off the ear of an Indian contemplating surrender, and Chitto Hadjo, still fighting in 1843, were among

254 the Miccosukee leaders, but the best known, certainly the most determined, was Arpeika or Sam Jones. The birthplace of this diminutive hillis haya is unknown. Late in 1835 white-haired, seventy-year-old Arpeika was on the Seminole Reservation counseling Osceola to take revenge on Thompson at Fort King and Miccosukee warriors to be patient, conceal themselves, and wait for Dade. Months and years passed; Arpeika moved from one secluded hammock to another, losing his property and his followers, but neither old age nor, when he was in his eighties, even possible senility altered his resolve.[17]

The historic or "true" Seminoles were those Lower Creeks who in the mid–eighteenth century had moved from Georgia into the Payne's Prairie–Alachua region. By the time of the Second Seminole War they had resided there for nearly a century and their principal chief Micanopy was a lineal or collateral descendant of Payne and Cowkeeper. Micanopy owned slaves, cattle, fields, and a truck house; perhaps fear of losing his property made him cautious. In any case both Indians and whites portrayed corpulent Micanopy, living at Pelackakaha, east of Dade's battlefield, as lethargic and indecisive.[18] This was not the case of Halpatter Tustenuggee (Alligator), a confederate of Micanopy, and it was not necessary to prod this war leader into action. Alligator was a Eufaula, who during his or his parents' lifetime had immigrated into central Florida from the Creek country.[19] Young dark-eyed Coacoochee (Wildcat), apparently Micanopy's nephew and "by far the most dangerous chieftain in the field," again and again, with a rifle in his hand and a scalping knife thrust in his sash, caused the white man grief.[20]

Tallahassees were one of the hostile Seminole components and included Nehestocomatta among their leaders. Though "Tallahassee" is a common and confusing name, apparently Tallahassees were primarily Hitchitis and Yuchis who in the late eighteenth century had migrated southward and settled at Tallahassee in north Florida before being driven farther south by Jackson around 1818. Almost two decades later they composed part of the Indians concealing themselves alongside the military road.[21]

Americans decreed that Spanish Indians were Seminoles and

must move beyond the Mississippi. The embittered, enterprising, six-foot-tall Spanish Indian war leader Chakaika made it
clear to the Americans that it was not his intention to relocate
where there was no salt water. As far as is known he was not at
Dade's massacre, but other Spanish Indians were.[22]

Yuchis were Lower Creeks, primarily from the Flint-Chat-
tahoochee region, who had migrated into Florida, often retaining
much of their separate language and identity. They joined the
Seminoles waiting for Dade. Accounts of the massacre do not
mention the presence of any prominent Yuchi leader. Two of the
foremost Yuchi warriors, Yuchi Billy (Billy Hicks) and Yuchi
Jack, who operated in the Saint Johns–Saint Marys region in East
Florida, apparently were not among those who confronted Dade.
At the outbreak of hostilities, however, Yuchi Billy went to Georgia and Alabama and brought over one hundred Yuchis with him
back to Florida; in the ensuing months these Yuchis caused
Florida whites grief enough.[23]

A number of Indian leaders—especially those arriving in Florida a few years before or just after Dade's massacre—continued
to be known as Creeks. Their number included Coe Hadjo, who
was later captured with Osceola; Miccopotokee, who led a small
band of hostile refugees in swamps above Fort King; Nokosc
Yahola, who fought in central Florida until captured at the end
of 1837; Pascofar, who did not submit until 1842 in the Florida
panhandle; and the Creek Prophet, Arpeika's advisor, who apparently never capitulated.[24] One could easily add to the list of
Creek war leaders. At no time was there an Indian commander
in chief, a generalissimo. Seminoles continued to be what they
always had been—an assemblage of southeastern remnant
tribes, who for a variety of reasons had found themselves in
territorial Florida. Their one common trait was that they often
did not have pure Muskogee ancestry; unless they were bilingual, however, they did not necessarily understand one another.

All this omits black Muscogulges. They killed their share of
Dade's command, and their conduct perhaps best explains why
Dade's men were caught off guard. Negroes were depicted by
abolitionists in heroic terms: living in Maroon communities or
independent settlements and valiantly striving to preserve their

256 African culture. When threatened they banded together and took up arms to become freedom fighters.

Black participation in the hostilities did not conform to this or any other stereotype. A percentage of the black Muscogulges or Indian-Negroes were highly acculturated, blacks or Negroes in name only, and in reality Indians, dressing like Muscogulges and belonging to a Muscogulge family, clan, and talwa. Like the Indians proper, some black Muscogulges fought each other, allied with whites, or struggled manfully against the Americans. Other black Muscogulges, Africans and Creoles alike, were conscious of their African ancestry, were aware that they were blacks or Negroes, not Indians, and thus often looked down upon and degraded by whites and to a lesser extent by Muscogulges. Blacks might dream about or hope to return to Africa, but that was a chimera. The reality was that they were, and were likely to remain, in the New World. Life among the Indians often seemed the best way to preserve something of their identity and their freedom. Warriors with Negroid features were among those awaiting Major Dade's approach. Some thought of themselves as Tigers, Alligators, and Potatoes; others as Hausas, Mandingos, and Fulanis.

The Negro Luis Pacheco was at Dade's ambush—not hidden behind saw palmettos but instead in the van guiding Dade's men. There has been much disagreement about details of Luis's early years and whose side Pacheco was really on. Likely a zambo, the slave Pacheco had been born on Francis P. Fatio's Saint Johns River plantation. His brother and sister lived with the Seminoles. Luis ran away in 1824, for a time lived among the Seminoles and the Spanish Indians, and then in some fashion again was enslaved. His new masters were American officers at Fort Brooke who used him as an interpreter, and the Spaniard Antonio Pacheco who employed Luis on his Sarasota Bay rancho. One can only guess whether in the mid-1830s, Luis, who was given his Spanish master's surname, was beginning to consider himself a Spanish Indian. In any case Dade, in a hurry to reinforce Fort King, needed a guide-interpreter, and Pacheco was available. The major and half his men fell in the first volley, but Pacheco survived. Captured by the Indians, he again lived with

Luis Pacheco. Reprinted by permission from *Edge of Wilderness: A Settlement History of Manatee River and Sarasota Bay,* © 1983 Janet Snyder Matthews. Courtesy the author.

258   them, with Jumper's band, and in 1838 he moved with Jumper
       and his party to the West. Luis had varied experiences as a slave
       and a freedman in Oklahoma, Arkansas, and Texas. Over a half
       century after Dade's massacre a wizened, white-bearded, ninety-
       three-year-old Negro appeared at the residence of Susan Fatio
       L'Engle in Jacksonville. A decade younger than Luis, she was
       the daughter of Luis's original master and had known Luis before
       he first ran off to the Indians. Pacheco (whose surname was now
       Fatio) described his remarkable career, all the while professing
       that he had not led Dade into a trap. When Luis died in 1895
       Susan buried him on the old Fatio Saint Johns River plantation
       at New Switzerland. Jacksonville citizens attended the funeral
       of the trusty and unfairly maligned "darky Fatio who had re-
       turned home to his missus." Perhaps the account Luis told the
       whites was accurate, or perhaps his story was a cover to allow
       him to discover what had happened to his Negro brother, sister,
       and wife, whom he had left behind many years ago. The answer
       lies buried at New Switzerland.[25]

       Lasting roughly seven years, the Second Seminole War ended
       not because there was a peace treaty, but because more than
       10,000 Muscogulges in Florida had died, moved to Oklahoma,
       or disappeared in remote swamps and piney barrens. Numerous
       works discuss the costly Second Seminole War, Osceola's cap-
       ture under a flag of truce, and the conduct of and bickering
       among regular officers whose names became better known dur-
       ing the Mexican and Civil Wars. Our purpose is not to redo this,
       but to consider the effects of Dade's massacre on Muscogulges
       in Florida and the Southeast. During the Second Seminole War,
       frustrated American commanders engaged in few pitched bat-
       tles. Several years later, when Winfield Scott, Thomas Jesup,
       and Zachary Taylor commanded American forces in Mexico,
       they fought as soldiers were supposed to: their artillery roared
       and their massed troops assaulted Chapultepec and the Halls of
       the Montezumas.

       Though one-sided, the encounter with Dade had lasted sev-
       eral hours. A week later troops under command of General
       Clinch set out to lay waste Seminole villages on the south side
       of the Withlacoochee River. As Clinch was crossing that river

Indians attacked his divided army, which with difficulty extricated itself, in the process suffering sixty-three casualties. In the ensuing months Clinch had to explain why his army, which was to overrun and lay waste the Seminole heartland, instead retired.[26] Two years later in December 1837 Seminole warriors made a stand in southern Florida on the north side of Lake Okeechobee. Forced to wade through swamps and sawgrass, soldiers were cut down by 500 entrenched and concealed Indians. Americans suffered 136 casualties; those of the Seminoles were substantially less.[27] These encounters or battles—Dade's massacre, Withlacoochee, Okeechobee, and perhaps one or two others—were anomalies. Each side suffered many deaths during seven years of hostilities, but small skirmishes and ambushes and especially diseases, in the Indians' case compounded by malnutrition, were the greatest killers—not battle casualties.

The Seminole population had steadily increased in the nineteenth century, and for a short time after Dade's ambush there was an additional spurt because of the migration of Upper and Lower Creeks into Florida. The case of a fugitive Alabama chief affords an example. Soldiers who had assembled him and his followers in preparation for removal demanded the Indians' guns. The chief (Echo Harjo?) was indignant, exclaiming that the Alabamians had robbed him of everything else and he would die before relinquishing his guns. He and 200 warriors—counting women and children between 800 and 1,000 total—fled to western Florida to seek refuge in inaccessible retreats spread out over 200 miles.[28] But in the latter half of 1836 most the of Alabama Creeks set out for their new homeland in the West, and the Florida Seminoles realized that their traditional Georgia and Alabama population reservoirs were drying up.

During the lengthy hostilities, troops hounded Seminole bands from one secluded hammock to another. Contemporary reports and folk tradition describe how Indian mothers smothered babies to keep them from disclosing their whereabouts. Abortions were more numerous than ever. At times American pursuers came upon the bodies of young children who had not been able to keep up, their nostrils and mouths stuffed with mudgrass.[29] Except under the most favorable circumstances,

260   Seminole warriors avoided pitched battles. Small encounters were the norm from one end of Florida to the other—at exposed sugar plantations on the Saint Johns River, new cotton plantations near Tallahassee, on roads used by couriers and wagoners en route from one army post to another, the lighthouse at Cape Florida on Key Biscayne, and exposed settlements west of the Apalachicola River in the panhandle. In 1836 nine Seminoles attacked the Johns's farmhouse not far from Jacksonville. Mr. Johns was killed, shot through the head. His young wife, Jane, apparently fatally shot, was in fact only seriously wounded. Though barely conscious she vividly remembered how a warrior grasped her hair with one hand, and using a long wooden-handled knife, deftly made a circular incision around her skull and ripped off her scalp. Eventually a rescue party discovered her and she was nursed back to health. Settlers in Florida and neighboring states marveled at accounts of her deliverance.[30]

Soldiers, sailors, friendly Indians, black spies, and double agents roamed, probed, and trampled over Florida to ferret out and destroy hostile Seminole bands. Hunting dogs often accompanied detachments attempting to pick up the Indians' trail. After several frustrating years American commanders imported Cuban bloodhounds, and a popular outcry of protest ensued. In the sixteenth century, Spanish conquistadores had used bloodhounds, and the practice had helped to create an anti-Spanish black legend. Soldiers of the new republic in the nineteenth century, critics charged, ought not cast themselves in the conquistadores' mold. Because of the furor, the dogs were hardly ever used. However, with the massacre of a nearby family in mind, the Florida governor in 1840 was anxious to unleash "blood hounds against [Indian] hell hounds."[31]

Military necessity forced Seminoles to seek refuge in hammocks deep in swamps, and it was fortunate for them that Florida was endowed with such terrain on which Muscogulges had long hunted and trapped. With some exaggeration Seminoles complained that they could not survive on the large reservation granted them in the 1823 treaty because most of the region was barren swampland. In 1835 a majority of the Seminoles lived on this reservation, and after the ambush of Dade and the Battle of

Withlacoochee, many Seminoles, including Osceola, withdrew to villages in the interior. American forces converged on or surrounded inhospitable, low-lying areas bordering the Withlacoochee River, and for the first year or so these were the most publicized Indian retreats. Seminoles insisted that if the Americans did not relent they would retire to the Big Swamp—the Everglades—and fight forever. To an extent this happened: in 1835 Arpeika, Coacoochee, and Alligator lived in villages in the Withlacoochee River Valley, but several years later they and their followers were scattered farther south among camps in the Everglades. The impression that essentially all Seminoles retired to the southern part of the peninsula, however, is misleading. Arpeika's village in 1841 was near Lake Okeechobee, but in the same year Octiarche's was on the Withlacoochee, and Alligator's was even farther north on the Steinhatchee. Other Seminoles took refuge in low-lying areas bordering Choctawhatchee Bay in the Florida panhandle. The largest swamp in northern Florida–southern Georgia was the Okefenokee, and the number of Muscogulges living in its interior increased after 1835.

One could mention other Florida refuges occupied by hard-pressed Muscogulge bands. Keeping to themselves, sometimes Indians were almost swallowed up by the inhospitable environment, though upon occasion warriors sallied forth to burn a plantation or ambush soldiers. Constantly patrolling and probing, the army and navy discovered some of these refuges, and after a brief skirmish burned the cabins. Whatever their exact locations, these retreats, these villages, were scattered all over Florida.

Despite their isolation and being separated by hundreds of miles, Muscogulges regularly kept in touch with each other, not only in Florida but also in Georgia and Alabama. Garrisoned forts, mounted patrols, steamboats, and light draft vessels on rivers and streams could not prevent Indians from going almost anywhere. Walking, running, riding horseback, or burying dugouts in the sand and digging them up after soldiers passed, in one fashion or another Muscogulges readily traversed great distances.

262   Occasionally one gets a glimpse of the Indian sanctuaries. Spies sometimes led soldiers to Seminole camps, and subsequent official reports described the fifty to one hundred cabins or huts laid out in an irregular fashion, perhaps with an identifiable square ground. Soldiers were surprised by fine crops of corn and rice about a foot high, along with potatoes and other vegetables, red and white flour from smilax and zamia, and signs of large herds of horses and cattle, all of which, though not many miles from military forts or white settlements, had long gone undetected.[32] Sometimes Seminoles were captured or met soldiers to parley. Accompanied by six warriors between sixteen and thirty years old, the Miccosukee Halleck Tustenuggee in 1839 came to Fort King to meet with General Macomb: the Indians were miserably poor, a "wicked and demon-like looking set of savages," but self-possessed in spite of everything. The men wore dirty and tattered cotton or deerskin shirts.[33] From time to time soldiers noticed that Seminole warriors were armed with bows and arrows. This did not mean that Indians had degenerated to a more primitive state but that they had no powder or that in dangerous times they had found it expedient to hunt silently.[34]

       During the Creek War Tustunnuck Hadjo in Alabama advised his fellow townsmen never to accept relocation beyond the Mississippi but instead to go to remote inaccessible regions on the Gulf Coast east of Pensacola, where the Indians could live off fish, game, and kunti, and grow a few vegetables in the sandy soil. An elderly Upper Creek matriarch took his advice, and leading a small band of eleven, including her children and grandchildren, moved to the Florida panhandle. After living in the woods for a year or more she emerged, and presented herself before friendly Indians and the local Indian agent: if our chief (Tustunnuck Hadjo) and his tribe could see us now with our new blankets and clothes given us by the agent he would know he was wrong. She urged friendly Creeks to find the rest of her clan and townsmen before the whites did and killed them. Oklahoma could be no worse.[35]

       Preserved in Seminole folklore is an account of how American soldiers relentlessly pursued the Indians farther and farther south. After reaching Lake Okeechobee the Indians divided, one party going the long way around the lake on horseback, and the other taking the shorter route on foot. When the two weary, nearly starved groups finally united, they decided to celebrate with a *wacka-wilanua-defiskilan*, "to kill cattle and get all messed up." Just as they prepared to eat, soldiers arrived; the warriors took up their arms, fought, retreated into a cypress swamp, fought again, and then after losing their cattle, lit pine torches and made their way at night out of the swamp to safety. Here they planted crops and lived unmolested for some time. Soldiers and sailors, however, once more discovered them. Hillis hayas again made war medicine, and additional fighting ensued. Some hard-pressed fugitives were driven toward the Atlantic coast where soldiers, waving a white flag, fed them and treated them kindly . . . until Indians were put on a ship that sailed away, never to be heard from. Arpeika had stayed behind, warning about the white man's white flags, but to no avail.[36]

At one time or another during the 1835–42 era, parties of Florida Indians, like the elderly grandmother, became discouraged. They either agreed to board a steamboat and go west, or else they were captured and forcibly sent away. The most famous was the Upper Creek tastanagi Osceola. Polemical and sentimental tracts have denounced his treacherous seizure under a flag of truce, and the true facts may never be known. For whatever reason—sickness, an attempt to deceive the whites and buy time, or the realization that he could not fight forever—late in 1837 Osceola let it be known that he was willing to parley. General Jesup arranged a meeting below Saint Augustine and ordered General Joseph Hernandez and his men to ride out and meet the Indian delegation. A Spanish Floridian whose family had risen from modest circumstances to prosperity, Hernandez resented the Indians' destruction of his plantations and carrying off his slaves. A white flag previously given to the Indians waved over Osceola's camp whose number included Coe Hadjo, seventy-one warriors, six women, and four black Seminoles. As the parley began, Hernandez's men unobtrusively surrounded the Indians and then, without firing a shot, captured them. Then captives and captors alike marched back to Saint Augustine

264   where the Indians were incarcerated in the stone Castillo de San
        Marcos. Osceola's two wives and two of his children joined the
        sick warrior, and after two months all were sent on to Fort
        Moultrie in Charleston, where George Catlin met and painted
        the Seminole chief before his death. Soldiers buried Osceola
        outside the fort and sent the surving Seminoles on to the West.
        Friends of the Indians and abolitionists castigated Jesup and
        Hernandez and eulogized the noble warrior. Typical white sen-
        timents coming out of the southeastern states—the old Mus-
        cogulge domain—denounced "False and hollow-hearted philan-
        thropists, who exhaust their sympathy on the Indians—while
        sitting by their firesides and on their carpeted floors."[37] Many
        an Indian, not just Osceola, was seized under a white truce flag.
            Hernandez had captured the Miccosukee Coacoochee (Wild-
        cat) along with Osceola, and these Indian war leaders may have
        hoped to make an arrangement with the whites short of emigra-
        tion. In his dark castillo cell Wildcat realized that this was not
        to be. Fifteen feet above the coquina cell floor was a narrow,
        barred window through which Wildcat and about twenty others,
        after removing the bars, slipped to freedom. In late November
        1837 Wildcat was confined in Saint Augustine; less than a
        month later he was two hundred miles to the south leading
        Miccosukees at the Battle of Okeechobee, doing more than his
        share to cause the 138 white casualties. However, he was cap-
        tured again in 1841 near Fort Pierce, and this time he urged his
        Miccosukee followers to come in and submit. Relatively few of
        the ten thousand Seminoles remained in Florida after six years
        of hostilities, and further resistance seemed pointless. As the
        American steamer bound for the West dipped below the horizon
        in October 1841, Wildcat finally lost sight of Florida.[38]
            Osceola fought in Florida until 1837 and Wildcat until 1841;
        but the diminutive Arpeika never gave up. Opposing the Amer-
        icans at every chance, he saw his following dwindle. Better than
        most of the Muscogulge people in Florida, Miccosukees could
        claim to be the ancient inhabitants of the land. As a Miccosukee
        medicine man Arpeika had a special commitment to preserve
        the Hitchiti culture and domain. Years of incessant warfare and
        possibly even senility took their toll, but only death when he

was at least ninety and perhaps over one hundred extinguished his recalcitrance. He was buried in the Southeast in the same general region where centuries ago the Master of Breath had severed his peoples' umbilical cord. By 1842 Wildcat and most of the hostile bands had departed for the West. Arpeika and his few followers in the Everglades and other Indians in inaccessible sanctuaries did not seem much of a danger, and Americans may not even have been aware of their existence. Unilaterally American authorities declared the long contest over and withdrew soldiers and sailors.[39]

The Muscogulge people in Florida and American military commanders realized that it was impossible to separate what was happening in Florida from events in Alabama and Georgia. The Second Seminole War in Florida and the Creek War in Alabama, both occurring in the 1830s, stemmed from similar causes, and involved the same Indian people; nevertheless they have been portrayed as distinct conflicts. Dade's massacre was in December 1835, and the main Creek outbreak in Alabama and Georgia did not occur until the following May, the most intense period being between May and June 1836. The Muscogulge people known as Creeks for the most part lived in Alabama, and were exasperated by fraudulent practices of land speculators, racial epithets, and Jackson's removal policy. A lesser number remained in Georgia. From the standpoint of local white authorities these Indians had ceded their lands and few had any legal right to be in the state. Even so a number of diehards were there and as such were among the most oppressed and angry of all the Muscogulges. Employed by whites to pick cotton, some were murdered in the fields. Others, forced off their lands, crossed the Chattahoochee into Alabama and, despite the fact that Indian canoes were illegal on that river, later returned to prey on settlers' cattle, crops, and sometimes the Georgians themselves. The bodies of two such Creeks who had been caught and killed were taken to Columbus and displayed conspicuously at the courthouse.[40]

Whether in Alabama or Georgia, the primary resistance came from Yuchis, Hitchitis, and other non-Muskogees. Three of the principal Indian leaders—Jim Henry, Neamathla, and Eneah

Micco (Neahmico)—were Hitchitis. Twenty-year-old Lower Creek mestizo Jim Henry was the youngest. His father, Antonio Rea, was a British or Spanish Indian countryman who had married a Hitchiti woman from Chehaw Town on the Flint River. Jim Henry's early years are obscure, but in his late teens he apparently was working as a clerk in a Columbus firm. If he did not see, he heard about the Creek corpses at the courthouse. Emerging as an important manufacturing and commercial center at the head of navigation on the Chattahoochee River, the bustling new city of Columbus spread out over the old Coweta heartland. A steamboat's shrill whistle could be heard coming from the river where Indians had formerly paddled dugouts. Jim Henry mulled this over, put down his ledger, decided to fight, and joined Neamathla.[41]

Although he was more than four times older and less headstrong than Jim Henry, Neamathla was no less resentful and hostile. Rather than remaining on his allotment in north Florida or moving to the Seminole Reservation, he and his followers had retired into Alabama and established a square ground and villages on Hatchechubbee Creek southwest of Columbus. Experience had made Neamathla respect American power, and from time to time he had negotiated with them: at Moultrie Creek outside Saint Augustine in 1823, and at Fort Mitchell in 1835 and 1836. But again and again Americans had made it clear that their vision of the Muscogulges' role in the Southeast was not Neamathla's. The Chattahoochee Valley was the Hitchiti motherland, and Neamathla would fight anyone—white or Indian—who threatened the Hitchitis' realm. Lieutenant Scott and his party had found this out to their cost in 1816. Neamathla was a chief of the second rank, but no ordinary one. His superior, his chief, the elderly Neamico, at once was as cautious, as dangerous, and as indignant as Neamathla.[42]

After talk and delay, Americans in 1835–36 began to assemble the Alabama Creeks and prepared to move them to new homes beyond the Mississippi. Led by Jim Henry, Neamathla, Neamico, and other Hitchiti and Yuchi micos, tastanagis, hillis hayas, and emathlas, thousands of Indians painted for war resisted, laying waste the populated region south of the Columbus-

Montgomery federal road, killing settlers, waylaying stage-coaches, and forcing virtually all survivors to flee. At least one-half of the Georgia farmers between the Chattahoochee and Flint rivers sprinted for safety. Worried about mounting tensions, Jonathan Sims, who lived below Columbus, asked local friendly Indians to come to his plantation and reassure him that all was well. But "not one showed up so I lay in the swamp." To their sorrow others did not follow his example and their corpses were found in burned cabins and fields.[43] The burning of Alabama and Georgia plantations, the carrying off of Negro slaves, and the destruction of livestock had much in common with what was happening in northern and central Florida.

With houses, stores, courthouses, and land offices encompassing ancient Muscogulge square grounds, new Alabama and Georgia towns on the Chattahoochee were closest to hostile Indians and most resented. Among their number were Columbus, Roanoke just to the south, and Irwinton even farther downstream. The Indians' destruction of farms and at times killing or wounding their owners alarmed Alabamians and Georgians, and they panicked when they learned in May 1836 that Indians had overrun Roanoke. Just before daybreak Jim Henry and 300 warriors had struck, surprising 100 sleeping inhabitants in this new town on the Georgia side of the Chattahoochee. They killed fifteen and wounded twenty more, burning houses in town and for miles around. Settlers who were able fled in every direction, some hiding in nearby streams with only their noses protruding. Survivors' tales unnerved citizens in Columbus and Irwinton. The founders of Columbus, enthusiastic boosters, who expected their city to become a cotton port and manufacturing center second only to Mobile, had ignored the Indians in their promotional literature. In the spring of 1836 they were taken aback as 2,000 refugees, including barefooted women and children in nightclothes, some of them having rushed by corpses lying in the road, crowded into the infant city, reminding all that the Indians could not be ignored.[44] Georgians and Alabamians rallied, hastily raised troops, attacked Roanoke, and drove off Jim Henry and his followers who were entrenched in a warehouse behind bags of cotton. At Roanoke and elsewhere along the

268   Chattahoochee, hostile Indians angrily fired at steamboats defiling the river with their jarring pulsations.[45] They burned and sank one at Roanoke, another a few miles below Columbus, and they killed and wounded passengers and crew members.

Various reasons explain why the Creek War, though causing destruction and alarm enough, was of short duration in contrast to the protracted Muscogulge struggle in Florida. One was the overwhelming force of at least thirteen thousand men quickly brought into the field against Jim Henry and Neamathla. That many Georgia militiamen who rushed to the Chattahoochee had no arms made little difference. Indian warriors headed by Opothleyahola assisted. Opotheyahola was a Tuckabatchee. Not a Muskogee, he also was not a Hitchiti or Yuchi. Alabamians put enormous military and economic pressure on Opothleyahola to help bring refractory Hitchitis and Yuchis into line, and Opothleyahola obliged, reasoning that if in this instance he did not do the white mans' bidding he and his followers were doomed. He did not like what Jackson was doing to the Indians, but he had enrolled a son in the Choctaw Academy and realized that without the government's largess he and his people seemed to have little future in either the East or the West.[46] White settlements in Alabama and Georgia surrounded hostile Creek villages, whereas southern Florida with few white inhabitants, lay open. Florida also contained more swamps and inaccessible areas than did Alabama and Georgia.

American commanders bickered about the proper strategy, but considering their commanding force it did not seem to make any difference. In overall command, General Scott wanted to seal off the southern Georgia-Alabama borders, attack the Creeks from the south, and prevent warriors from escaping to Florida.[47] "The Hitchiti tribe of the Creek Nation [is aiding the Seminoles] . . . warriors arrive in Florida like travellers with packs on their backs . . . watchfulness is everywhere necessary."[48] The danger was not just hostiles escaping southward to Florida. In February 1836 Seminoles had fought and more than held their own against General Gaines at the Battle of Camp Izard on the Withlacoochee, wounding the general himself. No more than two months later some of these defiant warriors (now

Opothleyahola. From Thomas L. McKenney and James T. Hall, *History of the Indian Tribes of North America* (1836–44). Courtesy National Anthropological Archives, Smithsonian Institution. Photo No. 45,111-F.

270   designated Creeks) painted themselves for war again and fought Georgians and Alabamians in the Chattahoochee River Valley, determined to be equally successful in the North.[49] Reports abounded that Osceola himself had returned home and was with these warriors.

General Jesup at Tuskegee was surrounded by Alabama militiamen fearful for the safety of their wives and children, and by a large friendly Indian force that could not long remain inactive and kept in the field. Anxious for glory, to become another Old Hickory, Jesup to Scott's exasperation prematurely attacked from the north. Marching from Tuskegee through the heart of the Yuchi-Hitchiti country, Jesup headed for Neamathla's villages on Hatchechubbee Creek.[50] An advance party under Thomas Woodward seized Neamathla and subsequently many of his followers. Their villages were put to the torch and prisoners marched off to Fort Mitchell.[51] Jim Henry held out longer: he was captured, then escaped to continue the struggle, but by July his forces had been scattered and defeated, and he walked in by himself to surrender.[52] Few pitched battles occurred, and by July 1836 the Creek War seemed over. Thousands of Creeks in the latter part of 1836 began their journey west, Neamathla's and Jim Henry's followers, some in irons, in the van.

Neamathla had much in common with Arpeika. Approximately the same age, both Hitchiti chiefs had lived in northern Florida and resisted whites, Americans and Spaniards alike. American pressure had forced Arpeika farther and farther south until he ended up in the Everglades, while Neamathla had moved northward into Alabama. They never put shackles on Arpeika, however.

It is too simple and really not accurate to assert that the Creek War ended in 1836, because hostilities continued in Alabama and Georgia. In 1837 Indians burned farmhouses in southern Georgia. In the same year 200 hostile Creek warriors returned from West Florida to southern Alabama in Barbour County and forced the outnumbered militia to flee.[53] In 1838 Georgia militia fought Creeks in the Okefenokee, and the following year Creeks attacked the settlement at Stefanalgee west of the Chattahoochee, killing a few civilians. One way to appreciate that the Creek War had not ended by July 1836 is to keep in mind that the Creeks did then what they had done in 1814— retired to Florida and continued the struggle. Scott's efforts to seal off the Florida border had only partially succeeded. Between 1837 and the mid-1840s refugee Creeks killed scores of Floridians living near the Georgia line from Jacksonville in the east to Pensacola in the west.[54] Nokose Yahola had fought as best he could against Jesup and Scott in Alabama, and then in the summer of 1836 he and his warriors slipped past armed patrols into Florida. Jesup finally captured the Seminole Nokose Yahola west of Saint Augustine late in 1837 and as quickly as possible imprisoned him in the Castillo de San Marcos.[55] Surviving sources allow us to follow the Lower Creek Octiarche's movements more closely. Despite the vigilance of patrolling steamboats and militia posted at crossing places, Octiarche, one side of his face painted red, the other black, and at least one hundred warriors furtively slipped across the Chattahoochee below Columbus, travelled, sometimes fighting their way, southeastward through Georgia to the Okefenokee, then turned about and headed across northern Florida until they reached Cook's Hammock on the Gulf Coast near the Steinhatchee River. Here these "Seminoles" lived until 1842, alternately lashing out at the Americans and threatening to put to death any peace emissary, and unobtrusively tending fields and cattle.[56] With greatest reluctance in 1836 some Alabama Creeks had agreed to assemble in camps in preparation for western removal. Followers of Echo Harjo (Osceola's kinsman) perhaps because Americans planned to disarm them, broke out of their camp. Militia set out after the fugitives, and the Indians not destroyed were driven into the swamps or fled to Florida.[57]

The southern migration of Muscogulges into Florida in small groups over little-used trails, frequently at night, remains obscure. Typically there were only enough horses for one-third to one-fourth of the refugees, and women and children often walked and were more likely to be captured. They have revealed some details about the Indian movements. A Creek mother and her two children making their way into Florida via the Okefenokee were captured eighteen miles northwest of Jacksonville.

272   Fearful of slowing down, twenty-five warriors in the fugitive party had promised to send a horse back, but local whites arrived on the scene first.[58] In 1836 whites caught up with another body of fugitives, probably numbering over one hundred, in Lowndes County, Georgia, near the Florida line. Ten warriors were killed, eight women and children captured, and the rest escaped. Prisoners were escorted to a nearby farmhouse. In the evening the Indian mother gave her children a drink from a coffee pot and a few hours later they all died. Infanticide was a Muscogulge practice that had survived since Mississippian times, but Georgians were shocked at the actions of this "unnatural mother," who escaped.[59] The Upper Creek grandmother who fled from Alabama to the Florida panhandle and described how she lived off fish, kunti, and game, moving from camp to camp until finally surrendering in 1838, has already been mentioned.

Since the American Revolution Muscogulges, especially those in the non-Muskogee moiety, had been encouraged and supported by Britain and at times by Spain. Americans were alarmed by reports that Seminoles were receiving munitions from Cuban fishermen "who swarm uninterruptedly along the coasts" and from British merchants in the Bahamas.[60] Though greatly exaggerated, there was truth in these accounts. Muscogulges determined to resist in the 1830s still dreamed of British aid from a latter-day Thomas Brown, William Bowles, or Alexander Arbuthnot. Largely a dream or myth, this expectation nevertheless was real in the minds of desperate Indians and can be seen by looking inside the Montgomery jail in 1836. During the early phase of the Creek War, scores of warriors were captured and imprisoned, and they awaited trial for inciting the Indians and murdering civilians. The mestizo Earle was one such incendiary. A Columbus silversmith until 1836, Earle in that year crossed the Chattahoochee into Alabama and rode about Neamathla's and Neamico's villages, distributing and, as best his command of the Indian tongue permitted, translating mysterious printed documents. As it turned out, these were musty copies of Admiral George Cockburn's 1813 proclamations, promising that British ships and redcoats were en route to the Gulf of Mexico to save the southeastern Muscogulges. Earle allegedly altered or crossed out the date.

Questioning Earle closely, alarmed authorities discovered to their amazement that he was Hillis Haya's son. He had been born in London, returned with his mother to Florida, and in the 1820s, like Neamathla, had moved northward to Alabama. There he married an Indian and at some point became a Columbus silversmith. Earle was the same age as the indomitable Creek war leader Jim Henry, and both worked in Columbus until 1836. Confusion persists concerning Earle. Opothleyahola avowed he was no Muskogee but a white man, and assuredly Earle did not much look like an Indian. But Earle and his mother had guarded Hillis Haya's personal possessions including Cockburn's proclamations. Like Hillis Haya, Earle was a silversmith and a savior or prophet. While awaiting trial Earle died in his Montgomery cell. Whether he was unceremoniously dragged out by his heels and thrown into an unmarked grave like Hillis Haya at Saint Marks is unknown. Before his death Earle could look out of his Montgomery prison and see where his father Hillis Haya, Tecumseh, and Alabama prophets had danced the dance of the Lakes Indians, all of which would have seemed foreign to white artisans, shopkeepers, lawyers, speculators, and jailers going about their business in a city now two decades old.[61]

One thing that had not changed, however, was that the Muscogulges fought among themselves in the 1830s with as much intensity as ever. As whites were turning Creeks out of their cabins and rounding them up for western removal, and in some instances even after Creek families had actually set out on their Trail of Tears, warriors collaborated with American soldiers in assembling other Indians and subduing those resisting. Hitchitis, Yuchis, and other non-Muskogees made up the nucleus of the hostiles, while friendly Indians were from the pure Muskogee moiety along with certain non-Muskogees who were not Hitchitis or Yuchis. The old internal tensions persisted, manifest in Alabama, Georgia, and Florida. One of the reasons the 1836 Creek War was short-lived was that Upper Creeks from Tuckabatchee, Nuyaka, Kialijee, and other Upper Creek towns on the Tallapoosa, as well as Paddy Carr and his followers on the Chattahoochee had turned on Hitchitis and Yuchis with a vengeance. The highly acculturated Paddy was particularly un-

274   happy because hostiles had carried off seventy-seven of his slaves.[62] Commanding friendly warriors, General Thomas Woodward captured Neamathla and brought him to Fort Mitchell, while Paddy Carr and friendly Lower Creeks rallied to protect Columbus from the likes of Earle and Jim Henry and patrolled the river to prevent hostiles from escaping to Florida.

This civil war was best seen in Florida. Almost 800 friendly Creeks fought in Florida alongside American soldiers going after Osceola, Wildcat, and Arpeika. The Upper Creek (Okchai?) Jim Boy, whose son was enrolled in the Choctaw Academy, raised 450 Creeks and in 1836 descended the Apalachicola River, boarded ship for Tampa, and after arrival at Fort Brooke plunged into the interior looking for hostiles and booty.[63] General Woodward, second in command of this regiment, accompanied them to the Apalachicola's mouth, but the general, notoriously involved in swindling all the Muscogulges, was forced to return home.[64] Lower Creek Paddy Carr was almost as deeply involved in land frauds as Woodward. Nevertheless during 1836 and 1837, wearing a scarlet turban with a strip of white cloth around the center to identify him as a friendly Indian, Carr led the Creeks in Florida: "Never [has] an officer, charged with a delicate and hazardous enterprise, served with more zeal and promptitude."[65]

Major David Moniac, whose kinsmen had died inside Fort Mims, had graduated from West Point in the 1820s. When the Creek and Seminole Wars broke out he volunteered for active duty and accompanied the Creek regiment into Florida, surprising white soldiers that he was not a white officer. When searching for a ford giving access to Wahoo Swamp, Moniac was cut down by the enemy, and the press lamented the passing of the valiant West Pointer. Newspapers made no mention, but it is safe to assume that the Seminole who killed Moniac took satisfaction in dispatching an American soldier and a Muskogee warrior with only one shot.[66]

Not only friendly Creeks in Alabama and Georgia but also those in Florida served against the Seminoles. Though Chief Blount had moved away, other friendly Creeks remained on the Apalachicola River and annually swept the coast eastward to the Suwannee or westward almost to Pensacola, trying to discover the haunts of fugitive bands. Friendly Creeks from several southeastern states visited Seminole camps to encourage hostiles to submit, and to gather intelligence. The Alabama Creek Yahola Hajo, nephew of the old red-stick exile Jumper, for days made his way through bogs and cypress swamps to confer with his fellow townsman Nocose Yahola, with Osceola, and with other warriors, most of whom had been born in Alabama. Yahola Hajo was unsuccessful and lucky to escape alive.[67]

Jesup viewed the Seminole War not as a civil conflict but in another light: "This, you may be assured, is a Negro, not an Indian war; and if it be not speedily put down, the South will feel the effects of it on their slave population before the end of the next season [1837]."[68] Abolitionist congressman Joshua R. Giddings from Ohio agreed with Jesup on this point if little else. In speeches and writings Giddings used the nineteenth-century Seminole wars to illustrate his crusade. He charged that all of the wars—the destruction of the Negro Fort, Jackson's 1818 incursion, and the protracted Second Seminole War—were brought on by the rapacity and inhumanity of white southern slaveowners. Giddings scrutinized government reports, got first-hand accounts from abolitionist colleagues, and used them to publish the *Exiles of Florida* in 1858. His exiles were Negroes or Indian-Negroes, and Giddings described how during the Second Seminole War these exiles—men, women, and children—often starving, had to flee from one hammock or burned out plantation to another. From time to time parties of exiles were captured and returned to whites who claimed them or sold them, mothers sobbing as they were sent in one direction, and their children and husbands in another. Giddings's contemporaries idealized Osceola as the noble savage, but Giddings insisted that the true heroes and freedom fighters were the exiles, including Gopher John, Abraham, and Cudjo, interpreters, military chieftains, and advisors to Indians and whites. Giddings exaggerated, but the Second Seminole War cannot be comprehended without considering his point of view.[69]

Most southern whites saw the exiles in a different light. In May 1839 General Alexander Macomb concluded a treaty once again "ending the Indian War" by allowing the Seminoles, in-

Gopher John, Seminole Interpreter

Gopher John. From Joshua Giddings, *Exiles* (1858). Courtesy Florida State University Library, Tallahassee.

Negro Abraham.

Abraham. From Joshua Giddings, *Exiles* (1858). Courtesy Florida State University Library, Tallahassee.

cluding black Seminoles, to remain at least temporarily in southernmost Florida. In reality, of course, there was no Seminole nation. Signed by Chitto Tustenuggee and Halleck Tustenuggee, this treaty affected only these war leaders and their friends and followers. Other Indian bands in the Everglades, Okefenokee, and westernmost Florida, whether classified as Seminoles or Creeks, did not feel bound by this treaty, and

278   perhaps even disavowed it. Aghast at the prospect of a permanent Maroon retreat in the territory, white Floridians, however,
denounced Macomb and chiefs who really had no authority,
merely having been "appointed . . . or elected by an enterprising
nigger."[70] Giddings regarded Sandy Perryman, the Negro interpreter at the treaty negotiations, and Wildcat's black followers,
still fighting three years after Dade's death, as more than "savage
niggers" who needed taming by white masters or returning to
Africa.

Giddings's portrayal of the Negroes was too simple and one-
sided. Black Muscogulge influence in the Southeast was pervasive, and many Indian-Negroes were essentially Indians and not
Africans. Culturally and genetically, blacks had been absorbed
or acculturated by the Muscogulges. They had Hitchiti, Yuchi,
and Muskogee spouses or parents, and they belonged to Wind,
Tiger, Alligator, and similar clans. They and their progeny became more and more Indian while unobtrusively introducing
African folklore and customs into Muscogulge society, and mod-
ifying the Indian culture itself. Considering themselves Indians
belonging to a particular clan, talwa, and moiety, acculturated
black Muscogulges fought on both sides in the Indian civil war.

Indian-Negroes also allied and collaborated with whites, and
in this respect their linguistic abilities served them in good
stead. As Alabama Creeks were forced off their lands and cheated
out of their allotments, Negro interpreters often acted as inter-
mediaries, and like the speculators they profitted from the corruption and intimidation. Joseph Bruner, "a colored man" employed as an interpreter, was awarded a half section in the Creek
domain for such efficacious services.[71] Florida Negroes gave
warning of impending Indian attacks, which allowed white masters time to escape to Saint Augustine. Eventually they warily
led parties back to burned-out plantations to survey damage and
round up livestock. Seldom did the United States Army pene-
trate the Florida interior without being accompanied by a Negro-
Indian spy-guide-interpreter. Opothleyahola hired out Negro
Sam to American forces in Alabama during the Creek War as an
interpreter, and Jim Boy furnished one of his Negroes to Jesup
in Florida for the same purpose. Unfortunately both were killed,

and the indignant owners demanded restitution.[72] Living on the
Withlacooche, the wealthy, Seminole-Negro Cudjo was acquainted with the terrain and location of Indian camps. During the Seminole War he furnished American commanders valuable information about the whereabouts and intentions of Osceola, Arpeika, and hostile black Seminoles, and as a result Cudjo lost much of his property. Army officers urged the government to reimburse "this honest . . . faithful . . . and valuable servant" for the loss of 115 cattle and 15 horses.[73]

Indian-Negroes sometimes seemed more Indian and at other times more Negro. Osceola presumably had a Negro wife who lived with him and the Indians in his village south of the Withlacoochee; a short distance away was a separate Negro village where blacks tended their fields and raised their children. An undetermined amorphous group of black Muscogulges was conscious that they were neither Indian nor white; they were blacks, Africans, Negroes, or whatever, but in any case separate. Looking out for their own interests, they were less concerned whether whites or Indians triumphed. Many had won freedom by running away from white plantations and joining the Indians, often as slaves; if whites promised them freedom these Negroes were prepared to desert the Indians. The Negro Abraham, who had lived with the Seminoles for years and risen to prominence, accepted Jesup's offer of liberty and money to join American forces.[74] Concerned with their own well-being, certain Indian-Negroes routinely switched sides or perhaps were double agents, simultaneously serving two masters. This worried and confused whites. In 1840–41 American commanders in southern Florida at one point put irons on Negro John and kept him in close confinement and at another released him and employed him as a guide-interpreter for expeditions into the Everglades.[75]

Despite the varied responses and conduct of black Muscogulges during the Creek and Seminole wars, a majority of the Indian-Negroes were associated or identified with hostile Muscogulges in Potato, Tiger, Alligator, and other clans that were so numerous among the non-Muskogees, rather than with whites and their friendly Creek allies. Some of those Creeks who fled to Florida in 1836 and swelled the Seminole population

280   were black Creeks.[76] Black Muscogulges were aware that the
       Southeast traditionally had been a promising region in which to
       go slave hunting, and that the spirit of the Goose Creek men
       still lived. Indian-Negroes with the hostiles contended they
       were free, that they had acquired their liberty through purchase,
       proclamations of British commanders, manumission by Indian
       owners, self-purchase, or in another fashion. But whether re-
       garded as Negroes or as Indians they were free. Their legal status
       in fact was bewildering. Whites insisted they were fugitives,
       that British proclamations were invalid, and that inheritance
       was traced through the male rather than the female line. There-
       fore Indians did not really own some of the slaves they claimed.
       In fact, Americans contended that most Indian-Negroes were in
       reality fugitive slaves.

          In the summer of 1837 Jessup reported that he had already
       returned nearly one hundred captive Negroes to their rightful
       owners. Others were imprisoned in Saint Augustine and Talla-
       hassee and then auctioned off with unseemly haste.[77] As in the
       days of Goose Creek men, Indians themselves often were the
       slave hunters. Immediately after the Creek War, Jim Boy and
       Yeleka Harjo asserted that they would be glad to take their
       friendly Creek warriors into Florida and quickly put down the
       Seminole uprising if only they could keep the booty, the most
       valuable being Indian-Negroes. After scores of Negroes were
       captured in this fashion Jesup ordered that friendly Creeks not
       keep the captives, but instead be reimbursed $20 per slave and
       that captives be disposed of in the Southeast or better still sent
       to Africa.[78] Sometimes black Muscogulges stayed in the South-
       east; on other occasions, because Americans were so anxious to
       remove the Indians, Negroes were allowed to accompany emi-
       grating parties of both friendly and hostile Indians. Debates over
       Indian-Negroes, exiles, or Maroons—along with the Creek and
       Seminole conflicts and the accompanying civil war—all helped
       set in motion the dispersal of most of the Muscogulge people
       from the Southeast, a major turning point in their unfortunate
       history.

Dispersal and Survival

The diaspora of the Muscogulge people was intertwined with Andrew Jackson's long career. Old Hickory was the symbol of national Indian policy, but General Winfield Scott, Georgia's Governor George Troup, Indian office head Thomas McKenney, missionaries Lee Compere and William Capers, and a welter of other descendants of Goose Creek men, all determined to make Muscogulge people serve the interests of western capitalism and convert to Protestantism.

Indians had resisted, though often in vain. A potent ally of white colonists over a long period, not overlooked but perhaps not sufficiently emphasized, was new disease introduced by Europeans and Africans. The greatest devastation had occurred in the sixteenth and seventeenth centuries, and the Muscogulge people, an assemblage of survivors, paradoxically were increasing at the time of nineteenth-century removal. Adoption and assimilation of neighboring tribes and increased immunity, due in part to intermarriage with Africans and Caucasians and in part to smallpox vaccination, were largely responsible for stopping the population loss. Whatever the Indian population in 1492, it was many times greater than that of the nineteenth-century Creeks and Seminoles. As Earle rode about the countryside distributing Cockburn's proclamations, Jackson and the heirs of the Goose Creek men could thank their old allies, those

282 sixteenth-century pathogens. It was also providential that Britain had abandoned notions of propping up the Muscogulges. All of this, coupled with the spectacular growth of the American population and Jackson's victory at Horseshoe Bend, made dispersal of the Muscogulge people inevitable after 1814. Fields of cotton were replacing herds of white-tailed deer, and there was little room left for commercial hunting. Cotton bales rather than hogsheads of skins were being exported to English factories.

Though a majority of the Muscogulge people departed in 1836, no single year or prescribed route marked their exodus. Western relocation had commenced in the late eighteenth century as Muscogulge hunting parties, like those of neighboring Cherokees and Choctaws, had crossed the Mississippi into Arkansas, Oklahoma, and Texas in a relentless search for game. Some of the hunting parties converted temporary camps into permanent villages. The departure of Indians from the Creek heartland intensified after 1814; and in the ensuing years one could find Peter McQueen and Hillis Haya in Florida, but Savannah Jack as we know had moved beyond the Mississippi.[1] Roley and Chilly McIntosh led several thousand Creeks to Oklahoma in the late 1820s, and Chief Blount escorted several hundred of his followers to Texas a few years later. In 1836 Opothleyahola, Neamico, and other chiefs conducted at least 14,000 Creeks to the West, while Black Dirt (Fuchalusti Hadjo) sailed from Tampa with 400 Seminoles. The western removal of the Muscogulges was far from complete by 1836; thousands of Creeks departed in the late 1830s, and the largest number of Seminoles left Florida in the early 1840s. In one fashion or another some Muscogulge people managed to remain in the Southeast for many years: some did not depart for the West until the 1850s; some not until after the Civil War; and, in isolated cases, some not even until the twentieth century.

Regular army officers, Indian department officials, and hired contractors who rounded up, organized, directed, fed, and transported Indians to the West have left their orders, account books, and reminiscences describing the Indians' "Trail of Tears." Often dating from 1836, these written records obscure the fact that many Muscogulges went to the West on their own. Indian hunting parties have already been mentioned. Almost nothing is known about how Savannah Jack got to the Red River after Horseshoe Bend except that no soldier showed him the way and no white contractor fed him en route. A twentieth-century Seminole tradition recounts how George Scott's Seminole parents, walking and riding ponies, took two years in the 1830s to get from Florida to Hitchita Town in Oklahoma.[2]

From Indian hunters and from chiefs sent out by the United States to view the land, Muscogulges had a good idea about the eastern Oklahoma and Texas terrain: it was well east of the 100° meridian, and it contained fertile soil, trees, and sufficient water. Muscogulges did not have to be literate and read Horace Greeley's *Tribune* in order to realize the promise of the frontier and take his advice of "Go west, young man." That the promise for Muscogulges was not that of white emigrants departing in trains of Conestoga wagons does not mean that such a dream—at least for some Indians—did not exist.

Riding, walking, freezing, and starving in their journey, Creeks comforted themselves by singing the hymn "We are going home to our homes and land; there is one who is above and ever watches over us. . . . "[3] Protestant missionaries won many converts in Oklahoma during the nineteenth and twentieth centuries, and such hymns were commonplace. Descendants of emigrants attending Baptist, Methodist, and Presbyterian services, regularly singing "We are going home," may have assumed that their ancestors had done likewise in 1836—as perhaps they had. It is possible, however, that Indians, especially those who constantly circled emigrant parties with eagle feathers on the ends of sticks, did not mean "we are going home [to Jesus]" but instead literally going home. According to tradition, Creek-speaking Muskogees proper had come from the West, crossed the Mississippi, and settled in the Southeast. LeClerc de Milfort, Alexander McGillivray's brother-in-law, related how he and Indian hunters accompanying him in 1781 had visited caves on the upper Red River from which the Muskogees had first emerged. In addition to the Muskogees, various Apache and Pueblo peoples in the Southwest believed that many centuries ago their ancestors had emerged from caves. These west-

284   erners also had matriarchal societies, emphasized dualism and opposites, and employed the symbolism of the numeral four in their rituals. Perhaps in the remote past all this could be traced to a common source in the United States Southwest or even Mexico.

One would not want to accept all of Milfort's assertions at face value, but his assertion that the Muskogees had come into the Southeast from the Red River or somewhere beyond the Mississippi was very much alive in 1802 when Milfort published his *Memoirs*.[4] Tuckabatchees, Koasatis, Yuchis, and Shawnees had arrived in the Southeast from the North; Hitchitis were the "original inhabitants," and black Muscogulges had come from Africa. These, who were not Muskogees, had not first come into the world from trans-Mississippian caves. True Muskogees, however, had.

A majority of the Muscogulges travelled to the West by two main routes: one primarily by land and the other by water. Alabama River wharves at Montgomery were a major departure point for the water route. Creeks made their way to Montgomery by land from Fort Mitchell, Tuskegee, or another assembly point fifty to one hundred miles away. The number of soldiers accompanying the Indians to Montgomery depended on whether the Creeks were hostile or friendly. Occasionally Upper Creeks arrived via the Coosa and Tallapoosa rivers. Montgomery citizenry came out to gawk at these "savages," many of whom had pillaged and killed during the recent war. At times angry citizens protested that the leaders should be imprisoned and executed for their crimes and never leave the state. Others observed that these children of the forest in fact were noble savages more sinned against than sinning, and that the drama enacted at local wharves was but the final, albeit inevitable, episode in their tragic history in the East.

The Indians' stay in Montgomery usually was brief. Whites in charge of feeding, collecting, protecting, and transporting the Indians were reasonably efficient, aware of compelling reasons for speeding their charges on their way. After the Indians had silently filed aboard barges and steamboats, giant paddlewheels began to churn, and the small armada descended the Alabama

River to Mobile. The vessels sailed by the crumbling old brick French fort at Mobile, anchoring just below the city where the Indians debarked. As quickly as possible they were transferred to oceangoing steamers and sailing ships, though local citizenry had time to ride or drive out in carriages to witness the spectacle.

From Mobile the small flotilla sailed out into the Gulf of Mexico, then westward toward New Orleans, which they usually reached by Lakes Borgne and Pontchartrain rather than the more difficult route up the Mississippi River. Indians debarking at Lake Pontchartrain marched several miles overland to the outskirts of New Orleans on the Mississippi to await steamboats for passage up the Arkansas River. The stopover in the New Orleans area might be protracted if the season were dry and the Arkansas River too low for steamboat travel. Hostile warriors were imprisoned in the New Orleans barracks or at Fort Pike at the eastern end of Lake Pontchartrain until time to leave. Friendly Indians such as Jim Boy were invited to attend the theater.

Eventually all departed, and with luck the 400-mile voyage upstream from New Orleans to Fort Gibson would be relatively swift. It was not unusual, however, for steamboats to ascend the Arkansas River to Little Rock or its vicinity and then not be able to proceed because of lack of water. Transferring belongings to pack animals, wagons, and ox carts, Muscogulges sometimes were forced to walk the final 150 to 200 miles.

There were many variations of this water route. Florida Muscogulges assembled not at Montgomery but at Tampa, Fort Lauderdale, Saint Augustine, the lower Apalachicola River, and even Charleston, before sailing for New Orleans. Transports entering the mouth of the Mississippi might sail by New Orleans up to Vicksburg or Natchez before stopping to transfer Indians to light draft steamboats. After traveling overland to Muscle Shoals on the Tennessee River, some Creeks—often old men, women, and children—boarded ship and went almost all the way to their new home by steamboat. Regardless of the variations, the Trail of Tears for thousands of Muscogulges was a water one via the Gulf of Mexico, Mississippi, Tennessee, White, and Arkansas rivers, and their memories and accounts

286   were of being crowded above and below deck, of frequent stops to bury those who had died from diseases, and occasionally of a boiler explosion, fire, or some other disaster. After being packed aboard the steamboat *Monmouth* in 1837, 611 of Jim Boy's friendly Creeks began their passage upstream from New Orleans. Rounding a bend in the Mississippi River, the *Monmouth* suddenly was rammed by another steamboat heading downstream, which split her in half, and separated the cabin from the hull. The *Monmouth* sank immediately. Miraculously all but two whites aboard survived, but 300 Indians died. After arriving in Oklahoma, Creek survivors told and retold their children about the horrors of abruptly being thrown into the water and of listening to their kinsmen's frantic cries.[5]

The other route to the West, the one more often taken by Upper Creeks, was by land. Indians, typically "friendly" Indians, congregated at a central talwa, though sometimes soldiers built a stockade to watch them and at the same time protect them from neighboring whites. Some young Creeks in the 1830s were still alive almost a century later, or at least their children were, and memories of what transpired in Alabama remained vivid. Oral traditions describe how overloaded wagons rumbled by Indian cabins and how mothers held infants in sacks hanging in front while men carried older children on their shoulders as Creeks began assembling at a nearby town or stockade—all the while an "awful silence" ensued.[6] At the appropriate time, usually during the latter half of 1836, parties of two or three thousand Indians, some riding ponies and even more walking, accompanied by overburdened wagons, soldiers, Indian agents, interpreters, and contractors paid $25 per head for provisions, set out. Averaging ten to fifteen miles per day, the Indians proceeded across Alabama, Mississippi, and sometimes Tennessee until they reached the Mississippi River at or near Memphis. The trip across the Mississippi was short but dangerous; more than one Indian died when his ferryboat wrecked and sank. Once across the river Indians struck out overland on the new but unfinished road to Little Rock, and from there followed the Arkansas River upstream to Fort Gibson. Some Creeks boarded steamboats at Memphis and completed the latter half of their journey by water, making forty to eighty miles a day if there were no obstacles.

Whatever route they took, many who started out never arrived in the West. The spectacular loss of life when the steamboat was split in two on the Mississippi and the deaths en route of prominent chiefs attracted the press's attention. Osceola's death at Fort Moultrie is the best example of the latter, but newspapers also reported that the Seminole Tiger Tail had died in New Orleans and the friendly Chief Holata Emathla, the Blue Warrior, was buried only twenty miles from his final western destination. Newspapers, especially southern ones, seldom mentioned that perhaps 10 percent of the Indians died en route, and this does not include those Indians who committed suicide before ever setting out. According to the press, those who died were the ones who remained behind and wandered about the woods in a drunken stupor, not realizing the advantages afforded by a new homeland in the West. Despite more intensive efforts at vaccination, smallpox, cholera, and many other diseases took a high toll on Indians crowded in stockades and aboard barges. For months or years these Indians had lived in swamps on a precarious diet. Emigrating parties getting off late in the season suffered losses due to inadequate clothing and shelter in the bitter cold and snow. Graves of Muscogulge men, women, and children marked all major routes to the West.

Relocating the Muscogulge people was a logistical undertaking that strained the federal bureaucracy and the free-enterprise system. Jackson's critics denouncing the spoils system could find grist for their mill when they considered those added to the federal payroll. From Alabama to Arkansas advertisements appeared in newspapers requesting that at the appropriate time farmers and merchants provide salt, corn, fodder, fresh beef, flour, wagons, and teams of horses or oxen. Thomas Woodward in Alabama and his counterparts in Little Rock, Arkansas, enthusiastically fulfilled requests of the government contractors, though Indians complained to no avail about short rations, that barrels of flour were actually lime, and that so-called healthy 500-pound steers weighed less than half that much and could hardly walk.[7]

288   Census officials in 1832 had gone among the Creeks to count them, to determine who was entitled to an allotment, and to get an idea of the wagons, shipping, and foodstuffs necessary for the journey. The results tabulated in 1833 listed 14,142 Upper Creeks and 8,552 Lower Creeks. Seminoles were conservatively estimated to number between 5,000 and 6,000.[8] These figures, approximations, were understated, partly because of the difficulty of determining exactly who was an Indian and partly because no attempt was made to count Indians in areas such as western Georgia or the Florida panhandle. After counting or enrolling the Indians, the government listed the heads of household's property, most of which could not be readily transferred to the West and must be bought. The United States would transport only sixty pounds of baggage at government expense. Property left behind included whatever speculators had not taken, along with houses or cabins, looms, cotton gins, cowbells, iron pots, pewter plates, cattle, hogs, sheep, geese, blankets, deerskins, yards of homespun, corn, potatoes, sugarcane, storehouses, summerhouses, sheds, corncribs, smokehouses, beehives, barns, fence rails, and fruit trees. Authorities sometimes purchased the Indians' rifles, upon occasion took these weapons by force, and at times allowed Indians to keep them on their journey. Indians attempted, frequently unsuccessfully, to keep rather than sell their ponies and slaves. Before emigration and for years after arrival in Oklahoma, litigation ensued about whether Muscogulges had been adequately paid for their lands and personal property and if sufficient cattle and guns had been furnished in the West to replace those given up in the East.

    The government made almost no effort to reimburse hostile Muscogulges. Neamathla's cabin, summerhouse, and crib on the Hatcheechubbee were put to the torch and his Negroes, whether long-time slaves or plunder in the 1836 war, were summarily taken from him. Troops searched for Osceola's cabin on the Withlacoochee merely to burn it on sight. Earle's compensation in his Montgomery jail was an unmarked grave, the same that his father Hillis Haya had received at Saint Marks. It did not pay to be a hostile.

    The annuity was used to prod Muscogulges to emigrate. Indian agents threatened to give the annuity to common Indians rather than in lump sums to chiefs unless the latter used their influence in behalf of removal. Similarly, they threatened not to pay annuities and other monies to any Indians until after they had departed. The United States stipulated that five years after 1832 there would be just one Creek nation—in Oklahoma—and that only Indians in the West would be entitled to annual payments.[9]

It was paradoxical that as the government was exerting financial pressure and inducements to get Muscogulges to leave, other whites were delaying emigration by imprisoning Indians for debt. One result of dividing Creek lands in Alabama into counties and of expanding the state's legal jurisdiction was that Indians, like whites, could be jailed for not meeting financial obligations. Some claims against the Indians were bona fide, others specious. Sale of lands and property, annuities, and treaty payments entitled Indians to large sums of money, and whites were determined to get what money and half-acre sections of land they considered to be their rightful share before the Indians departed. Threat of imprisonment was one way to force Indians to loosen their purse strings. Opothleyahola delayed emigrating for months so he could satisfy his creditors and keep out of jail.[10] Chief Blount tarried in New Orleans longer than he intended because creditors dogging his footsteps had had him thrown in jail.[11] Both whites and Indians were attracted to the American West and Mexican Texas as a means of escaping creditors.

Satisfying real or pretended financial obligations was merely part of the legal morass. Since 1790 the United States Census Bureau had listed "heads of households," which, except for widows and a few others, were male; and when Benjamin S. Parsons and Thomas J. Abbott went about the Creek country in 1832 they followed the same procedure. The male Indian head of household, entitled to half-section allotment, was paid for it, for improvements to the land, and for personal property, all of which ran counter to the Muscogulge tradition of women being heads of the families and communal ownership of the land. The fact that many Indians of both sexes regarded their clan as their true family added to the legal confusion.

American resolve to remove the Indians expeditiously was compounded with a sense of guilt, a commitment to do justice to the Indians, and a determination to pay them a fair price for their personal property and possibly even their land. This entailed imposing concepts of patrilineal descent and private property on all Muscogulges—not much of a problem for white Indian countrymen and wealthy acculturated male mestizo, mulatto, and Indian factors. Since the latter half of the eighteenth century, they had been making written or oral wills and bequeathing property to sons and daughters. However, even for this acculturated minority there was a problem: polygamy.

Polygamy was an ancient Muscogulge practice especially identified with the political, religious, and economic elite. In the late eighteenth and nineteenth century, it was customary, almost the norm, for prominent Indians to have several wives: William McIntosh and Paddy Carr had three each; Osceola, Alexander McGillivray, and William Weatherford at least two; and Holata Emathla, whose brother, Charlie Emathla, Osceola had killed, also had two. One of Osceola's wives was a Negro, as were spouses of other Indians. Easily shedding the heritage of their upbringing in meeting house and kirk, white Indian countrymen readily adopted Indian ways. Lachlan McGillivray had more than one wife; George Galphin four, two of whom were Indians; and Bowles at least two. As white law on the local or county level spread over the Muscogulge domain, polygamy became illegal in the sight of man and God. On the eve of removal, Indian wives, whose husbands perhaps had died and who claimed extensive property, were scattered about the Muscogulge country. White authorities accepted this reality, and they prosecuted Indians for debt but not for bigamy.

A related problem was when an Indian married his Negro slave and subsequently died. Sometimes authorities treated the widow like the head of the household, though more often she was treated like the cattle and fence rails. Chances of such female Negro heads of household reaching Oklahoma were slim, which helps to explain why Negro freedman Frank Berry, Osceola's grandson, in the 1930s was living in Florida rather than Oklahoma.[12] The long-term effect of removal was to quicken acculturation and to encourage Muscogulges to adopt white racial attitudes towards Negroes.

The initial group of officially organized Muscogulge emigrants was the McIntosh party, primarily Lower Creeks, who departed in the late 1820s. The first were in a hurry, going by land in the dead of winter, not willing to wait and see if the government would provide water transportation and make other arrangements. It rained constantly from November 1827 until the following February, and streams overflowed, inundating low-lying areas. Near the Mississippi it took 700 freezing Indians nearly a month to proceed 100 miles. Subsequent parties fared better. The following year 1,000 women, children, and infirm Indians boarded riverboats at Muscle Shoals and made most of the journey by water. The McIntosh faction was well-to-do, owning horses and wagons and cash to purchase more. Assembling at Fort Bainbridge and elsewhere in Alabama, up to 3,000, under Chilly and Roley McIntosh and their successors, trekked westward with their bulky wagons, slaves, horses, and ponies in a long file. Negro slaves belonged to McIntosh's partisans and to unlucky claimants left behind. By land, water, or some combination thereof, several thousand emigrants arrived in the West to see the stars and stripes waving over Fort Gibson. They established themselves on nearby Verdigris River bottomlands in the Three Forks region.[13] For some the most dangerous part of the three months' journey had been at the beginning. The army assembled Indians at Fort Bainbridge midway between Montgomery and Fort Mitchell, guarding them against angry Hitchitis, Yuchis, and Tuckabatchees. Even so, some unlucky McIntosh emigrants arrived at Fort Gibson without any ears.[14]

Authorities protected and facilitated the McIntosh faction's removal, hoping that this initial trickle of emigrants would soon become a flood. Montgomery citizens cheered and toasted Captain David Brearley, who, overcoming great obstacles, had conducted the early emigrants to Oklahoma. Emigrating agents and the press saw to it that reports of treatment in Oklahoma that reached the eastern Indians were favorable. Delila McIntosh, William's daughter, after reaching Oklahoma claimed as a result of her father's will that eight of the slaves brought West by

292 Sandy Grayson and sold to Kendall Lewis really belonged to her. They were returned to Delila, but Lewis also expected to be fully compensated by the government for these same slaves.[15] The press reported how well these Creeks were prospering and what a pity it was that those remaining in the East were so oppressed, living off roots, and starving. At least six years elapsed, however, before any significant additional bodies of Muscogulges arrived in Oklahoma. During this period no one was on the scene to dispute the fact that Chilly and Roley McIntosh were the Creek nation.

Departing in 1834, John Blount's followers on the lower Apalachicola River were the second group of organized Muscogulge emigrants. Before removal, the size of Blount's band had fluctuated as some had retired to the Upper Creek country to live with Jim Boy, and others had moved to the Seminole Reservation. Around 1830 Blount was the leader of 300 to 600 Indians. As we know, Blount resolved—even became anxious—to leave the Apalachicola. Some of his kinfolk were already in Oklahoma with the McIntosh group, and in 1829 he and other Apalachicola River chiefs considered an inspection trip to visit them. Texas, however, where his uncle had settled, held far more appeal, and the Tuckabatchee Blount set his eye on that Mexican province.

It was not a simple matter for the well-to-do Blount to put his affairs in order. Like George Washington, he had a wife who owned many slaves. The mestizo Blount had married Nelly Factor, daughter of the Black Factor, who had lived for many years near the forks of the Apalachicola River. After the Black Factor's death in 1816 Nelly claimed her father's slaves, and when John Blount married Nelly he felt entitled to them. In his own right Blount also possessed slaves. Resorting to Indian or white law as best served their interests, both Indians and whites claimed John and Nelly Blount's slaves and other property. Government officials badgered Blount to leave, threatening that he would lose his annuity and more if he did not, and at the same time creditors gladly would have thrown the chief in prison for debt if a jail had been at hand.[16]

At last in 1834 Blount and several hundred followers boarded a vessel, dropped down the Apalachicola into the Gulf of Mexico, and began sailing westward. New Orleans was the first stop, and it turned out to be a mistake, because Blount's creditors arrived there first and had authorities throw him and other headmen into jail. He eventually was released and continued his journey by water to Opelousas, Louisiana, and then overland to the Trinity River in East Texas. Wondering why he had waited so long to join his Koasati uncle Red Moccasin, the harried elderly Blount soon died.[17] As time passed, other Florida Indians also arrived on the Trinity. Yet despite persecution by whites and Indians alike, some of Blount's relations and descendants remained on the Apalachicola River in the vicinity of Blountstown and are still there today.[18]

Another group of Muscogulge emigrants were Indians who had relocated among the Cherokees in northwest Georgia and mountainous regions in adjoining states. As Alabamians and especially Georgians extended white law over Creek lands during the 1820s and 1830s an undetermined number of Creeks—but at least several thousand—had fled to the Cherokee country. For years Creeks and Cherokees alternately had allied and intermarried with each other or lifted one another's scalps. In earlier times, the Natchez, Tuskegees, Shawnees, and other remnant tribes had settled among both the Creeks and Cherokees and eventually became known, at least to whites, as Creeks and Cherokees. Muskogees and non-Muskogees alike had relations and partisans among the Cherokees: William McIntosh had a Cherokee wife, and non-Muskogees had close ties with Cherokees, especially those known as Chickamaugas. Some Creeks who joined the Cherokees avowed they really were not Creeks but Cherokees, and hoped that they would fare better as Cherokees. The Cherokee heartland lay in part of the destroyed Muskogee Coosa chiefdom, and if they were so inclined for a variety of reasons Creeks with some validity could insist that they should be considered Cherokees.

Since before 1800, Cherokees on their own initiative or at the government's expense had moved to Arkansas and Texas. The number of Cherokee emigrants increased in the 1820s and 1830s, and "Creeks" accompanied many of the Cherokee parties. The largest number of such Creek emigrants did not leave

294   the East until 1838 when soldiers sought out and rounded up
most of the Cherokees. Presumably a few Creeks successfully
hid out to become part of the eastern Cherokees in the Smoky
Mountains. Nevertheless, before and after 1836 as Cherokees
made their way by land and water through Tennessee, across
the Mississippi River, and up the Arkansas River, several thousand Creeks were in their midst. Such Muscogulges were part
of those Cherokees who saw the flag flying over Fort Gibson,
and they usually settled down with the Cherokees, though
sometimes with the Creeks.[19]

The relocation in the West of Creek refugees among the
Cherokees, along with the emigration of Blount's and McIntosh's followers, was but prelude to the great exodus of 1836.
Neamathla, Neamico, and their hostile Hitchiti and Yuchi adherents were the first to go that year. No delay ensued in com-
pensating them for lands, slaves, and property; the only legal
controversy was whether to hang imprisoned war leaders or send
them on their way. Soldiers escorted Neamathla, 300 warriors,
and 550 women and children from Hatcheechubbee Creek villages to Fort Mitchell. Other warriors soon joined Neamathla,
and all were kept under close, but not close enough, guard,
because large numbers of Indians escaped. Though 1,000 were
recaptured, others successfully made their way to Florida.[20] As
white settlers began returning to burned-out farms in mid-July
1836 and a measure of calm returned to the countryside, soldiers
set some 1,500 hostile Yuchis and Osochis in motion. Few Muscogulges with Negroid features were to be seen. Negroes had
been brought into Fort Mitchell, but whether they considered
themselves Indians or not, they did not depart with the prisoners. Three hundred of the most dangerous Indians were hand-
cuffed in pairs with a long chain passing down the middle to
connect them in a single file. The elderly Neamathla was one
of these. Head held defiantly high, he marched day by day toward
Montgomery without complaining or saying a word. Children
followed in wagons, while the women, some crying, walked. En
route, Neamico and 500 more hostiles joined the party, and the
number of Indians swelled to 3,000 after they all reached
Montgomery.[21]

Young Jim Henry was in their midst. This irrepressible war leader was blamed for white deaths at Roanoke and the burning of farms and killing of settlers in a broad region on both sides of the Chattahoochee River. Jim Henry was incarcerated in the same jail as Earle. The careers of these two mestizos had much in common: approximately the same age, both had worked in Columbus before becoming leaders in the Creek War, and eventually they ended up as cellmates in Montgomery.

In mid-July the hostiles were escorted aboard two steamboats and four barges. When the chains were struck from all but about fifteen of the warriors, some Indians attempted to escape. One was shot, another bayoneted, still another slit his own throat, and a few made good their bid for freedom. Nevertheless the boarding methodically proceeded. Indians were crowded into the barges under the July sun, and onlookers assumed that many would not make it to Oklahoma. Jim Henry remained behind, fearing that he would never leave the jail alive, because he knew that Georgians and Alabamians were demanding that he "meet the reward of his murderous conduct." Before he departed, his young wife visited him, and his jailers reported that their final separation was touching.[22]

Steamboats sped down the Alabama River, past the Holy Ground, sites of Alabama talwas and temple mounds, and over waters on which French bateaumen and Panton, Leslie, and Company employees had shipped goods to Fort Toulouse and the Upper Creeks. Passing under the guns of old crumbling brick French Fort Condé at Mobile, Indians debarked below the city. Whites were struck by the melancholy spectacle of white-haired, erect Neamathla, that "noble specimen of the savage." Relatively unscathed by the recent Creek War, Mobile citizenry were better able than other whites, whose farms had been burned and family members killed, to reflect dispassionately on the Indians' plight. The increasing number of ships coming into their port, and newspaper quotes of the high price of cotton on the Liverpool market also aided their humanity. Neamathla, who two decades previously had burned Lieutenant Scott's men at the stake, was evolving into a noble savage, who in a valiant endeavor had defended his doomed homeland. It was inevitable that the Indians must leave the East, but in their new western settlement the government should be generous and just to these unfortunates: "We shall . . . have no more of them in Mobile . . . we do not regret this . . . [but] we have been permitted for once to contemplate the red man of the forest in all his wild and native grandeur of character . . . we have seen what we have seen and many will be the day ere the impression that was made will be worn out from our memory."[23] The shackled Neamathla would not forget either.

With remarkable efficiency authorities had sent off several thousand hostiles from the Southeast, though not all accompanied Neamathla and Neamico. Jim Henry remained behind in Montgomery until he was eventually released and sent on to the West. He was fortunate. Six companions captured and brought into Fort Mitchell were turned over to civil authorities at Girard, Alabama, across from Columbus to answer for their crimes. They languished in jail until taken out on 29 November 1836 and hanged. Georgians and Alabamians congregated to witness the spectacle: "Doubtless some unlucky son of the forest suffered in the very midst of his innocence. But it cannot be helped—blood for blood, life for life, it is the golden maxim; the wails of the widow and the cry of the orphan sued for revenge in tones of thunder."[24]

After Neamathla and Neamico departed, many other Creeks followed, usually by land. That they had been neutral or friendly during the recent conflict made little difference. White settlers prematurely swarmed over Indian villages and farms while Creek families were making final preparations. Indian Toney protested that he had not sold and had certainly not been paid for his land, and he shot and killed the Macon County sheriff who was serving an eviction notice. Toney was rushed off to the Tuskegee jail for trial and to be protected from lynching.[25] Incidents such as this increased Opothleyahola's resolve to depart, and in September he and his 2,300 followers at Tuckabatchee got under way. Hillis hayas extinguished fires in the squares, carefully preserving the ashes and flints used by the talwa's fire makers. Placing them alongside copper plates and other sacred objects, medicine men wrapped them in deerskin bundles, which they strapped to their backs. Then without saying a word they led warriors and their families westward. White settlers in Tuscaloosa and other cities en route to Memphis came down to the road to watch the long procession of squalid, forlorn, miserable, and dejected walking and mounted Indians, accompanied by government wagons, Indian agents, and troops. When the procession camped for a few days to allow for rest and hunting, enterprising whites visited to exchange whiskey for the Creeks' gold and other possessions.[26] Opothleyahola led the first of the large overland parties, but others soon followed. Three thousand Indians assembled at Wetumpka on the Coosa not far from Fort Toulouse and in early September marched westward, crossing the Coosa and leaving behind the Upper Creek heartland. Four thousand Upper Creeks assembled at Talladega soon set off on the same route: "the whole nation is in motion," and by early December at least fifteen thousand Creeks had arrived in Oklahoma.[27]

Nevertheless many still remained in the Southeast. The Seminole population had increased sharply in 1836, and with few exceptions the Muscogulges in Florida were determined to fight or hide out. In Georgia and especially in Alabama other Muscogulges did the same thing. In addition Jim Boy's band of at least 3,500 were among those still in the East. His friendly Indians had furnished the bulk of the warriors for the 776-man Creek regiment sent to Florida. Old men, women, and children, however, remained behind in the Alabama Upper Creek country. General Jesup had advocated using Creek allies in the Florida campaigns, but other whites, especially those in Alabama, had misgivings, fearing warriors would go over to the Seminoles or join unsubdued Creeks in Alabama. Though their menfolk were away, families of friendly Creek warriors still occupied villages, retarding white development of the Black Belt.

Ann Cornells, one of Jim Boy's friendly Indians, lived near Tuskegee. Whites set her cabin on fire, stole two Negroes and a young Indian boy, and sent Ann fleeing for her life. A fifteen-year-old Creek girl from upper Eufaula town escaped from Alabama militiamen who tried to assault her, though she had been shot in the leg. Other Creek women were not as quick as this

298   nimble fifteen-year-old. A ninety-year-old man at Thlapthlako
        (Jim Boy's) Town had "his head stove in with . . . butts of mus-
        kets." Though their menfolk were still in Florida, families of
        Jim Boy's warriors were happy enough to assemble with only
        thirty-six hours' notice, and by March 1837, 1,900 were on the
        road. Boarding steamboats and barges they sailed down the Tal-
        lapoosa and Alabama rivers first to Fort Morgan below Mobile.
        Soon, however, they were transferred to Pass Christian eighty
        miles to the west on the Gulf to await the warriors' return. Creek
        families at Pass Christian were hostages for these Indian soldiers'
        good behavior in Florida.[28]

        In the late summer of 1837 Creek auxiliaries, many of them
        sick, after being discharged in Florida, joined their families. For
        months 3,500 friendly Indians were encamped at Pass Christian,
        awaiting arrival of the last Indians from Florida and news that
        the Arkansas River was high enough for steamboat travel. Jim
        Boy's Creeks erected tents and bark huts in woods close to the
        Pass Christian lighthouse, while in an adjoining open field bor-
        dering the white sandy beach, a large wooden hotel serving the
        finest wines was nearing completion. A diversion for the guests
        was the Indians: "idle, careless, and mendicant" warriors
        lounged about while women, busy at assorted tasks, were clean,
        neatly attired, and attractive. Jim Boy, whom they could not
        talk to because he did not speak English, was "a tall, fine looking
        savage." Despite prohibitions, white entrepreneurs sold Indians
        rum and whiskey, and both whites and Indians bet on the out-
        come of the ball game. During 1837–38 almost 4,000 Indians
        arrived at Pass Christian, though 15 percent or more would never
        see Fort Gibson. Graves were interspersed among the trees at
        Pass Christian and on the banks of the Mississippi River.[29]

        In the summer of 1837 550 Creeks who had hidden out with
        the Cherokees finally were rounded up and escorted to Muscle
        Shoals. Boarding steamboats and flatboats, still guarded by sol-
        diers, and sailing night and day, the Indians took less than a
        month to reach Fort Gibson. Losses of 15 percent were due
        almost as much to desertions as to diseases.[30]

        The last major group of Muscogulge emigrants were the Sem-
        inoles, almost 4,000 of whom between 1836 and 1843 were

relocated in the West. This figure does not include those like Osceola who left Florida but never arrived in Oklahoma. It was expected that most Seminoles, like most Creeks, would depart in 1836. As it turned out only 400 Seminoles, those of Black Dirt's band, emigrated that year, and the Seminole population actually increased. Black Dirt (Fuchalusti Hadjo) was a friend, perhaps a kinsman, of Charlie Emathla, whom Osceola had killed. Black Dirt and his followers withdrew to Fort Brooke and collaborated with American soldiers until they sailed away in May 1836. Though beset by disease and hardships, Black Dirt's journey to New Orleans and Fort Gibson was relatively swift.[31] The next year more than 500 additional Seminoles—those captured with Osceola and Wildcat and hostiles from south Florida brought into Tampa—were sent out of Florida. To prevent captives from escaping like Wildcat at Saint Augustine, some Indians were rushed off to Fort Moultrie and Castle Pinckney in Charleston harbor.

Osceola, the most famous, attracted considerable attention, attending a play in the local theater and sitting for portraitist George Catlin. Osceola, however, did not have long to live as the ministrations of a white physician and a hillis haya proved ineffectual. In a dignified ceremony, soldiers buried the Seminole warrior outside Fort Moultrie.[32] Early in 1838 vessels transported Micanopy and other Charleston prisoners on to New Orleans, and as time passed additional small Seminole parties were dispatched from Charleston. Major Isaac Clark, quartermaster and emigrating agent stationed in New Orleans, was surprised in April 1839 when without any warning three Seminole warriors arrived in irons. He informed superiors that he had no instructions and did not know whether to shoot or hang the prisoners . . . but of course he would follow orders.[33]

Small groups of Indians from West Florida, variously classified as Seminoles, Creeks, or Apalachicolas, voluntarily surrendered or were captured in the late 1830s, and were forwarded to New Orleans. Steamboats cruised up and down the Apalachicola River occasionally picking up isolated parties. Indians were fed, clothed, and well treated but not informed—until it was too late—that they were bound for Oklahoma.[34] Between 1836 and

1840 West Florida Indians from the Apalachicola River and Dog Island near the river's mouth, along with prisoners from Tampa, Saint Augustine, and Charleston, made the voyage to New Orleans and on to Fort Gibson or nearly so. Having died on a steamboat only forty miles below the fort, King Philip, Wildcat's father, was buried on the banks of the Arkansas, and warriors and soldiers fired one hundred guns over his grave.[35]

Spanish Indians were among those sent out of Florida before the great exodus of the early 1840s, and more than the usual pathos marked their removal. When General Jesup insisted that the "whole Seminole nation" leave, he included Spanish Indians on ranchos below Tampa. That male white Cubans had Christian Indian wives, children, and grandchildren made no difference, and by the end of 1837 ranchos, some a century old, were broken up. A few Indians escaped by sea to Cuba or other islands; some joined militant Seminole bands in the interior; but most Spanish Indians were shipped to Oklahoma. To no avail did Cuban fathers and grandfathers protest that their loved ones were being torn from them. After Spanish Indians had relocated to Oklahoma, from time to time dejected Cuban husbands arrived unannounced at Fort Gibson, still insisting that their wives and children were not Seminoles, and that their Indian families should be compensated and allowed to leave. Some Indian wives on the ranchos were members of Black Dirt's band. Paying no heed to Cuban and Indian husbands, Black Dirt's warriors forcefully took the women away, and they accompanied Black Dirt's group, which sailed from Tampa in 1836. Most Spanish Indians departed in 1837, though for years a trickle continued to arrive at Fort Gibson. They avowed they were not Seminoles—and hostile Seminoles concurred. Spanish Indians eventually disappeared, absorbed by the Seminoles and to a lesser extent by the Creeks. Contemporary western Seminoles and Creeks, however, still remember hardships encountered by their Spanish forebears on the Trail of Tears.[36]

Associated with Spanish Indians below Tampa were about fifty Upper Creeks who, in the era of the American Revolution, had migrated with two Spaniards from Tuckabatchee to Black Water Bay near Pensacola. Living on a small Spanish land grant, they provided fish and oysters for the Pensacola market. Having transformed themselves from commercial hunters to commercial fishermen, they were determined not to go to Oklahoma, and they vowed that they would sooner die or join hostile Creeks near Fort Mitchell. Because of their small numbers it is unclear whether Indians on the Black Water Bay rancho ever emigrated or instead unobtrusively retired to the interior, perhaps associating themselves with Upper Creeks in the piney barrens near Weatherford's plantation.[37]

The primary Seminole removal occurred during 1841 and 1842. Parties of Florida Indians who had voluntarily submitted or been captured in those years departed in groups of 100 to 400 from the panhandle, the Apalachicola River, Tampa, Miami, Fort Lauderdale, and Saint Augustine. By 1844 just over 3,800 had left the territory, and this figure did not include Indians not classified as Seminoles. Officers on Apalachicola River steamboats who picked up small groups of Indians in 1838 were instructed to send these Indians to the West "as parties of the Creek Nation, and in no other light."[38] Rather than going to Texas, part of Blount's followers had withdrawn to the Upper Creeks and emigrated with them. After arriving in Oklahoma, however, they insisted they really were Seminoles and petitioned the government to furnish the guns and blankets provided for in the 1832 Seminole removal treaty.[39] By the mid-1840s only small groups of Indians remained in Florida—in the Everglades, Okefenokee, Pensacola hinterland, and similar inhospitable, inaccessible areas, posing little threat, perhaps not even being noticed.

Remembrances of how they were treated—or mistreated—aboard ship, and of their ancestors' fierce resistance in the East stand out vividly in the consciousness of the Oklahoma Seminoles. Dick McGirt, who in the twentieth century lived in Tuckabatchee Town (Oklahoma), passed on the story of a Seminole who had come from Florida. The old warrior related how American soldiers had captured him, three other warriors, and their wives and children. Soldiers bound the four warriors closely, and guards taunted the captives by asking if they were afraid to die. When thrown into a small room aboard a ship bound for

"Sorrows of the Seminoles—Banished from Florida." Library of Congress, lot 9356. Courtesy Florida State Archives. Photo no. 5269.

New Orleans, the four Seminoles resolved to escape. Rushing out, two were shot, while the other two hid for a time in the lower part of the boat before jumping overboard to swim "the mighty river" to freedom. In the water one saw a large snake that had the head of a cow, perhaps a manatee (sea cow). Among the prophets, however, there was a tradition that the Great Serpent, the evil powers, the scum of the universe, and the Americans were the same.[40]

After the Second Seminole War wound down around 1843 and most hostile Creeks in Alabama and western Florida had been rounded up, small groups of eastern Muscogulges still continued to migrate to Oklahoma from the Southeast. Paddy Carr and his partisans had remained on the Georgia-Alabama frontier as long as possible. Carr was wealthy, and except for facial markings looked as much like a white as an Indian, and had served effectively with Jesup's army in Florida. Presumably he assumed or hoped that time would soon finish the process of acculturation and that he and his descendants could remain in the Chattahoochee Valley as whites. But this was not to be. During the era of the American Revolution there had been room on the frontier for George Galphin and his wives, but three-quarters of a century later the frontier in the vicinity of Columbus and Fort Mitchell was rapidly disappearing, and little room remained for Paddy and his spouses. At the head of nineteen Indians and their slaves, Paddy early in 1847 left for Oklahoma.[41] White Indian countrymen had more choice than Paddy. Bidding their Indian families good-bye, some remained behind in the East. Others, however, accompanied their families to Oklahoma, identifying themselves even more with the Indian way of life.

Additional Muscogulges followed Paddy. The brief Third Seminole War (1855–58) resulted in the expulsion of almost 300 more émigrés from the Everglades.[42] According to Seminole tradition several hundred additional Seminoles left Florida for Oklahoma soon after the Civil War ended in 1865. Whether these Indians had been living in northern or southern Florida and whether they were black Seminoles is unclear.[43] The elderly Creek George Abbot did not reach Oklahoma until just after World War I. His parents had moved from Alabama to eastern Louisiana where George was born in 1862. In 1919 George and his Cherokee wife moved on to Oklahoma, arriving there by train.[44]

Black Muscogulges were caught up in and affected by the Indian removal. Less room remained in the South for a zambo— or a mulatto or a mestizo—and differences persisted as to whether black Muscogulges were really Negroes or Indians. The zambo Sarah, daughter of Sam Factor, "a respectable old Indian," lived with her three children on the lower Apalachicola River. Slave raiders, considering that Sarah and her children, if they were not, ought to be Negroes, captured them in 1836 and sold

304 them near Columbus, Georgia.[45] Muscogulges on the Apalachicola River in 1838 asserted they were ready to leave except that part of their tribe was detained as slaves. Protests were in vain, and Indian husbands departed, leaving their wives and children behind to become part of the Old South's Negro population.

Whites and Indians alike claimed black Muscogulges, and this delayed western removal. Anxious to end the conflict in Florida, military commanders in 1837 and 1838 promised Seminoles that if they surrendered, black Seminoles could accompany them without danger. Small groups accepted the offer and sailed from Tampa. But interested whites followed them to New Orleans and persuaded the local sheriff to incarcerate the "fugitive slaves." Asserting that black Seminoles were prisoners of war rather than fugitives, after litigious delays army officers were successful in forwarding the Indian Negroes to Oklahoma.[46] But even the West did not necessarily provide security and stability for black Muscogulges, and whites and Creeks continued to insist they were slaves and carry them off.

Whether arriving by land or water, the first stop for emigrating Muscogulges was square, log Fort Gibson with blockhouses at two corners and outbuildings and gardens spread out over a considerable area on the Grand River above its intersection with the Arkansas. It was the port of entry, the Ellis Island, for more than 20,000 southeastern Muscogulges. Here they rested, received rations, clothing, agricultural implements, seed, annuity payments, and possibly guns and cattle to replace those given up in the East. Ox carts, wagons, and horses transported Indians on the final leg of their journey, usually much less than one hundred miles farther.[47]

Muscogulges arriving in Oklahoma "brought the old devil with them" from the East,[48] or as a Creek later characterized it "old prejudices cropped out from time to time" in the West.[49] Six hundred miles had not put an end to tribal, clan, and moiety rivalries, and they affected life in the West as they had in the East. Chilly and Roley McIntosh established the Creek National Council in the West. Seminoles—Hitchitis, Yuchis, Miccosukees—were expected to locate on the Creek preserve and be subject to the Muskogee-dominated National Council. As Roley and Chilly McIntosh protested to Americans in 1834: We don't want the Seminoles to have their own lands in the West. "If [we are] cut up into separate clans, then shall we be unhappy."[50] Fearing for their slaves, if not their lives, Alligator, Holatoochee, Coacoochee, and their Seminole followers settled among the Cherokees no more than fifteen miles from Fort Gibson. Though establishing new towns in the Creek Territory, Black Dirt and Micanopy kept their villages as far as possible from those of McIntosh.[51] Neamathla's and Neamico's followers, primarily Hitchitis and Yuchis, had similar ethnically based fears. The two Hitchiti leaders met with Roley McIntosh at Fort Gibson and agreed to be governed by—"to submit to"—the laws of the Creek nation, i.e. McIntosh's laws. The alternative was for soldiers to put shackles back on Neamathla and Neamico.[52]

Despite the American contention of a unified Creek nation, the realities of the Muscogulge condition had surfaced from time to time even before removal. Colonel John J. Abert, a federal agent supervising purchase of Indian allotments by the government, realized this: no common bond existed among the Creeks except for one or two closely related towns. Larger towns were generally strangers to one another with different languages and customs. In groups of 2,000 to 3,000, emigrating Creeks usually belonged to a single talwa and its satellites, and seldom needed to be bilingual to understand one another.[53] Conditions among Muscogulges in Florida were the same, except that numbers of Indians were proportionally smaller. Their diversity was made clear to army officers in 1837 who tried to conclude a removal treaty with the Seminole nation. Friendly Creek, Yahola Hajo, after visiting his uncle, Seminole chief Jumper, reminded negotiators that Seminoles acknowledged no authority of the chiefs to make any treaty unless all the heads of the families (clans) in the nation agreed.[54] Two years later the army captured and sent to New Orleans a group of approximately 250 Seminoles. Lieutenant John Sprague, who had helped capture the Indians, characterized these Seminoles quartered in the New Orleans barracks as remnants of six tribes—Seminoles, Creeks, Tallahassees, Miccosukees, Yuchis, and Hitchitis. "Now . . . they turned upon each other, and indulged in the gratification

306   of their vicious and savage passions."[55] Holata Emathla was not
with this group, but at the war's outset he had categorically told
the Americans that, though a Seminole and ready to emigrate,
he could not settle with Seminoles in Oklahoma. They would
kill him like they had his brother Charley Emathla.[56]

Opothleyahola's followers were the first large group of Muscogulges to arrive in Oklahoma in 1836 via the overland route.
These Upper Creeks were Tuckabatchees of the same fire. Having lived among the Upper Creeks, they had absorbed much of
the pure Muskogee language and culture. Though Tuckabatchees had turned on Hitchitis and Yuchis in the 1836 Creek War,
they earlier had been instrumental in "laying the Muskogee
William McIntosh to rest." As he approached Fort Gibson,
Opothleyahola realized, as did Roley and Chilly McIntosh long
on the scene, that the "old devil" was alive. In Alabama and
Oklahoma Opothleyahola protested that he could not live with
the McIntosh Creeks and instead hoped to settle in Texas.

Both Anglo-American *empresarios* and Mexican officials
wanted Opothleyahola and his followers to settle in eastern
Texas, the former to help develop their concessions, and the
latter to have Tuckabatchees—along with Koasatis, Alabamas,
Seminoles, Cherokees, and Shawnees also in Texas—serve as a
counterweight to Anglos and untamed Plains Indians. The
Tuckabatchee chief repeatedly tried to make necessary arrangements to have his annuity paid on foreign soil, and he was
conscious that creditors could not touch him in Texas. But
despite considerable efforts, Opothleyahola's attempt to relocate in Texas failed, frustrated in part by the fall of the Alamo
in 1836 and the Texan Revolution. Tuckabatchees settled down
on the Canadian River away from Roley and Chilly McIntosh,
each group hoping that the old devil and clan vengeance might
be restrained, that memories of how William McIntosh had been
laid to rest might be forgotten, and that Muscogulge people could
set about building a new life on the edge of the Great Plains.[57]

By the late 1840s with few exceptions which Muscogulge
people were to be known as Seminoles and which as Creeks had
been resolved. Pascofar's band was one of those arriving at Fort
Gibson. In 1836 he had fought as a Creek in Alabama, and he

continued resisting in southern Alabama and western Florida, until 1842 when he finally submitted in the Florida panhandle. As soon as Pascofar reached Oklahoma this Creek chief was designated a Seminole, and in the ensuing years he, along with Nocose Yahola, Octiarche, and other Creeks of 1836, became leading spokesmen for western Seminoles.[58]

Black Muscogulges accompanied almost every party arriving at Fort Gibson, their presence ensuring that the old devil would not die. Disagreement persisted as to whether they were free Indians—members of the Tiger, Alligator, and similar clans—or Negro slaves. Memories of the black Muscogulges' role in the Creek land frauds, the 1836 Creek War, and the Seminole conflict remained alive. Gopher John, whose horse was shot out from under him near Fort Gibson, could attest to this.

Talwas in Oklahoma continued to reflect the ethnic diversity of the Muscogulge people. Nevertheless, intimidation by United States soldiers stationed at nearby Fort Gibson, the external threat of Osages and other "wild" (Plains) Indians, and common hardships of building cabins, clearing and planting fields, and subsisting in a new environment, all restrained the old devil, that is, until some new crisis occurred. Firing at Fort Sumter in 1861 rattled Osceola's bones, and served as a catalyst to unleash the old devil. Both the North and the South bid for the Indians' support. More often than not the McIntosh-Muskogee moiety aligned itself with the Confederacy, while non-Muskogees tended to side with the north. Opothleyahola and the Tuckabatchees were pro-Union as were the Yuchis and other non-Muskogees. John Chupco, a veteran of the Florida wars, and several hundred Seminoles promptly joined Opothleyahola, and before the war ended two-thirds of the Seminoles and almost all of the black Seminoles were on the Union side. Hitchiti Billy Bowlegs fought alongside blue-coated soldiers in the West as energetically as he had struggled against them in Florida. Black Muscogulges usually sided with the North because blacks often had found it expedient to affiliate with the non-Muskogee moiety and the northern cause was identified with emancipation. The main exception were Negro slaves belonging to Chilly and Daniel McIntosh and their friends, who often had little

308   choice but to support the Confederacy. Sometimes families split along clan lines, the father fighting for the Confederacy and the mother and children joining Opothleyahola in Kansas.

The 1813–17 internecine civil war of the Muscogulges in the East broke out afresh in the West during 1861–65. Battlefields were not Horseshoe Bend, Fort Mims, the Negro Fort, Miccosukee, and Bowlegs Town on the Suwannee, but Round Mountain and Chustenahlah in northern Oklahoma. Opothleyahola's defeated followers retired to Kansas, and their retreat turned into a disaster, a rout, as warriors and their families froze and starved before finding a measure of security on the upper Verdigris. The fortunes of pro-Union Loyal Creeks (and Seminoles) improved as they and northern soldiers revenged themselves on McIntosh's partisans at Honey Springs near Fort Gibson. Some of the Seminoles, such as John Jumper, served the Confederacy; Jumper fought against Opothleyahola's followers in the West as his ancestors had in the East.

Following Appomattox peace came to or was imposed on the Muscogulge people. As with the Treaty of Fort Jackson after Horseshoe Bend, friendly as well as hostile Indians suffered. In 1814 friendly Indians more often than not had been Muskogees, and in 1865 they tended to be in the opposite moiety, but that made little difference. Creeks and Seminoles—friendly and hostile alike—were required to give up much of their Oklahoma lands and live on separate reduced holdings. Whatever their former status, black Muscogulges became free, a stipulation that caused the McIntosh party grief.[59]

Relative peace ensued until 1882 when the more conservative, traditional often non-Muskogee elements, with Isparhecher as their leader, raised the standard of revolt against Samuel Checote's followers, who frequently had a pro-Confederate, pro-McIntosh moiety heritage. Both Checote and Isparhecher were non-Muskogees and belonged to the Tiger clan. But in the East Checote had attended the Methodist mission school at Asbury, and as a youth in Alabama and subsequently in Oklahoma, he had rapidly adopted more and more of the culture of his white (mestizo) father and shed that of his Creek mother. Muscogulges were plunged into civil war (the Green Peach War), and peace was not restored until 1883 after a few dozen lives had been lost.[60] A similar cleavage among the Muscogulges could be seen in the nativistic movement and abortive rebellion of 1901 led by Crazy Snake (Chitto Harjo).[61] The ethnic moiety lines of division, sometimes distinct, sometimes blurred and confused, can be discerned in Crazy Snake's rebellion, the Green Peach War, the 1861 Civil War, the Creek-Seminole conflicts of the 1830s, the 1813 Creek War, Indian hostilities during the American Revolution, and in conflicts going back as far as written and oral accounts permit. Of course, distinct non-Muskogee tribes at times bitterly fought each other. It was possible to restrain but not kill the old devil.

Although Muscogulge traditions and ancient rivalries persisted in Oklahoma, Indians at the same time adopted or had imposed on them more and more of the white culture. This trend, long underway in the East, accelerated in Oklahoma, greatly influencing the conduct of Indians in both moieties. At an earlier period the tendency to adopt white culture readily could be seen in the Southeast with Alexander McGillivray and William McIntosh in the Muskogee moiety, and William Weatherford, Hillis Haya, and Jim Henry in the opposite. All were mestizos, and many could be mistaken for whites. Baptist, Methodist, and other Protestant missionaries made more converts in the West than at Withington and Asbury. Perhaps the most remarkable conversion was Jim Henry, who became a Methodist minister and in time a bishop. Georgia Methodists, who knew at first hand about the burnings and killings in the 1836 Creek War, visited Oklahoma, still not sure whether a pearly gate or a cell door was most appropriate for the bishop. English and Muskogee were languages used in Oklahoma mission schools, and a considerable number of Natchez, Alabama, Yuchi, and other non-Muskogee pupils had to master at least one of these new languages.

Though weakened, opposition to civilization and conversion persisted among traditional or conservative Indians, who often had non-Muskogee backgrounds. They resolutely attempted to retain their languages and separate identities. Every day elderly members of the Alabama town taught their young the dialect

310   spoken on the Alabama River in the old country, but in the long
run, theirs was a losing battle against Muskogee and English.
Whatever their ethnic backgrounds, hillis hayas attempted to
preserve and pass on tribal traditions and medical practices.
Customary training to become a medicine man included lengthy
instruction, eight days ritualistic fasting, purging, and solitary
meditation. Having completed this, the candidate sat on one
end of an east-west log to await "that thing" (a lizard-shaped
reptile), which would appear in the east, jump into his open
mouth, and enter his system. Young Adam Grayson from Ke-
chobadagu Town (Pharoah, Oklahoma), was not willing to wait
on the end of the log for "that thing," though he would have
liked to become a hillis haya.[62]

Some of the most violent criticism of the missionaries continued to come from acculturated Indians who were alarmed by
their preaching to slaves. Having damned missionaries in the
mid 1830s, Chilly McIntosh in 1861 became a colonel in the
Confederate Army and joined other Southerners who had no use
for such "abolitionists." Muscogulges in Oklahoma no longer
had to send their children away to the Choctaw Academy or
elsewhere for an education. Despite opposition, missionary
teachers at Tallahassee, Asbury, and Coweta in Oklahoma had
reason to be satisfied and were more successful than ever in
curtailing daily dances and ball play and in making English, if
not Muskogee, the lingua franca.[63]

In the West, the Muscogulges' economy both changed and
remained the same. Indians still planted maize, beans, and
squash, and a tall log mortar stood by Indian cabins to pound
corn for sofke and hoecake. Except for ceremonial purposes,
however, coffee largely supplanted the black drink. Indian
women known as Superlamy, Toaknulga, and Sofilamaja in the
East became Mrs. Tiger or Elizabeth Harjo in the West. Commercial hunting persisted, but to an extent buffalo replaced
white-tailed deer. Indian countryman Joseph A. Johnson had
remained in Chambers County, Alabama, while a majority of
his mestizo in-laws emigrated to the West, and he watched
eastern hunting lands disappear. In 1837 he asked his brother-
in-law to send back 1,000 good buffalo hides.[64] Southeastern

Muscogulges had been herdsmen and drovers until the moment of departure. When the Chisholm Trail and similar cattle trails were opened up through the Oklahoma Indian Territory, Muscogulges exchanged their long whips for lariats, but little else was new. They had seen cattle replace buffalo in the East and were not surprised when the same thing happened in the West.

Wild Indians in the East, "savages" with ragged clothing and tattered blankets, who had sallied forth from swamps and piney barrens to terrorize Alabamians, Georgians, and Floridians, became transformed into "civilized" Indians in Oklahoma. "Wild" Indians in the West were buffalo Indians (Plains Indians), primarily Osages. In 1831 Chilly McIntosh met with Osage chiefs at Fort Gibson in an attempt to prevent the spread of hostilities. The highly acculturated Chilly contrasted sharply with his Plains Indians counterparts. This, of course, was not the first time Creeks and Osages had encountered one another. Hillis Haya and Tecumseh had spoken in Osage villages before 1812 to urge unity, and after Fort Mims, Creek red sticks repeatedly urged Osages to join the struggle against the Americans. But Chilly was no red stick, and as far as he was concerned Creek negotiations with the Osages began when he sat down with them at Fort Gibson. Despite negotiations at Fort Gibson, Creeks and Seminoles joined Buffalo Bill and other whites in appropriating the western Indians' lands and indiscriminately slaughtering the buffalo; as a result, enraged Osages, Pawnees, and other Plains Indians retaliated. In time when a young Creek girl married a Sioux and lived in a tepee in far western Oklahoma, she, like many whites, was surprised that once you got to know such wild Indians they were not so savage.[65]

After removal was essentially completed in the 1840s, whites, including those residing in the Southeast and soldiers who had fought in the Seminole wars, manifested sympathy for and interest in the language and culture of the Indians who had been removed. Soldiers, missionaries, traders, and Indian agents had easy intercourse with Oklahoma Muscogulges, and they interviewed and reminisced with them. To his surprise Major Ethan Allen Hitchcock, while investigating frauds of white contractors supplying the Indians, discovered that Hillis Haya's

312 daughter, Milly Francis, poverty-stricken and with three surviving children, was living on the Arkansas River near Fort Gibson. In 1818 she had saved Duncan McCrimmon from being burned by Neamathla's and Hillis Haya's warriors on the Wakulla River. Milly's father had been executed at Saint Marks, and her brother Earle had died in a Montgomery jail. Sympathy for the distressed Milly, this latter-day Pocahontas who had rescued young McCrimmon, was aroused. In 1844 Congress granted this mestizo a ninety-six-dollar pension and a twenty-dollar medal for her conduct during the First Seminole War. Milly made no formal application for the pension, and for several years nothing happened. Creek agent James Logan, visiting her children in 1848, discovered that Milly, not quite fifty, had recently died of consumption. Two of her children, who had families of their own, spoke English. Milly's eldest son Joseph said he would be proud to accept the medal and would carefully preserve it. Some of Hillis Haya's progeny treasured Cockburn's belligerent proclamations; others a medal from the United States Congress.[66]

Hillis Haya had been executed in 1814, and Tecumseh, Hillis Haya's companion, had been killed a year or so previously. But Tecumseh's brother, Tenskwatawa, the Shawnee prophet, still lived, having moved to the Indian Reservation in eastern Kansas with the Shawnees. A widespread though overemphasized tradition persisted that Tenskwatawa was the true prophet of the early nineteenth century, and that Hillis Haya and the others were his disciples. White Indian agents interviewed the aged Tenskwatawa, and George Catlin painted his picture; all were interested in learning more about the fanaticism that had inspired warriors at the Prophet's Town on the Tippecanoe in the north and at the Holy Ground on the Alabama in the south, and that had motivated Creeks, with cow tails tied to their belts and oblivious to the white man's bullets, to rush headlong into the open gates at Fort Mims. Black Muscogulges, survivors of Fort Mims, were in Oklahoma and also in the East to relate accounts of what happened that awful day in 1813.[67]

Attention devoted to Oklahoma can give the false impression that all Muscogulges were relocated in this Indian Territory. However, Blount and his followers had joined the Koasatis on the Trinity River in eastern Texas, and Opothleyahola, before 1836 when Texas belonged to Mexico and later when it became independent, repeatedly had attempted to lead the Tuckabatchees to Texas. Busily acquiring Creek allotments in the East and pushing Indians off the land, white speculators simultaneously encouraged them to resettle in eastern Texas on enormous grants recently acquired from the Mexican government. At one time or another small groups of Alabamas, Koasatis, Taensas, Shawnees, large parties of Cherokees, and other non-Muskogees did move to Texas, or perhaps to Louisiana.

Indian countryman James Moore remained in eastern Alabama, though his mestizo children emigrated—John to Oklahoma, Peggy and Catherine to Texas, and Jackson died near Shreveport en route to Texas. Thousands of Americans who had migrated into Mexican Texas revolted in 1836, and nine years later became citizens of the United States. This deterred Muscogulges who otherwise might have moved to Texas. Peggy wanted brother John to join her, but John declined: "that territory will soon be a white settlement . . . it will not do for any Indian blood to go to live [in Texas] at the present time."[68]

Mexico retained control of adjoining, thinly settled Coahuila, an arid, mountainous province not likely soon to become white man's country. The Seminole Coacoochee (Wildcat) realized this. As a Seminole in Oklahoma he feared McIntosh's Creeks and worried about their designs on black Seminoles in his midst. Encouraged by Mexicans bestowing generous land grants, Wildcat and Gopher John, collaborating with Kickapoos and miscellaneous other Indians, led their followers from Oklahoma to Coahuila, fighting a rearguard action against pursuing Creeks who were angry that Seminoles, especially those who were black, were attempting to escape the Creek National Council's jurisdiction. Nevertheless, commencing in the 1840s, Seminoles alternated between Oklahoma and Coahuila. In the 1930s and later, Seminoles, especially conservative or traditional ones "not civilized," still felt Mexico had more to offer than Oklahoma, whose landscape was being filled with oil rigs. Seminoles, largely black Seminoles, live in northern Coahuila today.[69]

Some Muscogulges stayed in the East and relocated to nearby

314   islands, primarily Cuba and the Bahamas. Like those accompanying Wildcat, many were Afro-Indians or black Muscogulges. Black Seminoles had long associated the Bahamas with freedom. At the end of the American Revolution and during the War of 1812 British officers who had promised Southern blacks liberty often had come from or passed through the Bahamas. Aboard privateers, merchant ships, and in their oceangoing dugouts, black Seminoles who were sailors repeatedly sailed over to the Bahamas and back again. In the Bahamas they first heard about Britain's abolishing the slave trade in 1807, and it was there that they perceived specifically what this meant for blacks.

As time passed, more and more black Florida Seminoles stayed in the islands. The broad outline of this movement, of this southern underground railroad, can be seen. After the destruction of the Negro Fort on the Apalachicola River in 1816 and Jackson's invasion two years later, it seemed probable that the United States would acquire Spanish Florida. In consequence many black Seminoles moved farther south down the peninsula. Their Maroon settlements could be found around Tampa Bay, at Angola on Sarasota Bay, and elsewhere on the Gulf Coast, and also at Biscayne Bay and the Keys on the Atlantic. Fishermen, turtlers, privateers, soldiers of fortune trying to liberate Spanish America, and wreckers carried parties of harried Negroes over to the Bahamas.[70] Zephaniah Kingsley, probably the largest slave trader in Florida in the 1820s with a plantation north of Saint Augustine, complained that two of his slaves had run off to the Bahamas.[71] How they got there or their point of departure is unknown; perhaps they used a dugout canoe. Other black Seminoles did, and such dugouts long survived on Andros Island, symbols of black Seminoles' journey to freedom.[72]

Cuba was another terminus of Florida's "underground railroad." The institution of slavery was entrenched there, and Cuba did not have the same reputation for freedom as did the Bahamas. Nevertheless black Seminoles, particularly those associated with fishing ranchos on Florida's Gulf Coast, had easy access to Havana and took advantage of the opportunity. In many instances black Seminoles regarded themselves as free but realized that southern planters and McIntosh's followers had different ideas. As American soldiers and McIntosh's Creeks raided deeper and deeper into the Florida peninsula, Cuba looked more attractive.

Most black Seminoles who relocated in the islands are ciphers, though occasionally litigation, instituted or supported by abolitionists, affords details. Mitchell Roberts, a black Seminole who in the 1850s testified in the Bahamas, is an example. He disclosed that he had been born in Florida, had joined the Royal Colonial Marines during the War of 1812, and had served at the British (Negro) Fort on the Apalachicola River. He fortunately was not present when it blew up in 1816, and he accompanied blacks who moved from the Apalachicola River to Tampa Bay. In 1820, two years after Andrew Jackson and McIntosh's Creeks had swept into Florida, Roberts departed for the Bahamas, where he presumably spent his remaining days.[73]

Roberts's testimony in the 1850s concerned Ben Newton, another black Seminole. In 1820 Newton's free black mother, Elizabeth Newton, resided at Tampa where she apprenticed young Ben to a Bahamian ship captain. In some fashion another ship captain got hold of Ben, took him to Cuba, and sold him as a slave. Ben protested that he was free to no avail, that is until the 1850s, when he escaped from his plantation and fled to the United States consulate in Havana. Abolitionists in the Bahamas and New York heard about Ben and took up his case. Unfortunately Ben died before the courts had time to rule in his favor. The only time he had ever been truly free was as a young black Seminole in Florida. His aged mother, Elizabeth, who had maintained her freedom both in Florida and Andros Island, never saw Ben again and could only bemoan his death.[74]

Part of the Seminole diaspora from Florida resulted in black Seminoles' hoeing cotton or serving as domestics on antebellum Georgia and Alabama plantations. The wars and removal of the 1830s had resulted in many uprooted and displaced Muscogulge children who were held by whites. John P. Booth, a new settler at Irwinton (Eufaula), was indignant when charged with keeping an eleven-year-old girl as a slave. He insisted the destitute child had been abandoned in 1837 by hostile Indians returning from Florida to Alabama, and as a humanitarian measure he took her

316   in: "I [don't consider her] a slave, she is not permitted to associate
with my Negroes more than my own children. She has had more
religious instruction than my critics."[75] Over a hundred miles to
the east in Lowndes County, Georgia, Mr. Williams was less
subtle, avowing that he had been at great pains to capture a small
Indian girl and he was going to keep her.[76]

Born on the Flint River in Sumter County, Georgia, in 1858,
the "Negro" H. A. Allen some years after the Civil War went to
Oklahoma as a freedman, a Baptist minister, and also a black
Seminole. His mother was a Seminole Indian-Negro and his
grandmother a Creek or black Muscogulge. The latter had
moved into Florida and married Chief Bowlegs, prominent in
the First Seminole War. Born in Florida, as a young girl Allen's
mother had been carried off by Indians or whites, sold in Georgia,
and became a house servant on a large plantation. A white man
who rose to be an outstanding lawyer in Americus became the
father of H. C. Allen. The Trail of Tears of Allen's Indian-Negro
mother, however, had taken her only from northern Florida to
southern Georgia.[77]

Southern whites had made it clear that they intended to keep
Indian children "for the benefit of their present and future services,"[78] and although details are murky, a number of Creek-
Seminole children and adults remained in the Muscogulge
homeland to become part of the Old South's Negro population.
One of Osceola's wives was in this category, and in the 1930s
the aged former Negro slave, Frank Berry, Osceola's grandson,
told something about his Negro grandmother's career with the
Indians.[79] A zambo from Russell County, Alabama, Abraham
Jones, 112 years old in the 1930s, recounted how as a young boy
he had intently observed a long procession of Creeks with wagons, military escort, and few possessions slowly pass by. Alabama whites decreed that Abraham was a Negro, and he had
remained behind, watching the wagon's dust settle on the
horizon.[80]

The destruction and dispersal of the Muscogulge people occasionally resulted in remarkable odysseys. Young John Bemo,
"a full blood Seminole," Osceola's nephew, was captured near
Saint Marks during the nineteenth-century Indian wars.

Adopted by a French seaman, Jean Bemeau (Bemo), John saw much of the world before enrolling in a Philadelphia school to prepare for the Baptist ministry. Dressed as an Indian, he lectured before large audiences in the East prior to moving to Oklahoma in the early 1840s. John married a Creek, and like H. C. Allen spent his remaining days winning over Creeks and Seminoles, including black Indians, to the Baptist fold.[81]

Young Bemo initially went to Philadelphia, but another Indian, youthful Nikkanochee journeyed even farther afield. His father, Econchatti Mico, and his uncle, Osceola, were Creeks who had migrated into Florida in the early decades of the nineteenth century. During the bitter fighting of 1836 in northern Florida, American soldiers captured Nikkanochee and brought him to Saint Augustine. The English doctor, land speculator, and promoter, Dr. Andrew Welch, first adopted Nikkanochee, then in a few years took him to England and enrolled him in school, and subsequently apprenticed him to a ship captain bound for the South Seas. After arriving in Australia, Nikkanochee ran away. Something of a P. T. Barnum–type showman, Doctor Welch had had plaster casts of Nikkanochee's head made in England. (Welch's Saint Augustine colleague, Dr. Frederick Weedon, had cut off and preserved Osceola's head.) In any case, after sailing from England, Nikkanochee saw no reason to contact Welch, his white father and benefactor, and the young Seminole vanished from sight.[82]

Muscogulges remained in the Southeast both as Negroes and as whites. According to a yarn that may or may not be true, after a full day of hunting and drinking, three white frontiersmen threw themselves down in a log shelter to rest and sober up. Suddenly in the middle of the night two of the hunters rushed headlong out of the crude shelter, fleeing blindly through the woods, leaving clothes and other possessions behind, later remarking they did not realize that their companion was an Indian until he began to gobble. The reputation of a Muscogulge warrior's spine-chilling turkey-gobble war whoop, which he emitted after taking a scalp or completing some heroic exploit was widespread.[83] Other Muscogulges, however, did not gobble, and continued undetected in the Southeast as whites.

318   Despite Jackson's removal bill, some Muscogulges who were identified as Indians nevertheless remained in the Southeast. Withdrawing into swamps and piney barrens and not molesting whites, they lived almost unnoticed. The largest, most cohesive group was located above Pensacola near Poarch, Alabama. An amalgam of Creeks who had moved to southern Alabama in the late eighteenth century, of Indians who had retired to the region with Weatherford, or who after 1836 had fled to this area to escape hostilities, they attracted little attention until large timber companies arrived on the scene in the late nineteenth century. Emerging from obscurity, these Muscogulges in 1984 were recognized by the national government as the Poarch Band of Creeks. By then, however, they had lost their native language and most of their previous culture. The same acculturation applied to other groups of Muscogulges, such as members of the Florida Tribe of Eastern Creek Indians in north Florida, who organized and asserted themselves in the twentieth century.[84]

Seminoles scattered about the southern Florida Everglades are the best known, though not necessarily the largest, group of Muscogulge people to remain in the Southeast. From the 1840s until well into the twentieth century they lived in relative isolation and, like Spanish Indians, had time to develop a unique subculture, which for the Seminoles included adapting to conditions in a semitropical region where there were no hickory nuts or acorns, developing new methods of agriculture and hunting, living in small camps rather than large towns, and wearing loose-fitting, brightly colored cotton shirts and long skirts made by intricate strip sewing (patchwork). The summerhouse was particularly suited to southern Florida and easily evolved into the open-sided chickee. Unlike the Spanish Indians, these Seminoles were never abruptly expelled. Better than in any other place one could find in the Everglades a Seminole nation and a distinct culture. Less ethnic diversity existed among these Muscogulges than among those elsewhere. For the most part, the Yuchis, Spanish Indians, Choctaw remnants, and other tribes or groups had moved to Oklahoma or the islands or had been annihilated. White and Indian slavers repeatedly had swept through the Seminole country, carried off prisoners, and forced

most but not all Negroes to flee. A twentieth-century morpho-
logical and serological study reveals that the Negroes' genetic
contribution to Indians in the Everglades was probably small,[85]
and an 1847 census discloses only four Yuchi warriors.[86]

One would not want to overemphasize the cohesiveness and
uniqueness of southern Florida Indians. Fundamental cleavages
persist: Miccosukee (Hitchiti) speakers outnumber Creek speakers by two to one, and this ratio is reflected in the thousand or
so members of the officially recognized Seminole tribe. Virtually
all of its members, however, speak both Indian languages. Several hundred Miccosukee speakers have organized themselves
and are recognized as a separate Miccosukee nation. Still other
Miccosukee speakers, generally the most traditional or conservative southern Florida Indians, have refused to be incorporated
into any tribe and adamantly insist, as historically they have
every right to do, that they are the true Seminoles. Miccosukee
speakers, probably numbering less than 1,000, tend to be the
most conservative Seminoles, and this helps explain why the
Bible has yet to be translated into Miccosukee. There are at least
three distinct groups of southern Florida Indians: Hitchiti-
Creek–speaking Seminoles; Miccosukee–speaking Miccosukees, and Miccosukee–speaking Seminoles. The lapse of two
centuries has not made it easier to characterize the Muscogulge
people.[87]

Oklahoma Seminoles after 1845 had an autonomous government, and after 1856 one that was completely separate from that
of the Creeks, with a Seminole council house near Wewoka.
Nevertheless, the Oklahoma Seminole components were more
diversified than those of Seminoles in Florida, even though today
Hitchiti speakers in Oklahoma have almost disappeared. The
black Seminole presence in Oklahoma was considerable, and
overnight the Creek Pascofar and other Creeks became prominent Seminole spokesmen in the West. The elderly Seminole
Louis Graham recounted in the twentieth century how his
ancestors had come from Florida to Oklahoma. But he—and
they—were not really Seminoles; they were part of "a lost tribe
of the Choctaw tribe."[88] Manifesting less ethnic diversity, the
Seminole-Miccosukee experience in the Everglades in the late

320   nineteenth and twentieth centuries reflected a break with the past.

British officials before the American Revolution, and Washington, Jefferson, Hawkins, and others after 1775 had maintained the existence of a unified Creek nation. When the Creeks moved to Oklahoma, established their National Council house at Okmulgee and utilized lighthorsemen as a rudimentary national police, a Creek nation became more of an actuality. The McIntosh faction and the Muskogee moiety increased its power as non-Muskogee elements that had not dispersed lost influence. Some of them were absorbed by Muskogees, while others in effect became whites. Living by themselves, the Seminoles in Florida and Oklahoma were largely non-Muskogees, while the Koasatis, Alabamas, Shawnees, Taensas, and Wildcat's followers had moved to Texas and Coahuila. Tuckabatchees were driven to Kansas with great loss of life, though survivors eventually returned to Oklahoma. Black Muscogulges had fled to the Bahamas and Cuba to escape slave raids by McIntosh's Cowetas, while those Creeks and Seminoles who joined the Cherokees in Oklahoma often did so to get away from these same Cowetas. All these migrations magnified the power of the McIntosh, pure Muskogee moiety at the Creek National Council in Oklahoma, and allowed this dominant group to absorb more quickly remaining non-Muskogee elements. The sovereign Creek nation was abolished in 1907 when Oklahoma became a state. Nevertheless contemporary Oklahoma Creeks to an extent are bound together by the western Creek nation's experiences and traditions—proceedings in the House of Kings and House of Warriors in the council house at Okmulgee and exploits of the Indian police, the lighthorsemen. The significance of clan and ethnic heritage diminished, however, and Oklahoma Creeks became less aware of their history in the Southeast. In the twentieth century, Oklahoma Creeks from the same clan intermarried, and had to be reminded of or in some instances did not even know the name of their clans. This would have been almost unthinkable at an earlier period.

Despite the dispersal of many non-Muskogees, the more rapid absorption of non-Muskogees by Muskogees proper, the many converts to Christianity, and the collective loss of Indian culture, old patterns, traditions, divisions, and ways of doing things survived in Oklahoma, perhaps imperceptibly so. Opothleyahola's Tuckabatchees and other tribes had brought their sacred ashes to the West, rekindling fires in new Oklahoma talwas at Tuckabatchee, Broken Arrow, Coweta, Cusseta, Hickory Ground, Hitchiti, Miccosukee, Yuchi, Tuskegee and many other towns. Twentieth-century Muscogulges still lived in these towns, or if they had moved away, they still symbolically remained attached to their ancestral homes. Much of the knowledge of Oklahoma Creeks was written by or transmitted to whites by Muskogee speakers. The white novelist Hamlin Garland, an observer at the last session of the National Council in 1905, became nostalgic when considering what had befallen the Creek nation.[89] He and other whites tended to assume that Creek history and the history of the Muscogulge peoples were synonymous. Yet this was not what Yuchi-speaking Maxey Simms of Sapulpa, Oklahoma, had in mind in the late 1920s when he described how "some day the sun will rise in the east and look for her children . . . if she sees that not even one of the Tsoyaha [Yuchi] is living . . . she will cry and cover her face."[90] The old devil refused to die; tribal particularism and diversity remained a feature in Muscogulge society; and even in Oklahoma a centralized Creek state was often a myth. From the earliest days of the republic the United States had attempted— and in many respects had failed—to create unified nations out of diverse peoples. The Creek nation was one of the first, but by no means the last, of such attempts, and, in the case of numerous other Indian peoples, the Muscogulge experience proved prophetic.

Abbreviations

Adm.	Admiralty
ADAA	Alabama Department of Archives and History
AGI	Archivo General de Indias
AHN	Archivo Histórico Nacional
AHQ	*Alabama Historical Quarterly*
ANC	Archivo Nacional de Cuba
AR	*Alabama Review*
ASP, IA	*American State Papers, Indian Affairs*
ASP, MA	*American State Papers, Military Affairs*
BL	British Library
CL	William L. Clements Library
CO	Colonial Office
CSP, Col.	*Calendar of State Papers, Colonial Series*
EFP	East Florida Papers
FHQ	*Florida Historical Quarterly*
FO	Foreign Office
FSUL	Florida State University Library
GDAH	Georgia Department of Archives and History
GHQ	*Georgia Historical Quarterly*
GHS	Georgia Historical Society
HR	House of Representatives
IPHC	Grant Foreman, Indian Pioneer History Collection
JAH	*Journal of American History*
JNH	*Journal of Negro History*
LC	Library of Congress
LR	Letters Received
LS	Letters Sent

M	Microcopy
MPHC	*Michigan Pioneer and Historical Society Historical Collections*
NA	National Archives and Records Service
NASP, IA	*New American State Papers, Indian Affairs*
NL	Newberry Library
NLS	National Library of Scotland
NMM	National Maritime Museum
NYHS	New York Historical Society
OIA	Office of Indian Affairs
PAC	Public Archives of Canada
PLP	Panton, Leslie, and Company Papers
PRO	Public Record Office
RG	Record Group
SAC	Southeast Archeological Center
SCHGM	*South Carolina Historical and Genealogical Magazine*
UFL	University of Florida Library
UOWHC	University of Oklahoma Western History Collection
UWFL	University of West Florida Library
WMQ	*William and Mary Quarterly*
WO	War Office

Notes

CHAPTER I

1. Minutes taken from General McGillivray respecting the Creeks, Aug. 1790, Ynox Papers 26, FSUL.
2. Crane, "Origin of the Name of Creek Indians," pp. 339–42.
3. Swanton, "Social Organization of the Creek Confederacy," p. 68.
4. Sturtevant, "Creek into Seminole," pp. 96–105.
5. John Stuart to William Howe, Pensacola, 16 June 1777, Carleton Papers 586, FSUL; Estado en que se hallava la plaza de San Augustin, 29 Oct. 1780, 176G14 EFP.
6. Swanton, *Indians of the Southeastern United States*, p. 218.
7. Fairbanks, *Ethnohistorical Report on Florida Indians*, pp. 127–289.
8. Young, "Topographical Memoir on East and West Florida," p. 82.
9. Joseph M. White to James Barbour, Augusta, 4 June 1830, LR, OIA, M234, roll 290: 71; T. Hartley Crawford to William Armstrong, 7 Mar. 1839, LR, War Dept., Western Supt., M640, roll 2.
10. Congress of principal chiefs and warriors, Upper Creek Nation, Pensacola, 29 Oct. 1771, CO 5/73; Swanton, *Indians of the Southeastern United States*, pp. 28, 138–39.
11. Emisteseguo to Charles Stuart, in Stuart to ?, 2 Dec. 1770, CO 5/72.
12. Ware and Rea, *George Gauld*, p. 62.
13. Adair, *History*, p. 285.
14. Higginbotham, "Origins of the French-Alabama Conflict," pp. 121–22.
15. Barnard Letters, p. 11, GDAH.
16. Speck, "Ethnology of the Yuchi Indians," pp. 7–8; James Oglethorpe to Trustees, Frederica, 18 May 1736, *Collection of the Georgia Historical Society* 3 (1873): 35–36.

326

17. Bartram, *Travels*, Naturalist's ed., pp. 245, 292–94.
18. The history and influence of the large number of Shawnees who lived in the Southeast is not well understood or appreciated. See, however, Charles Callendar, "Shawnee," pp. 622–35; and Howard, *Shawnee!*
19. Hawkins "Sketch of the Creek Country," Hawkins, *Letters*, ed. Grant, 1:300.
20. Brain, "Natchez Paradox," p. 220; James Glen to president and assistants, S.C., Oct. 1750, *Ga. Col. Rec.*, ed. Candler, 26:62.
21. Swanton, "Religious Beliefs and Medical Practices of Creek Indians," pp. 503–10; Adair, *History*, pp. 187–88; journal, 13 Jan. 1693, *Journals of the Commons House of Assembly of South Carolina, 1693*, ed. Salley, p. 12.
22. Swanton, *Early History of the Creeks*, pp. 201–7; Green, *Politics of Indian Removal*, p. 40.
23. Swanton, *Early History of the Creeks*, pp. 272–74.
24. Swanton, "Social Organization of the Creek Confederacy," p. 46.
25. An account of hunting parties visiting the Red River is in Milfort, *Memoirs*, pp. 53–54.
26. Romans, *History of East and West Florida*, p. 280; Holmes, *José de Evia*, p. 35.
27. Howard, *Oklahoma Seminoles*, pp. 110–11.
28. White, *Roots of Dependency*, p. 38.
29. Haas, "Creek Inter-Town Relations," pp. 481–82.
30. Swanton, *Early History of the Creeks*, pp. 277–78.
31. Eschochabey to Stuart, May 1769, CO 5/70; Boyd and Latorre, "Spanish Interest in British Florida," pp. 110–12; David Taitt, "Journal of Travels from Pensacola," p. 524.
32. Crawford, *Mobilian Trade Language*, p. 100. I am indebted to James M. Crawford, Charles Daniels, and Emmanuel J. Drechsel for help concerning the etymology of "stinkard."
33. Swanton, "Social Organization of the Creek Confederacy," pp. 107–241; and Hudson, *Southeastern Indians*, pp. 185–96, discuss complexities of the southeastern clan system.
34. Hawkins, Journal, 20 Dec. 1796, in Hawkins, *Letters*, ed. Grant, 1:24.
35. The best account of culture associated with the temple mounds is Howard, *Southeastern Ceremonial Complex*.
36. Adair, *History*, pp. 435–38; a recent study on the origins and usages of maize is Hardeman, *Shucks, Shocks, and Hominy Blocks*.
37. Sleight, "Kunti," pp. 46–49; Dobyns, *Their Number Become Thinned*, pp. 63–64.
38. Swanton, "Social Organization of the Creek Confederacy," pp. 109, 115.
39. Bartram, "Observations on Creek and Cherokee Indians," pp. 26, 67–77.
40. Many Creek stories reflect the importance of tobacco. See Swanton, *Myths and Tales of Southeastern Indians*, p. 20.
41. Schoolcraft, *Historical and Statistical Information*, 1:269, 271.

42. Hardman, "Primitive Solar Observatory at Crystal River," p. 164.
43. Stiggins Narrative, Draper Mss., Ga., Ala., and S.C., IV, roll 30:1, FSUL.
44. Wagner, *Yuchi Tales*, p. 149.
45. Hudson, *Southeastern Indians*, pp. 123–34.
46. Ibid., p. 302.
47. Ibid., p. 128.
48. Wagner, *Yuchi Tales*, p. 150.
49. Gatschet, *Migration Legend*, p. 38; James Oglethorpe to Samuel Wesley, Old Palace Yard, 19 Nov. 1734, *Newman's Letterbooks*, ed. and trans. Jones, p. 514.
50. Swanton, "Religious Beliefs and Medicinal Practices," p. 624.
51. Adair, *History*, pp. 49–50.
52. Fairbanks, "Black Drink among the Creeks," pp. 134–35.
53. Lee Compere to Thomas L. McKenney, Montgomery, 4 Feb. 1828, LR, OIA, M234, roll 237, 149–50.
54. There were many variations to the busk. Two contemporary descriptions are Hawkins, "Sketch of the Creek Country," in Hawkins, *Letters*, ed. Grant, 1:322–24; and Bartram, *Travels*, Naturalist's ed., pp. 323–24.
55. Wright, *Only Land They Knew*, pp. 126–50.
56. The best example of black Maroon communities in the Southeast is among those Creeks who became known as Seminoles. This is discussed in Wright, "Black Seminoles."
57. Swanton, "Social Organization of the Creek Confederacy," pp. 276–307.
58. Helpful in understanding the importance of a talwa is Opler, "The Creek 'Town,'" pp. 165–75.
59. Bartram, "Observations on Creek and Cherokee Indians," pp. 55–56.
60. Fairbanks, *Ethnohistorical Report*, pp. 225–29.
61. Hawkins, "Sketch of the Creek Country," in Hawkins, *Letters*, ed. Grant, 1:319–20.
62. Swanton, "Social Organization of the Creek Confederacy," pp. 198–99.
63. Pictures of three mortars and pestles are in Swanton, *Indians of the Southeastern United States*, plates 72–73.
64. Swan, "Position and State of Manners in the Creek Nation," 5:276–77; Speck, "Ethnology of the Yuchi Indians," p. 67.
65. Swan, "Position and State of Manners," p. 277; J. Otto Fries to John M. Cheney, Cowbone Camp, Fla., 9 July 1900; Kersey, "Florida Seminoles and Census of 1900," p. 152.
66. Gatschet, "Tchikilli's Kasihta Legend," pp. 4–5; Bartram, "Observations on Creeks and Cherokees," p. 18.
67. Romans, *Natural History*, p. 102.
68. John Galphin to Bowles, 17 Sept. 1788, in John Hambly to John Leslie, St. John's, Conception, 28 Sept. 1788, 116L9, EFP.
69. Emisteseguo to Charles Stuart, in Stuart to ?, 2 Dec. 1770, CO 5/72.
70. Bartram, *Travels*, Naturalist's ed., p. 143; Julian Carballo to Arturo O'Neill, Apalache, 4 Mar. 1792, AGI, Cuba, 40, PLP.
71. Goggin, "Seminole Negroes of Andros Island," pp. 204, 206.

328   72. Downs, "British Influences of Creek and Seminole Men's Clothing,"
          pp. 46–63; see also portraits in Fundaburk, *Southeastern Indians.*
       73. Description of ball games are in Pope, *Tour*, pp. 49–51; and Williams,
          "Journal," p. 20.
       74. Swanton, "Religious Beliefs and Medical Practices," pp. 522–34.

CHAPTER 2

   1. Account of goods left . . . at Augusta . . . by late commissioners of the
      United States, 6 Oct. 1789, Knox Papers, 25:8, FSUL.
   2. Cowettas to Samuel Elbert, Coweitter, 17 Aug. 1785, Creek Indian Let-
      ters, p. 84, GDAH.
   3. Gatschet, *Migration Legend*, p. 79.
   4. Alexander Arbuthnot's journal, 23 Oct. [1817?], *British and Foreign
      State Papers*, 6:497.
   5. Meriwether, *Expansion of South Carolina*, pp. 69–70.
   6. Patrick Tonyn to John Stuart, St. Augustine, 8 Sept. 1778, CO 5/80:31.
   7. Lachlan McGillivray's affidavit, 21 May 1784, PRO, Audit Office 13/36,
      no. 1528, f.560.
   8. William Panton to ?, St. Augustine, 13 Sept. 1776, Archives of State of
      Maryland, Md. Historical Soc., PLP.
   9. Panton to John Leslie, Pensacola, 28 Aug. 1793, Lockey Collection, UFL.
  10. Wright, "Queen's Redoubt Explosion," pp. 183–90.
  11. Opinion on McGillivray's monopoly of commerce with Creek Indians,
      29 July 1790, *Papers of Jefferson*, ed. Boyd, 17:288–89.
  12. An act for the better regulation of the Indian Trade in the province of
      West Florida, 19 May 1770, *Minutes, Journals, and Acts of West Flor-
      ida*, ed. Rea and Howard, pp. 379–83.
  13. Henry Laurens to William Cowles, Westminister, 24 Dec. 1773, *Papers
      of Laurens*, ed. Hamer et al., 9:209–10.
  14. Crane, *Southern Frontier*, pp. 109–12.
  15. Wright, "Queen's Redoubt Explosion," pp. 178–79.
  16. Coker and Watson, *Indian Traders of Spanish Borderlands*, pp. 31–48.
  17. Lachlan McGillivray's affidavit, 21 May 1784, PRO, Audit Office 13/36,
      NO. 1528, F.560.
  18. George Galphin to Council of Safety, 9 Aug 1775, *SCHGM*, 1:124.
  19. Tonyn to Stuart, 8 Sept. 1778, CO 5/80.
  20. Whitaker, ed. and trans., *Documents Relating to the Commercial Pol-
      icy of Spain in the Floridas*, pp. xxvi–xxx.
  21. The best account of this firm is Coker and Watson, *Indian Traders of
      Spanish Borderlands.*
  22. Jonathan Halsted to William Davy, Ft. Wilkinson, 20 Sept. 1805, Letter

Book, Creek Trading House, f.91. The standard history of the factory   329
system is Peake, *History of the Indian Factory System.*

23. Panton to Luís de las Casas, Pensacola, 16 June 1783, B116L9, EFP;
Peake, *History of the Indian Factory System*, pp. 11–13.

24. Coker and Watson, *Traders of the Spanish Borderlands*, p. 216; Thomas
Davy and Joseph Roberts to William Davy, London, 4 Aug. 1806, LR,
Supt. of Indian Trade, T58.

25. Bills of sale, manifests, and customs records scattered throughout the
voluminous PLP best reveal the diversity of European goods exchanged
with the Muscogulges.

26. Estevan Miró and Martin Navarro to José de Gálvez, New Orleans, 24
Mar. 1787, Lockey Collection, UFL.

27. John Bartram visited Galphin in 1765 and briefly described Silver Bluff,
J. Bartram, *Diary of a Journey*, pp. 25–26, 64–65; figs. 12, 13.

28. Coker, "Religious Censuses of Pensacola," p. 57; Carondelet to Panton,
New Orleans, 16 Apr. 1796, Cruzat Papers, PLP; present state of the
houses and lots in Pensacola, 16 Dec. 1799, Greenslade Papers, PLP.

29. Boyd, "Events at Prospect Bluff," p. 63.

30. John Bowles to William A. Bowles, New Providence, 21 Apr. 1792, AGI,
Cuba, leg. 205.

31. Romans, *Natural History*, chart facing p. 104; Alden, *John Stuart*,
p. 17.

32. Panton to ?, St. Augustine, 13 Sept. 1776, Archives of the State of
Maryland, Md. Historical Soc., PLP.

33. Panton to Adam Gordon, Pensacola, 24 July 1799, Greenslade Papers,
PLP.

34. Juan de Courville to Juan Hindman, Pensacola, 2 Apr. 1803, AGI, Cuba,
leg. 617, PLP.

35. W. J. Harris to Timothy Barnard, 29 Oct. 1798, Letter Book, Creek
Trading House, p. 170.

36. Journal of occurrences in the Creek agency . . . , 2 Apr. 1802, in Hawkins,
Letters, ed. Grant, 2:419.

37. Thomas Brown to John Stuart, Chehaws, 29 Sept. 1776, CO 5/78.

38. Abigail Adams to Mary Cranch, New York, 8 Aug. 1790, *New Letters
of Abigail Adams*, ed. Mitchell, p. 57.

39. Stiggins Narrative, Draper Mss., Ga., Ala., and S.C., IV, roll 30:1 FSUL;
Woodward, *Reminiscences*, pp. 143–65.

40. G. W. Grayson Ms., Smock Coll., UOWHC.

41. McGillivray to Charles McLatchy, Little Tallassee, 25 Dec. 1784, 116L9,
EFP, PLP.

42. Hawkins to John Armstrong, Creek Agency, 23 Aug. 1813, in Hawkins,
Letters, ed. Grant, 2:658.

43. Barnard Letters, p. 6, GDAH.

330   44. Journal, 26 Jan. 1797, in Hawkins, *Letters*, ed. Grant, 1:40; declaraciones referentes a Guillermo Bowles, AGI, Cuba, leg. 1395.

45. Alexander McGillivray to Halloing King of Cowetas, Tuckabatchee, 14 April 1786, Creek Indian Letters, p. 101, GDAH; James Durouzeaux to Edward Telfair, Coweta, 5 June 1786, ibid., pp. 114–15.

46. Alexander McGillivray to Arturo O'Neill, Little Tallassee, 26 Oct. 1785, AHN, leg. 3898, exp. 1, PLP.

47. Letter from Cheehaw, Oakmulgey, Oheeche, and Hitcheta town, Cheehaugh Town, 27 June 1786, Creek Indian Letters, p. 124, GDAH; Alexander McGillivray to William Clark, Tuckabatchee, 24 Apr. 1785, ibid., p. 89; Woodward, *Reminiscences*, p. 13.

48. Almost no description of hunting camps is in Hawkins, *Letters*, ed. Grant, which contains the most extensive compilation of the agent's writings.

49. Bartram, *Diary of a Journey*, p. 41.

50. William Lindsay testimony, 9 Dec. 1836, *ASP, MA*, 7:140.

51. Anthony Wayne to Henry Knox, Richmond, 20 Mar. 1790, Knox Papers 26, FSUL.

52. Mad Dog (Efau Haujo) to John Forbes, Tuckabatchee, 31 May 1801, *FHQ* 13 (1934): 166.

53. Adair, *History*, p. 331.

54. Alexander McGillivray to Panton, Apalachee, 19 Dec. 1785, AGI, Cuba, 198, PLP.

55. Swanton, *Indians of the Southeastern United States*, pp. 442–48.

56. Jonathan Halsted to Abraham D. Abrahams, Ft. Wilkinson, 6 Dec. 1804, Letter Book, Creek Trading House, p. 268, NA; Halsted to Levi Shiftall, Ocmulgee Trading House, 8 Dec. 1807, ibid., p. 311.

57. "The Creek Nation, Debtor to John Forbes and Co. . . . . Journal of John Innerarity," *FHQ* 9 (1930): 79.

58. McGillivray to Estevan Miró, Little Tallassee, 28 Aug. 1788, AGI, Cuba 2361, PLP.

59. Thomas Portell to Vicente Folch, San Marcos, 4 Oct 1799, Lockey Coll., UFL; John Hambly to John Leslie, St. Johns, Conception, 26 Apr. 1789, Buckingham Smith Papers, NYHS, PLP.

60. Edward Price to John Harris, Coleraine, 20 Jan. 1797, Letter Book, Creek Trading House, p. 12, NA; Hawkins to Panton, Tuckabatchee, 7 Feb. 1801, Greenslade Papers, PLP.

61. Hawkins to Silas Dinsmoor, Tuckabatchee, 7 June 1798, in Hawkins, *Letters*, ed. Grant, 1:199.

62. Timothy Barnard to Hawkins, Tuckabatchee, 10 Oct. 1801, LR, Sec. War, M271, roll 1:59.

63. William Bunce to Wiley Thompson, Tampa, 9 Jan. 1835, LR, OIA, M234, roll 288:251.

64. Robert L. Crawford to John Robb, Tuscaloosa, 15 Sept. 1832, ibid., roll 223:56.

65. Certificates of valuation of improvements, Chattahoochee, Oct. 1838, ibid., roll 291:9–84.
66. Brown to Lord North, St. Augustine, 8 Jan. 1784, enclosure, CO 5/82.
67. Minutes of executive council, 25 Mar. 1778, *Ga. Col. Rec.*, ed. Candler, 2:63.

CHAPTER 3

1. Thwaites, ed., *Journals of Lewis and Clark*, 1:186; Jackson, ed., *Letters of Lewis and Clark*, 1:503.
2. Jefferson, *Notes on the State of Virginia*, p. 56.
3. Robert Leslie to John Leslie, Appalachy, 4 Mar. 1794, Buckingham Smith Papers, NYHS, PLP.
4. Woodward, *Reminiscences*, pp. 144, 160.
5. John Crowell to John Eaton, Creek Agency, 22 Jan. 1831, LR, OIA, M234, roll 222:467, 68.
6. James Burges to Robert Leslie, Flint River, 1 July 1793, EFP, PLP.
7. George McIntosh interview, [1937], IPHC, 7:72–73.
8. A good account of Afro-Indians in the Caribbean is Gullick, *Exiled from St. Vincent*.
9. Chief Neamathla speech to governor of Florida, *Myths and Tales*, by Swanton, p. 75.
10. "Origin of Races," *Myths and Tales*, by Swanton, p. 74. Attitudes towards blacks are discussed in Sturtevant, "Seminole Myths of the Origins of Races," pp. 80–86; and in Dundes, "Washington Irving's Version of the Seminole Origin of Races," pp. 257–64.
11. Swanton, "Social Organization," p. 31.
12. Grayson ms., Smock Coll., pp. 19–20, UOWHC.
13. Lee Compere to Thomas L. McKenney, Withington Station, 20 May 1828, LR, OIA, M234, roll 221:704–6.
14. Vignoles, *Observations upon the Floridas*, p. 137.
15. R. C. Gatlin, to W. I. Worth, New Orleans, 10 Jan. 1843, LR, OIA, M234, roll 289:346.
16. Hartley and Hartley, *Osceola*, pp. 117–18; Frank Berry narrative, *Slave Narratives*, 17:27–28.
17. Buker, "Mosquito Fleet's Guides," p. 324; Porter, "Negro Abraham," p. 11.
18. George Galpin will, 6 Apr. 1782, Creek Indian Letters, 1:8–15, GDAH.
19. Polly Russell testimony, Cowetuh Tallahassee, 19 Mar. 1799, Hawkins, Independence Letterbook, pp. 56–57, SAC.
20. Andrew Bryan to John Rippon, Savannah, 23 Dec. 1800, *JNH* 1 (1916): 87.
21. John Leslie codicil, 7 Aug. 1798, PRO, B11/1411, PLP.
22. Zephaniah Kingsley Will, 20 July 1843, UFL.

332

23. Juan Ruiz de Apodaca to Miguel de Lardizabal y Uribe, Havana, 20 Oct. 1815, Lockey Coll., UFL.

24. Meyer, *Life and Times of Richard M. Johnson*, pp. 317–22.

25. Act of friendship between Robert Johnson and Creeks, 15 Dec. 1736, *Journal of Commons House*, ed. Easterby, p. 110; Negro Act, 7 Mar. 1755, *Ga. Col. Rec.*, ed. Candler, 18:138. For the whites' fears of Indians and blacks see Willis, "Divide and Rule," pp. 157–76.

26. Daniel Pepper to William H. Lyttelton, Ockhoy, 30 Mar. 1757, *Documents Relating to Indian Affairs*, ed. McDowell, 2:357.

27. Wright, "Southern Black Loyalists."

28. John Forrester to Mr. Garvin, in Hammond to Quesada, 2 Aug. 1792, Lockey Coll., UFL.

29. Daniel McGillivray to Panton, Little Tallassee, 18 Sept. 1799, Forbes Papers, Mobile Public Library, PLP.

30. John Miller to O'Neill, 1 Sept. 1788, Lockey Coll., UFL.

31. Robert Leslie to John Leslie, Appalachy, 4 Mar. 1794, Buckingham Smith Papers, PLP.

32. TePaske, "The Fugitive Slave," pp. 1–12.

33. Minutes of governor and council, Savannah, 4 Dec. 1771, *Ga. Col. Rec.*, ed. Candler, 12:146.

34. Henry Laurens to Stephen Bull, Charleston, 16 Mar. 1776, *SCHGM* 4(1903):205–6.

35. Mary Bonelly Leonardy testimony, 10 Oct. 1835, LR, OIA, M234, 800:298.

36. Simmons, *Notices of East Florida*, pp. 44–45.

37. President and assistants, 9 Feb. 1748, *Ga. Col. Rec.*, ed. Candler, 6:209.

38. Wright, "Southern Black Loyalists."

39. The most recent accounts of Brown are in Olsen's "Loyalists and the American Revolution," pp. 201–19, and his "Thomas Brown, Loyalist Partisan," pp. 1–19, 183–208.

40. Wright, "Dunmore's Loyalist Asylum," pp. 370–79.

41. Edward Nicholls to Alexander Cockrane, Apalachicola Bay, 12 Aug. 1814, Cochrane Papers, 2328, NLS; Cochrane to Nicholls, *Tonnant* off Apalachicola, 3 Dec. 1814, ibid., 3346.

42. Bullard, *Black Liberation on Cumberland Island*, pp. 127–30.

43. Brumbaugh, "Black Maroons in Florida."

44. Turner, *Africanisms in Gullah Dialect*, is the most complete linguistic study of African survivals among the southern blacks. See also Wood, *Black Majority*, pp. 181–86.

45. Alex Blackston interview, 14 Oct. 1937, IPHC, 90:373.

46. Simmons, "Journal," p. 36.

47. Hawkins, journal, 25 Dec. 1796, in Hawkins, *Letters*, ed. Grant, 1:29.

48. John Whitehead to John Clark, Waynesboro, 26 Jan. 1820, LR, Sec. War, roll 3:164–68.

49. Edmund Doyle to John Innerarity, Prospect Bluff, 11 July 1817, "Panton Leslie Papers," *FHQ* 18 (1939): 137.

50. Philip A. Lewis interview, 4 May 1937, IPHC, 6:216–22.

51. *Ga. Gazette*, 10 Jan. 1770, in *JNH* 24 (1939): 252.

52. John DeLacy to Bowles, 11 Mar. 1802, Lockey Coll., UFL.

53. Ibid.; Thomas Perryman to Vicente Folch [1804?], Lockey Coll., UFL.

54. Alexander Cornell to Hawkins, Tuckabatchee, 19 Sept. 1812, Lockey Coll., UFL.

55. George K. Walker to Archibald Smith, Tallahassee, 20 Apr. 1837, LR, OIA, M234, roll 288:386.

56. Porter, "Billy Bowlegs," pp. 238–39.

57. Polly Russell testimony, Cowetuh Tallahassee, 19 Mar. 1799, Hawkins, "Independence Letterbook," pp. 56–57, SAC.

58. R. C. Gatlin to William J. Worth, New Orleans, 10 Jan. 1843, LR, OIA, M234, roll 289:346; Alexander Cummings to Matthew Arbuckle, Ft. Gibson, 14 July 1840, ibid., p. 184.

59. Archibald Smith, Jr. to Cary A. Harris, Gadsden Co., 14 May 1837, ibid., roll 288:388.

60. LR, Western Supt., M640, roll 3:858; decision . . . the case of Matthew Solana . . . , 19 Oct. 1843, LR, OIA, M234, roll 806:269.

61. David Randon declaration, 19 May 1798, Hawkins, Independence Letterbook, p. 1, SAC.

62. Bartram, "Observations on the Creek and Cherokee Indians," p. 38.

CHAPTER 4

1. The persistence of French Canadian trade with the Cherokees is briefly mentioned in Brown, *Old Frontiers*, p. 265.

2. De Vorsey, *Indian Boundary in Southern Colonies*, p. 22.

3. Governor's speech to Gun Merchant and other Indian chiefs, Savannah, 4 Jan. 1763, *Ga. Col. Rec.*, ed. Candler, 9:14.

4. The most recent account of McGillivray is Green, "Alexander McGillivray." Green believes that McGillivray was a Koasati rather than an Abihka, p. 43.

5. Robert Johnson to Board of Trade, Charleston, 12 Jan. 1720, *CSP, Col.* 31:302.

6. Chief Cowkeeper is often regarded as founder of the Seminole nation, yet as late as 1774 the East Florida lieutenant governor addressed him as one of the "head men of the Creek nation." Moultrie to Cowkeeper, Feb. 1774, CO 5/571.

7. Montault de Monberaut, *Memoire*, pp. 9–14.

8. Johnson, *British West Florida*, pp. 9–23, 37–42.

9. John Stuart to Board of Trade, Charleston, 10 July 1766, *N.C. Col. Records*, ed. Saunders, 7:237–40.

10. De Vorsey, *Indian Boundary*, pp. 181–203.

11. Ibid., pp. 212–15.

334

12. John Stuart to Lord Dartmouth, Charleston, 3 Jan. 1775, CO 5/76; Thomas Grey deposition, St. Augustine, 10 Oct. 1775, CO 5/555.

13. De Vorsey, *Indian Boundary,* pp. 149–51; Jones, *License for Empire,* pp. 42–53.

14. Abstract of letter, David Taitt, Pallachicola, 21 Sept. 1782, CO 5/74.

15. Abernethy, *Western Lands,* p. 116.

16. Stuart to Gage, Charleston, 18 Jan. 1775, Gage Papers, CL, 125; Stuart to Dartmouth, Charleston, 3 Jan. 1775, CO 5/76.

17. Moultrie to Cowkeeper and other headmen of Creek nation, Feb. 1774, CO 5/571:101.

18. Stuart to Emisteseguo and Neahlatchko, in Stuart to Dartmouth, Charleston, 15 Dec. 1774, CO 5/76.

19. Escochabey to Stuart, May 1769, CO 5/70; Stuart to Dartmouth, Charleston, 20 May 1775, CO 5/76; Boyd and Latorre, "Spanish Interest in British Florida," pp. 110–12.

20. David Holmes journal, 6 Aug. 1778, CO 5/80.

21. Oche Haujo (Alexander Cornells) to Benjamin Hawkins, Tuckabatchee, 27 May 1798, Deputy Supt. Gen., R G 10, A5b, PAC.

22. Proceedings of a general council of the several Indian nations, Glaize, 30 Sept. 1792, Supt. Gen. and Insp. Gen. VIII, R G 10, A5a, PAC.

23. Taitt, "Journal," p. 541; Woodward, *Reminiscences,* p. 9.

24. Coker and Coker, *Siege of Mobile,* p. 59; O'Neill, to Bernardo de Gálvez, Pensacola, 17 June 1781, AGI, Cuba, leg. 36.

25. Tonyn to Henry Clinton, St. Augustine, 2 May 1780, Carleton Papers, 2707, FSUL.

26. Searcy, *Georgia-Florida Contest,* pp. 28, 108, 177.

27. Council, 5 July 1776, *Ga. Rev. Rec.,* ed. Candler, 1:154; William McIntosh to Alexander Cameron, Broken Arrow, 6 July 1777, CO 5/78.

28. Chiefs of Upper Creeks to Brown, Tallassee, 30 Dec. 1783, CO 5/82.

29. Bonner, "William McIntosh," p. 116.

30. William McIntosh to Stuart, Hitchitaws, 3 Apr. 1778, CO 5/79.

31. Lyon, *Louisiana in French Diplomacy,* pp. 79–126.

32. Green, "McGillivray," pp. 41–60.

33. Wright, *Only Land They Knew,* p. 214.

34. Green, *Politics of Indian Removal,* p. 37.

35. Assembly journal, 23 Feb. 1784, *Ga. Rev. Rec.,* ed. Candler, 3:540; James Durouzeaux to Vicente Folch, Coweittaw, 8 May 1802, Lockey Coll., UFL; Hoboithle Mico to George III, Apalachicola River, 1 Sept. 1811, CO 23/58. The Tallassee Tame King's background is uncertain. Tallassee was a new town founded in the eighteenth century on the Tallopoosa River across from Tuckabatchee. Its population, which fluctuated considerably, contained diverse components, including Muskogee emigrants from Little Tallassee and elsewhere, Hitchitis, Yuchis, Shawnees, and various other groups. Presumably Muskogee was the dominant language. Because of the Tame King's close association with Hitchitis and

Yuchis among the Lower Creeks and among the Seminoles, we can   335
assume that he was a Hitchiti or Yuchi. When the Tame King's younger
contemporary Osceola came to Florida, Osceola had a close and apparently natural association with Miccosukees (Hitchitis). The relocation
of Indians, so pronounced in the sixteenth century, persisted in the
eighteenth, and unfortunately relatively little is known about Tallassee.
Even so we can make an educated guess that the Tame King was either
a Hitchiti or Yuchi who spoke Muskogee as either his first or second
language.

36. Assembly journal, 23 Feb. 1784, *Ga. Rev. Rec.*, ed. Candler, 3:540;
Green, *Politics of Indian Removal*, pp. 32, 34. Circumstantial evidence
strongly indicates that the Fat King was a Hitchiti (or possibly a Yuchi),
in any case not a Muskogee. When he asserted during the American
Revolution that the Lower Creeks were pro-American, or at least neutral,
he meant not the Cowetas but the Hitchitis, Yuchis, and Apalachicolas
(later known as Seminoles). The Fat King was a Bowles supporter, and
the Hitchitis and Yuchis were among Bowles's adherents. During the
eighteenth century there was southward drift of Hitchitis and Yuchis
into Florida. In the late 1790s Hawkins sent the Fat King on missions to
the Seminoles, presumably because they were his kin and they spoke
his language.

37. Mrs. Hugh Henry interview, 13 Mar. 1937, IPHC, 5:25; Swanton, *Indians of the Southeastern United States*, p. 137.

38. Cline, *Florida Indians*, 2:236; map 16.

39. Wright, *Britain and the American Frontier*. pp. 11–49.

40. Milfort, *Memoirs*.

41. Thomas Brown to Guy Carleton, St. Augustine, 12 Jan. 1783, Carleton
Papers, 6742, FSUL.

42. John Stuart to Augustine Prevost, Pensacola, 24 July 1777, CO 5/78.

43. Council, Detroit, 10 July 1783, minutes of Detroit councils, 1781–90,
RG10, A4, PAC; Winthrop Sargent to Arthur St. Clair, Ft. Steuben, 17
Aug. 1790, *Territorial Papers*, ed. Carter, 2:301.

44. Statement by John Strother, 1792(?), *St. Clair Papers*, ed. Smith, 2:302.

45. George Wellbank to Alexander McKee, Cowetah Old Town, 6 Feb. 1793,
Upper Canada, Indian Off., M.G. 19, F 16, 1, PAC.

46. Ockillissa Chopka, Houthlie Opoi Micco, and Tustinicia Opoi to McKee,
12 Apr. 1793, ibid. These letters were dictated to George Wellbank,
Bowles's lieutenant. The Indians were Bowles's partisans, among whom
the Yuchis, Shawnees, and Hitchitis were prominent. Shawnees probably delivered the letters to Canadian authorities.

47. Woodward, *Reminiscences*, p. 60.

48. Driesback to Lyman Draper, Baldwin Co., Ala., July 1874, Draper Mss.,
Ga., Ala., and S.C., IV, roll 31:62, FSUL.

49. Folch to McGillivray, Fuerte de San Esteban, 14 June 1789, AGI, Cuba,
52, PLP.

336

50. Francis Fatio, Jr. to Enrique White, St. Augustine, 12 Nov. 1801, EFP 197B16.
51. Creek chiefs to Louisiana governor, Ochualafau, 5 Oct. 1802, Lockey Coll., UFL; Woodward, *Reminiscences*, pp. 43–44.
52. Timothy Barnard to Edward Telfair, 1786, Barnard Letters, p. 55.
53. DeLacy to Bowles, Miccosukee, 9 Dec. 1801, Add. Mss. 27859, BL; Miller, *Quesada*, p. 91.
54. Whitaker, *Spanish-American Frontier*, p. 167.
55. Diego de Vegas to O'Neill, St. Marks, 22 Dec. 1788, AGI, Cuba, leg. 40.
56. Declaración de Lucas Perez, in Zéspedes to Espeleta, 1 Nov. 1788, Lockey Coll., UFL.
57. Luís de Bertucat to O'Neill, St. Marks, 18 Aug. 1790, West Papers, PLP.
58. Holmes, *Gayoso*, pp. 151–54.
59. O'Neill to Sonora, Pensacola, 11 July 1787, Caughey, *McGillivray*, p. 157.
60. Panton, Leslie, and Co. to Hawkins, Pensacola, Hawkins, Independence Letterbook, p. 75, SAC; Hawkins to Panton, near Ft. Wilkinson, 10 July 1800, ANC, Fla., leg. 1, exp. 12, #13, Cuban transcripts, LC.
61. John Forbes to Dearborn, Pensacola, 5 Sept. 1806, *ASP, IA*, 1:750–51.
62. John Innerarity to [John] Sanderson, Pensacola, 23 Nov. 1810, West Florida Papers, PLP; Hoboithle mico to George III, Prospect Bluff, 1 Sept. 1811, CO 23/58.
63. Daniel McGillivray to Panton, Hickory Ground, 13 Oct. 1800, *FHQ* 11 (1932):36–37; Doster, *Creek Indians*, 1:84; Swanton, "Social Organization of Creek Confederacy," pp. 115, 158.
64. Representations of Bowles . . . to George III, Osborn's Hotel, 3 Jan. 1791, FO 4/9; Paredes and Plante, "Economics, Politics, and Subjugation of the Creek Indians," p. 6.
65. Appropriation of Creek lands in Georgia and Alabama in the 1820s and 1830s and the Creek War of 1836 resulted in numerous Muscogulges' seeking refuge in Florida and a great increase in the Seminole population. Population estimates are based on lists of Seminoles who emigrated to Oklahoma and on accounts of Creeks fleeing into Florida.

CHAPTER 5

1. Swan, "Position and State of Manners in the Creek Nation," p. 258.
2. Adair, *History*, p. 490.
3. A scholarly, annotated recent edition is Bartram, *Travels of William Bartram*, Naturalist's ed., ed. by F. Harper.
4. "W. B." (William Bartram), "Some hints and observations concerning the civilization of the Indians or aborigines of America," 1792?, Knox Papers, 47:51, FSUL.
5. The United States and the Indian tribes, 1792(?), ibid., 53:164.

6. Knox to U.S. Congress, 26 July 1788, *NASP, IA*, 6:29–30.
7. Knox to James Seagrove, 11 Aug. 1792, *ASP, IA*, 1:257.
8. Andrew Jackson to John McKee, Poplar Grove, 16 May 1794, *Papers of Andrew Jackson*, ed. Smith and Owsley, 1:48–49.
9. Ibid., p. 49.
10. Coulter, "Elijah Clarke's Foreign Intrigues," pp. 267–72.
11. McGillivray to Zéspedes, Apalache, 10 Dec. 1785, *East Florida Documents*, ed. Caughey, p. 745.
12. John Martin to Tallassee King, Headmen, and Warriors of Upper and Lower Creek Nation, Savannah, 19 July 1782, *GHQ* 1 (1917): 314–15.
13. Kings, Chiefs, and Head Warriors of Creek and Cherokee Nation to George III, Coweta, 1789, CO 42/87.
14. A. McGillivray to McLatchy, Little Tallassee, 25 Dec. 1784, EFP, 116L9.
15. James Durouzeaux to Edward Telfair, Coweta, 5 June 1786, Creek Indian Letters, p. 114, GDAH.
16. McGillivray to Panton, Little Tallassee, 20 Sept. 1788, J 1 Case #11J6, PLP.
17. Smith, "James Seagrove and Mission to Tuckabatchee," p. 42.
18. Coleman, *American Revolution in Georgia*, pp. 240–45.
19. Thomas Brown to Lord North, St. Augustine, 30 July 1783, CO 5/82.
20. The text of the 1790 Creek treaty, not including the secret articles, is in Kappler, ed., *Indian Affairs*, 2:25–28. The secret articles are in Miller, ed., *Treaties*, 2:344.
21. Freeman, *Washington*, 6:222–24, 272–73.
22. Washington's diary, 1 July 1790, *Diaries of Washington*, ed. Fitzpatrick, 4:132–33; Howard to McGillivray, Philadelphia, 18 July 1790, AGI, Cuba, leg. 182.
23. Wright, "Creek-American Treaty," pp. 381, 394.
24. Ibid., pp. 391–93.
25. Miller, ed., *Treaties*, 2:344.
26. Knox to James Seagrove, War Dept., 16 Sept. 1793, *ASP, IA*, 1:366–67.
27. Treaty of San Lorenzo, 27 Oct. 1795, *Treaties*, ed. Miller, 2:319–21.
28. Creek treaty, Coleraine, 29 June 1796, *Indian Affairs*, ed. Kappler, 2:46–50.
29. Price to Thomas Freeman, 9 June 1798, Letter Book, Creek Trading House, NA.
30. Creek treaty, Ft. Wilkinson, 16 June 1802, *Indian Affairs*, ed. Kappler, 2:58; Creek treaty, Washington, 14 Nov. 1805, ibid., p. 85.
31. Treaty with the Creeks, New York, 7 Aug. 1790, ibid., 2:26.
32. Stipend to the Creek Nation for 1806, LS, Sec. War, M15, roll 2:182.
33. Eustis to Hawkins, War Dept., 29 Mar. 1811, ibid., 3:73.
34. Horsman, *Expansion and American Indian Policy*, pp. 66–83, 104–8.
35. Dearborn to Hawkins, War Dept., 9 May 1808, LS, Sec. War, M15, roll 2:377.
36. Hawkins journal, 15 July 1804, in Hawkins, *Letters*, ed. Grant, p. 477.

338

37. Hawkins journal, 16 Feb. 1797, ibid., 2:47–48.
38. Hawkins to Alexander Cornells, Coweta Tallahassee, 5 Nov. 1799, ibid., 1:268.
39. Henry Dearborn to Hawkins, War Dept., 10 Nov. 1804, LS, Sec. War, M15, roll 2:27.
40. Ibid.
41. Hawkins to ?, Cusseta, 1 July 1798, Hawkins, *Letters*, p. 485.
42. John Innerarity to [John] Sanderson, Pensacola, 23 Nov. 1810, West Florida Papers, PLP.
43. General abstract of debts due Panton, Leslie, and Co., 20 Aug. 1803, LR, Sec. War, M271, roll 1.
44. ? to Dearborn, St. Stephens, 1 Oct. 1803, ibid., p. 242.
45. John Forbes to Dearborn, Pensacola, 5 Sept. 1806, *ASP, IA*, 1:750–51.
46. Dearborn to Hawkins, War Dept., 12 Feb. 1805, LS, Sec. War, M15, roll 2:41.
47. Diary of John Innerarity, 14 Oct.–1 Nov. 1812, Greenslade Papers, PLP.
48. Francis P. Fatio to Hawkins, St. Augustine, 4 Sept. 1801, LR, Sec. War, M271, roll 1:34.
49. David Taitt, "Journal of Travels from Pensacola," p. 524; Brown to Lord North, St. Augustine, CO 5/82.
50. Hambly, "Visit to the Indian Nations," p. 61; Smith, "Seagrove Mission," pp. 54–55.
51. Journal of a voyage to the Creek Nation from Pensacola, 1803, AGI, Cuba, leg. 2372.
52. Hoboithle Mico to George III, Apalachicola River, 1 Sept. 1811, CO 23/58.
53. James Innerarity to William Simpson, Pensacola, 24 Sept. 1804, *FHQ* 10(1931): 102–8.
54. Forbes to Dearborn, Pensacola, 5 Sept. 1806, *ASP, IA*, 1:751.
55. Ellicott, *Journal*, pp. 213–26.
56. Report by Tustunee Haujo and Robert Walton to Hawkins, Coweta Tallahassee, 4 Nov. 1799, Hawkins, "Independence Letterbook," pp. 89–91, SAC.
57. Dearborn to Hawkins, War Dept., 9 May 1808, LS, Sec. War, M15, roll 2:378.
58. Journal of a voyage to the Creek nation from Pensacola, 1803, AGI, Cuba, 2372.
59. Pound, *Hawkins*, pp. 209–10.
60. Stiggins Narr., Draper Mss., Ga., Ala., and S.C., IV, roll 30:1, FSUL.
61. Matthew Elliott to Isaac Brock, Amhurstburg, 12 Jan. 1812, *MPHC* 15(1931): 68; Reuben Attwater to William Eustis, Detroit, 21 Jan. 1812, *Territorial Papers*, ed. Carter, 10:377.
62. Hawkins to David B. Mitchell, Creek Agency, 13 Sept. 1812, Hawkins Letters, p. 169, GDAH.

CHAPTER 6

1. Owsley, *Struggle for the Gulf Borderlands*, pp. 34–40; Pickett, *History of Alabama*, pp. 528–43; Doster, "Letters Relating to Tragedy of Fort Mims," pp. 269–85.
2. Swanton, "Religious Beliefs and Medical Practices," pp. 614–21.
3. Ibid.; Robert Grierson to Hawkins, Hilibi, 23 Sept. 1813, Hawkins Letters, p. 254, GDAH.
4. Tecumseh Papers, Draper Mss., 10YY, roll 58:91, FSUL.
5. Pickett, *History of Alabama*, p. 532.
6. Stiggins Narrative, Draper Mss., Ga., Ala., and S.C., IV, roll 30:1, FSUL.
7. Tucker, *Tecumseh*, p. 364.
8. Tecumseh Papers, Draper Mss., 4YY, roll 58:21, FSUL.
9. Mooney, "Ghost-Dance Religion," p. 682.
10. Tecumseh Papers, Draper Mss., 10YY, roll 58, FSUL; Tucker, *Tecumseh*, pp. 193–94.
11. Report of J. C. Warren to David B. Mitchell, 10 Apr. 1813, Lockey Coll., UFL.
12. Tucker, *Tecumseh*, p. 216.
13. John Innerarity to James Innerarity, Pensacola, 27 July 1813, Greenslade Papers, PLP.
14. Mooney, "Ghost-Dance Religion," p. 676.
15. Hawkins to William Eustis, Creek Agency, 3 Oct. 1811, in Hawkins, *Letters*, ed. Grant, 2:592–94.
16. Alexander Cornells to Hawkins, near Ft. Hawkins, 22 June 1813, Hawkins Letters, pp. 203–6; GDAH, Hassig, "Internal Conflict in the Creek War," p. 260.
17. Patrick, *Florida Fiasco*, pp. 85–97, 129–43.
18. Hawkins to Mitchell, Creek Agency, 24 Aug. 1812, Hawkins Letters, p. 166, GDAH.
19. Cornells to Hawkins, Tuckabatchee, 19 Sept. 1812, Lockey Coll., UFL.
20. Hawkins to Mitchell, Ocmulgee Ferry, 31 May 1813, Hawkins Letters, p. 198, GDAH; Porter, "Negroes and the East Florida Annexation Plot," pp. 195–98.
21. Edward Nicholls to J. P. Morier, near Eltham, 25 Sept. 1815, WO 1/143.
22. John B. Warren to Melville, Bermuda, 25 Feb. 1813, Warren Papers, NMM.
23. Bonner, "McIntosh," pp. 115–25; Green, *Politics of Indian Removal*, pp. 54–59, 71.
24. Stiggins Narrative, Draper Mss., Ga., Ala., and S.C., IV, roll 30:1, FSUL.
25. Woodward, *Reminiscences*, pp. 87–102; Tecumseh Papers, Draper Mss., FSUL.
26. Hunter, *Manners and Customs of Indian Tribes*, p. 56; diary of John Innerarity, 14 Oct.–1 Nov. 1812, Greenslade Papers, PLP; Tucker, *Tecumseh*, p. 216.

340

27. Green, *Politics of Indian Removal*, pp. 39–42.

28. Woodward, *Reminiscences*, pp. 40, 102, 109.

29. William Munnings to earl of Bathurst, Nassau, 30 Sept. 1819, CO 23/68.

30. Porter, "Negro Abraham," pp. 295–338.

31. John Innerarity to James Innerarity, Pensacola, 27 July 1813, Greenslade Papers, PLP.

32. Pickett, *History of Alabama*, pp. 521–25.

33. Halbert and Ball, *Creek War*, pp. 170–71.

34. Pickett, *History of Alabama*, pp. 539–42.

35. Halbert and Ball, *Creek War*, p. 164.

36. Natives of Creek nation petition to President Madison, Alabama River, 29 May 1815, LR, Sec. War, M271, roll 1:840.

37. Talesee to Hawkins, Creek Agency, 5 July 1813, Hawkins Letters, p. 210, GDAH.

38. John Floyd to Mary H. Floyd, camp, South Chattahoochee, 5 Dec. 1813, Floyd, "Letters," p. 235; Owsley, *Struggle for Gulf Borderlands*, pp. 51–60.

39. Davis, "Elotchaway, East Florida," p. 148.

40. Pickett, *History of Alabama*, pp. 588–92; Owsley, *Struggle for Gulf Borderlands*, pp. 79–82.

41. Hugh Pigot to Cochrane, *Orpheus*, New Providence, 8 June 1814, PRO, Adm. 1/506.

42. Treaty with the Creeks, 9 Aug. 1814, Ft. Jackson, *Indian Affairs*, ed. Kappler, 2:107–10. McIntosh signed for himself and for three others.

43. Extract from minutes of occurrences at Fort Jackson, Fort Jackson, 7 Aug. 1814, Documents, Ratified and Unratified Treaties, M494, roll 1, NA.

44. Halbert and Ball, *Creek War*, p. 253.

45. Dreisback narrative, July 1874, Draper Mss., Ga., Ala., and S.C., FSUL.

46. Charles Cameron to Lord Bathurst, Nassau, 23 Mar. 1816, CO 23/63.

47. Sugden, "Southern Indians in War of 1812," p. 287.

48. Henry Goulburn to John W. Croker, Downing St., 19 Jan. 1814, Cochrane Papers, 2342, NLS; Alexander Cochrane to John Lambert, *Tonnant*, 3 Feb. 1815, WO 1/143; John Forbes to George Cockburn, 26 Feb. 1815, Cumberland Island, WO 1/144.

49. John Innerarity to John Forbes, Pensacola, 22 May 1815, Forbes Papers, Mobile Public Library, PLP.

50. Sebastian Kindelan to Cockburn, St. Augustine, 18 Feb. 1815, WO 1/144.

51. Forbes and Co., Pensacola, to Forbes and Co., London, 1 Feb. 1814, Greenslade Papers, PLP; James Innerarity to John Forbes, Mobile, 12 Aug. 1815, *FHQ* 12 (1934): 127–29.

52. Thomas McKee to John Johnson, Montreal, 26 Sept. 1814, Deputy Supt. Gen., RG10, A5b, PAC; speech by deputy supt. general of Indian affairs, Burlington, 24 Apr. 1815, ibid.

53. Bathurst to George Prevost, War Dept., London, 27 Dec. 1814, Claus   341
Papers, 10, PAC.
54. Wright, "Note on the First Seminole War," p. 571.
55. Hawkins to George Graham, Creek Agency, 1 Aug. 1815, in Hawkins,
Letters, ed. Grant, 2:743–46.

CHAPTER 7

1. Abernethy, *South in the New Nation*, p. 465.
2. Wright, "Note on the First Seminole War," pp. 567–74.
3. Boleck to governor of East Florida, Sahwahnah, 18 Nov. 1816, *British
and Foreign State Papers*, 6:222–23.
4. Abernethy, *Formative Period in Alabama*, pp. 25, 66.
5. Natives of Creek Nation, petition to President Madison, Alabama River,
29 May 1815, LR, Sec. War, M271, 1:838–39.
6. Stiggins Narr., Draper Mss., Ga., Ala., and S.C., IV, roll 30:1, FSUL.
7. William Bibb to Calhoun, St. Stephens, 23 Jan. 1817, *Papers of Calhoun*,
ed. Hemphill and Meriwether, 2:89; Jackson to Calhoun, Ft. Montgomery, 2 June 1818, *ASP, MA*, 1:708.
8. George Graham to Gaines, War Dept., 30 Oct. 1817, LR, Sec. War, M271,
2:506.
9. Bathurst to Charles Cameron, 8 June 1816, in Statement of correspondence . . . 1816–17, FO 5/127.
10. Alexander Arbuthnot to John Arbuthnot, Ft. St. Marks, 2 Apr. 1818,
British and Foreign State Papers, 6:433.
11. Doyle to Innerarity, Prospect Bluff, 11 July 1817, "Panton, Leslie Papers,"
FHQ 18(1939): 135.
12. Ibid., 17 Aug. 1817, p. 140.
13. Hambly and Doyle testimony, Ft. Gadsden, 2 May 1818, *ASP, MA*, 1:715.
14. Claim no. 339, 29 May 1789, CO 5/562, PLP.
15. John Quincy Adams, *Memoirs*, 4:74.
16. Forbes, *Sketches of the Floridas*, pp. xvi–xxix.
17. Power of attorney for the Indian chiefs to Arbuthnot, Ochlockonee
Sound, Creek Nation, 17 June 1817, *ASP, MA*, 1:726:27.
18. Arbuthnot to governor of Havana, 17 June 1817(?), *British and Foreign
State Papers*, 6:444–45.
19. Nicholls to J. P. Morier, Eltham, 25 Sept. 1815, WO 1/143.
20. Arbuthnot to Nicholls, Sawahnee, Lower Creek Nation, 30 Jan. 1818,
British and Foreign State Papers, 6:489–91.
21. 26 Aug. 1817, Ibid., p. 420.
22. Cappachimico, McQueen, Charlie Tastonoky, et al., to Charles Bagot,
with enclosures, Sawahnee Town, 8 Nov. 1816, CO 23/66.
23. Jairus Loomis to Daniel T. Patterson, Bay St. Louis, 13 Aug. 1816, *British
and Foreign State Papers*, 6:379–81.
24. Giddings, *Exiles of Florida*, pp. 42–44.

342

25. Gaines to Calhoun, Ft. Scott, 2 Dec. 1817, *ASP, MA*, 1:687.

26. Davis, "Milly Francis," pp. 254–65.

27. An expanded version of the 1818 laws, written down in 1825, is in Waring, ed., *Laws of the Creek Nation*, pp. 17–27.

28. Bowleck to governor of East Florida, Sahwahnah, 18 Nov. 1816, *British and Foreign State Papers*, 6:223; Cappachimicco and Boleck to governor of the Bahamas, ibid., p. 439.

29. Gaines to Seminole chiefs, Aug. 1817, ibid., p. 436.

30. Gaines to Calhoun, Ft. Scott, 4 Dec. 1817, *ASP, MA*, 1:688.

31. Calhoun to Gaines, War Dept., 9 Dec. 1817, LR, Sec. War, M271, roll 2:513; Remini, *Jackson*, 1:346–53.

32. Jackson to Calhoun, Ft. Gadsden, 25 Mar. 1818, *ASP, MA*, 1:699.

33. 20 Apr. 1818, Ibid., pp. 700–701.

34. Woodward, *Reminiscences*, p. 161; Jackson to Calhoun, Bowlegs Town, 20 Apr. 1818, *British and Foreign State Papers*, 6:470.

35. Jackson to Calhoun, near St. Marks, 8 Apr. 1818, ibid., p. 410.

36. Crider, "Borderland Floridas," pp. 234–36.

37. Woodward, *Reminiscences*, p. 168; Jackson to Calhoun, Bowlegs Town, 20 Apr. 1818, *ASP, MA*, 1:700–701.

38. Jackson to Calhoun, Ft. Gadsden, 5 May 1818, *British and Foreign State Papers*, 6:475–76.

39. Proceedings of the trial are in ibid., vol. 6.

40. William Rabun to Calhoun, Milledgeville, 1 June 1818, *ASP, MA*, 1:774.

41. Woodward, *Reminiscences*, p. 167.

42. Crider, "Borderland Floridas," pp. 249–55.

43. Jackson to Calhoun, Ft. Montgomery, 2 June 1818, *ASP, MA*, 1:707.

44. Calhoun to Mitchell, War Dept., 21 July 1818, LS, Sec. War, M15, roll 4:186–87.

45. Woodward, *Reminiscences*, pp. 41, 44.

46. Brumbaugh, "Black Maroons in Florida."

47. Mitchell to Calhoun, Milledgeville, 7 Dec. 1819, LR, Sec. War, M271, 2:1516.

48. McIntosh, et al., talk, Washington, 23 Feb. 1819, ibid., pp. 1238–39.

49. Green, *Politics of Indian Removal*, pp. 52–57.

50. McIntosh and other Creek chiefs to Calhoun, Washington, 9 Mar. 1819, *Papers of Calhoun*, ed. Hemphill and Meriwether, 3:646.

51. Calhoun to Creek delegation, War Dept., 28 Mar. 1819, ibid., pp. 700–701.

52. McIntosh and other Creek chiefs to Calhoun, Washington, 9 Mar. 1819, ibid., p. 646.

53. John Bidwell to Joseph Planta, Portsmouth, 17 Sept. 1818, FO 5/140.

54. Bemis, *John Quincy Adams*, pp. 327–28.

55. William Hamilton to Croker, 15 Sept. 1818, FO 5/140.

56. Jackson to Calhoun(?), camp, 14 miles from St. Marks, 9 Apr. 1818, *ASP, MA*, 1:700.

57. William V. Munnings to earl of Bathurst, Nassau, 30 Sept. 1819, CO 23/ 168; William Gibson to Joshua Brooke, Nassau, 4 Oct. 1819, CO 23/69.

58. Stiggins Narrative, Draper Mss., Ga., Ala., and S.C., IV, roll 30:1, FSUL.

CHAPTER 8

1. Sprague, *Origin of the Florida War*, p. 20. The 1832 Creek census listed almost 23,000 Indians. However, in the preceding fourteen years some 4,000 had moved beyond the Mississippi, while at the same time an undetermined but considerable number had relocated in the West Indies or joined the Cherokees. Perhaps 4,000 were stretched out for hundreds of miles across southern Georgia and Alabama. Florida Muskogulgees including those in the panhandle, numbered around 8,000, while perhaps 3,000–5,000 black Muskogulgees lived somewhere in the Southeast. A not inconsiderable number of Muskogulgees lived relatively unnoticed among blacks and whites. Considering the difficulties of modern census takers, we can assume the 1832 census takers missed some Indians when they visited the various Creek towns. An overall estimate of 50,000 or more for all southeastern Muskogulgees, including those who were black or were nearly white, seems realistic.

2. Francis Richard deposition, Alachua Co., 6 Mar. 1829, LR, OIA, M234, roll 800:103.

3. Jesup to William Bunce, Tampa, 15 May 1837, LR, OIA, M234, roll 289:54–55.

4. Woodward, *Reminiscences*, p. 110.

5. David Tate to David Moniac, 23 Apr. 1822, *AHQ* 19 (1957): 407–8.

6. Jackson to Calhoun, Pensacola, 17 Sept. 1821, *Papers of Calhoun*, eds. Hemphill and Meriwether, 6:373.

7. Treaty of Moultrie Creek, 18 Sept. 1823, *Indian Affairs*, ed. Kappler, 2:205.

8. *Floridian*, 30 July 1836.

9. Duncan G. Campbell and James Meriwether to Creek Chiefs, 9 Dec. 24, *NASP, IA*, 6:312–13.

10. Calhoun to Creek deputation, Dept. War, 28 Mar. 1819, *Papers of Calhoun*, eds. Hemphill and Meriwether, 3:700–1.

11. A. Hamill to Capers, Yellow River Mission, 25 Mar. 1823, LR, OIA, M234, roll 219:202.

12. Details of the Moravians' efforts on the Flint River are in Records of the Moravian Mission, Box 195, folder 4, roll 25, FSUL. See also Mauelshagen and Davis, ed. and trans., *Partners in the Lord's Work*, pp. 16–70.

13. An exhibit of the state of the school at Tuckabatchee, 30 Sept. 1824, LR, OIA, M234, roll 772:460; Compere to Luther Rice, Withington Station, 26 Aug. 1825, ibid., pp. 652–53.

14. Compere to James Barbour, 2 Sept. 1825, ibid., p. 457.

344

15. Second annual report of the missionary committee of the South Carolina conference, 26 Feb. 1823, *NASP, IA*, 7:38.

16. Report . . . S.C. Conference of the Methodist Episcopal Church, 21 Feb. 1822, ibid., p. 95.

17. Caper's Journal, Waring Papers, 1287, no. 127, GHS.

18. Report . . . S.C. Conference of the Methodist Episcopal Church, 21 Feb. 1822, *NASP, IA*, 7:95.

19. Talk of Florida delegation of Indians to Barbour, 17 May 1826, LR, OIA, M234, roll 800:14.

20. McKenney, *Memoirs*, 2:16.

21. Henderson, quarterly report, Choctaw Academy, 1 Aug. 1832, *NASP, IA*, 13:70.

22. Barbour to Thomas Henderson, War Dept., 21 Sept. 1826, ibid., p. 34; Henderson Quarterly report, 1 Nov. 1833, ibid., pp. 82–84.

23. Johnson to War Dept., Great Crossings, 20 Aug. 1826, ibid, p. 45; Barbour to Henderson, War Dept., 21 Sept. 1826, ibid., p. 46.

24. Abstract . . . 8 Indian boys to be educated at the Choctaw Academy, LR, OIA, M234, roll 288:132; Choctaw Academy, 1 Apr. 1837, ibid., 778:226.

25. McKenney to Henderson, War Dept., 7 Feb. 1828, *NASP, IA*, 13:46–47.

26. War Dept. Regulations, 29 Feb. 1820, *NASP, IA*, 2:581.

27. Exposition of United States Commissioners, Milledgeville, 12 Nov. 1825, *NASP, IA*, 8:397; Compere to Barbour, Withington, 2 Sept. 1825, LR, OIA, M234, roll 772:457.

28. John Tipton to Barbour, Fort Wayne, 2 June 1827, *NASP, IA*, 13:50.

29. Henderson to Elbert Herring, Choctaw Academy, 12 Oct. 1833, LR, OIA, M234, roll 776:228–29; Johnson to Herring, 9 Nov. 1833, ibid., pp. 237–39.

30. David Mitchell to Calhoun, Creek Agency, 3 Feb. 1818, *Papers of Calhoun*, eds. Hemphill and Meriwether, 2:115.

31. David Tate to David Moniac, 23 Apr. 1822, *AHQ* 19 (1957): 407–8.

32. Woodward, *Reminiscences*, p. 160.

33. McKenney, *Memoirs*, 1:188–90.

34. John Hogan to George Gibson, Ft. Mitchell, 9 May 1835, *ASP, MA*, 6:724.

35. Gadsden to Calhoun, St. Augustine, 11 June 1823, LR, Sec. War, M234, roll 4:570–71.

36. Jackson to Calhoun, Pensacola, 17 Sept. 1821, *Territorial Papers*, ed. Carter, 22:207.

37. Calhoun to Duval, War Dept., 18 Aug. 1822, ibid., pp. 518–19.

38. Jackson to Calhoun, Pensacola, 17 Sept. 1821,, ibid., p. 206.

39. Reply of Neamathla to talk, St. Marks, 20 Mar. 1823, LR, Sec. War, M234, roll 4:834–35.

40. Sprague, *Florida War*, p. 73.

41. Treaty of Ft. Moultrie, 18 Sept. 1823, *Indian Affairs*, ed. Kappler, 2:203–7.

42. Wiley Thompson to Duval, Tallahassee, 1 Jan. 1834, LR, Sec. War, M234, roll 290:79.
43. Treaty of Ft. Moultrie, 18 Sept. 1823, *Indian Affairs*, ed. Kappler, 2:203–7.
44. Joseph M. White to George Graham, Washington, 25 Dec. 1827, *Territorial Papers*, ed. Carter, 23:959.
45. Cowe Mathla, Pos Harjoe, Holati Thlocoe, et al. to John Eaton, Ft. Bainbridge, Creek Nation, 12 Apr. 1829, LR, OIA, M234, roll 237:263–64.
46. William Walker to McKenney, Montgomery, 18 Mar. 1828, ibid., 221:885–87.
47. Declaration of chiefs, Seminole Agency, 20 Oct. 1828, ibid., 800:49.
48. Irving, *Works*, 1:153–55.
49. Blount to Joseph M. White, 10 Dec. 1827, LR, OIA, M234, roll 2:316–20; Wiley Thompson to Herring, Elberton, 6 Aug. 1834, ibid., 288:195.
50. Kappler, ed., *Indian Affairs*, 2:214–17.
51. Duncan Campbell to Calhoun, Washington, 8 Jan. 1825, Documents, Ratified and Unratified Treaties, T494, NA; Address from twenty-four Indians, Pike Co., Ga., 17 May 1825, *NASP, IA*, 7:340–41.
52. Green, *Politics of Indian Removal*, pp. 96–97.
53. Alexander Lasley, Jim Fife, Spoko Cago, et al., testimony, Ashville, Ala., 14 May 1825, LR, OIA, M234, roll 219:1595.
54. Timothy P. Andrews to James Barbour, Milledgeville, 2 June 1825, *NASP, IA*, 7:194.
55. Kappler, ed., *Indian Affairs*, 2:214–17.
56. *Arkansas Gazette*, 23 June, 11 Nov. 1828.
57. For a recent discussion of the removal bill controversy see Remini, *Jackson*, 2:257–66.
58. Treaty of Payne's Landing, 9 May 1832, *Indian Affairs*, ed. Kappler, 2:344–45; Treaty of Ft. Gibson, 28 Mar. 1833, ibid., pp. 394–95.
59. Creek delegation to Calhoun, Brown's Hotel, 10 Dec. 1825, *NASP, IA*, 8:305.
60. Compere to McKenney, Withington, 29 Sept. 1829, LR, OIA, M234, roll 773:948.

CHAPTER 9

1. Wilson Lumpkin to Cass, Milledgeville, 5 Feb. 1834, LR, OIA, M234, roll 224:81–83.
2. I. H. Howard to ?, Pole Cat Spring, Creek Nation, 1 Feb. 1834, Sanford Papers, ADAH.
3. Alfred Balch to Benjamin F. Butler, 14 Jan. 1837, *NASP, IA*, 9:502–7; Benjamin P. Tarver to M. A. Craven, Columbus, 1 Mar. 1835, ibid., p.

513; Eli S. Shorter, et al. to Cass, Columbus, 16 Oct. 1825, ibid., pp. 522–25; Young, *Redskins*, p. 73–98.

4. Testimony, Irwinton, 18 Feb. 1834, Sanford Papers; Thomas J. Abbott to John Crowell, Eufaula, 13 Oct. 1832, LR, OIA, M234, roll 233:165; Young, *Redskins*, p. 77.

5. Opothleyahola et al. to Jackson, 13 June 1835, LR, OIA, M234, roll 224:275–81.

6. James D. Westcott to Abraham Bellamy, Tallahassee, 2 Feb. 1832, ibid., 288:60–61.

7. Ibid.

8. Scattered information concerning Charlie Emarthla is in Creek treaty, 15 Nov. 1827, *Indian Affairs*, ed. Kappler, 2:286; Mahon, *Second Seminole War*, pp. 79, 99–101; Laumer, *Massacre!*, pp. 23, 71.

9. James A. Everett to John Eaton, Ft. Valley, 25 May 1829, LR, OIA, M234, roll 222:147.

10. Petition to Congress by inhabitants of St. Augustine, Mar. 1836, *Territorial Papers*, ed. Carter, 25:265–66.

11. Andres Pappy and Joseph S. Sanchez, depositions, 19 Apr. 1842, LR, OIA, M234, roll 289:351–54; Jane Murray Sheldon narrative, 1890, *FHQ* 8 (1930): 189.

12. Laumer, *Massacre!*, pp. 134–50.

13. *Mobile Daily Commercial Register*, 11 Jan. 1836.

14. *Army and Navy Chronicle*, 28 Jan. 1836.

15. Hartley and Hartley, *Osceola*, pp. 138–40.

16. Motte, *Journey into Wilderness*, p. 283.

17. Mahon, *Second Seminole War*, pp. 127–28.

18. Porter, "Cowkeeper Dynasty," pp. 344–49.

19. Jesup to John Bell, Washington, 3 May 1841, LR, OIA, M234, roll 800:464; Mahon, *Second Seminole War*, p. 127.

20. Sprague, *Florida War*, pp. 98, 293.

21. Hawkins, *Letters*, ed. Grant, 1:37–38; Jesup to Poinsett, Garey's Ferry, 10 Oct. 1837, *ASP, MA*, 7:884.

22. William Bunce to Thompson, Tampa, 9 Jan. 1835, LR, OIA, M234, roll 288:251; Sturtevant, "Chakaika and the 'Spanish Indians'," pp. 37–53.

23. Motte, *Journey into Wilderness*, pp. 120–23; 277–79.

24. J. C. Casey to Carey A. Harris, Tampa Bay, 1 Oct. 1837, LR, OIA, M234, roll 290:125.

25. *Austin, Texas, Commercial Journal*, Aug. 1861, in *Pioneer Florida*, by McKay, 2:480–81; Matthews, *Edge of Wilderness*, pp. 80, 397; *Florida Times Union*, 30 Oct. 1892, 8 Jan. 1895.

26. Mahon, *Second Seminole War*, pp. 108–12.

27. Ibid., pp. 227–29.

28. Call to Daniel Boyd, Walker's Town, 7 Mar. 1838, LR, OIA, M234, roll 239:97–98.

29. *Mobile Daily Commercial Register*, 19 Aug. 1836.

30. Welch, *Narrative of Jane Johns*, pp. 13–15.
31. Robert R. Reid to legislative council, Tallahassee, 28 Feb. 1840, *Territorial Papers*, ed. Carter, 26:113.
32. Court of inquiry, Frederick, Md., Feb. 1837, *ASP, MA*, 7:416; *Mobile Daily Commercial Register*, 22 Apr. 1836.
33. White, ed., "Macomb's Mission to the Seminoles," p. 168.
34. Hitchcock, *Fifty Years*, p. 170.
35. Archibald Smith to Harris, Apalachicola Agency, 7 Feb. 1838, LR, OIA, M234, roll 239:281.
36. Evans, ed., "Seminole Folktales," pp. 483–85.
37. *Mobile Daily Commercial Register*, 18 Jan. 1836.
38. Porter, "Seminole Flight from Fort Marion," pp. 113–33.
39. Mahon, *Second Seminole War*, pp. 310–21.
40. John Hogan to Cass, Ft. Mitchell, 1 Feb. 1836, 24th Cong., 1st Sess., HR, Doc. 276:66–67.
41. Woodward, *Reminiscences*, pp. 45–46; Valliere, "Creek War of 1836," p. 481.
42. Ibid., p. 466; Hogan to Cass, Mobile, 8 Mar. 1836, 24th Cong., 1st Sess., HR, *Doc.* 276:348–55.
43. Jonathan Sims to Major Mitchell, Ft. Mitchell, 9 Apr. 1836, Creek Indian Letters, 4:1273, GDAH.
44. *Floridian*, 28 May, 31 May 1836.
45. *Mobile Daily Commercial Register*, 20, 30 May 1836; 29 June 1836; William Schley to Cass, Milledgeville, 17 May 1836, 24th Cong., 1st Sess., HR *Doc.* 276:265.
46. Chiefs of Tuckabatchee Town to Cass, LR, OIA, M234, roll 225:46–48.
47. Deposition of A. H. Kenan, 27 Nov. 1836, *ASP, MA*, 7:170.
48. *Mobile Daily Commercial Register*, 28 Jan. 1836.
49. S. A. Billings, E. A. Dunn, John Morgan, et al., petition, Irvinton, 12 Apr. 1836, 24th Cong., 1st Sess., HR, *Doc.* 276:259.
50. Deposition of William Schley, 3 Jan. 1837, ibid., pp. 174–76; Jesup to Scott, Camp Hatchychubby, 20 June 1836, ibid., pp. 337–38.
51. Jesup to Francis P. Blair, Ft. Mitchell, 20 June 1836, ibid., p. 336; Jesup to Cass, 25 June 1836, ibid., pp. 347–48.
52. Valliere, "Creek War," p. 481.
53. *Floridian*, 18 Feb. 1837.
54. Ibid., 16 Dec. 1837, 28 Apr., 28 July 1838, 18 May 1839; *Florida Herald and Southern Democrat*, 27 Dec. 1838, 30 May 1839.
55. Jesup to Poinsett, Ft. Mellon, 15 Dec. 1837, *ASP, MA*, 7:891.
56. Sprague, *Florida War*, pp. 505–6.
57. *Army and Navy Chronicle*, 22 Sept. 1836.
58. Ibid., 8 Sept. 1836.
59. *Mobile Daily Commercial Register*, 19 Aug. 1836.
60. Ibid., 18 Jan. 1836.
61. Hogan to Alfred Balch and T. Hartley Crawford, Mobile, 28 Dec. 1836,

348

NASP, IA, 9:507–8; Crawford's report, near Tuskegee, 9 Jan. 1837, ibid., p. 545.

62. *Floridian,* 30 July 1836.
63. "Alabama Indian Chiefs," pp. 13–15.
64. Jesup to Poinsett, St. Augustine, 3 Oct. 1837, *ASP, MA,* 7:883.
65. Motte, *Journey into Wilderness,* p. 102.
66. Brannon, "Removal of Indians," p. 99.
67. Jesup to Poinsett, Tampa Bay, 15 June 1837, *ASP, MA,* 7:875.
68. Jesup to Benjamin F. Butler, Volusia, 9 Dec. 1836, ibid., p. 821.
69. Giddings, *Exiles of Florida,* p. 39ff.
70. *Florida Herald and Southern Democrat,* 6 June 1839; White, ed., "Macomb's Mission," pp. 178–83.
71. Young, *Redskins,* pp. 75–76; Creek treaty, 4 Apr. 183 ʻ. *Indian Affairs,* ed. Kappler, 2:342.
72. Crawford to Armstrong, 16 July 1840, LR, Western Supt., M640, roll 3:142; Judge Bryan to William Medill, Washington, 2 Dec. 1846, ibid., 6:151.
73. Joseph W. Harris to commissioners of Indian Affairs, 13 Sept. 1836, LR, OIA, M234, roll 288:393.
74. Porter, "Negro Abraham," pp. 23–25.
75. Buker, "Mosquito Fleet's Guides," pp. 312, 316–22.
76. John B. Hogan to Scott, Ft. Mitchell, 1 Feb. 1836, *ASP, MA,* 7:519.
77. Jesup to Roger Jones, St. Augustine, 20 July 1837, *ASP, MA,* 7:842; *Florida Herald and Southern Democrat,* 13 Aug. 1836.
78. *Mobile Daily Commercial Register,* 1 Aug. 1836; Jesup to Poinsett, St. Augustine, 22 Sept. 1837, *ASP, MA,* 7:882.

CHAPTER 10

1. Woodward, *Reminiscences,* pp. 41, 44.
2. George Scott interview, IPHC, 103:160–62.
3. Mary Hill interview, Okfuskee Town, Okemah, Okla., 19 Apr. 1937, IPHC, 5:106–7.
4. Milfort, *Memoirs,* pp. 37, 54.
5. *Floridian,* 18 Nov. 1837.
6. Mary Hill interview, IPHC, 5:106–7.
7. *Arkansas Gazette,* 26 Aug. 1836.
8. Benjamin S. Parsons and Thomas J. Abbott, 1832 Census of Creek Indians, T275, NA; Duval to Eaton, Tallahassee, 9 June 1829, *Territorial Papers,* ed. Carter, 24:231; Fairbanks, *Ethnohistorical Report,* p. 272.
9. John Hogan to George Gibson, Ft. Mitchell, 9 May 1835, *ASP, MA,* 6:724–25.
10. Opothleyahola to Jesup, Indian Camp, 26 Aug. 1836, LR, OIA, M234, roll 239:430–31.
11. H. Sockett to Cass, New Orleans, 22 July 1834, ibid., 288:164.

12. Frank Berry narrative, Jacksonville, 18 Aug. 1936, *Slave Narratives,* 17:27–30.
13. D. Brearly to Peter Porter, Western Agency, 12 Dec. 1828, LR, OIA, M234, roll 237:136; Cowemathla, et al. to Eaton, Ft. Bainbridge, 12 Apr. 1829, ibid., 263–64; *Arkansas Gazette,* 23 June 1828.
14. Cowemathla, et al. to Eaton, Ft. Bainbridge, 12 Apr. 1829, LR, OIA, M234, roll 237:263–64.
15. Creek council, 21 May 1832, ibid., 225:224; *Arkansas Gazette,* 9 Dec. 1828.
16. Legal controversy surrounding ownership of Blount's and Nelly Factor's slaves is in LR, OIA, M234, roll 287:222–38.
17. Sockett to Cass, New Orleans, 22 July 1834, ibid., 288:163–64.
18. *Florida Muskogee (Creek) News,* July 1984; Andrew B. Ramsey, personal communication, 28 Nov. 1984.
19. Creeks residing in Cherokee nation to John Ross, Red Clay, 12 Aug. 1837, *NASP, IA,* 9:610; A brief review of the . . . Cherokee Nation, Payne Papers, 9:72–3, NL.
20. Jesup to ?, Ft. Mitchell, 1 Oct. 1836, Indian Depredations, 4:1442–44, GDAH.
21. *Floridian,* 16 July 1836, *Mobile Daily Commercial Register,* 8 July 1836.
22. *Arkansas Gazette,* 16 Aug. 1836; *Army and Navy Chronicle,* 11 Aug. 1836.
23. *Mobile Daily Commercial Register,* 14 Sept. 1836.
24. *Floridian,* 31 Dec. 1836.
25. *Mobile Daily Commercial Register,* 1 Aug. 1836.
26. *Arkansas Gazette,* 14 Oct. 1836; *Army and Navy Chronicle,* 22 Sept. 1836.
27. Ibid., *Arkansas Gazette,* 22 Nov. 1836.
28. George G. Reynolds to ?, Ft. Morgan, Mobile Point, 31 Mar. 1837, *ASP, MA,* 7:867–69.
29. *Mobile Daily Commercial Register,* 28 July 1837.
30. Edward Deas, journal, Ft. Gibson, 5 June 1837, LR, OIA, M234, roll 238:250–80.
31. *Army and Navy Chronicle,* 12 May 1836.
32. Hartley and Hartley, *Osceola,* pp. 241–49.
33. Isaac Clark to Crawford, New Orleans, 6 Apr. 1839, LR, OIA, M234, roll 291:89.
34. Archibald Smith to Harris, Apalachicola Agency, 7 Feb. 1838, ibid., 239:280.
35. *Florida Herald and Southern Democrat,* 21 July 1838.
36. Casey to Jesup, Seminole Agency, Tampa Bay, 4 June 1837, LR, Adjutant Gen. Office, RG94, PAC; James Logan to Armstrong, Creek Agency, 19 May 1840, LR, Western Supt., M640, roll 3:315–16; Tatekke Tiger interview, 17 Nov. 1937, IPHC, 36:482.
37. Smith to Harris, 12 Mar. 1837, LR, OIA, M234, roll 290:231.

350

38. Crawford to Secretary of War, War Dept., OIA, Jan. 1844, *Territorial Papers*, ed. Carter, 26:848; Boyd to George Hutter, Crooked River, 31 May 1838, LR, OIA, M234, roll 239:134.
39. Opothleyahola et al. to Armstrong, Tuckabatchee council house, 2 Jan. 1840, LR, Western Supt., M640, roll 3:298.
40. Dick McGirt interview, Tuckabatchee Town, 29 May 1937, IPHC, 7:46–47; Edmunds, *Shawnee Prophet*, pp. 24, 38.
41. Muster roll of a company of Creek Indians, 23 Feb. 1849, LR, OIA, M234, roll 240:428.
42. Covington, "Episode in the Third Seminole War," pp. 45–59; Kersey, *Pelts, Plumes, and Hides*, pp. 5–7.
43. Mrs. Leister Reed interview, IPHC (1937):113:290.
44. George Abbot interview, 20 May 1937, ibid., 12:11–14.
45. Smith to Harris, Apalachicola Agency, 26 Feb. 1838, LR, OIA, M234, roll 239:284.
46. Giddings, *Exiles of Florida*, pp. 192–232; *Florida Herald and Southern Democrat*, 19 May 1838.
47. Agnew, *Fort Gibson*, pp. 160, 175–76.
48. John P. Moore to James Moore, Arkansas, Creek Nation, n.d., "Echoes 'Trail of Tears,' " ed. Hoole, p. 225.
49. Grayson ms., Smock Coll., p. 43, UOWHC.
50. Roley McIntosh, Foshutchee Micco, Chilly McIntosh, et al. to Cass, Washington, 6 June 1834, *ASP, MA*, 6:472.
51. Creek census [1843], LR, Western Supt., M640, roll 4:1175; Arbuckle to R. Jones, Ft. Gibson, 8 Oct. 1839, Payne Papers, 6:164, NL.
52. *Arkansas Gazette*, 4 Oct. 1836.
53. John J. Abert to Cass, Creek Agency, 3 July 1833, LR, OIA, M234, roll 223:423.
54. Jesup to Poinsett, Garey's Ferry, 17 Oct. 1837, *ASP, MA*, 7:886.
55. Sprague, *Florida War*, p. 501.
56. Mahon, *Second Seminole War*, pp. 93, 101.
57. Opothleyahola et al. to Andrew Jackson, Council Ground, Ala., 13 June 1835, LR, OIA, M234, roll 224:275–81.
58. Treaty with the Creeks and Seminoles, 4 Jan. 1845, *Indian Affairs*, ed. Kappler, 2:552.
59. Debo, *Creek Indians*, pp. 142–76; McReynolds, *Seminoles*, pp. 289–318.
60. Agnes Kelley interview, 1937, IPHC, 32:106; Debo, *Road to Disappearance*, pp. 270–80.
61. Bolster, "Smoked Meat Rebellion," pp. 37–55; Agnes Kelley interview, 19 Aug. 1937, IPHC, 32:107.
62. Adam Grayson interview, Kechobadagee Town, Pharoah, Okla., 14 Oct. 1937, IPHC, 84:331–33.
63. Roley McIntosh, Little King, Chilly McIntosh, et al. to Arbuckle, Western Creek Nation, 31 Aug. 1836, LR, Western Supt., M640, roll 1:57; Morgan and Strickland, eds., *Oklahoma Memories*, p. 47.

64. Joseph A. Johnson to Jackson Moore, Sept. 1837, "Echoes from 'Trail of Tears,'" ed. Hoole, p. 144.

65. *Arkansas Gazette,* 25 May 1831.

66. An act granting a pension to "Milly," an Indian woman of the Creek nation, 17 June 1844, LR, Western Supt., M640, roll 6:419; James Logan to S. Rutherford, Creek Agency, 3 Sept. 1848, ibid., 721–22; Hitchcock, *Traveler in Indian Territory,* pp. 102–7.

67. Edmunds, *Shawnee Prophet,* pp. 179–89; Tony Morgan interview, *American Slave,* ed. Rawick, 1:473.

68. John P. Moore to James Moore, Arkansas, Creek Nation, 16 Jan. 1838, "Echoes from 'Trail of Tears,'" ed. Hoole, p. 229.

69. Marchey Yetchie interview, 12 Nov. 1937, IPHC, 52:70; Porter, *Negro on the Frontier,* pp. 424–59.

70. William P. Duval to Calhoun, St. Augustine, 23 Sept. 1823, LR, Sec. War, M271, roll 4:536–37.

71. Waters Smith, affidavit, St. Augustine, 19 Feb. 1829, LR, OIA, M234, roll 800:93.

72. Goggin, "Seminole Negroes of Andros Island," p. 206.

73. Kersey, "Seminole Negroes of Andros Island Revisited," p. 174.

74. Ibid., pp. 171–75.

75. John P. Booth to John Bell, Irwinton, 30 May 1841, LR, OIA, M234, roll 240:138–40.

76. Henry Blair to William Schley, Thomasville, 12 Sept. 1836, Indian Depredations, 4:1377, GDAH.

77. H. A. Allen interview, 22 Mar. 1937, IPHC, 1:87–88.

78. Robert M. Cherry to William Medill, Montgomery, 11 Jan. 1846, LR, OIA, M234, roll 240:382.

79. Frank Berry narrative, Jacksonville, 18 Aug. 1936, *Slave Narratives,* 17:27–29.

80. Abraham Jones narrative, 10 May 1937, ibid., 5:234.

81. W. A. Evans interview, 22 Jan. 1937, IPHC, 24:40–42.

82. What is known about the young Seminole is in Welch, *Narrative of Osceola Nikkanochee.*

83. Harry Kernal interview, 28 Apr. 1937, IPHC, 32:185; Howard and Lena, *Oklahoma Seminoles,* pp. 175, 197.

84. "Technical Reports regarding the Poarch Band of Creeks," p. 1141; Ellsworth and Dysart, "West Florida's Forgotten People," pp. 422ff.

85. Pollitzer, Rucknagel, Tashian, et al., "Seminole Indians of Florida," pp. 65, 76–80.

86. Covington, "Florida Seminoles in 1847," pp. 52–53.

87. Buswell, "Florida Seminole Religious Ritual," pp. 13–14.

88. Louis Graham interview, 28 May 1937, IPHC, 4:144.

89. Underhill, "Hamlin Garland and Final Council of the Creek Nation," pp. 511–20.

90. Wagner, *Yuchi Tales,* pp. 149–50.

Bibliography

I. MANUSCRIPTS

ANN ARBOR, MICHIGAN
William L. Clements Library
  Gage Papers
ATLANTA, GEORGIA
Georgia Department of Archives and History
  Creek Indian Letters, Talks, and Treaties
  Creek Letters. Edited by T. J. Peddy (typescript)
  Indian Depredations, Claims against the Creek Indians from the Counties
    of Lee, Baker, Early, Marion, and Muscogee. Edited by J. E. Hays
    (typescript)
  Unpublished Letters of Timothy Barnard, 1784–1820. Edited by Louise
    F. Hays (typescript)
  Unpublished Letters of Benjamin Hawkins, 1807–15. Edited by Louise F.
    Hays (typescript)
CHICAGO, ILLINOIS
Newberry Library
  John Howard Payne Papers
EDINBURGH, SCOTLAND
National Library of Scotland
  Cochrane Papers
GAINESVILLE, FLORIDA

354   University of Florida Library
      Zephaniah Kingsley Will
      Joseph B. Lockey Collection
   GREENWICH, ENGLAND
   National Maritime Museum
      John B. Warren Papers
   LONDON, ENGLAND
   Public Record Office
      Admiralty 1 (in letters)
      Audit Office 12 (loyalists' claims)
      Audit Office 13 (loyalists' claims)
      Colonial Office 5 (America and West Indies)
      Colonial Office 23 (Bahamas)
      Colonial Office 42 (Canada)
      Foreign Office 4 (United States)
      Foreign Office 5 (United States)
      War Office 1 (in letters)
   MONTGOMERY, ALABAMA
   Alabama Department of Archives and History
      J. W. A. Sanford Papers
      William Weatherford vs. Weatherford, Howell, et al., 10 Mar. 1852, case
         1229
   NORMAN, OKLAHOMA
   University of Oklahoma Western History Collection
      Grayson Family Paper Collection
      Eloise D. Smock Collection
   OTTAWA, CANADA
   Public Archives of Canada
      Claus Papers
      Deputy Superintendent General, R.G. 10, A5b
      Superintendent General and Inspector General, R.G. 10, A5a
      Upper Canada, Indian Office, MG19, F16, 1
   PENSACOLA, FLORIDA
   University of West Florida Library
      Panton, Leslie, and Company Papers
   SAVANNAH, GEORGIA
   Georgia Historical Society
      Antonio J. Waring, Jr. Papers
      George Galphin Account Books, Silver Bluff
   SEVILLE, SPAIN
   Archivo General de Indias
      Cuba
   TALLAHASSEE, FLORIDA
   Florida State University Library
      Sir Guy Carleton Papers, Public Record Office, London (microfilm)

Lyman Draper Manuscripts, State Historical Society of Wisconsin, Madison (microfilm)

355

East Florida Papers, Library of Congress (microfilm)

Henry Knox Papers, Massachusetts Historical Society, Boston (microfilm)

Indian Pioneer History Collection, Oklahoma Historical Society (microfilm)

Records of the Moravian Missions among the Indians of North America, Archives of the Moravian Church, Bethlehem, Pennsylvania (microfilm)

Southeast Archaeological Center, National Park Service

Benjamin Hawkins, "Independence Letterbook." Transcribed by Bernard Berg. Independence National Historical Park, Philadelphia (typescript)

WASHINGTON, D.C.

Library of Congress

Spanish transcripts

Cuba

Archivo Histórico Nacional

National Archives and Records Services (microfilms)

Census of Creek Indians, 1832, T275

Documents Relating to the Negotiation of Ratified and Unratified Treaties with various Indian Tribes, 1801–69, T494

Letter Book, Creek Trading House, 1795–1816, M4

Letters Received by the Adjutant General's Office, RG94

Letters Received by the Office of Indian Affairs, 1824–81, M234

Letters Received by the Office of the Secretary of War on Indian Affairs, 1800–1823, M271

Letters Received by the Superintendent of Indian Trade, 1806–24, T58

Letters Received by Western Superintendency, 1832–51, M640

Records of the Secretary of War, Letters Sent Relating to Indian Affairs, 1800–1824, M15

II. NEWSPAPERS

Arkansas Gazette, 1828–48

Army and Navy Chronicle, 1835–42

Florida Herald and Southern Democrat, 1835–41

The Florida Muskogee (Creek) News, 1984–86

Florida Times Union, 1892–95

Floridian, 1835–42

Mobile Daily Commercial Register, 1835–40

Muscogee National News (Oklahoma), 1984–86

356   III. BOOKS AND ARTICLES

Abernethy, Thomas P. *The Formative Period in Alabama, 1815–1828.* Montgomery, 1922.

———. *The South in the New Nation.* Baton Rouge, 1961.

———. *Western Lands and the American Revolution.* New York, 1937.

Adair, James. *The History of the American Indians.* Edited by Samuel C. Williams. Johnson City, 1930.

Adams, John Q. *Memoirs of John Quincy Adams, Comprising Portions of His Diary from 1795 to 1848.* Edited by Charles F. Adams. 12 vols. Philadelphia, 1874–77.

Agnew, Brad. *Fort Gibson: Terminal on the Trail of Tears.* Norman, 1979.

"Alabama Indian Chiefs," *Alabama Historical Quarterly* 13 (1951): 5–91.

Alden, John R. *John Stuart and the Southern Colonial Frontier: A Study of Indian Relations, War, Trade, and Land Problems in the Southern Wilderness, 1754–1775.* Ann Arbor, 1944.

American State Papers, Indian Affairs. 2 vols. Washington, 1832–34.

American State Papers, Military Affairs. 7 vols. Washington, 1832–60.

Bartram, John. *Diary of a Journey through the Carolinas, Georgia, and Florida, from July 1, 1765 to April 10, 1766.* Edited by Francis Harper. Transactions of the American Philosophical Society, nos. 33, pt. 1. Philadelphia, 1942.

Bartram, William. "Observations on the Creek and Cherokee Indians, 1789." *Transactions of the American Ethnological Society* 3, pt. 1 (1853):1–81.

———. *Travels in Georgia and Florida, 1773–1774: A report to Dr. John Fothergill.* Edited by Francis Harper. Philadelphia, 1943.

———. *The Travels of William Bartram.* Naturalist's Edition. Edited by Francis Harper. New Haven, 1958.

Bemis, Samuel F. *John Quincy Adams and the Foundations of American Foreign Policy.* New York, 1949.

Bolster, Mel H. "The Smoked Meat Rebellion," *Chronicles of Oklahoma* 31 (1953): 37–55.

Bonner, James C. "William McIntosh." In *Georgians in Profile: Historical Essays in Honor of Ellis Merton Coulter*, edited by Horace Montgomery, Athens, 1958.

Boyd, Julian P., ed. *The Papers of Thomas Jefferson.* Princeton, 1950–.

Boyd, Mark F. "Events at Prospect Bluff on the Apalachicola River, 1808–1818," *Florida Historical Quarterly* 16 (1937): 55–96.

———, and José N. Latorre, "Spanish Interest in British Florida, and in the Progress of the American Revolution," *Florida Historical Quarterly* 32 (1953): 92–130.

Brain, Jeffrey P. "The Natchez Paradox," *Ethnology* 10 (1971): 215–22.

Brannon, Peter A. "Removal of Indians from Alabama," *Alabama Historical Quarterly* 12 (1950): 91–117.

British and Foreign State Papers, 1818–1819. vol. 6. London, 1835.

Brown, John P. *Old Frontiers: The Story of the Cherokee Indians from Earliest Times to the Date of Their Removal to the West, 1838.* Kingsport, 1938.

Buker, George E. "The Mosquito Fleet's Guides and the Second Seminole War," *Florida Historical Quarterly* 57 (1979): 308–26.

Bullard, Mary R. *Black Liberation on Cumberland Island in 1815.* DeLeon Springs, 1983.

Calendar of State Papers, Colonial. Edited by W. N. Sainsbury, J. W. Fortescue, C. Headlam, et al. London, 1860–.

Callendar, Charles. "Shawnee," *Handbook of North American Indians.* Vol. 15. Edited by Bruce G. Trigger. Washington, 1978.

Candler, Allen D., ed. *The Colonial Records of the State of Georgia.* 26 vols. Atlanta, 1904–16.

———. *The Revolutionary Records of the State of Georgia.* 3 vols. Atlanta, 1908.

Carter, Clarence E., ed. *The Territorial Papers of the United States.* Washington, 1934–.

Caughey, John W., ed. *East Florida, 1783–1785. A File of Documents Assembled and Many of Them Translated by Joseph Byrne Lockey.* Berkeley, 1949.

———. *McGillivray of the Creeks.* Norman, 1959.

Clark, C. B. " 'Drove Off Like Dogs'—Creek Removal." In *Indians of the Lower South: Past and Present,* edited by John K. Mahon, 118–24. Pensacola, 1975.

Cline, Howard F. *Florida Indians.* 2 vols. New York, 1974.

Coker, William S. "Religious Censuses of Pensacola, 1796–1801," *Florida Historical Quarterly* 61 (1982): 54–63.

———, and Hazel P. Coker. *The Siege of Mobile, 1780, in Maps.* Pensacola, 1982.

———, and Thomas D. Watson. *Indian Traders of the Southeastern Spanish Borderlands.* Gainesville, 1985

Coleman, Kenneth. *The American Revolution in Georgia, 1763–1789.* Athens, 1958.

Coulter, E. Merton, "Elijah Clarke's Foreign Intrigues and the 'Trans-Oconee Republic,' " *Proceedings of the Mississippi Valley Historical Association* 10 (1920): part 1.

Covington, James W. "An Episode in the Third Seminole War," *Florida Historical Quarterly* 45 (1966): 45–59.

———, ed. "The Florida Seminoles in 1847," *Tequesta* 24 (1964): 49–57.

Crane, Verner W. "The Origin of the Name of the Creek Indians," *Journal of American History* 5 (1918): 339–42.

———. *The Southern Frontier, 1670–1732.* Durham, 1928.

"The Creek Nation, Debtor to John Forbes and Co., Successors to Panton, Leslie, and Co., A Journal of John Innerarity, 1812," *Florida Historical Quarterly* 9 (1930): 67–95.

358   Crawford, James M. *The Mobilian Trade Language*. Knoxville, 1978.

Davis, T. Frederick. "Elotchaway, East Florida, 1814," *Florida Historical Quarterly* 8 (1930): 143–55.

———. "Milly Francis and Duncan McKrimmon: An Authentic Florida Pocahontas," *Florida Historical Quarterly* 21 (1943): 254–65.

Debo, Angie. *The Road to Disappearance: A History of the Creek Indians*. Norman, 1941.

De Vorsey, Louis, Jr. *The Indian Boundary in the Southern Colonies, 1763–1775*. Chapel Hill, 1966.

Din, Gilbert C., and Abraham P. Nasatir. *The Imperial Osages: Spanish Indian Diplomacy in the Mississippi Valley*. Norman, 1983.

Dobyns, Henry F. *Their Number Become Thinned: Native American Population Dynamics in Eastern North America*. Knoxville, 1983.

Doster, James F. *The Creek Indians and Their Florida Lands, 1740–1823*. 2 vols. New York, 1974.

———, ed. "Letters Relating to the Tragedy of Fort Mims: August–September, 1813," *Alabama Review* 14 (1961): 269–85.

Downs, Dorothy. "British Influences on Creek and Seminole Men's Clothing, 1733–1858," *Florida Anthropologist* 33 (1980): 46–65.

Drechsel, Emanuel J. "The Question of the *Lingua Franca* Creek," *1982 Mid-America Linguistics Conference Papers* (1983): 388–400.

Dundes, Alan. "Washington Irving's Version of the Seminole Origin of Races," *Ethnohistory* 9 (1962): 257–64.

Easterby, James H., ed. *The Journal of the Commons House of Assembly, 1736–*. Columbia, 1951–.

Edmunds, R. David. *The Shawnee Prophet*. Lincoln, 1983.

Ellicott, Andrew. *The Journal of Andrew Ellicott, Late Commissioner on Behalf of the United States during Part of the Year 1796, the Years 1797, 1798, 1799, and Part of the Year 1800. . . .* Philadelphia, 1814.

Ellsworth, Lucius F., and Jane E. Dysart. "West Florida's Forgotten People: The Creek Indians from 1830 until 1970," *Florida Historical Quarterly* 59 (1981): 422–39.

Evans, Hedvig T., ed. "Seminole Folktales," *Florida Historical Quarterly* 56 (1978): 473–94.

Fabel, Robin F. A., and Robert R. Rea. "Lieutenant Thomas Campbell's Sojourn among the Creeks, November, 1764–May, 1765," *Alabama Historical Quarterly* 36 (1974): 97–111.

Fairbanks, Charles H. *Ethnohistorical Report on the Florida Indians*. New York, 1974.

———. "The Function of Black Drink among the Creeks." In *Black Drink, A Native American Tea*, edited by Charles M. Hudson, 120–49. Athens, 1979.

Fitzpatrick, John C., ed. *The Diaries of George Washington, 1748–1799*. 4 vols. Boston, 1925.

Floyd, John. "Letters of John Floyd, 1813–1838," *Georgia Historical Quarterly* 33 (1949): 228–269.

Forbes, James G. *Sketches, Historical and Topographical, of the Floridas, More Particularly East Florida, 1821.* Edited by James W. Covington. Gainesville, 1964.

Foreman, Grant. *Indian Removal: The Emigration of the Five Civilized Tribes.* Norman, 1952.

Freeman, Douglas S. *George Washington: A Biography.* 7 vols. New York, 1948–57.

Fried, Morton H. "The Myth of Tribe," *Natural History* 84, 4 (1975): 12–20.

Fundaburk, Emma Lila, ed. *Southeastern Indians: Life Portraits; A Catalog of Pictures, 1564–1860.* Luverne, 1958.

Garbarino, Merwyn S. *Big Cypress: A Changing Seminole Community.* New York, 1972.

Gatschet, Albert S. *A Migration Legend of the Creek Indians, with a Linguistic, Historic, and Ethnographic Introduction.* New York, 1969.

———. "Tchikilli's Kasihta Legend in the Creek and Hitchiti Languages with a Critical Commentary and Full Glossaries to Both Texts," *Transactions of the Academy of Science of St. Louis* 5 (1888): 33–239.

Giddings, Joshua R. *The Exiles of Florida, or the Crimes Committed by Our Government against the Maroons, Who Fled from South Carolina and Other Slave States, Seeking Protection under Spanish Laws.* Edited by Arthur W. Thompson. Gainesville, 1964.

Goggin, John M. "The Seminole Negroes of Andros Island, Bahamas," *Florida Historical Quarterly* 24 (1946): 201–6.

Green, Michael D. "Alexander McGillivray." In *American Indian Leaders,* edited by R. David Edmunds, 41–63. Lincoln, 1980.

———. *The Politics of Indian Removal: Creek Government and Society in Crisis.* Lincoln, 1982.

Gullick, Charles J. M. R. *Exiled from St. Vincent: The Development of Black Carib Culture in Central America up to 1945.* Malta, 1976.

Haas, Mary R. "Creek Inter-Town Relations," *American Anthropologist* 42 (1940): 479–89.

Halbert, Henry S., and Timothy H. Ball. *The Creek War of 1813 and 1814.* Edited by Frank L. Owsley, Jr. University, Alabama, 1969.

Hambly, John. "Visit to the Indian Nations: The Diary of John Hambly." Edited by Daniel J. J. Ross and Bruce S. Chappell, *Florida Historical Quarterly* 55 (1976): 60–73.

Hamer, Philip M., George C. Rogers, Jr., David R. Chesnutt, et al., eds. *The Papers of Henry Laurens.* Columbia, 1968–.

Hardeman, Nicholas P. *Shucks, Shocks, and Hominy Blocks: Corn as a Way of Life in Pioneer America.* Baton Rouge, 1981.

Hardman, Clark, Jr. "The Primitive Solar Observatory at Crystal River and Its Implications," *Florida Anthropologist* 24 (1971): 135–68.

Hartley, William, and Ellen Hartley. *Osceola: The Unconquered Indian.* New York, 1973.

360   Hassig, Ross. "Internal Conflict in the Creek War of 1813–1814," *Ethno-history* 21 (1974): 251–71.

Hawkins, Benjamin, *Letters, Journals, and Writings of Benjamin Hawkins*. Edited by C.L. Grant. 2 vols. Savannah, 1980.

——. *Letters of Benjamin Hawkins, 1796–1806*. *Collections of the Georgia Historical Society* 9 (1916).

——. "A Sketch of the Creek Country, in the Years 1798 and 1799." *Collections of the Georgia Historical Society* 3, pt. 1 (1848).

Hemphill, William E., and Robert L. Meriwether, eds. *The Papers of John C. Calhoun*. Columbia, 1959–.

Hewitt, J. N. B. "Notes on the Creek Indians." Edited by John R. Swanton. *Bureau of American Ethnology Bulletin* 123: 123–59.

Higginbotham, Jay. "Origins of the French-Alabama Conflict, 1703–1704," *Alabama Review* 31 (1978): 121–36.

Hitchcock, Ethan A. *Fifty Years in Camp and Field: Diary of Major General Ethan Allen Hitchcock, U.S.A.* Edited by W. A. Croffut. New York, 1909.

——. *A Traveler in Indian Territory: The Journal of Ethan Allen Hitchcock*. Edited by Grant Foreman. Cedar Rapids, 1930.

Holmes, Jack D. L. *Gayoso: The Life of a Spanish Governor in the Mississippi Valley, 1789–1799*. Baton Rouge, 1965.

——. *José de Evia y sus reconocimientos del Golfo de México, 1783–1796*. Madrid, 1968.

Hoole, W. Stanley, ed. "Echoes from the 'Trail of Tears,' 1837," *Alabama Review* 6 (1953): 135–52.

Horsman, Reginald. *Expansion and American Indian Policy, 1783–1812*. East Lansing, 1967.

Howard, James H., and Willie Lena. *Oklahoma Seminoles: Medicines, Magic, and Religion*. Norman, 1984.

——. *Shawnee! The Ceremonialism of a Native Indian Tribe and Its Cultural Background*. Athens, Ohio, 1981.

——. *The Southeastern Ceremonial Complex and Its Interpretation*. Missouri Archaeological Society Memoir 6. Columbia, 1968.

Hryniewicki, Richard J. "The Creek Treaty of November 15, 1827," *Georgia Historical Quarterly* 52 (1968): 1–15.

Hudson, Charles M. *The Southeastern Indians*. Knoxville, 1976.

Hunter, John D. *Manners and Customs of Several Indian Tribes Located West of the Mississippi*. Philadelphia, 1823.

Irving, Washington. *The Works of Washington Irving*. 10 vols. New York, n.d.

Jackson, Donald D., ed. *Letters of the Lewis and Clark Expedition with Related Documents, 1783–1854*. 2 vols. Urbana, 1962.

Jacobson, Daniel, Howard N. Martin, and Ralph Henry Marsh, *(Creek) Indians: Alabama—Coushatta*. New York, 1974.

Jefferson, Thomas. *Notes on the State of Virginia*. Edited by Thomas P. Abernethy. New York, 1964.

Johnson, Cecil. *British West Florida, 1763–1783*. New Haven, 1943.   361

Jones, Dorothy V. *License for Empire: Colonialism by Treaty in Early America*. Chicago, 1982.

Jones, George F., ed. and trans. *Henry Newman's Salzburger Letterbooks*. Athens, 1966.

Kappler, Charles J., ed. *Indian Affairs. Laws and Treaties*. 2 vols. Washington, 1903.

Kersey, Harry A., Jr. "Florida Seminoles and the Census of 1900," *Florida Historical Quarterly* 60 (1981): 145–60.

———. *Pelts, Plumes, and Hides: White Traders among the Seminole Indians, 1870–1930*. Gainesville, 1975.

———. "The Seminole Negroes of Andros Island Revisited: Some New Pieces to an Old Puzzle," *Florida Anthropologist* 34 (1981): 169–76.

Laumer, Frank. *Massacre!* Gainesville, 1968.

Littlefield, Daniel F., Jr. *Africans and Creeks: From the Colonial Period to the Civil War*. Westport, 1979.

Lyon, Elijah Wilson. *Louisiana in French Diplomacy, 1759–1804*. Norman, 1934.

MacCauley, Clay. "The Seminole Indians of Florida." *Fifth Annual Report of the Bureau of American Ethnology, 1883* (1887): 469–531.

McDowell, William L., Jr. ed. *Documents Relating to Indian Affairs*. 2 vols. Columbia, 1958–70.

McKay, Donald B. *Pioneer Florida*. 3 vols. Tampa, 1959.

McKenney, Thomas L. *Memoirs, Official and Personal; with Sketches of Travels among the Northern and Southern Indians*. 2 vols. New York, 1846.

McLoughlin, William G. *The Cherokee Ghost Dance: Essays on the Southeastern Indians, 1789–1861*. Macon, 1984.

McReynolds, Edwin C. *The Seminoles*. Norman, 1957.

Mahon, John K. *History of the Second Seminole War, 1835–1842*. Gainesville, 1967.

Matthews, Janet S. *Edge of Wilderness: A Settlement History of Manatee River and Sarasota Bay, 1528–1885*. Tulsa, 1983.

Mauelshagen, Carl, and Gerald H. Davis, eds. and trans. *Partners in the Lord's Work: The Diary of Two Moravian Missionaries in the Creek Indian Country, 1807–1813*. Atlanta, 1969.

Meriwether, Robert L. *The Expansion of South Carolina, 1729–1765*. Kingsport, 1940.

Meyer, Leland W. *The Life and Times of Colonel Richard M. Johnson of Kentucky*. New York, 1932.

Milfort, Louis LeClerc. *Memoirs, or a Quick Glance at My Various Travels and My Sojourn in the Creek Nation*. Translated by Ben C. McCary. Savannah, 1972.

Miller, David Hunter, ed. *Treaties and Other International Acts of the United States of America*. Washington, 1931–.

362   Miller, Janice B. *Juan Nepomuceno de Quesada: Governor of Spanish East Florida, 1790–1795.* Washington, 1981.

Mitchell, Stewart, ed. *New Letters of Abigail Adams, 1788–1801.* Boston, 1947.

Montault de Monberaut, Henri. *Mémoire Justificatif: Indian Diplomacy in British West Florida, 1763–1765.* Edited and translated by Milo B. Howard and Robert R. Rea. University, Alabama, 1965.

Mooney, James. "The Ghost-Dance Religion and the Sioux Outbreak of 1890." *Fourteenth Annual Report of the Bureau of American Ethnology, 1892–93* (1896): pt. 2, 641–1140.

Morgan, Anne H., and Rennard Strickland, eds. *Oklahoma Memories.* Norman, 1981.

Motte, Jacob R. *Journey into Wilderness: An Army Surgeon's Account of Life in Camp and Field during the Creek and Seminole Wars, 1836–1838.* Edited by James F. Sunderman. Gainesville, 1953.

Neill, Wilfred T. "The Galphin Trading Post Site at Silver Bluff, South Carolina," *Florida Anthropologist* 21 (1968): 42–54.

The New American State Papers: Indian Affairs. 13 vols. Wilmington, 1972.

Nuñez, Theron A., Jr. "Creek Nativism and the Creek War of 1813–1814," *Ethnohistory* 5 (1958): 1–48, 131–75, 292–301.

O'Donnell, James H. "Alexander McGillivray: Training for Leadership, 1777–1783," *Georgia Historical Quarterly* 49 (1965): 172–86.

Olsen, Gary D. "Loyalists and the American Revolution: Thomas Brown and the South Carolina Backcountry, 1775–1776," *South Carolina Historical Magazine* 68 (1967): 201–19; 69 (1968): 44–56.

———. "Thomas Brown, Loyalist Partisan, and the Revolutionary War in Georgia, 1777–1782," *Georgia Historical Quarterly* 54 (1970): 1–19, 183–208.

Opler, Morris E. "The Creek 'Town' and the Problem of Creek-Indian Political Reorganization." In *Human Problems in Technological Change. A Casebook,* edited by Edward H. Spicer, 165–80. New York, 1952.

Owsley, Frank L., Jr. *Struggle for the Gulf Borderlands: The Creek War and the Battle of New Orleans, 1812–1815.* Gainesville, 1981.

"The Panton Leslie Papers," *Florida Historical Quarterly* 12–18 (1933–39).

Paredes, J. Anthony, and Kenneth J. Plante. "Economics, Politics, and the Subjugation of the Creek Indians: Final Report for the National Park Service." Tallahassee, 1975.

———. "A Reexamination of Creek Indian Population Trends, 1738–1832," *American Indian Culture and Research Journal* 6 (1982): 3–28.

Patrick, Rembert W. *Florida Fiasco: Rampant Rebels on the Georgia–Florida Border, 1810–1815.* Athens, 1954.

Peake, Ora B. *A History of the United States Indian Factory System, 1795–1822.* Denver, 1954.

Perdue, Theda. *Slavery and the Evolution of Cherokee Society, 1540–1866.* Knoxville, 1979.

Pickett, Albert J. *History of Alabama and Incidentally of Georgia and Mississippi from the Earliest Period.* Birmingham, 1962.

Pollitzer, William S., Donald Rucknagel, Richard Tashian, et al. "The Seminole Indians of Florida: Morphology and Serology," *American Journal of Physical Anthropology* 32 (1970): 65–81.

Pope, John. *A Tour through the Southern and Western Territories of the United States of North-America.* Edited by J. Barton Starr. Gainesville, 1979.

Porter, Kenneth W. "Billy Bowlegs (Holata Micco) in the Seminole Wars," *Florida Historical Quarterly* 45 (1967): 219–42, 391–401.

———. "The Cowkeeper Dynasty of the Seminole Nation," *Florida Historical Quarterly* 30 (1952): 341–49.

———. "The Founder of the 'Seminole Nation,' Secoffee or Cowkeeper," *Florida Historical Quarterly* 27 (1949): 362–84.

———. "The Negro Abraham." In *The Negro on the American Frontier,* by Kenneth W. Porter, 295–338. New York, 1971.

———. "Negroes and the East Florida Annexation Plot, 1811–1813." In *The Negro on the American Frontier,* by Kenneth W. Porter, 183–204. New York, 1971.

———. *The Negro on the American Frontier.* New York, 1971.

———. "Seminole Flight from Fort Marion," *Florida Historical Quarterly* 22 (1944): 112–33.

———. "The Seminole in Mexico, 1850–1861." In *The Negro on the American Frontier,* by Kenneth W. Porter, 424–60. New York, 1971.

Pound, Merritt B. *Benjamin Hawkins, Indian Agent.* Athens, 1951.

Rawick, George P., ed. *The American Slave: A Composite Autobiography.* Supplement. Series 1. 12 vols. Westport, 1978.

Rea, Robert R., and Milo B. Howard, Jr., eds. *The Minutes, Journals, and Acts of the General Assembly of British West Florida.* University, Alabama, 1978.

Remini, Robert V. *Andrew Jackson.* 3 vols. New York, 1977–84.

Romans, Bernard. *A Concise Natural History of East and West Florida, 1775.* Edited by Rembert W. Patrick. Gainesville, 1962.

Salley, Alexander S., Jr., ed. *Journals of the Commons House of Assembly of South Carolina.* 25 vols. Columbia, 1907–49.

Saunders, William L., ed. *The Colonial Records of North Carolina.* 10 vols. Goldsboro, 1886–90.

Schoolcraft, Henry R. *Historical and Statistical Information respecting the History, Condition, and Prospects of the Indian Tribes of the United States.* 6 vols. Philadelphia, 1851–57.

Searcy, Martha C. *The Georgia-Florida Contest in the American Revolution: 1776, 1777, and 1778.* University, Alabama, 1985.

Simmons, William H. "Journal of Dr. W. H. Simmons," *Florida Historical Quarterly* 1 (1908): 28–36.

364 ———. *Notices of East Florida, with an Account of the Seminole Nation of Indians.* Edited by George E. Buker. Gainesville, 1973.

Slave Narratives: A Folk History of Slavery in the United States, from Interviews with Former Slaves. 17 vols. St. Clair Shores, 1976.

Sleight, Frederick W. "Kunti, A Food Staple of Florida Indians," *Florida Anthropologist* 6 (1953): 46–52.

Smith, Daniel M. "James Seagrove and the Mission to Tuckaubatchee, 1793," *Georgia Historical Quarterly* 44 (1960): 41–55.

Smith, George G. *The Life and Times of George Foster Pierce.* Sparta, 1888.

Smith, Sam B., and Harriet C. Owsley, eds. *The Papers of Andrew Jackson.* Knoxville, 1980–.

Smith, William H., ed. *The St. Clair Papers: The Life and Public Services of Arthur St. Clair, Soldier of the Revolutionary War, President of the Continental Congress, and Governor of the North-Western Territory, with His Correspondence and Other Papers.* 2 vols. Cincinnati, 1882.

Speck, Frank G. "Ceremonial Songs of the Creek and Yuchi Indians." *Anthropological Publications of the University of Pennsylvania* 1 (1911): 155–245.

———. "The Creek Indians of Taskigi Town," *Memoirs of the American Anthropological Association* 2 (1907): 99–164.

———. "Ethnology of the Yuchi Indians," *Anthropological Publications of the University of Pennsylvania* 1 (1909): 1–154.

Spoehr, Alexander. "Changing Kinship Systems: A Study in the Aculturation of the Creeks, Cherokee, and Choctaw," Field Museum of Natural History, pub. 538 (1947).

Sprague, John T. *The Origin, Progress, and Conclusion of the Florida War.* Edited by John K. Mahon. Gainesville, 1964.

Sturtevant, William C. "Chakaika and the 'Spanish Indians': Documentary Sources Compared with Seminole Tradition," *Tequesta* 13 (1953): 35–73.

———. "Creek into Seminole." In *North American Indians in Historical Perspective,* edited by Eleanor B. Leacock and Nancy O. Lurie, 92–128. New York, 1971.

———. "The Medicine Bundles and Busks of the Florida Seminole," *Florida Anthropologist* 7 (1953): 31–70.

———. "Seminole Myths of the Origin of Races," *Ethnohistory* 10 (1963): 80–86.

Sugden, John. "The Southern Indians in the War of 1812: The Closing Phase," *Florida Historical Quarterly* 60 (1982): 273–312.

Swan, Caleb. "Position and State of Manners and Arts in the Creek, or Muscogee Nation in 1791." In *Historical and Statistical Information,* by H. R. Schoolcraft, 5:251–83. Philadelphia, 1851–57.

Swanton, John R. *Early History of the Creek Indians and Their Neighbors.* Washington, 1922.

———. *The Indians of the Southeastern United States.* Washington, 1946.

———. *Myths and Tales of the Southeastern Indians*. Washington, 1929.   365
———. "Religious Beliefs and Medical Practices of the Creek Indians," *Forty-second Annual Report of the Bureau of American Ethnology* (1928): 473–672.
———. "Social Organization and Social Usages of the Indians of the Creek Confederacy," *Forty-second Annual Report of the Bureau of American Ethnology* (1928): 23–472.
Taitt, David. "Journal of David Taitt's Travels from Pensacola, West Florida to and through the Country of the Upper and Lower Creeks, 1772." In *Travels in the American Colonies*, edited by Newton D. Mereness, 492–565. New York, 1916.
"Technical Reports Regarding the Poarch Band of Creeks of Atmore, Alabama." Accompanying *Federal Register Notices* 49, no. 5, 9 January 1984.
TePaske, John J. "The Fugitive Slave: Intercolonial Rivalry and Spanish Slave Policy, 1687–1764." In *Eighteenth-Century Florida and Its Borderlands*, edited by Samuel Proctor, 1–12. Gainesville, 1975.
Thwaites, Reuben G., ed. *Original Journals of the Lewis and Clark Expedition, 1804–1806*. Vol. 1. New York, 1904.
Tooker, Elisabeth. "Clans and Moieties in North America," *Current Anthropology* 12 (1971): 357–64.
Tucker, Glenn. *Tecumseh: Vision of Glory*. New York, 1956.
Tuggle, William O. *Shem, Ham, and Japheth: The Papers of W. O. Tuggle*. Edited by Eugene Current-Garcia and Dorothy B. Hatfield. Athens, 1973.
Turner, Lorenzo D. *Africanisms in the Gullah Dialect*. Chicago, 1949.
Underhill, Lonnie E. "Hamlin Garland and the Final Council of the Creek Nation," *Journal of the West* 10 (1971): 511–20.
United States Congress, 24th congress, 1st session, House of Representatives. *Document 276*.
Valliere, Kenneth L. "The Creek War of 1836: A Military History," *Chronicles of Oklahoma* 57 (1979): 463–85.
Vignoles, Charles B. *Observations upon the Floridas*. Edited by John H. Moore. Gainesville, 1977.
Viola, Herman J. *Thomas L. McKenney: Architect of America's Early Indian Policy, 1816–1830*. Chicago, 1974.
Wagner, Günter. *Yuchi Tales*. New York, 1931.
Wallace, Anthony F. C. "Revitalization Movements," *American Anthropology* 58 (1956): 264–81.
Ware, John D., and Robert R. Rea. *George Gauld: Surveyor and Cartographer of the Gulf Coast*. Gainesville, 1982.
Waring, Antonio J., ed. *Laws of the Creek Nation*. Athens, 1960.
Waselkov, Gregory A., Brian M. Wood, and Joseph M. Herbert. *Colonization and Conquest: The 1980 Archaeological Excavations at Fort Toulouse and Fort Jackson, Alabama*. Montgomery, 1982.
Welch, Andrew. *A Narrative of the Early Days and Remembrances of*

366

Osceola Nikkanochee, Prince of Econchatti, a Young Seminole Indian, Son of Econchatti-mico, King of the Red Hills in Florida. Edited by Frank Laumer. Gainesville, 1977.

———. *A Narrative of the Life and Sufferings of Mrs. Jane Johns, Who Was Barbarously Wounded and Scalped by Seminole Indians in East Florida.* Edited by Frank Laumer. Gainesville, 1977.

Whitaker, Arthur P., ed. and trans. *Documents Relating to the Commercial Policy of Spain in the Floridas, with Incidental Reference to Louisiana.* DeLand, 1931.

———. *The Spanish-American Frontier: The Westward Movement and the Spanish Retreat in the Mississippi Valley.* Gloucester, 1962.

White, Frank F., Jr., ed. "Macomb's Mission to the Seminoles: John T. Sprague's Journal Kept during April and May, 1839," *Florida Historical Quarterly* 35 (1956): 130–93.

White, Richard. *The Roots of Dependency: Subsistence, Environment, and Social Change among the Choctaws, Pawnees, and Navajos.* Lincoln, 1983.

Williams, John Lee. "Journal of John Lee Williams," *Florida Historical Quarterly* 1 (1908): 37–44, 18–29.

Willis, William S., Jr., "Divide and Rule: Red, White, and Black in the Southeast." In *Red, White, and Black: Symposium on Indians in the Old South,* edited by Charles M. Hudson, 99–115. Athens, 1971.

Wood, Peter H. *Black Majority: Negroes in Colonial South Carolina from 1670 through the Stono Rebellion.* New York, 1974.

Woodward, Thomas S. *Woodward's Reminiscences of the Creek, or Muscogee Indians, Contained in Letters to Friends in Georgia and Alabama.* Montgomery, 1859.

Wright, J. Leitch, Jr. *Britain and the American Frontier, 1783–1815.* Athens, 1975.

———. "Creek-American Treaty of 1790: Alexander McGillivray and the Diplomacy of the Old Southwest," *Georgia Historical Quarterly* 51 (1967): 379–400.

———. "Lord Dunmore's Loyalist Asylum in the Floridas," *Florida Historical Quarterly* 49 (1971): 370–79.

———. "A Note on the First Seminole War as Seen by the Indians, Negroes, and Their British Advisors," *Journal of Southern History* 34 (1968): 565–75.

———. *The Only Land They Knew: The Tragic Story of the American Indians in the Old South.* New York, 1981.

———. "The Queen's Redoubt Explosion in the Lives of William A. Bowles, John Miller, and William Panton." In *Anglo-Spanish Confrontation on the Gulf Coast during the American Revolution,* edited by William S. Coker and Robert R. Rea, 177–93. Pensacola, 1982.

Young, Hugh. "A Topographical Memoir on East and West Florida with Itineraries of General Jackson's Army, 1818," edited by Mark F. Boyd and Gerald M. Ponton, *Florida Historical Quarterly* 13 (1934): 16–50, 82–104, 129–64.

Young, Mary E. *Redskins, Ruffleshirts and Rednecks: Indian Allotments in Alabama and Mississippi, 1830–1860.* Norman, 1961.

IV. UNPUBLISHED PAPERS AND DISSERTATIONS

Brumbaugh, Roderick. "Black Maroons in Florida, 1800–1830." Paper delivered at Organization of American Historians Annual Meeting. Boston, 1975.

Buswell, James O. "Florida Seminole Religious Ritual: Resistance and Change." Ph.D. dissertation, St. Louis University, 1972.

Crider, Robert F. "The Borderland Floridas, 1815–1821: Spanish Sovereignty under Siege." Ph.D. dissertation, Florida State University, 1979.

DePratter, Chester B. "Late Prehistoric and Early Historic Chiefdoms in the Southeastern United States." Ph.D. dissertation, University of Georgia, 1983.

Green, Michael D. "The Creek Nation and the Removal Crisis." Manuscript article.

Usner, Daniel H., Jr. " 'Fragments of This Erratic Race': The presence of American Indians in New Orleans before 1900." Manuscript article.

Wright, J. Leitch, Jr., "Black Seminoles." Paper delivered at 44th International Congress of Americanists, Manchester, 1982.

———. "Southern Black Loyalists." Paper delivered at Conference on American Loyalists. St. Augustine, 1975.

Index

378

In the *Indians of the Southeast* series

CPSIA information can be obtained at www.ICGtesting.com
Printed in the USA
LVOW040031311012

305165LV00001B/1/A